Immigration to Denmark

Immigration to Denmark

International and national perspectives

by David Coleman and Eskil Wadensjö

with contributions by
Bent Jensen and Søren Pedersen

THE ROCKWOOL FOUNDATION RESEARCH UNIT

AARHUS UNIVERSITY PRESS

Copyright: Aarhus University Press, 1999
Word-processed by Flemming Hedegaard Rasmussen and Lotte Bülow
Printed by Morsø Folkeblad, Nykøbing M, Denmark
ISBN 87 7288 775 3

AARHUS UNIVERSITY PRESS
University of Aarhus
DK-8000 Aarhus C
Fax (+ 45) 8619 8433

73 Lime Walk
Headington, Oxford OX3 7AD
Fax (+ 44) 1865 750 079

100 Main St.
Oakville, CT 06779
Fax (+ 1) 860 945 9468

Foreword

In 1997, the Rockwool Foundation decided that 'immigrants and their living conditions' should be given a high priority among the areas in which the Foundation, through research projects, seeks to present reliable and balanced social scientific knowledge to political decision-makers and to the public debate.

Some of the major questions to be answered by such research would include how the encounter between the new citizens and their descendants on the one hand and Danish society on the other takes place — and how it affects living conditions for immigrants and their descendants. An important factor here is the process of integration into the Danish labour market, where the previous research by the Rockwool Foundation Research Unit and the rich possibilities for analysis afforded by existing statistics, argued strongly for a joint effort in some areas.

In July 1998, therefore, the Research Unit initiated a new research project, whose most important data source will be an extensive interview survey among all the major groups of immigrants and refugees, including their descendants, in Denmark. The results — supplemented by the conclusions from other analyses — will be presented in spring 2000.

The demographic part of the project was largely unknown territory for the Research Unit. It was therefore with great pleasure that we were able to persuade Professor Poul Chr. Matthiessen (D.Sc. (Econ)), former professor of demography at the University of Copenhagen — now chairman of the board at the Carlsberg Foundation — to act as consultant for the project.

Among the demographic works, which, at the suggestion of Poul Chr. Matthiessen, were included in the project's planning phase, was a UN report (*UN, 1994. European Population Conference. Proceedings. Vol.1.* New York and Geneva) which, among other things, contained a contribution on international migrations at the beginning of the 1990s. The author of this contribution was David A. Coleman, Reader in Demography at Oxford University. We were subsequently able to persuade Dr. Coleman to update and expand on his contribution to the UN conference, resulting in an account by one of the leading experts in the field of the current situation, both as regards international migration in general, immigration to Europe in particular, and the political efforts of European countries to draw up an actual immigrant policy.

David Coleman's new analyses (in chapters 1, 2 and 3) are presented in what will be the first publication from the Rockwool Foundation's new immigrant project — in both a Danish and an English version. The two identical books have been jointly edited by Poul Chr. Matthiessen and myself.

The Danish Ministry of Economic Affairs, which in 1997 published an analysis of the economic consequences of immigration in 1995, has at short notice very kindly given us access to data for three selected years in the 1990s. This has thus made it possible for the author who is responsible for this sub-topic, Professor Dr. Eskil Wadensjö, Stockholm University — one of the pioneers of national economics within this research area — to complete the first part of his planned publication in time for inclusion in this book (as chapter 7).

Søren Pedersen (MA (Econ)), of the Research Unit, presents in chapter 4 a statistical overview of the historical development in immigration to Denmark over the last 3-4 decades, with a special focus on scale, structure and integration into the labour market. Bent Jensen, also of the Research Unit, presents an analysis (chapters 5 and 6) of the newspaper debate on the immigrant problem during these decades in selected representative Danish dailies.

In addition to these authors, Professor Poul Chr. Matthiessen and the Ministry of Economic Affairs, I would also like to extend warm thanks to various other persons/institutions who have provided valuable assistance to this first publication:

The Department of Population at Statistics Denmark, especially its head, Lars Borchsenius, and two members of staff, Anita Lange and Marius Ejby Poulsen, but also including — as usual in these projects — the entire service, including the library and management, and its director, Jan Plovsing.

Chapters 4, 5 and 6 (on immigration to Denmark and the debate in the media) have benefited from the expert advice on immigrant and refugee legislation of Jens Vedsted-Hansen (LLD), University of Copenhagen.

Jette D. Søllinge, a press historian, has given invaluable assistance to Bent Jensen in his work on chapters 5 and 6 on the newspaper debate about 'foreigners'. She has also read and commented on various drafts of these chapters, and contributed an outline of appendix 5.1.

At the Research Unit itself, I owe a special thank you to Hanne Lykke, institute secretary, who has collected, corrected and prepared the manuscript for publication, while Claus Larsen, a researcher at the Unit, Niels-Kenneth Nielsen and Sebastian Stenderup, two students of economics, have contributed analyses and comments to various parts of the manuscript. Bent Jensen, MA, in addition to writing chapters 5 and 6, has also been responsible for contact with the two — professional and patient — publishers, Aarhus University Press and Spektrum.

The project has, of course, been carried out by the Research Unit in complete scientific independence of both Statistics Denmark and the Rockwool Foundation.

However, such a generous financial framework for the analyses would have been difficult without the great willingness and interest of the Foundation. I would therefore like to warmly thank the Foundation's staff, including Director Poul Erik Pedersen, and not least the board, chaired by Director Tom Kähler, for making such good working conditions possible and for the usual good working relations between the Foundation and the Research Unit.

Copenhagen, March 1999   Gunnar Viby Mogensen

Contents

Chapter 3
Migration Policies

CHAPTER 1

International Migration in the context of global demographic change

David Coleman

Preface

The purpose of the following three chapters is to put international migration to Denmark into an international context. The first chapter will consider contemporary global and European demographic and migration processes, of which Denmark cannot escape being a part. The second chapter will describe and analyse recent migration patterns and trends and their evolution, concentrating on Europe. The third chapter will present the policy responses developed by European governments in their attempt to control the migration processes impinging upon them and to deal with the novel problems presented by large numbers of immigrants, particularly those from outside Europe.

1.1 Introduction

For migration to occur there must be people, motivation and means. Much of the migration which presses upon the West comes from remote countries where populations are poor and usually numerous and rapidly growing. Poor populations with high growth rates are assumed to be likely to migrate to rich countries with low population growth rates. We start in this chapter, by examining global population and migration processes. The bicentenary of Malthus' Essay fell last year. His assertion about the connection between growth in the number of people and poverty remains relevant. Migration is one way of avoiding that poverty; one indeed not much considered by Malthus as the means scarcely existed in his world and economic disparities between countries were less marked. However, in the century after the essay was published, about 50 million Europeans crossed the Atlantic in search of better opportunities. Today, poor people in rapidly growing populations are prime candidates as migrants to richer countries, as long as the means to move — information, resources, transport and ability to enter — are there. We will see later that these connections do not go unchallenged. But whatever the mechanisms, the countries of origin of migrants to Europe are not in doubt. What is happening to their populations today, and what does the future hold?

1.2 Population trends outside Europe

For the last few decades world population has been growing at the rate of about 2% per year. This is a development absolutely unique in history and one which is clearly unsustainable for anything other than a very short time in historical terms. No-one will need reminding of the concern, excitement and controversy which world population growth has generated. The time taken to add a further billion to the world's population had fallen from 30 years in 1960 to 15 years in 1975 and 12 years in 1987. That dismal statistic will remain at about 12-13 years until around 2050 — but that means a diminishing rate of growth. Growth rates probably peaked at just over 2.0% around 1970. During the 1980s it had at last become clear that a majority of the world's couples — as well as a majority of its governments — had already decided for their own reasons that Malthus was right and that their family size needed some prudential restraint.

This reduction in traditional, large family size to a controlled level of two children or even less, following earlier decline in the death rate, is known as the 'demographic transition'. The exact sequence of the process is still controversial, but demographic transition usually follows economic and social modernisation and the acceptance of new ideas and new knowledge, particularly about the possibility and availability of family planning itself. The demographic transition is complete in the developed countries and is at various intermediate stages in most of the rest of the world. Of course it remains a supposition that the birth rate will fall, or continue to fall, in the third world until it reaches the equivalent of a two-child family or less. But most demographers, and almost all official population projections, assume that it will. National populations at a lower and lower threshhold of economic development are beginning to reduce their fertility (Bongaarts and Watkins 1996). Accordingly the 1990s became the first decade in the 20th century — and for centuries before that — when the annual absolute increase of the human population began to fall. The peak annual increase in the annual number of human beings occurred around 1990 at about 87 million. Now the latest UN estimates (United Nations, 1998) suggest that the annual increase in population is down to about 78 million per year, equivalent to a growth rate of 1.4%. The crisis, according to some, is over and indeed population growth may be even more modest in future than these UN projections suggest (Chesnais, 1997).

Unfortunately that will not help the issue of migration pressure very much. The annual increase of 78 million people, expected to be still as high

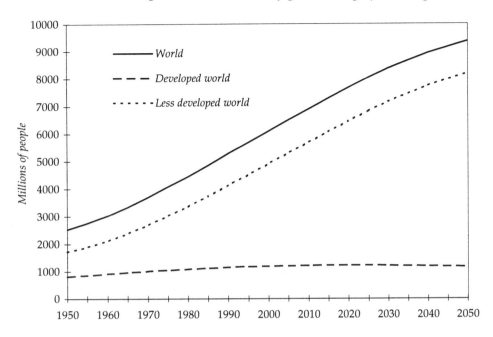

Figure 1.1 World Population Estimates and Projections 1950-2050.

Source: UN 1997 World Population Prospects: the 1996 Revision. Medium variant.
Note: Data beyond 1996 are projections.

as 40 million even by 2050, is almost entirely concentrated in the third world — that is, the sending countries. Of the world's population of 5.70 billion around 1995, only 1.18 billion were in the receiving countries of the 'developed world' as defined by the United Nations. All the rest — 4.52 billion — and almost all the future increase, is in the actual or potential sending countries of the less developed world (see Table 1.1 and Appendix Table 1.1).

Note that 'Western' Europe as defined in Figure 1.2 and in Figure 1.3 applies in the former, broad political sense to all European countries North, West and South only omitting the former Iron Curtain states of Eastern (including Central) Europe. On this broad definition 'Western' Europe includes all the countries of Northern, Western and Southern Europe as defined by the United Nations (UN) including the three Baltic States, and Albania and the former Yugoslavia. The Baltic States on the new UN definition are included in Northern Europe; Albania and Yugoslavia were always included in the UN subdivision 'Southern' Europe. In the tables which follow, the subdivisions of Europe, Eastern, Southern, Western and Northern Europe are used according to the current United Nations definitions — for component countries see Appendix Table 1.2.

By a commonplace of technical demography, population growth, once started, is uncommonly difficult to stop (so, for the same reasons, is po-

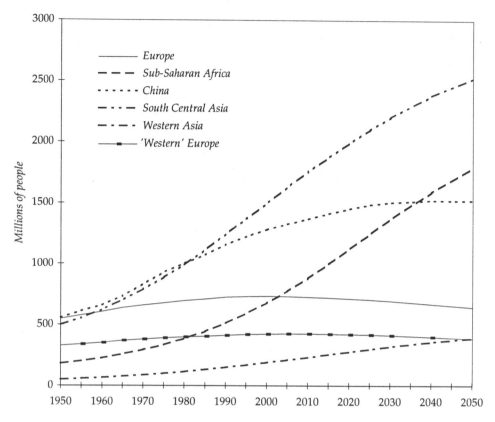

Figure 1.2 Population estimates and projections for major regions.

Source: UN 1997 World Population Prospects: the 1996 Revision. Medium variant.
Note: Data beyond 1996 are projections.

pulation decline). A population growing at 2-3% per year, as most of the third world has been doing since the 1950s, generates a youthful population with a high degree of built-in future growth. This population momentum or inertia means that even if a population growing at 2% per year were to adopt a replacement-level fertility overnight (say about 2.3 children per woman) it would still continue growing in size for another 60 years or so, with an increase in population of almost 40%. This arises because each succeeding generation of mothers for many decades is larger than the previous one. With constant numbers of children each this growing number of mothers produces an increasing number of babies per year for some decades. This 'demographic momentum' underwrites the otherwise troublesome and uncertain business of population projection. Future population increase is partly due to the momentum built into the population — almost unavoidable — and partly due to the uncertainty as to the timing of fertility reduction, which is subject to the pace of economic and social development and to the effects of government programmes to reduce the birth rate.

Because the greatest part of the future increase will be in the least developed countries, world population growth is thereby concentrated on those populations, economies and environments least able to bear the burden. That potentially increases migration pressure. The most dramatic increases will be, above all, in tropical Africa, where the worlds greatest nature reserve of non-controlled ('natural') fertility is to be found — that is, of populations not planning the numbers of their children. Even around 1990, the family planning surveys in the Demographic and Health Surveys programme show that very small proportions of married women are using modern contraception in large areas of West and Central Africa (Burundi 1987 1% , Nigeria 1990 4%, Sudan 1990 6%). Southern and parts of East Africa have been the front-runners in the limitation of fertility (South Africa, Kenya, Zimbabwe, Botswana). Because Africa's fertility transition is so late, sub-Saharan African population, relatively minor on the world scene around 1950, will overtake that of China by about 2025 and will by then approach that of South Central Asia (India, Pakistan, Bangladesh, the Central Asian Republics and their neighbours) (Figure 1.2).

Other areas which will gain disproportionately in number, although from a smaller base, include the Middle East — which also has some of the lowest rates of family planning and highest birth rates in the world. The reduction of the birth rate in Egypt has until recently been disappointing to those in charge of government programmes. The Total Fertility Rate (TFR) — a measure of the average family size expected if current birth rates remain constant — has fallen in Egypt to 3.6 in 1995 from 5.3 in 1980. If unwanted births could be avoided, however, the TFR would be 2.6 (Demographic and Health Surveys, 1997). Some of the poorest Asian countries (especially Muslim countries) form a third group with persistent high fertility. Pakistan, for example, has not followed the example of Bangladesh (Bongaarts & Amin, 1997): Progress there in family planning was not unambiguously discernible in 1996, with TFR still about 6 (Kantner & He, 1996).

A great turning-point was achieved in the last decade when half the world's couples of reproductive age, according to surveys, have now adopted modern means of family planning. Birth rates are coming down over most — but not all — of the third world. That includes not just the well-known economic success stories of Thailand, Chile and now even some southern African countries, but also some of the poorest countries. Sri Lanka began a fertility decline decades ago. The population of Bangladesh, fifth poorest country in the world, has reduced its birth rate from one equivalent to 7 children per woman at the end of the 1970s to about 3.5 today.

1.3 Demographic fault-lines: The Mediterranean

The world's populations are arranged across the globe in such a way that poor, fast-growing ones closely confront rich, slow-growing ones on two obvious fronts and a third potential one. The Mediterranean, claims Chesnais (1995) is the biggest demographic fault-line in the world, where realms separated by a wide gulf in terms of their culture and demography are separated only by modest geographical distance. Despite their high level of development compared with the countries of tropical Africa, their proximity to Europe and the (past) influence of France, the countries of North Africa have been relatively slow to modernise their birth rates. Family planning programmes were introduced relatively late or ineffectively, retarded by a combination of socialist and nationalist sentiment on the part of newly independent governments and low rates of acceptance on the part of Muslim rural populations. Elsewhere in the Middle East, Lebanon and Israel are in a much more developed state in these respects, with more moderate fertility (Appendix Table 1.1). That of Israel is still relatively high (2.9) thanks to recent immigration of non-European Jews, the higher fertility of the Arab population and to a generally elevated birth rate among the Jewish population (Anson & Meir, 1996) compared with Europe. But the migration links of Israel are mostly from the former Soviet Union and out to the USA and little more will be said about it. Lebanese emigration has been less driven by population growth (highly differentiated between different religion groups, but recently uncounted because of its political sensitivity) than by the violence of recent decades.

1.3.1 Turkey

In Turkey, overall fertility has fallen relatively fast in recent decades to a TFR of about 2.5 by 1995. Nonetheless considerable regional variation remains between West and East and city and country. Demographic momentum still gives Turkey considerable natural increase (the difference between annual births and deaths) and population growth.

Annual natural increase has been about 900,000 in recent years — more than all Western Europe put together. That taxes Turkey's capacity for job creation, adding to the more acute migration potential arising from the war between the Turkish government and its Kurdish population, whose asylum claims form the greater part of Turkish migration streams today. Turkey is an interesting example of a 'semi-developed' country with reduced fertility and partial industrialization but still with considerable migration potential. There is of course considerable debate as to Turkey's place in Europe. Its exclusion from the EU arises to a considerable extent from fear of the migration potential which could be mobilised by closer association (Martin, 1991; Hönekopp, 1993). Other considerations include the hostility of the Greeks, for whom the memories of Ottoman oppression are still sharp, and unease about the treatment of the Kurdish minority, although indignation about the ex- tirpation of the culture of the remaining Christian minorities there and else- where in the Middle East is much more muted (Dalrymple, 1997). Most of the latter have found refuge in the United States. Nonetheless Turkey is included in the member states of the Council of Europe, and included in the UN Economic Commission for Europe, along with the former Soviet Central Asian Republics and Israel, despite being classified geographically by the UN (along with Israel) as part of Western Asia.

1.3.2 North Africa and the Middle East

Because of their youthful age structure, populations of the countries of the Southern shore of the Mediterranean will experience considerable further growth. Birth rates in North Africa are declining: In Algeria the TFR fell below 4.7 around 1990, in Tunisia 3.3 and in Morocco 4.4 (together, these three countries comprise the 'Maghreb'). But these rates are still relatively high given the state of development of those countries. Population growth is still linear and strongly upwards. From approximate equality of population around the year 2000, the countries to the South of the Mediterranean from the Maghreb to Turkey are expected to exceed the population of Western Europe by almost 60% in 25 years' time (Figure 1.3). 'Western' Europe is here defined essentially as Europe west of the old Iron Curtain: All Europe except for Central and Eastern Europe, including (on the new UN definition) the Baltic States, Albania and former Yugoslavia.

The population of that 'Western' region is expected to peak in about 2005. Annual growth rates of labour force and population are very different in the two areas. For example the annual average increase in the labour force in the EU to 2000 is estimated at 0.45 million, that in the Southern Mediterranean is estimated at 2.2 million. Annual natural increase in Turkey is about 0.9 million, to which should be added a further natural increase of 1.5 million for the Maghreb countries and 1.7 million for the rest of the countries of the Southern Mediterranean (4.3m in all for the Mediterranean third world). But even allowing for reduction of fertility to a TFR of about 2 by 2025, the annual natural increase for that area by 2025 is likely still to be over 4 million (United Nations, 1997). The chances of those countries creating an extra four million jobs per year over the next 35 years seem to be low.

Some new projections by the French demographer Youssef Courbage (1998) have claimed that the United Nations projections are over-stated and need to be reduced. The Courbage projections are based upon a consideration of the rise of education in most of the Southern Mediterranean countries, especially among females, and its likely effect in reducing fertility further than forecast by the UN. But the effects are relatively modest and do not detract

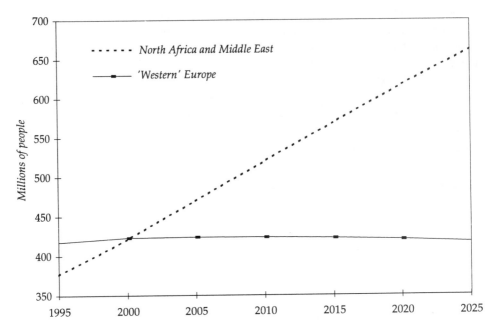

Figure 1.3. Population projections: Northern and Southern shores of the Mediterranean, 1995-2025.

Source: UN 1997 World Population Prospects: the 1996 Revision. Medium variant.
Note: Data beyond 1996 are projections.

from the general proposition that future population growth will be substantial. The difference between the mean of the Courbage projections and the UN medium variant amounts to 37 million in 2010 or 7% and 62 million or 9.5% in 2025. Such a reduction in migration or migration pressure of up to 10% would be good news but would not substantially change the position. The effect on migration is possibly even more muted than these revisions would suggest. We are concerned primarily with young adults, either as potential migrants or spouses or dependants. All likely potential initiators of migration for at least the next 15 years or so have already been born, as have those who will be seeking work. Their increase is already built into the age structure. Unless they migrate as dependants, the only factors affecting their numbers will be changes in mortality, which at those ages is unlikely to make much difference. The Courbage projections — not in this respect much different from the UN ones — envisage the annual increase of the age-groups entering the workforce (or trying to) increasing from about 8.2 million today to about 10 million in 2005-10, an increase of 21% (up to 8 million in net terms, taking retirement into account). The net number of persons seeking work each year under the Courbage projections peaks at 8 million in 2005 and is forecast to decline to 6 million by 2025.

However, there will be a change in the main potential emigrant-sending countries. The populations — and therefore the workforces — of some countries in the Middle East are likely to go on increasing much more and for much longer than others, thanks to the tardiness of their fertility decline and the consequent high population momentum. These include Iraq, Jordan, Palestine and the Israeli Arabs, Yemen, Saudi Arabia and the Gulf States. A collective reduction in supply of labour after 2010 can only be assumed if the states of this area mop up each others' surplus, so preventing it exerting pressure outside the region. That is not implausible even though the oil states' demand for labour may dry up with the oil. Nonetheless new external pressures are likely to emerge from states now little thought of in terms of migration to the West, quite apart from the unpredictable stability of countries in that part of the world, almost none of which have democratic governments.

At present, the Middle East occupies a paradoxical place as one of the world's demographic hot-spots which nonetheless sends relatively few migrants except from obvious politically troubled areas such as Palestine, the Lebanon and Iraq. Thanks to oil this region is unique in having high fertility, high population growth rates and high levels of income. Through rentier status, high fertility can float on the back of oil money for some time to come without provoking much emigration, or even fertility decline, except for annual migration of the rich to Europe during the hot season. Political instability rather than the conventional economic/demographic connection may be the more likely cause of future migration, if some of the autocratic oil states collapse. The Gulf crisis of 1991 provoked a huge out-movement of about 2 million Palestinians, Yemenis and other guest workers to (mostly impoverished) home countries (van Hear, 1998). Few attempted to enter Europe.

1.4 Demographic fault-lines: China, Central Asia and Africa

The equivalent fault-line in the Western hemisphere, the Rio Grande, is outside the scope of the chapter. However, one further demographic boundary needs a mention, that of the steppe, desert, mountains and plains of the immense boundary between Russia on the one side and the republics of Central Asia and of China on the other. This 4000 mile frontier, impassable in some places, easy in others, joins what is now defined as Eastern Europe to the growing populations of Central Asia and of China. At present Russian Siberia or Russia proper might be thought to be an unlikely destination. Nonetheless the Russian Migration Service estimated that there were 500,000 illegal immigrants from the third world, including China, in Russia in 1994, and the authorities in Belarus estimated that there had been between 100,000 and 400,000 illegal entries between 1993-95 (cited in Salt, 1997, p. 22).

1.4.1 China

The demographic gulf with China, in terms of growth rates, is now modest, although even the smallest growth rate (now about 1%) of China's population implies a natural increase in absolute numbers which is very large: Population momentum is expected to increase China's population by a further 200 million before growth stops. China's economy, although starting at a lower point, is growing faster than Russia's. Nonetheless the pressure of China's huge population on resources is greater — hence its draconian population policies. China is famous for a remarkable series of family planning policies culminating in the one-child policy of 1979. This policy was intended to undercut the effects of demographic momentum noted above by bringing fertility to a level well below replacement, not elsewhere thought of in the ambitions of family planning programmes. While never fully implemented, contradicted by other policies such as the 'rural responsibility' system of agricultural reform, and now abandoned in its original form, the one-child family policy and other developments have been followed by a remarkable fall in China's fertility down to a TFR as low as 2.3 or even 1.7 (Lin & Liu, 1997). That of course falls substantially short of the original plan, but that was never really feasible.

Despite this extraordinarily radical fall there is plenty of natural increase left in the Chinese demographic system. Population growth rate in the late 1990s is estimated to be about 1.1% and is projected to fall to 0.8% in 2000-5 and to zero in 2025-30, based on a fall of TFR to 1.8. Population projections expect China's population to increase by about 14 million per year, peaking at 1.52 billion in about 2035. The labour force (males 16-59 and females 16-54), 681 million in 1990, is projected to grow to a peak of about 893 million in 2020, an increase of 31%. That exceeds greatly the total labour force in the entire developed world.

This growth is expected to provoke severe problems of unemployment and migration from country to city, as well as pressure on resources. Its recent economic reforms and relaxation of the registration system which bound welfare to residence, have unleashed a huge 'floating population' of 80 million internal migrants. There are estimated to be 50 million rural-urban migrants, claimed to be the largest flow in history, of whom 20-30 million are living in cities illicitly (Roberts, 1997). At present there are still controls on emigration, although it is alleged that the Chinese authorities connive at illegal emigration to the West. Many of these attempt to leave for the west through Russia or more directly, frequently supported by family money and employing traffickers. When these controls are relaxed, if ever they are, even a small fraction of the 'floating population', if mobilised for international migration, would present a substantial new problem.

Much attention has already been claimed by the dozens of shiploads of illegal would-be immigrants headed for the US arranged by traffickers. Many more, however, have crossed into Russia either heading for Western Europe as transit migrants or in order to benefit from opportunities in Russia and Eastern Europe. Chinese feature strongly in the estimate of 500,000 people illegally resident in the Russian Federation. About 10,000 are reported to have made it (illegally) to Hungary, 20,000 to Prague alone in the Czech Republic, on the lookout for investments, small businesses and money-laundering outlets (Salt, 1997, p. 20). Russia's potential economic recovery is great if it can solve its political problems; as China modernises it may unleash a great number of mobile unemployed onto the world's migration routes. Indeed it has already begun to do so.

1.4.2 Central Asia and Transcaucasia

The countries of West and Central Asia have considerable numerical importance (84 million in West Asia, mostly in Turkey; 53 million in Central Asia, where Kazakhstan and Uzbekistan predominate demographically — Table 1.1, Appendix Table 1.2). Until recently, the Central Asian States, most of which have not completed the demographic transition, had high but varied levels of population growth, most except for Kazakhstan growing at over 2% per year natural increase. All had shown some 'westernization' of fertility in recent decades. Kazakhstan (with a population 40% Russian) most of all, Tadzhikistan least of all (Tolts 1995). The Transcaucasian republics had somewhat more 'western' levels of fertility and natural increase, with Azerbaijan and Armenia growing at a late pre-transitional rate of about 1.5% in the mid 1980s, and Georgia 0.8%.

However, population growth in the Central Asian countries, normally numerically equivalent to natural increase in the absence of much international migration, has recently been thrown into disarray, being reversed in some years around 1989 and in the early 1990s. Short-term population decline followed the break-up of the Soviet Union, with the departure of substantial numbers of persons of Russian nationality to Russia, some under duress, and the accelerated departure of *Aussiedler* to Germany. Tadjikistan, along with other countries of the former Soviet Union (Armenia, Azerbaijan, Chechnya, Georgia and Moldova), have additionally been affected by conflicts, although the refugees created by the fighting (about 900,000 in all these places since 1989) have not impinged much on Europe. Emigration of Russians from Central Asia has turned Russia into a major immigrant country, as noted in Chapter 2. That emigration has had a particular effect on the population of Kazakhstan, which has large Russian and *Aussiedler* populations, reversing its population growth in 1994-95 as it did that of Kirghizstan in 1993-94. These processes, re-inforced by warfare and internal conflict, also provoked population decline in Georgia and Azerbaijan in 1994 and 1993 respectively, the latest years for which data appear to be available.

These may well be transient episodes. If so, population growth through natural increase will soon resume its previous high though declining trend in the Central Asian Republics. If the position of the Russian minorities in those countries were not secured, the potential demographic effects would be considerable, both on the Central Asian republics and on Russia itself. If the Russians left, the Central Asian Republics would lose most of their skilled and scientific manpower. The disparity between the slow population growth of the European part of the USSR, and the fast-growing mostly Muslim Central Asian republics, was often cited as a growing source of instability which would eventually threaten the survival of the Soviet Union. This demographic disparity has now become an international one. So far there seems little evidence of new large-scale movement of Central Asians, as opposed to Russians, from their Republics either into the Russian Federation or into Western Europe. But as demographic inertia doubles its population in the next 35 years, it will be a space to watch.

1.4.3 Africa

The late onset of fertility reduction in tropical Africa will propel that region into the front rank of world population, at least demographically speaking, even if the same population growth will help to keep it economically depressed. Traditional African fertility patterns, probably by reason of the high disease burden of Africa, are among the highest in the world, although by no means uniform. Total Fertility Rates (TFR) of 7 were common and some still remain at that level. In the early stages of transition, which often enhance birth rates, African TFR peaked at just above 8 in Kenya in the 1970s, according to the World Fertility Survey, a record only ever equalled by North Yemen. That gave a population growth of about 4% per year. Apart from South Africa, no sub-Saharan African country showed a trend towards controlled and lower fertility until the 1980s, when the Demographic and Health Surveys revealed clear declines in Kenya, Zimbabwe, and Botswana (Oosthuizen, 1997). These, as might be expected, are among the most developed countries in a weakly developed part of the world, with reasonably stable government, close to South Africa and in the case of Kenya and Zimbabwe, with substantial white minorities. Further surveys in the same series have now shown declines in other countries. Population projections assume the inception of family planning, and the eventual completion of the transition, in all the remaining sub-Saharan African countries. But because of the youthful age structures built up by previous high levels of growth — in many counties over 50% of the population are aged under 15 — and because of the slow pace of family planning acceptance in rural societies based on tribe and kinship, the

African population will increase to rival that of India and China by the first few decades of the next century.

1.5 Eastern Europe — a missed opportunity

As our focus is on migration, let us first look at those regions of Europe which might be expected to send migrants to the West — namely the poorer regions of Central and Eastern Europe and of the former Soviet Union. In fact the countries of those regions, as well as being obvious potential and actual sending countries, have also in a number of unexpected ways turned into receiving countries as well. But to return to the demography, the expectation of migration from Eastern Europe to the West has depended in recent years mostly on economic and political factors — the huge gulf in earnings, and potential mobilization by political liberation from 1989.

Demographic pressure by any objective standard has been weak. In fact, throughout the post-war period the communist governments of the countries of Eastern Europe devised pro-natalist policies to enhance population growth and avert the low fertility to which their populations were inclined by the 1960s. They wished to enhance the labour force as in practice and in theory the most important means of increasing output, and also for strategic reasons. Despite decades of intermittent pro-natalist policy, despite lack of economic progress, despite large rural populations and in a few cases (Romania) explicit attempts to prohibit abortion and access to contraceptives, birth rates could scarcely be kept at replacement level.

Probably as a long-term result of a totalitarian system of government which deprived individuals of market choice and access to information, and allocated so much of national product to state spending on heavy industry and armaments with a corresponding low status for medicine, death rates ceased to fall as early as the 1960s and in many cases (Hungary, Soviet Union) started to worsen — a unique situation in the world. Consequently, with low birth rates and markedly high death rates, the populations of Eastern Europe and the Soviet Union had low rates of natural increase even by 1989 and have little demographic inertia following fifty years of falling fertility.

Lacking an economic boom in the 1950s and 1960s, at least in terms of personal consumption, those countries correspondingly lacked a 'baby boom' generation. While that generation will be a handicap to the West from 2020 onwards, when it is in retirement, it has through the age structure kept natural increase positive for longer than otherwise would have been the case. The age structures of the Eastern and Western parts of Europe are indeed somewhat complementary, insofar as if they are added together a more regular population pyramid is obtained. This fuelled some modest speculation about the possibility of East-West migration supplying some of the West's demographic deficits. But closer scrutiny (Coleman, 1993) showed large-scale migration to be unlikely, although for reasons discussed below, there has been substantial migration to Germany.

Since 1989, birth rates in many of these countries, particularly the European Republics of the former Soviet Union, have fallen rapidly to become among the lowest in Europe, while the death rates in some of these countries, have risen to worse than third world levels. As a consequence, most of the former Soviet Republics, Romania and Bulgaria, have slipped into considerable natural decline, where deaths substantially exceed births. Although, as will be described later, these countries now receive immigrants as well as send them, the officially registered population has started to decline. The pressure to emigrate follows from economic differentials and a (possibly temporary) excess of population over employment, not from any current or foreseeable increase in population size in absolute terms.

1.6 Population trends in Western Europe

Western Europe is one part of the world's migration system. Almost all countries in the world are involved in sending or receiving migrants – usually both. Other major migration systems are centred on North America, the Middle East, the Southern cone of Latin America, the (until recently) fast-growing Asian economies and others (Macura and Coleman, 1994). These will not be considered further here. Attention will be concentrated upon the demographic situation in the Western European countries in the context of migration streams.

1.6.1 Fertility, natural increase and immigration

The overall demographic situation in recent years is shown in Table 1.1 and in more detail in Appendix Table 1.2. There is quite a varied pattern of birth rates and rates of growth. Although almost all birth rates are below replacement rate, some countries are not far off replacement, others have births rates so low that, despite some demographic momentum, the native population is already declining. Thus Northern Europe still shows relatively vigorous growth; Southern Europe is either in numerical decline or on the edge of it. However the most vigorous growth is found in the country with the most chronically low birth rate — Germany. Quite apart from having swallowed East Germany, the German population has grown fastest because of its huge immigration. So to understand patterns of current and future growth we must look at the two components of growth, natural increase and net immigration.

About 80% of the total population increase of about 1.038 million in 1996 in the EU countries was due to immigration, as in all recent years. Net migra-

Table 1.1 Basic population data for European regions and selected others, around 1996.

	Population size (millions)	Crude birth rate per 1000	Crude death rate per 1000	Rate of natural increase per 1000	Net migration per 1000	Total fertility rate	e_0m	e_0f	Population projections (millions) 2025	2050
Eastern Europe	309.4	9.7	12.7	-3.0	1.5	1.39	63.4	73.9	284.2	256.0
Southern Europe	144.2	10.1	9.3	0.9	1.0	1.34	73.2	79.7	136.6	119.2
Western Europe	181.3	11.1	10.0	1.1	2.3	1.48	73.6	80.5	184.0	167.5
Northern Europe	94.0	12.2	10.8	1.4	1.2	1.69	73.6	79.4	95.3	93.9
North America	294.6	14.5	8.6	6.0	2.8	2.01	72.7	79.1	368.9	383.9
West Asia	84.1	20.7	6.6	14.0	0.0	2.45	69.8	75.1	113.4	128.3
Central Asia	52.8	25.3	7.9	17.5	-7.5	2.70	63.5	71.1	78.7	94.8
Australia and New Zealand	21.7	14.5	7.1	7.4	6.1	1.87	74.5	80.4	28.8	30.6
East and South East Asia	201.8	11.6	6.4	5.2	2.6	1.53	74.2	80.9	184.6	171.5
Developed World total	1246.9	9.2	9.7	-0.5	4.5	1.63	70.9	78.4	1282.3	1222.4

Sources: Mostly Council of Europe, Eurostat, national statistical yearbooks except for Central Asia (UN ECE, for 1995) and Israel and Turkey (UN, for 1995). UN World Population Prospects 1996 revision. Medium variant.
Definitions: Population given is usually mid-year total.
Abbrevations in headings: e_0m, e_0f : Expectation of life at birth (males, females).
Note: Latest data for Central Europe usually 1994 or 1995. For constituent countries see Appendix Table 1.2. Central Asia included through membership of UN ECE Region. Developed world: All regions except West and Central Asia.

tion, although lower than in the early 1990s, was still 727,000 in 1996 — over double the natural increase. This does not include the total of illegal im migrants, estimated to be about 350,000 per year in the early 1990s (Widgren, 1994). An important part of the natural increase comes from the resident foreign population themselves. These contribute about 10% of births, thanks to the higher fertility rates and more youthful age structures. The population growth of the native populations of the EU states are correspondingly less. As immigrant populations grow, and as long as their fertility remains incompletely assimilated to Western levels, their contribution to the growth rate and to the total population can be expected to increase.

At the other end of the scale, some countries in Eastern Europe are losing population both by natural decrease and by net emigration (although this may be overstated — illegal or irregular and therefore uncounted immigration probably comprises the greater part of migration to those countries). In Southern countries and Germany, natural decline is compensated by substantial immigration. The population of Germany in particular has increased substantially from immigration since the 1980s, even though deaths of German citizens have exceeded births in many years. The demographic contribution of immigration to Spain and especially to Italy is probably substantially undercounted, because a higher proportion is irregular.

The fourth category is a group of North and Western European countries with, on average, modest residual natural increase and substantial immigration both regular and from asylum-claiming, with some additional illegal immigration. In all these countries the intrinsic rates of natural increase are negative — only marginally in the case of Norway — but the momentum of past age structure still generates residual natural increase and will do so for the next decade or more. Most population growth, however, now comes from immigration.

1.6.2 Population decline and population ageing

These trends foreshadow the end of population growth and the beginning of decline for many countries in Western Europe. The fall of fertility and the constant improvement in expectation of life has caused an unavoidable ageing of the population, which is now general in the developed world. Population ageing is a complex process, driven both from the bottom — declines in the number of births — and from the top — increases in survival of the elderly. Short-run events — baby booms and the movement of war-damaged cohorts into old age — can confuse or reverse long-term trends. Median age in the North American/European countries is about 36.3 years for women and 33.4 for men. Countries can share a similar median age of population without having had a similar population history. Median age can be high even without a large elderly population, if birth rates have fallen. German women have the oldest median age (40.4); this is almost matched both by Italy (39.7) and more surprisingly by Greece (38.3), where the birth rate has fallen sharply since the 1980s.

The aged dependency ratio (population aged 65+ as percent of population aged 15-64), however, reflects more the size of the top end of the population, in relation to the productive age groups. It does not give the same rank-orders of countries. Here the highest dependency ratios are still those of the traditionally older populations of North Western Europe: Sweden (27), Norway (25) and the UK and Belgium (24). Italy, Greece and Spain are not far behind, however, at 22. Germany's modest aged dependency ratio reflects a deficit of men over 60, who were wartime casualties. Lower dependency ratios (20 or under) are found in North America (high birth rates). In Eastern Europe and the Balkans, the proportion of children in the population is still twice that of old people, or almost so. In Italy, the proportion of elderly (uniquely in the world) now narrowly exceeds that of children (15.6% compared with 15.4%) and the gap will grow. These indices of ageing are changing rapidly. The low-

Table 1.2 Population projections of Europe and its neighbours, 1995-2050.

	Population size (millions)				
Region	*1995*	*2005*	*2015*	*2025*	*2050*
Eastern Europe	309.4	302.6	294.7	284.2	256.0
Southern Europe	143.4	144.5	141.8	137.2	119.9
Western Europe	181.0	185.3	185.4	184.1	167.6
Northern Europe	93.4	94.0	94.8	95.6	94.2
North America	296.6	319.9	345.2	369.0	384.1
North Africa	158.1	192.5	225.6	256.7	317.3
Western Asia	167.7	208.5	252.7	297.4	387.0
Central Asia	52.8	61.5	70.8	78.7	94.8

Source: United Nations 1997.
Note: Regions are as follows:
North Africa: Algeria, Egypt, Libya, Morocco, Sudan, Tunisia, Western Sahara.
Western Asia: Armenia, Azerbaijan, Bahrain, Cyprus, Gaza strip, Georgia, Iraq, Israel, Jordan, Kuwait, Lebanon, Oman, Qatar, Saudi Arabia, Syria, Turkey, United Arab Emirates, Yemen.
Central Asia: Kazakhstan, Kirghizstan, Tadjikistan, Turkmenistan, Uzbekistan.

fertility countries of Southern Europe, and (despite their high death rates), those of Eastern Europe will soon acquire the highest dependency ratios. Aged dependancy ratios in North America, in those Balkan countries with relatively high birth rates and in the Irish Republic will increase more slowly.

This inevitable ageing has often led to suggestions that Europe needs the immigration which most governments are today attempting to limit, and that Western countries will have to turn progressively to immigrants as their main hope for population stabilisation and for the preservation of their age structures from unsustainable levels of dependency. We will consider those propositions in a later chapter.

1.6.3 Implications for the future

The UN (1997) projection forecasts continuing decline in the populations of Eastern and Southern Europe. The population of Western Europe is expected to grow slowly until 2025 and then decline rather fast. That of Northern Europe, however is expected to grow slightly by 2025 and then fall back to its 1995 level by 2050. The same population projections forecast the stabilisation of the populations of the major sending areas much later, sometime around the late 2060s. Europe must therefore prepare for at least another half century of demographic divergence, and potential migration pressure from the third world.

1.6.4 Is low fertility inevitable?

Long-term decline (over 20 years) in the projected European workforce derives from the assumption of continued low fertility. That assumption may be wrong. In the 1980s, fertility rose in a number of developed industrial countries. Such increases had been forecast on a number of grounds. Average responses to survey questions on 'ideal' and 'expected' family size have been above 2.0 children in most European countries since such questions began to be asked routinely in the early 1970s. Current low fertility may be due, in some degree, to the delay, rather than the cancellation of births. The peak age at childbearing has risen from 22 to 28 in Germany since 1968. A rise in fertility — though possibly transient — should appear when the delay in child-bearing ceases. Second and higher order births have not fallen to low levels, as they would do if final family size was really shrinking. They remain about 55% of all births in most Western countries. This suggests that once women have a first birth they usually go on to have more. Demographers still do not have the proper tools to meet the needs of policy makers in this area. Delay in the timing of births depresses the Total Fertility Rate (TFR), the conventional period measures of fertility. While cohort measures of fertility give a more stable and higher picture of family size over time, they can only reflect the fertility behaviour of women born up to about 1955, not those currently in their peak years of child-bearing. Period measures of fertility based on parity (the probability of having a first, second, third, etc., baby) may give a better measure of current fertility. The TFR based on parity data for Britain and for France is closer to 2.0 than the conventionally calculated TFR of 1.7 (Murphy and Berrington, 1993; Rallu and Toulemon, 1993).

1.7 Population and migration processes

A major demographic premiss is assumed in discussing the migration implications of demographic change. This is that migration is to a substantial degree driven by population growth, either directly or by its effects in inflating potential workforces above the local demand for labour. Therefore if population growth slackens to an appreciable degree, then migratory pressures will correspondingly fall, possibly *pro rata*. While it is highly plausible that migratory pressures follow from population growth, it is clearly only one component of a complex chain of processes. In fact it may well be that it is only by adopting economists' *ceteris paribus* assumptions that any such prediction can be made.

This uncertainty is a poor reflection on the theoretical position of migration and its causation in demography (Massey, Arango, Hugo, Kouaouci, Pellegrino, & Taylor, 1993). Demographic aspects of migration theory are poorly developed. In none of the mainline models of the causes of migration generally used by geographers and economists do we see much about population pressures as such, despite their almost invariable citation as a prime cause of migration. Indeed some empirical analyses have failed to find a clear relationship between them. It may be assumed to be a key factor in the growth and maintenance of labour supply, tending to keep unemployment high and growing and wage levels low. Adverse effects of rapid population growth on unemployment and capital adequacy have been prominent in the demographic literature and in population policy-making, presented as one of the chief drawbacks of population growth. Such considerations have moved third world governments to introduce policies to reduce fertility and thereby reduce population growth. It is paradoxical therefore that they feature so little in migration theorizing.

1.7.1 Population pressure

As most of the immigrants from outside Europe, and especially those that European governments worry about, come from poor countries with high rates of population growth, the notion of 'migration pressure' from those countries seemed an obviously suitable model. The term 'migration pressure' has been used in the migration literature and in government policy making for many years. Until recently, however, few attempts have been made to define it. Some definitions have broadened out the initial definition based on labour economics. One defines migration pressure as a mismatch between the willingness of destination counties to accept the available supply of those willing to migrate and the number wishing to emigrate from sending countries (Schaeffer, 1993). Another definition emphasizes the difference in the relative demand arising from the opportunities of moving from one country to another (Straubhaar, 1993). Political instability emerges as one important driving force (Weiner, 1985). It is also noted that willingness to accept immigrants depends not just on the employment situation but also on 'political mood' (Appleyard, 1994, p. 297). The ethnic dimension looms large in many aspects of international migration, and not just in the well-known case of the German ethnic migrants from the former Soviet Union. Many Turkish immigrants to Germany, especially illegals and asylum claimants, are not Turks in the strict sense but Kurds, to the Turks a troublesome minority which the Turkish government would perhaps like to see removed to Germany. These definitions do not make it easy to measure 'migration pressure'; one approach could be to regard pressure as the number of applications to emigrate while actual migration reflected demand for immigrants by the respective countries. (Stahl, Ball, Inglis, & Gutman, 1993).

None of this is very satisfactory. Many of these formulations of migration pressure neglect the fact that most immigration into Europe is not related to the labour market directly, but to hopes on the part of the immigrants of improvement in lifestyle, health, welfare — not excluding employment — by moving from an insecure poor environment to a safe developed one. As we will see, most of the migration is not primarily economic at all, but for family reunion — almost invariably taking place within the richer host country of one of the spouses, not the poor sending country — and involves non-working women and children. Such migration of dependants and spouses is not particularly welcome to the host countries but their freedom of option is limited by their adherence to various 'human rights' declarations. Neither can those definitions easily cope with the high level of illegal immigration or with its counterpart, asylum-claiming. Perhaps because of their origin in economics and in particular from countries of immigration (the US, Australia) the authors of some of those concepts do not take into account negative demand for migrants, which appears to predominate among European governments and their electorates. Much current migration, including much regular migration, takes place contrary to general policies aimed at reducing it which in liberal democracies are frustrated by political considerations — pressure from existing immigrants, pressure from their sending country governments, or obligations incurred from international conventions (Freeman, 1994).

1.7.2 Neoclassical economics — wage inequalities and migration

Mainstream migration theory derives from neoclassical economics. According to this, economic inequality in the sending country compared with the receiving country is the basic driving force behind migration. This viewpoint is derived from a macroeconomic form of neoclassical economics, based on rational responses to scarcity and surplus of labour and of capital. Migration will arise to equilibrate differences in labour supply and the employment of capital. Labour will move from where it is in surplus and poorly paid to capital-rich countries where it is in short supply, but better rewarded. Capital will move from areas where it is in surplus to where it is scarce (and where labour is correspondingly cheap). Hence migration would be expected to occur from the poorer countries in Figure 1.4 to the richer ones, as indeed it does. Both processes will tend to reduce the migratory flows in due course; net migration will cease when the returns to capital and to labour are similar in different countries (Johnson, 1990). Highly skilled migration, involving 'human capital' may follow a different pattern, and persist even between equally rich countries, partly because of international divisions of labour and specializations in goods and services, and also because of the rise of multinational companies (Salt & Ford, 1993).

Labour moves to growth areas to an extent depending on distance, wage differentials, attachment to home and the 'foreignness' of the destination, as well as smaller-scale frictional factors such as planning restrictions on new housing. As a result of such frictional factors, considerable under-employment

Table 1.3 GDP and foreign population in main receiving countries, 1996.

Receiving country	Population foreign %	GDP per capita USD
Austria	9.0	28110
Belgium	9.0	26440
Denmark	4.7	32100
France	6.3	26270
Germany	8.9	28870
Italy	2.0	19880
Luxemburg	34.1	45360
Netherlands	4.4	25940
Norway	3.6	34510
Portugal	1.7	10160
Spain	1.3	14350
Sweden	6.0	25710
Switzerland	19.0	44350
UK	3.4	19600

Sources: OECD 1998, PRB 1998.
Note: Population foreign refers to legally-resident persons of foreign citizenship.

and low participation rates (especially in the periphery) and labour shortage and high participation rates (especially in the core) co-exist within the EU (UN ECE 1991) and within individual countries. The data in Tables 1.3 and 1.4 show that there is no simple relationship between the wealth of receiving countries, the poverty of sending countries and migration.

On the neoclassical view, the labour market is the key. Sophisticated re-formulations, however, acknowledge that there is more to labour migration than individual optimizing behaviour and a response to wage differentials in a perfect market. Much migration occurs as a result of imperfections and asymmetries in world markets and financial institutions, preventing the flow of goods and capital and provoking persons to move instead. That may turn distance into a positive, not a negative factor. Family rather than individual decision-making, remittances, income uncertainty and relative deprivation are also important (Stark, 1991). The neoclassical model in its original form was irrelevant to migration choices in many sending countries; for example in India 'almost all decisions are made in a collective manner by the extended family or the community in the village' (Premi & Mathur, 1995, p. 627).

Most migration to Europe is not the labour migration that economists prefer to deal with. Neoclassical and related models do not incorporate demo-graphic trends directly and would only forecast a reduction of immigration pressure from the Maghreb and Middle East insofar as lower fertility and population growth had an effect upon wage rates (raising them) or labour

Table 1.4 GDP, population growth and number of migrants from main sending countries, 1996.

Sending country	No. of its citizens in Europe (1000s)	% of its citizens in Europe (current total)	GPD per capita USD
Algeria	641.7	2.1	1520
Morocco	1134.1	4.1	1290
Tunisia	283.8	3.0	1930
Turkey	2633.3	4.1	2830
fr Yugoslavia	1876.0	7.8	4000

Sources: OECD 1998, PRB 1998.

supply and unemployment (lowering them). In practice, while variation in migration over time, especially to the United States (Kuznets, 1958; Easterlin, 1961), has been successfully related to economic demand and other economic factors (Thomas, 1954), these models have been quite poor at predicting or modelling differences in levels of migration, where historical and cultural factors have clearly been important in linking sending and receiving populations. Above all, neither the rapid rise of migration to industrial countries from the mid-1980s, nor its less sharp reduction from the early 1990s, can be attributed to any commensurate change in economic or demographic conditions in the sending or the receiving countries.

In fact, under classical economics, many more people should have migrated than have done. One of the puzzles of international migration is why there are only 100 million people (out of 5.7 billion) living in countries outside that of their citizenship (Hammar & Tamas, 1997, p. 1) and not many more. Not only is migration from poor to rich countries less than economic theory suggests it should be, but at least some of the stages of economic growth in poor countries do not seem to reduce migration. Furthermore migration rates vary considerably between countries at the same economic level and once started continue independent of changing economic conditions (Malmberg, 1997, p. 22).

On the basis of neoclassical economics, however, the expectation is certainly that migration will not only continue in the medium term but may even increase, only partly for demographic reasons. The economic disparities present and future are clear enough. For example between North Africa and Western Europe, real GDP differences per capita are of the order of tenfold (Fig. 1.4). Unemployment there, in the 1960s not that different from European levels, has been increasing and is forecast to increase further. Contributing factors include poor current and projected economic growth, further demographic increases in the labour force and structural changes, including the

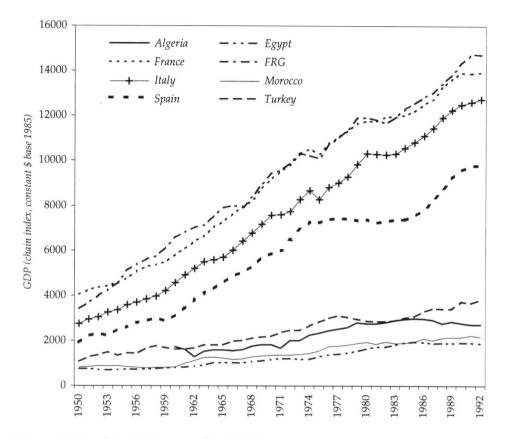

Figure 1.4. Trends in GDP per capita, 1950-93.

Source: Penn world table.

ending of guaranteed graduate state employment in some countries. By 1990 unemployment had reached 21% in Algeria and about 15% in Egypt and the whole Arab region. Furthermore, unemployment in countries without welfare systems is a much more severe penalty than in the West (Fergany, 1997). All these factors emphasize the status of the Mediterranean as the biggest socio-economic and demographic fault-line in the world (Chesnais, 1995).

1.7.3 Dual labour market/ethnic segmentation

The dual labour market model (Piore, 1979) is a variant of the economic model, emphasizing demand-pull factors from rich countries and the different roles of work to immigrants and to natives. Structural conditions in the labour markets of rich countries are held to create a constant demand for low-wage workers which can only be satisfied by continuous immigration from poor countries. This is claimed to arise because contrary to neoclassical theory, it is difficult to raise the wages of the lowest-paid workers doing undesirable jobs (the so-called 3D jobs — dirty, dangerous and degrading). To maintain prestige differentials, all other wages above have to be raised at the same time. Foreign workers from low-wage countries are not affected by these considerations, treating jobs merely as sources of income for themselves and their families without being concerned about prestige aspects. This creates continuous demand-pull from rich countries for willing third world immigrants to do 'dirty' jobs. This 'segmented' labour market becomes permanent as native workers are even less attracted to 'immigrant' jobs. This causation might even be reversed, so that the arrival of immigrants for other reasons, who take such jobs, make them thereby no longer acceptable to local labour. Bohning (1972) suggested that was the case in the not particularly '3D' jobs in the German motor industry, for example. Traditional sources of native supply (teenagers, women) dry up partly for demographic reasons, and the original immigrant workers move up and out, thanks to integration policies and 'human rights' regimes facilitating upward mobility, creating demand for their replacement.

At its worst, this can create a permanently reinforced ethnic underclass, often illegally employed and illegally present, and increasingly supplied by the trafficking arm of the migration industry. This form of migration, arising out of structural demand in industrial economies, may be seen as potentially permanent. This model emphasizes the demand-pull nature of labour-oriented migration and predicts that migration of this kind will be little affected by reductions in fertility until these substantially reduce the potential supply of poor recruits. It assumes considerable rigidities in the domestic labour market and the impossibility of changing the rank-order of wage hierarchies. This may be true of the more sclerotic and protected labour markets of some continental economies but is not true everywhere. In some countries (e.g. Austria, Fassmann, 1997) there is considerable ethnic segregation in the labour market, in others (e.g. Great Britain) there is much less. It may not be easy to separate the 'dirty jobs' element from the more straightforward economic effects. For example there is considerable migration to Germany in perfectly 'respectable' manual trades (e.g. building) arising from the very high costs of employing German labour, among whom there is considerable unemployment. In their pure sense, dual labour markets can only arise in societies where immigrants are obliged, formally or informally, to live apart from the rest of the population, and where there is no real or effective policy of integration intended to open up all opportunities to all comers. Japan and the Gulf States are good examples. Austria itself might be a European example with a weak commitment to integration.

Protected labour markets with high levels of 'social protection', compensation for dismissal and high unemployment benefit may have the paradoxical consequence that they create high levels of domestic unemployment while also encouraging continued inflows of often illegal labour which can enable employers to evade high payroll costs. Spain and Italy may be examples. Both problems might be eased with lower levels of 'job protection' and welfare. However such moves are unlikely under the policies encouraged by the European Union to increase and to 'harmonize' such areas of 'social protection'.

1.7.4 Individual and family motivation

Inspecting migration from the other end of the telescope helps us to see migration as only one of a number of options to be considered by individuals and families. A microeconomic approach can embrace a wide variety of rational choice calculations and motivations for betterment of migrants, along with the informal calculations of the costs and advantages of migration by potential migrants. That allows the more general advantages (e.g. welfare, education) of successful migration to be included in the model, not just formal labour market considerations, and also its costs, of transport, illegal trafficking fees, acquisition of minimal human capital, risks of removal (Todaro & Maruszko, 1987). This is based on the proposition, however implicit, that the unequivocal beneficiary of migration — possibly the only one — is the migrant.

This formulation also brings employment rates into focus and at least partly introduces the notion of the costs of the migration process, hitherto regarded as friction-free. This enables the effects of barriers or controls to be considered, at least through the costs which they impose on migrants which may, if the controls are effective, be infinite or insurmountable. This formulation also allows the cost of information to be incorporated, an important consideration as easy access to information, difficult to introduce into classical economic models, is thought to have been an important cause of the 1980s migration explosion (Hollifield, 1992). However the multiplicity of factors in such models, however plausible, hardly lend them to statistical testing.

1.7.5 The social dimension of migration — chains and networks

Migration from poor countries once begun tends to be perpetuated by processes such as chain migration and the institutionalization (more recently criminalization) of migration, almost irrespective of the details of the economic situation. The post-war experience of industrial countries shows this very clearly, and the details of the process have been described in a number of studies (e.g. Hugo, 1995). According to network theory (Gurak & Caces, 1992), chain migration is the phenomenon whereby the presence of earlier settlers from the sending country in any receiving country greatly facilitates further large flows by increasing information and opportunities and by reducing costs. It is particularly potent in relation to third world populations where ex-

Table 1.5 Foreign citizens from the Maghreb and Middle East resident in Europe around 1995. Selected countries only, not including naturalized persons.

Nationality	Thousands
Algeria	642
Egypt	22
Iran	150
Iraq	31
Lebanon	59
Morocco	1136
Tunisia	281
Turkey	2629
Total	**4950**

Western European countries with Maghreb/Middle East foreign populations > 100,000

Belgium	246
France	1591
Germany	2302
Italy	157
Netherlands	343

Source: OECD 1997.
Note: The data for France are from 1990.

tended families, household-based economy and the importance of lineage and kinship are major organizers of social and economic life, and where migration is best seen as an adaptive strategy by families and households, not just individuals (Hugo, 1995). Such chains pull in more migrants by greatly reducing the costs of search for information, transport, jobs, accommodation and facilitating the avoidance or evasion of immigration control by being able to claim dependant or relative status. That helps to explain the continuation of migration irrespective of the ups and downs of the economy, as long as gross differences in income and GDP persist.

Most regular migration to Europe in the 1990s is not directly job-related at all, but instead is dominated by the migration of dependants usually facilitated by chain migration. As colonies of immigrants age they grow into ethnic minorities and generate a further form of chain migration — that is marriage migration. As children and young immigrants grow up in ethnic enclaves, in many cases they retain traditional preferences for arranged marriages — or have them imposed by parents (for example by Turks in France, where outgroup marriages are almost unknown). Such unions — increasingly involving husbands — are also in demand in the sending country in order to evade immigration controls. In these ways, because of entitlements guaranteed under 'human rights' considerations, chain processes make it difficult to stop migration from third world countries into democracies once it has started, even when labour migration is ostensibly over (Freeman, 1994).

1.7.6 Chain migration — the migrants within

The potential for migration from the third world is evident from the large populations from the areas already resident in Europe. For example looking at the populations of the Maghreb and Middle East resident in Europe, we see about 5 million foreign citizens in the data of Table 1.5, not counting the millions who have been naturalized. In the 1990s, between 37 and 45% of all regular immigrants to France came from Turkey, Lebanon, Algeria, Morocco and Tunisia together. Immigrants from Turkey are prominent in flows to Germany.

The family connection also operates in an economic guise, so that its survival in the sending country may be dependent upon remittances sent home from workers abroad and from the diversification of risk in sources of income which this permits, especially in societies lacking social security. Such considerations mean that migration might continue even in the absence of gross wage differentials (Stark & Bloom, 1985; Stark, 1991).

The institutionalization of migration generates domestic immigrant pressure groups, agents and advisory bodies to minimize the effects of controls or to side-step them, encouraged by 'humanitarian' and 'civil liberties' organisations and other groups — part of the multi-billion dollar 'migration industry' described by Salt & Stein (1997). In the United Kingdom at least, it is apparent to the author of this report that criticism of the effects of the migration process is discouraged by censorship imposed and self-imposed by publishers and others through fear of impinging race relations laws. Information on its negative consequences may be suppressed, for example the statistics on street crime by race which in Britain had been published by the Metropolitan Police until 1988. Migration is also supported by criminal elements in the form of traffickers in what has become a multi-billion pound people-smuggling activity, providers of false documents and asylum legends (Salt, 1997; Salt & Stein, 1997). On the other side of the migration industry is a growing body of individuals and lobbyists and solicitors occupationally dependent on the continuation and encouragement of migration.

1.8 Changing the balance

Political events at both ends of the migratory process are at least as important as economic processes. Abroad, continued population growth, economic weakness and political instability in the third world, and the latter two factors in Eastern Europe, sustain immigration pressures. But the recent increases and declines in migration and asylum-claiming are not easy to understand in terms of these underlying factors, which have not changed commensurately. The processes whereby migrants are mobilized (IOM, 1993), what determines who stays and who migrates, on the basis of what information, are still poorly understood. Migrants have become more easy to mobilize, and asylum-claiming more attractive, as immigrant bridgeheads grow in size and become more numerous, as information becomes more widely available and as European internal barriers become weaker.

Such information, for example on whether and how potential migrants respond to amnesties, multicultural policies or other initiatives, changes in rules and so on, might be a new key to moderating flows. The political structure and principles of Western democracies, and the influence of focused pressure groups, can make it particularly difficult for these democracies to control migration effectively. Populations of immigrant origin in receiving countries are important actors in the migration process as well as those of potential migrants in sending countries.

Does it follow from this general association that family planning and development aid to poorer countries would accelerate their migration transition to the lower levels of emigration typical of richer countries? It would seem obviously so. But family planning programmes are affected by a wide variety of political processes, in which sensitivity about richer countries imposing family planning on poorer ones is salient. Most discussion in this area has been directed to economic development aid as a damping-down factor on emigration pressures — (more) aid in place of migration (Tapinos, 1991; Bohning and Schloeter-Paredes, 1994). Foreign development aid is easily justified in its own right. But it is also suggested that it is in the self-interest of receiving countries, because of its supposed effects on migration.

The first problem with this view is that aid and investment programmes, however efficient, can only increase economic growth by perhaps one percentage point. That is a modest rate of improvement by comparison with the income gap and it would still take many years to close it sufficiently to moderate economic motivations for migration. Furthermore, some migration analyses suggest that the short-term consequences of bilateral aid may increase, not reduce, migration flows (Martin, 1992). The US Commission for the Study of International Migration and Co-operative Economic Development (Teitelbaum, 1990) concluded that aid and investment would be likely to lead to an increase, in the short term, in immigration to the aiding country, especially if the investment was close to a border. This arises from a number of processes: Destabilization of traditional rural society and economy leading to rural-urban migration, which raises expectations and opportunities to migrate, economic growth which makes air tickets more affordable, specific contacts with rich countries though enterprises newly located in the sending countries, better transport to borders and out of the country. The Commission estimated that such a 'migration hump' effect might last for up to 15 years.

Free trade has a greater capacity to expand economic growth than does international aid. While therefore more effective in damping economic migration in the long run, it is also likely to generate a similar short-term increase in migration pressure (Russell & Teitelbaum, 1992). For example, the North American Free Trade Area (NAFTA) which is intended, among other things, to encourage investment and economic growth in Mexico may have effects on migration similar to those of aid. One study forecasts a similar 'hump' of increased migration, relatively small and limited in duration, followed by a longer-term reduction, compared to the position without NAFTA (Martin, 1993). However, it will take between 15 and 20 years for the decline in migration to emerge.

If this is correct, then in its short-term effects, investment is not a substitute for controls on immigration. Even with foreign aid, the economic and demographic disparities between sending and receiving countries cannot abate substantially for some decades. The gap does not need to be completely closed, however, for migration pressures to moderate, as experience within the EU shows.

1.9 Conclusions

This chapter has reviewed the global demographic scene, its potential for migration and the role of theory in accounting for the causes of present migratory flows and predicting their likely future. Major differences exist in wealth and in the rate of population growth between the richer and poorer countries. For a variety of economic and demographic reasons these differentials are bound to persist for many decades. In general terms, according to classical economic theory, migration is expected to develop between countries or regions which differ substantially in wage levels and in the relative abundance or scarcity of labour, and should persist until these differentials have been removed or moderated. It is therefore no surprise, given the substantial differences in wages and living standards between the developed and the less developed countries, and the rapid growth in the population and labour forces of the latter, that there should be major migration flows to the richer group of countries.

However, the actual situation is much more complex. Migrants are attracted not just by wages but also by more general conditions of life, including welfare, security and educational opportunities, in the developed world. The majority of regular immigrants from poor countries are now not workers but spouses and dependants, and they are joined by a substantial number of asylum-claimants and illegal immigrants. On the other hand, migration flows can co-exist with high levels of unemployment in the receiving countries. Social protection and high labour costs in the West can contribute to this situation, encouraging demand for clandestine labour.

Conventional economic migration theory by itself cannot well account either for the details of the pattern of migration nor for many of its trends, for example the increase in migration from the 1980s up to about 1992, nor indeed for its decline in the mid-1990s. We also need to explain why so many potential migrants do not attempt to move. We still lack a satisfactory comprehensive theory to account for migration trends or to forecast them. But it is at least clear that wider considerations need to be taken into account, including political, cultural and policy patterns and changes both in the sending and in the receiving countries. Populations of potential migrants have been mobilized by political changes in the sending countries and in the receiving countries, including the rise of entitlement in the host countries through the 'rights' revolution. However, this would have had little effect without the diffusion of knowledge through modern media and links with existing immigrant communities, which facilitate 'chain' migration.

The rapid diffusion to potential sending countries of information about transport links and changing entitlements has been further accelerated by the growth of trafficking and other legal and illegal developments in the migration industry. Growing immigrant populations in the receiving countries have also been important in generating persistent flows, through arranged marriage and other processes. Their presence, together with the long-term persistence of economic and demographic disparities, should ensure that while the details of flows might change, pressure to migrate will persist for decades to come. It is unlikely that these pressures could in any important way be alleviated by measures to accelerate economic growth in the sending countries.

References

Anson, J., & Meir, A. (1996). Religiosity, Nationalism and Fertility in Israel. *European Journal of Population*, 12(1), 1-25.

Appleyard, R. (1994). Emigration Dynamics in Developing Countries. *International Migration*, 33(3/4 special issue Emigration Dynamics in Developing Countries), 293-311.

Bohning, W. R. (1972). *The Migration of Workers in the UK and the European Community*. London: Oxford University Press.

Bohning, W.R., & Schloeter-Paredes, M.-L. (Eds.), (1994). *Aid in Place of Migration?* Geneva: International Labour Office.

Bongaarts, J., & Amin, S. (1997). *Prospects for Fertility Decline and Implications for Population Growth in South Asia*. New York: The Population Council.

Bongaarts, J., & Watkins, S.C. (1996). Social Interactions and contemporary fertility transitions. *Population and Development Review*, 22(4), 639-82.

Chesnais, J.C. (1995). *Le crépuscule de l'Occident: démographie et politique*. Paris: Robert Laffont.

Chesnais, J.-C. (1997). Transition de la prospérité et transition de la pauvreté: l'universalisation de la baisse de la fécondité. In IUSSP (Ed.), *International Population Conference Beijing 1997*, 269-85. Liège: IUSSP.

Coleman, D. A. (1993). Contrasting age-structure differences of Western Europe and of Eastern Europe and the former Soviet Union: demographic curiosity or labor resource? *Population and Development Review*, 19(3), 523-56.

Courbage, Y. (1998). L'avenir démographique de la rive sud de la Mediterranée (et les pays voisins). Reflexion sur les incidences socio-économiques et géopolitiques. Turin, Fondazione Giovanni Agnelli.

Dalrymple, W. (1997). *From the Holy Mountain: A Journey in the Shadow of Byzantium.* London: Harper Collins.

DHS (1997). New Findings from Egypt Assess Women's and Children's Health. *Demographic and Health Surveys Newsletter*, 8(2), 1-2, 9.

Faßmann, H. (1997). Is the Austrian Labour Market Ethnically Segmented? *European Journal of Population*, 13(1), 17-31.

Fergany, N. (1997). Dynamics of Demography and Development in the Mediterranean Basin: Implications to the Potential for Migration to Europe. In Council of Europe (Ed.), *Mediterranean Conference on Population, Migration and Development*, 211-42. Strasburg: Council of Europe.

Freeman, G. S. (1994). Can Liberal States control Unwanted Migration? *Annals of the American Association for Political and Social Sciences* (534), 17-30.

Gurak, D.T., & Caces, F. (1992). Migration Networks and the Shaping of Migration Systems. In M. Kritz, L. L. Lim, & H. Zlotnik (Eds.), *International Migration Systems: A global approach*, 150-76. Oxford: Clarendon Press.

Hammar, T., & Tamas, K. (1997). Why do people go or stay? In T. Hammar, G. Brochmann, K. Tamas, & T. Faist (Eds.), *International Migration, Immobility and Development*, 1-20. Oxford: Berg.

Hollifield, J.F. (1992). *Immigrants, Minorities and States: The political economy of post-war Europe.* Cambridge, Mass. Harvard University Press.

Hönekopp, E. (1993). The Effects of Turkish Accession to the EC on Population and Labour Market. *InterEconomics, March/April 1993*, 69-73.

Hugo, G. (1995). Migration as a Survival Strategy: The Family Dimension of Migration. In United Nations (Ed.), *Population Distribution and Migration. Procedings of the UN Expert Group Meeting on Population Distribution and Migration, Santa Cruz, Bolivia 1993*, 168-82. New York: United Nations.

IOM (1993). *Profiles and Motives of Potential Migrants. An IOM Study undertaken in Four Countries: Albania, Bulgaria, Russia and Ukraine.* Geneva: International Organisation for Migration.

Johnson, J.H. & Salt, J. (Eds.), (1990). *Labour Migration. The International Geographical Mobility of Labour in the Developed World.* London: David Fulton.

Kantner, A., & He, S. (1996). Levels and Trends in Fertility in South Asia: A Review of Recent Evidence. In IUSSP (Ed.), *Comparative Perspectives on Fertility Transition in South Asia. Proceedings of an IUSSP Seminar at Rawalpindi / Islamabad 1996*, 1-38. Liège: IUSSP.

Kuznets, S. (1958). Long Swings in the Growth of Population and in related Economic Variables. *Proceedings of the American Philosophical Society*, 102(1), 25-52.

Lin, F., & Liu, J. (1997). China's Fertility Transition and the Prospect of Population Situation. In IUSSP (Ed.), *Symposium on the Demography of China*, 97-126. Peking: China Population Association.

Macura, M., & Coleman, D. A. (Eds.), (1994). *International Migration: regional processes and responses,*. New York and Geneva: United Nations.

Malmberg, G. (1997). Time and Space in International Migration. In T. Hammar, G. Brochmann, K. Tamas, & T. Faist (Eds.), *International Migration, Immobility and Development*, 21-48). Oxford: Berg.

Martin, P.L. (1991). *The Unfinished Story: Turkish labour migration to Western Europe*. Geneva: International Labour Office.

Martin, P.L. (1993). *Trade and Migration: NAFTA and Agriculture*. Institute for International Economics.

Massey, D.S., Arango, J., Hugo, G., Kouaouci, A., Pellegrino, A., & Taylor, J. E. (1993). Theories of International Migration: A Review and Appraisal. *Population and Development Review*, 19(3), 431-66.

Murphy, M., & Berrington, A. (1993). Constructing period parity progression ratios from household survey data. In M. Ni Bhrolchain (Ed.), *New Perspectives on Fertility in Britain. Studies on Medical and Population Subjects*, No 55, 17-32. London: HMSO.

Martin, P.L. (1992). Foreign Direct Investment and Migration: the Case of Mexican Maquiladoras. In IOM (Ed.), *Tenth IOM Seminar on Migration: Migration and Development*. Geneva: International Organization for Migration.

OECD (1998). *Trends in International Migration. Annual Report 1998 edition*. Paris: OECD.

Oosthuizen, K. (1997). Similarities and differences between the fertility decline in Europe and the emerging fertility decline in sub-Saharan Africa. In IUSSP (Ed.), *International Population Conference Beijing 1997*, 1063-90). Liège: IUSSP.

Penn world table. *Quarterly Journal of Economics*, May 1991.

Piore, M.J. (1979). *Birds of Passage: Migrant Labor in Industrial Societies*. Cambridge: Cambridge University Press.

PRB (1998). World Population Data Sheet. Washington D.C. Population Reference Bureau Inc.

Premi, M.K., & Mathur, M.D. (1995). Emigration dynamics — the Indian context. *International Migration*, 33(3/4 Special Issue: Emigration Dynamics in Developing Countries), 627-66.

Rallu, J.-L., & Toulemon, L. (1993). Les mesures de la fécondité transversale. 1. Construction des différents indices. *Population*, 48(1), 7-26.

Roberts, K. (1997). China's 'tidal wave' of migrant labor: What can we learn from Mexican undocumented migration to the United States? *International Migration Review*, 31(2), 249-93.

Russell, S.S., & Teitelbaum, M.S. (1992). *International Migration and International Trade. World Bank Discussion Paper 160*. Washington DC: World Bank.

Salt, J. (1997). *Current Trends in International Migration in Europe. Consultant's Report to the Council of Europe November 1997*. Strasburg: Council of Europe.

Salt, J., & Ford, R. (1993). Skilled International Migration to Europe: the shape of things to come? In R. King (Ed.), *Mass Migration in Europe: the legacy and the future*, 293-309. London: Belhaven.

Salt, J., & Stein, J. (1997). Migration as a Business: The case of Trafficking. *International Migration*, 35(4).

Schaeffer, P.V. (1993). A definition of migration pressure based on demand theory. *International Migration*, 31(1), 43-72.

Stahl, C.W., Ball, R., Inglis, C., & Gutman, P. (1993). *Global Population Movements and their Implications for Australia*. Canberra: Australian Government Publishing Service.

Stark, O. (1991). *The Migration of Labor*. Cambridge, Massachusetts: Basil Blackwell.

Stark, O., & Bloom, D.E. (1985). The New Economics of Labor Migration. *American Economic Review*, 75, 173-78.

Straubhaar, T. (1993). Migration Pressure. *International Migration*, 31(1), 5-41.

Tapinos, G. (1991). Can International Co-operation be an alternative to the Emigration of Workers? In *International Conference on Migration*. Rome: OECD.

Teitelbaum, M.S. (1990). *Unauthorized Migration: An Economic Development Response. Executive summary, Report of the Commission for the Study of International Migration and Co-operative Economic Development*. Washington: US Government Printing Office.

Thomas, B. (1954). *Migration and Economic Growth*. Oxford: Oxford University Press.

Todaro, M.P., & Maruszko, L. (1987). Illegal migration and US immigration reform: A conceptual framework. *Population and Development Review*, 13, 101-14.

Tolts, M. (1995). Modernization of Demographic Behaviour in the Muslim Republics of the Former USSR. In Y. Ro'i (Ed.), *Muslim Eurasia: Conflicting legacies*. London: Frank Cass, pp 231-53.

UN ECE (1991). *Economic Survey of Europe in 1990-1991*. New York: United Nations Economic Commission for Europe.

United Nations (1997). *World Population Prospects: The 1996 Revision*. New York: United Nations.

United Nations (1998). *World Population Estimates and Projections, 1998*. New York: United Nations.

van Hear, N. (1998). *New Diasporas: The mass exodus, dispersal and regrouping of migrant communities*. London: UCL Press.

Weiner, M. (1985). On International Migration and International Relations. *Population and Development Review*, 2(3), 441-55.

WHO (1997). *The World Health Report*. Geneva: WHO.

Widgren, J. (1994). *The Key to Europe: a comparative analysis of entry and asylum policies in Western countries*. Stockholm: Fritzes.

CHAPTER 2

International Migration to Europe in the late 1990s

David Coleman

2.1 Introduction

2.1.1 Aims and scope of the chapter

This second chapter describes population movements to Europe and some aspects of the diverse immigrant populations which they have already generated. In doing so it attempts to evaluate the consequences of this migration, to see how it relates to European demographic or labour force needs and its effects upon the ethnic and demographic future of Europe's populations. A third chapter will investigate the policy responses to the new migration and to the immigrant or ethnic minority populations which it has created.

Here the term 'Western' Europe refers to all the European countries (including the Mediterranean countries) which were not part of the former East bloc. Eastern Europe refers to the former East bloc (including East Germany up to 1991). Neither is taken to include Turkey or Israel.

In the early 1990s Western Europe was at the peak of an unexpected increase in international migration. Older streams of immigration, for example for family reunion, once thought to be diminishing, began to increase. They were supplemented by new patterns of regular migration, including marriage migration to provide spouses through arranged marriages for the growing immigrant minorities in many European countries. Regular labour migration also increased, in particular for German reconstruction, a flow otherwise apparently perverse in view of growing unemployment. Outside regular streams, larger numbers of people began to enter Europe claiming asylum, many having earlier entered illegally or overstayed. Illegal immigration itself took on new dimensions. By the mid-1990s, the peak of migration appeared to have passed and numbers both of regular immigrants and of asylum-claimants had fallen, especially numbers net of return migration, although they remain at a high level at the end of the decade.

We cannot state confidently why either the upswing or the downswing in migration occurred as they did, although the latter is almost certainly a response to policy measures intended to moderate flows considered to be excessive. However that may be, the foreign populations already in Europe, and still entering it, present European societies with economic, social and cultural challenges which will occupy their governments for decades to come.

Immigrants came from a wider range of geographical origins than before, not only a wider range of third-world countries but also from Eastern Europe and the former Soviet Union, where a whole new migration space had opened up with the collapse of communism and its controls. Those Eastern European countries not only sent migrants, almost at once they began to receive them across their unregulated borders in large numbers for the first time in the post-war period. Small wonder that these events provoked an equally unexpected revival of interest in the otherwise neglected study of migration (Fassmann and Münz, 1992; Okolski, 1991; Böhning, 1992; Livi-Bacci, 1991; van de Kaa, 1991; Coleman, 1993).

2.2 Cautionary tales on migration data

2.2.1 Data on flows

Warnings on the inadequacy of migration data are a regrettable necessity in any publication on international migration (International Migration Review, 1987; Zlotnik and Hovy, 1991; Poulain, 1993, Salt et al., 1993). For demographic purposes, an international migrant is defined by the United Nations as one who (irrespective of birthplace or nationality) has entered a country with the intention of staying at least 12 months and who has been away for at least 12 months. This excludes the labour migration of seasonal workers, and all 'border' migration. But few countries in Europe (the UK with its International Passenger Survey is one of them) gather statistics on this basis. Instead most statistics on migration are gathered as a by-product of control or of population registration by national governments.

The volume of international passenger movement is immense — there are over 50 million international passenger movements both in and out of the UK each year, about the same as the population of the country. At any given time there are about 500,000 international passengers in the air between destinations. Statistical recording of all such vast movement is perfunctory. Only a small proportion can be described as 'migratory' — about 200,000 per year in each direction in the UK case (ONS, 1997).

Typically, in response to these problems, most published data on international migration are not based on counting the flows of migrants past frontiers, but instead through registration systems. Inflows of foreign population is measured by new registrations, outflows by the cancellation of old ones, and net migration by the difference between the two. That is the basis of the majority of 'migration' data reported in the annual SOPEMI system (OECD, 1998). SOPEMI is the 'Système d'Observation Permanente des Migrations Internationaux', a network of national correspondent experts reporting annually to the OECD. Along with the migration data from Eurostat, the annual SOPEMI report is the most comprehensive compilation of data on international migration and policies relating to migration. Immigration data of this kind depends on there being a registration system in the first place (there is none in the UK, for example) and focuses attention only on persons of foreign nationality (admittedly the centre of policy interest in migration matters) and on immigrants who match the criteria for registration of residence (in terms of length of stay, for example). German practice here tends to inflate the apparent volume of migration into and out of Germany because of the short period of qualification for residence, for example. But despite that there is no doubt that migration flows to Germany, in any sense, are large. German migration flows have also been affected by unification. In 1989, for example there were 344,000 *Übersiedler* immigrants from East Germany, persons accepted as German nationals under the Basic Law but nonetheless international migrants. Such migration (abated after unification made it partly redundant) is now of course internal migration, not international.

The output of data depends on the diverse aims and definitions of the legislation. Because these aims and rules each have unique legal and political histories, the data published on international migration by different countries often refer to different categories of people and are difficult to compare (Salt, Singleton & Hogarth, 1993). For example, UK immigration law makes no mention of the word 'immigrant' and the statistics published by the Home Office refer to persons 'given leave to enter' the country, most of whom had been resident for some time already. Until the latest SOPEMI report, these data were presented as 'immigration' data. The gaps in the consolidated tables in the annual SOPEMI reports (OECD, 1998) and in this chapter testify to these defects, although the coverage and quality have improved greatly in recent years.

Eurostat now publishes a comprehensive analysis of migration to and within the EU. Even so, data on movement between EU countries has been very unsatisfactory. Out of a possible 132 sets of data on migration between EC countries at the end of the 1980s, for example, data were available for 96 (73%) of the immigration streams and 88 (67%) of the emigration streams. But of 62 possible comparisons of data on movement between specific EC countries, in only six of the streams were the figures for emigration and immigration numerically compatible (Poulain, 1993). Other real migrant flows do not enter any statistics. For example, there are no immigration controls on person entering the UK from Ireland and no (direct) data on them, because the law does not require it. The situation in Eastern Europe, where law, administration and statistics have had to be built up from scratch, provokes even more complaint (Kupiszewski, 1996).

Without legal control on emigration in most open societies there are no corresponding emigration statistics. Outward movement is patchily recorded; for example by the voluntary sample of the International Passenger Survey (IPS) in the UK (ONS, 1997). Over the years these data have been plagued by problems, such that some researchers refuse to use them (Peach, 1981). Recent large-scale illegal overstaying or 'switching' from short-term pretexts for entry to permanent ones have caused the estimates of net immigration based upon them to be nearly doubled (Coleman, 1997). There are no emigration data from France and many other countries. European countries of emigration (Portugal, Spain) which used to regulate and measure emigration were and remain correspondingly poor on immigration control and immigration statistics. All East European countries had strict controls on emigration before 1989; some restrictions still apply (e.g. Romania). As these remaining controls do not necessarily benefit departing resident, they are often avoided. Official data on outward labour migration are usually underestimates (Martin, 1991) where they exist at all.

Typically, outside the EU and Nordic countries, nations exercise some control on incoming labour movement to protect their own labour forces, so that would-be labour migrants must obtain an official work permit. That creates a limited set of separate labour migration statistics (Salt et al., 1993) although in the EU and the Nordic countries they only apply to labour migrants from outside those areas. Only a few countries (New Zealand and Australia) yet link records of those who enter to those who depart. In those cases it is easy; geographical distance deters the passing trade, total volumes are modest and a high proportion of entrants are for settlement. In many European countries much of the post-war labour migration was planned on a guest worker basis, thus generating statistics on return migration. (Kubat, 1984; United Nations, 1982). For example, between 500,000 and 900,000 Turkish workers have returned to Turkey, mostly from Germany, and between 1981-87 net migration between Yugoslavia and Germany was –52,000 (Okolski, 1991).

2.2.2 Data on stocks

International migration leads to the creation of immigrant populations initially of foreign nationality: Workers, students, families, spouses, asylum-claimants, illegals. Depending on their responses to their new environment and the policies of the government of the host society, they may retain 'immigrant' characteristics for more than one generation and come to be regarded as new 'ethnic minorities', or they and their children may remain 'foreigners'. Data on these populations comprise the second source of data on immigrants; those relating to 'stocks' rather than to 'flows'. As we saw above changes in 'stock' data are used indirectly to measure the intensity of the flows of immigration as well. Data on population of foreign nationality come from censuses, from statistics on national or health insurance, from continuous registration systems, or from the annual EU Labour Force Surveys. These sources usually also provide data on birthplace. But in most European countries, 'nationality' is the main criterion in determining immigrant stocks. However immigrants need not be foreigners, and foreigners need not be immigrants. Many immigrants have been naturalized and no longer count as 'foreigners' in citizenship terms. Others, as in Commonwealth citizens in the UK, or citizens of overseas territories of the Netherlands and of France (the 'DOM-TOM'; 'Domaines d'outre-mer/Territoires d'outre-mer'), were not foreigners to begin with.

In countries which follow the *ius sanguinis*, that is, a right of citizenship or of residence based on ancestry rather than birthplace, e.g. Germany and Austria, children of foreign immigrants born in the receiving country do not automatically acquire its citizenship but may remain foreigners, although not immigrants. In addition, persons born outside a country but who enter it under special provisions relating to their national or ethnic origin, 'ethnic return migrants' such as German *aussiedler*, or Jews migrating to Israel, may feature as a special category in flow statistics but then become statistically invisible as they are not 'foreigners'. The use of nationality criteria rather than foreign birthplace underestimates the population of foreign origin in some countries in Europe but can overestimate the number of immigrants in others.

A few countries in Europe, and all the English-speaking countries overseas, also use the notion of 'ethnic group' (Castles, 1991; Department of Statistics, 1993; Statistics Canada & US Department of Commerce, 1993; Coleman and Salt, 1996). Such persons may be neither foreign nor immigrant. Even where the term is not used officially it is coming into use anyway through social science (Castles, Booth, & Wallace, 1984; Cross, 1992; Kalibova, 1996), sometimes as a gesture of commitment to a particular view of the appropriate treatment of immigrant populations. In the Netherlands in 1991 there were 692,000 foreigners but 876,000 members of defined ethnic minority groups targeted by the Netherlands minorities policy. Many of them (e.g. Surinamese and Antilleans) are not foreigners. In Great Britain in 1991 there were 3.75 million persons born outside the UK, 3.1 million members of various official 'ethnic minority' groups and 1.79 million foreigners (Salt, 1996a, table 5.2a). These categories were substantially non-overlapping; 2/3 of the immigrants did not belong to the ethnic minority groups; most members of the ethnic minority groups were not foreigners. In the Anglo-Saxon countries 'ethnic' group memberships in the census and surveys are self-ascribed, usually from a limited list.

Many continental countries such as France do not collect 'ethnic' statistics, considering the concept to be divisive, and objectionable on principle (Haut Conseil à l'Integration, 1991). Nonetheless attempts are made to reconstruct

Table 2.1 Naturalization in selected European countries 1987-96.

Table 2.1a Numbers of naturalizations (thousands)

Country	1987	1988	1989	1990	1991	1992	1993	1994	1995	1996	Total 1987-96
Austria	8.2	8.2	8.5	9.2	11.4	11.9	14.4	16.3	15.3	16.2	119.6
Belgium	1.6	1.7			8.5	46.4	16.4	25.8	26.1	24.6	151.1
Denmark		3.7	3.3	3.0	5.5	5.1	5.0	5.7	5.3	7.3	43.9
France	33.9	74.0	82.0	88.5	95.5	95.3	95.5	126.3	92.4	109.8	893.2
Germany	37.8	40.8	68.5	101.4	141.6	179.9	199.4	259.2	313.6	302.8	1645.0
Italy					4.5	4.4	6.5	6.6	7.4	7.0	36.4
Netherlands	19.3	9.1	28.7	12.8	29.1	36.2	43.1	49.5	71.4	82.7	381.9
Norway	2.4	3.4	4.6	4.8	5.1	5.1	5.5	8.8	11.8	12.2	63.7
Spain	9.1	8.1	5.9	7.0	3.8	5.3	8.4	7.8	6.8	8.4	70.6
Sweden	20.0	18.0	17.6	16.8	27.7	29.3	42.7	35.1	32.0	25.6	264.8
Switzerland	12.4	11.4	10.3	8.7	8.8	11.2	12.9	13.8	16.8	19.4	125.7
UK	64.9	64.6	117.1	57.3	58.6	42.2	45.8	44.0	40.5	43.1	578.1
All					400.1	472.3	495.6	598.9	639.4	659.1	4373.9

Table 2.1b Percent of foreign population naturalized

	1987	1988	1989	1990	1991	1992	1993	1994	1995	1996
Austria		2.5	2.5	2.4	2.5	2.2	2.3	2.4	2.1	2.2
Belgium	0.2	0.2			0.9	5.0	1.8	2.8	2.8	2.7
Denmark		2.7	2.3	2.0	3.4	3.0	2.8	3.0	2.7	3.3
Germany	0.8	1.0	1.5	2.1	2.7	3.1	3.1	3.8	4.5	4.2
Italy					0.6	0.5	0.7	0.7	0.8	0.7
Netherlands	3.3	1.5	4.6	2.0	4.2	4.9	5.7	6.3	9.4	11.4
Norway	1.9	2.7	3.4	3.4	3.5	3.5	3.6	5.4	7.2	7.6
Spain		2.4	1.6	2.8	1.3	1.5	2.1	1.8	1.5	1.7
Sweden	5.0	4.5	4.2	3.7	5.7	5.9	8.5	6.9	6.0	4.8
Switzerland	1.3	1.2	1.0	0.8	0.8	1.0	1.1	1.1	1.3	1.5
UK	3.5	3.5	6.4	3.2	3.4	2.4	2.3	2.2	2.1	2.1

Sources: OECD 1998 table A.1.7, OECD 1989 table F.
Note: Rate of naturalization for France cannot be calculated except for census years. In the census year 1990 the rate was 2.7 / 100. For France from 1988 onwards, figures are estimates.

the population of foreign descent for the purposes of estimation and projection. Divergent principles employed to this end can stir up passions. Official INED projections in 1980 were accused of having incorporated a 'statistical genocide' which eliminated 1,893,000 foreigners from the projected 2015 population (Bourcier de Carbon and Chaunu, 1986). Recent exchanges in the journal 'Population' revealed strong feelings about the appropriate way

to regard and compute the population of foreign origin (Le Bras, 1997; Tribalat, 1997), and in particular how far persons who had become naturalized
should still be regarded as to any extent 'foreign'. Thanks to a long history of
immigration, about 10.2 million residents of France in 1986, whether born in
France or not, could claim at least one foreign grandparent (Tribalat, Garson,
Moulier-Boutang & Silberman, 1991, p. 257).

2.2.3 The influence of naturalization

Totals of 'foreign' population are by definition net of naturalization, which di-
minishes the statistical visibility of the population of foreign origin and which
has proceeded at a rapid pace in some countries (Table 2.1), see Reinans and
Hammar, 1995. Whether or not naturalization reflects any important
adaptation on the part of its subjects to life in the host country, or serves to
promote it, and thereby turns 'foreigners' into 'natives' in some real sense, is
a separate issue. It is explored further in Chapter 3. In the UK, few of the 1.3
million immigrants from the New Commonwealth, and none of their 1.2
million descendants, are counted as 'foreigners'. Most therefore do not appear
in the totals above. Being 'Commonwealth Citizens' they were not technically
'foreigners' even on arrival, and most have been naturalized by an easy
process. In France, the pace of naturalization per year (109,800 in 1996, not
including 'automatic' naturalizations), is somewhat higher than the rate of
regular immigration, and has been over the last inter-censal period. The Netherlands too is naturalizing foreigners even faster than they arrive (83,000 in
1996, 11 % of the total foreign population). Since around 1990 a change of policy in Germany has brought annual naturalizations up to 303,000 in 1996.

This process can create the odd and misleading impression that the population of foreign origin is diminishing. The number of persons of foreign
birthplace naturalized in the last ten years alone in Western Europe would
add at least 3 million more to the 'foreign' total of 22.4 million given above.
The extent to which this is the case depends on the naturalization process and
nationality law in each country. That in turn depends upon national attitudes
to the definition of national identity. Table 2.2 shows that in the cases of the
Netherlands, Sweden and Great Britain, the number of immigrants (persons
born abroad) is about double the number of foreign citizens, primarily thanks
to high rates of naturalization. At the 1986 census there were 3.95 million immigrants in France, of whom a third (1.23 million) had acquired French
nationality. Where naturalization has not been pursued so vigorously or has
more demanding criteria, for example in Norway and in Denmark, the totals
of 'foreigners' and of immigrants are closer to each other.

The position is further complicated by the fact that the foreign total for
some counties (e.g. Germany) includes a substantial number of persons who
are not immigrants, but who are born in the host country of foreign parents.

Table 2.2 Proportion of population of foreign citizenship, and born abroad, selected countries, 1990s.

Country		Population (millions)	Born abroad (thousands)	Born abroad (percent)	Foreign nationality (thousands) (percent)		Foreign as % of immigrant
Belgium	1996	10.157	...	...	911.9	9.0	...
Denmark	1996	5.236	259.2	5.0	237.7	4.5	91.7
France	1990	56.577	...	...	3596.9	6.4	...
Germany	1996	81.678	...	...	7314.0	9.0	...
Netherlands	1995	15.424	1407.1	9.1	757.1	4.9	53.8
Norway	1996	4.381	246.9	5.6	157.5	3.6	63.8
Sweden	1996	8.841	943.8	10.7	526.6	6.0	55.8
Great Britain	1991	54.889	3746.1	6.8	1791.0	3.3	47.8

Sources: OECD 1998, table B.1.5, B.1.6; Council of Europe 1998.

That will tend, other things being equal, to lead to 'foreign' totals, ʒiving an excessive, not an understated estimate of the immigrant population, more akin to an 'ethnic minority' population concept. Data based on the latter concept are only available for a very few countries, including Great Britain, the English-speaking countries abroad and the Netherlands. In Great Britain the ethnic minority population is defined by reference to exclusively non-European groups of immigrant origin, who numbered 3.1 million (6%) of the population of England and Wales in 1991 (Owen, 1996).

2.3 International migration to Europe: patterns and trends

Since the 1950s, the Western European countries have been the focus of two overlapping international migration systems. The first is that between the developed countries of Europe and between them and equivalently rich developed counties outside it. These migrations, an inevitable consequence of trade, academic and other contacts between open societies, has developed and proceeds relatively unremarked and uncontroversial. Migration between economic equals seldom causes problems.

2.3.1 Migration between Western European countries

Migration between neighbouring countries in the same region has, at least in the case of the EU countries, been surprisingly modest in the last decade or more, given the almost complete removal of formal barriers to migration. The 1960s and 1970s had been dominated by guest-worker movements from the fringes of Europe to the centre, and later by migration from outside Europe and the immigration of their dependents and still later by new spouses. But

Highly-skilled and some low-skilled labour migration continues, retirement migration of British and Germans is important in Spain. More students study abroad. There is modest demand for new 'guest workers' but most are not from EU countries. Old guest workers from Italy, Spain and Greece have returned to their now much more prosperous homelands in large numbers, although more of those from Portugal, as well as Turkey and Yugoslavia, have remained. Despite strong regional differences in wages and unemployment, and the further encouragement of the Single European Act, an equilibrium of about 600,000 international movements per year within the EU seems to have developed, balancing economic incentives with cultural and personal barriers to movement.

However, some increase became apparent from around 1990, especially among the highly skilled and professional. This movement, disproportionately towards the central part of the EU, may partly be due to the growth of European institutions (Poulain, 1996). German reunification also unleashed a transient burst of labour demand in the early 1990s, attracting labour from within and outside the EU. In an unusual development, London has become a popular destination for young French workers; one in ten workers in the metropolis is foreign, much more than the national average. Proponents of EU economic and monetary union claim that it will stimulate overall European economic performance. However the effects on regional disparities are hard to predict. In the absence of exchange rate adjustments, economic downturns in particular countries would have to be compensated by more substantial labour market adjustments; either lower wages, or more out-migration, or higher unemployment (Rhein, 1995).

Free movement is only agreed for new members of the EU when it is deemed that their economic development and other characteristics are sufficiently on a par with those of other member states to ensure only moderate levels of migration. Such was the case with Spain, Portugal and Greece. If similar requirements of convergence and of delays in full freedom of movement are imposed on the new Central and Eastern European applicants to the EU, then migration from them may be equally modest. Before transition, international migration between the European member countries of COMECON was surprisingly modest (Macura, 1974) given the obvious opportunities for securely controlled migration and the regional imbalances of labour supply and demand. There was some overseas recruitment from fraternal communist countries abroad, for example Vietnam. Eastern and Central Europe was relatively free of the migration turmoil of Western Europe, although of course it was also relatively free of the economic growth and liberal political systems which provoked it. That has all now changed, although as noted below the consequences for international migration to the West have been relatively modest. The most interesting developments are those whereby Eastern Europe has itself become an immigration region, a topic to which we turn below.

Table 2.3 Gross inflows of foreign population into Western Countries 1980-96 (selected countries only). Thousands. Generally asylum-seekers are not included. For details of more countries and of intervening years, see Appendix Table 2.1

Country	1980	1982	1984	1986	1988	1990	1992	1994	1996
Austria	...	...	...	...	...	...	...	276.9	224.2
Belgium	46.8	36.2	37.2	39.3	38.2	50.5	55.1	56.0	51.9
Denmark[1]	...	13.0	17.9	17.6	13.8	15.9	16.9	15.6	...
France[2]	59.4	144.4	51.4	38.3	44.0	102.4	116.6	91.5	74.0
Germany[3]	523.6	275.5	331.1	478.3	648.6	842.0	1207.6	774.0	708.3
Hungary	...	...	...	...	23.5	37.2	15.1	12.8	9.4
Luxemburg	7.4	6.4	6.0	7.4	8.2	9.3	9.8	9.2	...
Netherlands[4]	78.5	39.7	37.3	52.8	58.3	81.3	83.0	68.4	77.2
Norway[5]	11.8	14.0	12.8	16.8	23.2	15.7	17.2	17.9	17.2
Sweden[6]	...	...	26.1	34.0	44.5	53.2	39.5	74.7	29.3
Switzerland[7]	70.5	74.7	58.6	66.8	76.1	101.4	112.1	91.7	74.3
UK[8]	69.8	53.9	51.0	47.8	49.3	52.4	52.6	55.	61,7
UK[9]	173.7	201.7	201.1	250.3	216.0	266.8	215.9	193.6	216.4
Canada	143.1	121.1	88.2	99.2	161.9	214.2	252.8	223.9	226.1
USA	530.6	594.1	543.9	601.7	643.0	1536.5	974.2	804.4	915.9

Notes: Data generally from population registers except for Austria, France, UK, Canada, USA. Data from annual SOPEMI reports can differ substantially from data given in earlier reports (e.g. Denmark, Norway, Sweden).

1. Entries of foreigners staying in Denmark for more than one year. Asylum-seekers and refugees with provisional permit not included.
2. Up to 1989, includes entries of new foreign workers with permanent and provisional work permits, and family reunification. After 1990, provisional work permits not included, but spouses of French nationals, parents of French children, refugees and those eligible for a residence permit are included.
3. Data includes reunited Germany after 1990.
4. Register data include asylum-seekers with provisional stay permits, recognized refugees, those admitted on humanitarian grounds. Asylum-seekers in reception centres excluded.
5. Foreigners intending to spend more than 6 months in Norway.
6. Residence notification entries for less than one year are not included (mostly citizens of other Nordic countries).
7. Foreigners with annual residence permits and permanent permits returning to Switzerland after a temporary stay abroad. Includes (up to 31 Dec 92) holders of permits of less than 12-month duration. Seasonal and frontier workers excluded. 92, 93 Clerc 94. P.8.
8. Data on non-British citizens from Home Office Control of Immigration Statistics; 'Accepted for Settlement' only. Most persons 'accepted' will have actually entered the UK in previous years.
9. Gross inflow data from the International Passenger Survey. Sample of persons (all nationalities) intending to (re)enter the UK for at least 12 months. (United Nations definition). Asylum-seekers not included except for the small number recognized and accepted for settlement.

Sources: OECD 1998 and earlier SOPEMI table A.2, INS Statistical Yearbook table 1.
Statistics Canada Report on the Demographic Situation in Canada 1994 table A 8.

2.3.2 Migration from outside Western Europe

The second migration system, not independent of the first, is of large-scale international migration to core European countries from the fringes of Europe and from outside Europe altogether (Bohning, 1972; Salt & Clout, 1976). It is by no means without precedent; there were considerable flows of labour migrants from Poland, Greece and Italy to Germany and France before the second and even before the first world war, at a time when those sending countries were more economically marginal than they are now. Nonetheless the scale of the post-war migration is new, as are its lasting consequences, arising substantially from the fact that the immigrant populations are not European. It is to these populations that most interest, and most policy, is addressed.

The background to this large-scale post-war international migration to Europe from outside is too well known to need detailed repetition. 'Temporary' guest-worker recruitment extended beyond Europe's fringe during a historically unique period of economic expansion. Already past its peak and provoking some domestic disquiet, that ceased in most countries around 1973 at the time of the first oil crisis. Not all was organised; some was spontaneous, some of it even then illegal. The resultant populations were made permanent by the growing obligation to permit family reunion, the continued chain migration of new spouses and others from the countries of origin, processes which continue strongly today. Not all countries or flows fit this sequential pattern. Some countries (e.g. the UK) recruited very little and only privately but received large flows from former colonial populations entitled to easy entry and mobilized by post-war conditions, a process also affecting France and the Netherlands. By the early 1980s, however, all these pressures appeared to be moderating.

2.3.3 Migration flows since the 1980s

But then, by contrast with its relatively stable internal migration regime, Europe experienced a marked increase in immigration legal, irregular and illegal (Tables 2.3, 2.4). This has turned almost all European countries, including the former sending countries of the Mediterranean, into *de facto* countries of immigration, including even the Irish Republic, although most of its immigrants are return migrants.

The numbers of regular migrants into Western European countries, dependants and new spouses but also including an unusual number of new labour migrants, increased substantially up to 1992. In that year about 1.5 million persons entered Western European countries lawfully, for purposes which might loosely be called 'immigration'. In addition to about 1.2 million dependants, spouses and labour migrants there were about 240,000 ethnic migrants

Table 2.4 Net inflow of foreign population into selected Western countries, 1980-96. Thousands. Asylum-seekers not included, except where indicated.

Country	1980	1982	1984	1986	1988	1990	1992	1994	1996
Belgium	...	...	...	7.5	6.0	23.4	26.9	21.9	19.5
Denmark	0.4	–0.1	4.0	11.0	8.5	10.5	12.1	10.5	...
Finland	–1.2	7.3	4.2	1.7	1.3	5.6	8.9	6.1	4.5
Germany	312.0	–75.4	–151.1	130.5	289.5	376.4	592.9	152.5	148.9
Luxemburg	...	...	...	1.9	2.9	3.8	4.2	3.9	...
Netherlands	53.0	3.2	8.0	29.2	36.9	60.7	60.3	45.7	54.8
Norway[1]	4.1	5.7	3.8	8.4	13.9	5.9	9.1	8.3	7.2
Sweden[2]	9.6	2.0	8.7	18.6	32.7	37.0	26.3	59.0	14.9
Switzerland[3]	6.8	12.1	3.0	14.0	20.3	41.8	31.7	27.5	6.6
UK[4]	28.0	32.0	45.0	49.0	32.7	65.8	22.8	52.9	...
UK[5]	...	...	...	70.0	71.8	118.2	68.9	99.3	...
Total	...	...	...	271.8	444.7	630.9	795.2	388.3	...
Germany %	...	...	...	48.0	65.1	59.7	74.6	39.3	...

1. Foreigners intending to spend more than 6 months in Norway.
2. Some short-duration entries are not counted (mostly citizens of other Nordic countries).
3. Foreigners with annual residence permits and permanent permits who return to Switzerland after a temporary stay abroad. Includes (up to 31 Dec 92) holders of permit of less than 12 months duration. Seasonal and frontier workers excluded.
4. Data from International Passenger Survey; UN immigration criterion, 'non-British' citizenships. ONS MN no 22 table 2.1.
5. Corrected data on 'non-British' citizens taking account of 'visitor switchers' entering on short-term pretext and remaining for marriage, post-entry asylum claims, etc. ONS Series MN no 22 table A.
Sources: OECD 1998 and earlier SOPEMI.

entering under various constitutional provisions. The majority of these were *Aussiedler* of German origin moving to Germany from Eastern Europe and the former Soviet Union. On top of those regular streams there were 692,000 asylum claims — the highest number ever recorded before or since. According to Widgren (1994, p. 19) if the 370,000 people fleeing Yugoslavia who were given temporary protection outside the asylum system are added, and an estimate made of over three hundred thousand illegal immigrants or illegal overstayers, the total gross inflow to Western Europe in 1992 would amount to about 2.9 million. It is important to remember, however, that emigration and return flows are also strong, and the net regular immigration that year was probably under 1 million, amounting to roughly 50% of the gross figure.

Mass migration to Europe is especially a German phenomenon. About 60% of regular migrants and about the same proportion of irregular ones have migrated to Germany. In addition, both the *Aussiedler* migration and the attraction to Germany of asylum-claimants are specific consequences of German law. Both have now been modified and the flows stabilized or reduced, as chapter 3 will detail. Germany's strong economy naturally attracts the lion's share of Europe's international migrants. Given unemployment at 11%, it will be preoccupied with their absorption for the foreseeable future. These include the large number of German migrants from East to West Germany before unification (*Übersiedler*) — about 340,000 in 1989, before the addition of the total population of East Germany (17 million) from October 1990. On top of that came ethnic German *Aussiedler* from Eastern Europe and the former Soviet Union — a cumulative total of 1.509 million from 1990-95 inclusive, although now arriving at a lower rate than in the early 1990s (218,000 in 1995; Hönekopp, 1997). With 408,000 net immigrants in 1995 (foreign inflow 788,000), 12% unemployment and persistent difficulties in reviving the former East Germany, West Germany is according to some researchers unlikely to need any additional increases in its labour force from migration until 2010 at least (Kühlewind, 1995 pp. 8, 9).

1993 seems to have been a turning point in the trend of both regular and irregular immigration into Europe, and may mark the beginning of a new period in immigration. Almost all components of migration which can be counted — especially labour migrants under work permit and asylum-claimants, have declined since the peak year of 1992.

Labour migration to most countries which provide data has declined (Italy, UK, Denmark are exceptions) (Table 2.5, also Table 4.4 in chapter 4). The tenfold increase to Germany since the mid-1980s was especially stimulated by the reconstruction process in the former East Germany and by the foreign policy need to develop contacts with the east; in this case through various employment programmes for Poles. The demand from reconstruction has now slackened; the employment programmes with the East have been curtailed in the light of domestic recession. In 1996, however, labour migration was still much higher than in the mid-1980s.

Net migration declined in proportional terms much more, particularly to Germany and to Switzerland, where the total declined to a third or less of its peak value. That indicates an acceleration of emigration or of return migration of previous immigrants. The United Kingdom did not share in this reduction. In fact correction of the net immigration figures to the UK from the International Passenger Survey, to include overstayers who switched from short-term entry to long-term through marriage or asylum-claiming, has doubled the previous estimates and put them firmly on an upward trend at least up to the mid-1990s. However, although more truthful as a description of migration, the inclusion of some asylum-claimants makes them less comparable with other countries' figures.

In most countries the number of asylum claims in 1997 was considerably lower than the peak years of 1992-93, with some fluctuations in between (Table 2.6). This is most marked in the most important asylum country (Germany) where claims in 1997 were a quarter of the total in 1992. The UK, despite some controversial but obvious ineffectual new legislation, was once again a perverse exception comparing 1997 to 92/93, although 1991 remains the highest yet recorded. The reductions in other countries are believed to follow changes in the procedures and legislation on asylum to deter unfounded claims and prevent asylum shopping in many countries, including a constitutional change in Germany, discussed further in Chapter 3.

2.4 Foreign population

The cumulative effects of past immigration have given the EU countries 22.4 million legally resident foreigners in 1996 (Eurostat 1997), of whom about 5 million were citizens of other European Union countries. 2.9 million were from Central and Eastern Europe, mostly from former Yugoslavia. Over 8 million were from outside Europe: 4.9 million from Turkey and the Maghreb, about 0.9 million from Asia. 36% of the total number of foreign residents and more than half of the non-EU nationals come from the Maghreb, Turkey and Yugoslavia (Table 2.7). While old immigrants have mostly stayed, new sources of immigration adding to and not replacing old ones, have given Western European countries a bigger and more diverse immigrant or foreign origin population than ever.

This total of 22 million also included about 800,000 persons from Yugoslavia receiving 'temporary protection'. It does not include the large number of ethnic German return migrants (*Aussiedler*), of whom 837,000 entered Germany between 1993 and 1996, mostly from the former Soviet Union. They are entitled to citizenship and are not counted as foreigners. Neither does the total above include most of the cumulative total of 5 million asylum-claimants since 1980 (strictly speaking 'claims' — some are duplicated). Although the great majority of these asylum claims were and are rejected as unfounded, most claimants, 80% according to Widgren, remain in Europe anyway, staying as they entered mostly in an illegal position. Illegal immigration, especially to Italy, Spain and Greece, is a common alternative to asylum-claiming, depending on opportunities, and has evidently increased as European countries have changed their administration and laws to deter bogus claims. In Italy in 1987-88, there were thought to be 850,000, in Spain 294,000, in Greece 70,000 and in Portugal 60,000 (ISOPLAN 1989). Minimal past estimates come from the response to 'regularization' programmes. In three separate episodes since 1987, Italy has regularized the presence of 484,000 illegal immigrants, and Spain has done the same to 173,000, and will doubtless do so again. In Italy the most numerous groups after the additional 'amnesty' of 1990 were Moroccans (69,821), Tunisians (38,837), Egyptians (12,441), Senegalese (24,174) Filipinos (22,889) and Yugoslavs (18,612) with representation from most countries of the third world. The International Labour Office estimated that there were 2.6 million illegal immigrants in Europe in 1991, similar to an estimate

Table 2.5 Gross inflows of foreign labour into Western countries (selected countries only), 1982-96. Thousands.

Country	1982	1983	1984	1985	1986	1987	1988	1989
Austria[1]	57.2	52.7	55.2	60.3	18.0	15.3	17.4	37.2
Belgium[2]	2.3	1.8	1.7	1.9	2.2	2.4	2.8	3.7
Denmark[3]	...	...	...	...	...	...	3.1	2.7
France Permanents[4]	97.0	17.3	10.8	9.7	9.9	10.7	12.7	15.6
France APT[5]	1.1	1.0	1.2	1.4	1.5	1.9	3.1	
Germany[6]	25.9	24.4	27.5	33.4	37.2	48.1	60.4	84.8
Hungary[7]...	...	...	...	...	...	...	...	25.3
Ireland[8]	...	...	...	...	...	...	...	1.2
Italy[9]	...	...	...	...	...	...	...	...
Luxemburg[10]	...	...	...	...	8.4	10.5	12.6	14.7
Spain[11]	...	...	...	...	...	...	...	
Switzerland[12]	...	...	...	...	29.4	33.6	34.7	37.1
UK Long-term[13]	...	...	...	...	7.9	8.1	10.4	13.3
UK Short-term[14]	...	...	...	...	8.0	9.4	11.8	12.2
UK trainees	...	...	...	...	2.8	2.9	3.8	4.2
UK Total	...	...	...	...	18.7	20.4	26.0	29.7

Total to Europe, excluding Denmark, Hungary, Ireland, Italy and Spain

Total (see above)	...	...	...	...	125.2	142.5	168.5	225.9
Germany %	...	...	...	...	29.7	33.8	35.8	37.5

of 2.5-3 million made in 1995 (Inter-Governmental Consultations 1995; Salt, 1996, pp. 8-9).

Foreigners comprise between 1.5% (Spain) and 19% (Switzerland) of the populations of the larger Western European countries, and 34% in the case of Luxemburg. Germany has received by far the greatest share of immigration to Western Europe (about 60%), and also of asylum-claims. Foreign population in Germany, 4.45 million in 1980, had increased to 7.31 million in 1996 (excluding ethnic Germans), the largest in Western Europe. Nonetheless Germany does not have the highest proportion of foreigners in its population. As noted above, Switzerland and Luxemburg have higher propertions. The foreign population in Belgium (9%) was the same as in Germany and was 4% in the Netherlands and Norway. In Spain and Italy, despite their discovery as countries of immigration, only about 1% and 2% respectively of (legal) residents are foreign, although in those countries a high proportion of immigrants are illegal and uncounted. In absolute numbers, Germany has the largest foreign population (7.31m) excluding ethnic Germans. In Eastern Europe, persons of foreign nationality typically comprise much less than 1% of the population, although substantial European minorities exist (Courbage, 1995); some ancient and indigenous, others arising from much earlier migrations or 20th century boundary changes, e.g. those of the Versailles treaty, which turned a large Romanian minority in Hungary into a large Hungarian minority in Romania.

Table 2.5 continued ...

Country	1990	1991	1992	1993	1994	1995	1996	Total
Austria[1]	103.4	62.6	57.9	37.7	27.1	15.4	16.3	633.7
Belgium[2]	...	5.1	4.4	4.3	4.1	3.0	2.2	41.9
Denmark[3]	2.8	2.4	2.4	2.1	2.1	2.2	2.7	22.5
France Permanents[4]	22.4	25.6	42.3	24.4	18.3	13.1	11.5	341.3
France APT[5]	3.8	4.1	3.9	4.0	4.1	4.5	4.8	40.4
Germany[6]	138.6	241.9	408.9	325.6	221.2	270.8	262.5	2211.2
Hungary[7]	51.9	41.7	24.6	19.5	18.6	18.4	14.5	214.5
Ireland[8]	1.4	3.8	3.6	4.3	4.3	4.3	3.8	26.7
Italy[9]	...	125.5	123.7	85.0	99.8	111.3	129.2	674.5
Luxemburg[10]	16.9	16.9	15.9	15.5	16.2	16.5	18.3	162.4
Spain[11]	19.8	85.0	52.8	17.4	23.5	36.6	...	235.1
Switzerland[12]	46.7	46.3	39.7	31.5	28.6	27.1	24.5	379.2
UK Long-term[13]	16.1	12.9	12.7	12.5	13.4	15.5	16.9	139.7
UK Short-term[14]	13.8	12.6	14.0	13.3	12.9	15.6	16.8	140.4
UK trainees	4.8	3.5	3.4	3.5	3.8	4.4	4.0	41.1
UK Total	34.7	29.0	30.1	29.3	30.1	35.5	37.7	321.2

Total to Europe, excluding Denmark, Hungary, Ireland, Italy and Spain

	1990	1991	1992	1993	1994	1995	1996	Total
Total (see above)	366.5	431.5	603.1	472.3	349.7	385.9	377.8	3648.9
Germany %	37.8	56.1	67.8	68.9	63.3	70.2	69.5	60.6

Notes: Data from selected countries only. Data for EU member states apply only to labour migrants from non-EU countries.
1. Work permits for new labour migrants and for those already resident. Includes seasonal workers. From 1986 data only refer to new entries. Comparable data 50.8 1986, 46.8 1987, 52.1 1988.
2. Permits to first-time immigrants in paid employment. Greece included until 1987, Spain and Portugal until 1992.
3. Residence permits for employment. Nordic citizens not included.
4. Foreign workers subject to control by Office des migrations internationales (OMI). 1982 data include 'regularizations'.
5. APT provisional work permits not to exceed 6 months. Renewable, for traineees, students etc.
6. New work permits issued. Include newly entered workers, contract workers and seasonal. Includes Greece up to 1987, Spain and Portugal up to 1992. Data refer to United Germany from 1991.
7. Grants of work permits including renewals.
8. Work permits issued including renewals.
9. Permits to new arrivals plus existing residents entering labour market.
10. Arrivals of new workers and existing residents starting work.
11. Includes initial permits for 1 year (renewable) and similar permit for self-employed. Excludes EU after 1992.
12. Includes new arrivals with a residence permit, holders of settlement permit returning after short stay abroad. Excludes issues of annual permits to seasonal workers.
13. Long-term permits (up to 4 years) mostly to highly skilled workers.
14. Short-term permits mostly for students doing temporary/part-time work, or to trainees.
Source: Mostly OECD SOPEMI report 1998 Table A.2.1 and earlier.

Table 2.6. Gross inflows of asylum-seekers to selected countries, 1980-97. Thousands.

Country	1980	1981	1982	1983	1984	1985	1986	1987	1988	1989
Austria	9.3	34.6	6.3	5.9	7.2	6.7	8.6	11.4	15.8	21.9
Belgium	2.7	2.4	3.1	2.9	3.7	5.3	7.6	6.0	5.1	8.0
Czech Republic	...	...	...	...	...	...	...	...	...	...
Denmark	...	...	...	0.8	4.3	8.7	9.3	2.8	4.7	4.6
Finland	...	...	...	0.0	0.0	0.0	0.0	0.1	0.1	0.2
France*	18.8	19.8	22.5	22.3	21.6	28.8	26.2	27.6	34.3	61.4
Germany	107.8	49.4	37.2	19.7	35.3	73.8	99.7	57.4	103.1	121.3
Ireland	...	...	...	...	...	...	...	...	...	...
Italy	...	...	...	3.1	4.6	5.4	6.5	11.0	1.4	2.2
Netherlands	1.3	0.8	1.2	2.0	2.6	5.6	5.9	13.5	7.5	13.9
Norway	0.1	0.1	0.1	0.2	0.3	0.8	2.7	8.6	6.6	4.4
Poland	...	...	...	...	...	...	...	...	...	...
Portugal	...	...	...	...	...	...	...	0.2	0.3	0.1
Spain*	...	...	...	...	...	...	2.8	3.7	4.5	4.0
Sweden	...	...	...	4.0	12.0	14.5	14.6	18.1	19.6	30.0
Switzerland	6.1	5.2	7.1	7.9	7.4	9.7	8.5	10.9	16.7	24.4
UK + dep	10.0	2.9	3.6	4.3	4.2	6.2	5.7	5.9	5.7	16.8
UK*	10.0	2.9	3.6	4.3	3.9	4.4	4.3	4.3	4.0	11.6
Total	156.1	115.2	81.1	73.1	103.2	165.7	198.2	177.1	225.2	313.3
Canada	...	...	...	5.0	7.1	8.4	23.0	35.0	45.0	19.9
United States	26.5	61.6	33.3	26.1	24.3	16.6	18.9	26.1	60.7	101.7

Because immigrants mostly settle in major cities and do not then diffuse even-ly across the geographical space of each country of settlement, they comprise very high proportions of the populations of many major European cities (Champion, 1994; Coleman, 1995a): 29% of the population of Frankfurt, 24% of Stuttgart, 22% of Munich in 1995 (Grunheid and Mammey, 1997, table 33) and 20% of the population of Greater London in 1991 (Owen, 1996, table 4.5, 'ethnic minority' population). Most of this large foreign population, more numerous than five of the present EU member states, has accumulated since the 1950s.

2.5 Components of migration

2.5.1 Geographical sources of immigration

Non-European immigrants come from most parts of the third world, directly or through Eastern Europe. Some areas predominate over others. North Africa and the Middle East are two of the most important sources of long standing, sending migrants to Europe, especially to France (Algeria) to Germany (Tur-key) and to the Netherlands (Morocco and Turkey). Each year from 1990 to

Table 2.6 continued ...

Country	1990	1991	1992	1993	1994	1995	1996	1997	Total
Austria	22.8	27.3	16.2	4.6	4.2	5.1	6.0	6.7	220.7
Belgium	13.0	15.2	17.4	26.3	14.5	11.6	12.4	11.6	168.8
Czech Republic	1.8	2.0	0.9	2.2	1.2	1.4	2.0	2.1	13.6
Denmark	5.3	4.6	13.9	14.3	6.7	5.1	5.9	5.1	96.0
Finland	2.5	2.1	3.6	2.0	0.8	0.9	0.7	1.0	13.9
France*	54.7	47.4	28.9	27.6	26.0	20.2	17.2	21.4	526.4
Germany	193.1	256.1	438.2	322.6	127.2	127.9	116.4	104.4	2390.5
Ireland	0.1	...	...	0.1	0.4	0.4	1.2	3.9	6.1
Italy	4.7	31.7	2.6	1.6	1.8	1.8	0.7	1.4	80.4
Netherlands	21.2	21.6	20.3	35.4	52.6	29.3	22.9	34.4	291.9
Norway	4.0	4.6	5.2	12.9	3.4	1.5	1.8	2.3	59.6
Poland	...	...	...	...	0.5	0.8	3.2	2.9	7.4
Portugal	0.1	0.2	0.6	2.1	0.8	0.5	0.3	0.4	5.6
Spain*	8.6	8.0	11.7	12.6	11.9	5.7	4.7	3.7	82.0
Sweden	29.4	27.4	84.0	37.6	18.6	9.0	5.8	9.6	334.3
Switzerland	35.8	41.6	18.0	24.7	16.1	17.0	18.0	23.9	299.2
UK + dep	38.2	73.4	32.3	28.0	42.2	55.0	37.0	41.5	412.9
UK*	26.2	44.8	24.6	22.4	32.8	44.0	29.6	32.5	310.2
Total	435.3	563.2	693.9	554.6	328.9	293.1	256.1	276.3	5009.4
Canada	36.7	32.3	37.7	21.1	21.7	25.6	25.7	23.9	368.2
United States	73.6	56.3	104.0	144.2	146.5	154.4	128.2	79.8	1282.8

Note: Most of the increase in asylum-claimants from 1991-92 was from former Yugoslavia (102,000 in 1991 to 210,000 in 1992).
* UK figures from Home Office excludes dependants. Others include dependants except France, Spain, US, Australia, Canada.
UK total including dependants estimated by IGC and confirmed by ref to table 2.5 in the HO Asylum Stats.
US data are asylum cases filed, fiscal year. INS Statistical Yearbook table 28. Refugee status applications are different and given at table 23.
Sources: OECD 1998 table A 1.4 and earlier, Inter-Governmental Consultations.

1993 about 100,000 lawful migrants entered France from that area, for example, although the number was reduced in 1994 (Tribalat 1996). West Africa is a more recent source of immigrants, particularly of asylum-claimants. Other sources are particularly salient in particular countries; Turks (including Kurds) to Germany, South Asians to the United Kingdom. While these traditional flows continue, source countries are becoming more diverse (Münz, 1995), particularly with the spread of asylum-claiming and trafficking in immigrants. Asian origins are becoming important; immigrants from the Philippines, China, South Asian countries and elsewhere are becoming numerous in Italy and some of the Eastern European transit migration countries.

2.5.2 Central and Eastern Europe

Eastern Europe was the natural labour hinterland for Western Europe's economic expansion in the 1950s and 1960s. Eastern European workers had
contributed to the substantial labour migration of the early 1900s, when continental European economies were expanding fast: By 1910 there were about
1.26 million foreign workers in Germany, for example, compared with 207,000
in 1871, at least 300,000 of them Poles (O'Brien, 1992). France also has a
history of pre-war immigration. In 1931, as today, the foreign population was
6% of the total (including 320,000 Poles and 910,000 Italians). After the war
huge population displacements involved the forced migration and resettle-
ment of 25 million people (Kosinski, 1970; Stola, 1992) as the Red Army
pushed the frontiers of Western Europe westward. Western Europe had many
more refugees and displaced persons, including workers, than their wrecked
economies could then accommodate. By the late 1940s Britain recruited about
100,000 temporary workers, mostly displaced persons from Eastern Europe.
Many returned home. That, it may be noted, was the only 'guest worker' episode in recent British migration history.

But the Iron Curtain, and the Fortress Eastern Europe behind it, put a stop
to any easy post-war repetition of this natural movement. The major early exception was the mass movement of population from East to West Germany
in search of political freedom and economic opportunity. This illegal movement (3.1 million net from 1950-61) could hardly be stopped until the building
of the Wall in 1961. That emigration had halted East German population
growth and was enough to meet West German workforce needs until 1955
(Rudolph, 1992; Mammey, 1990). Later on, there were two further episodes of
emigration from the otherwise closed communist societies of Eastern Europe.
From 1981 up to the peak year of 1988, about 653,000 Poles left Poland, about
360,000 to Germany (Korcelli, 1992), showing the failing grip of the
government. Most stayed away having got out with short-term visas, others
were persons claiming German origin. There was also substantial emigration
from former Yugoslavia, especially Croatia, mostly guest workers to Germany
recruited by agreement with Tito's freelance form of communist government.
Otherwise, emigration was on a modest scale: in 1987 about 1000 emigrants
from Hungary, 2,300 from Czechoslovakia (Okolski, 1991; Redei, 1990); perhaps 75% being related to the ethnicity of the migrant (Salt, 1996b).

Central and Eastern Europe only became a general migration area in 1989.
One of the surprises of the 1990s was then the relatively muted level of migration from Eastern Europe and the former Soviet Union, and the extent to
which much of it remains ethnic migration. At the time of the 1993 European
Population Conference convened by United Nations Economic Commission
for Europe (UN ECE) and the Council of Europe, newspaper headlines had
threatened the imminent departure of 6, 15 or even 20 million Russians to the

West as soon as their passports were provided (Coleman, 1993). Some surveys had shown extraordinary proportions wishing to leave Russia (50% being 'ready to leave the country' in 1991, 9% having 'decided to leave the country' in 1992, with another 38% wishing to but 'fearful of finding no work'), mostly younger, urbanized and in elite jobs. Some estimates suggested that the peak would be reached in 1993-94 when up to 1.5 million people might leave each year. If the economic situation improves, that should decline to 600,000 emigrants (Brubaker, 1992) — forecasts not realized in the event. More reasonably it was assumed that there would be considerable pressure to migrate westwards from the damaged economies of Central and Eastern Europe, even if lack of labour demand in the West (Coleman, 1993b) would require such migration to be illegal. The justification of asylum-claiming had disappeared in most of the former Iron Curtain countries, although that has not prevented large numbers of Romanian, Czech and Slovak gypsies from using it as a pretext to enter the West.

But although (official data) on East-West streams are higher than in the severely constrained days of the cold war, they are still relatively small and after an initial increase at the beginning of transition, have mostly been declining since 1993. Official emigration data (not the whole story, of course) shows Romanian emigration down to 26,000 in 1995 compared with a peak of 97,000 in 1990; Bulgarian emigration down to 55,000 in 1995 compared with 88,000 in 1990 (the interpretation of recent Bulgarian emigration is, however, complicated by emigration of Bulgarian Turks to Turkey at the beginning of the decade); Czech emigration down to just 400 in 1995 from 4100 in 1990 (Salt, 1997). Even in the early 1990s, surveys showed a low inclination to emigrate in some countries (e.g. Hungary; Szoke, 1992). Some of the movement is ethnic in character, and the biggest East-West regular migration stream in the 1990s has still been ethnic migration from the former USSR; that of the *Aussiedler* to Germany, and of Jews mostly to Israel and to the US. Numbers of *Aussiedler* from the former Soviet Union rose from 460 in 1985 to 147,950 in 1990 and stabilized at about 200,000 per year since (209,000 in 1995 — partly thanks to new policies by the German government (see Chapter 3). The small scale of (legal) emigration from the former Soviet Union to some selected Western countries shown in Table 2.8 contrasts with the major ethnic outflow to Germany, the US and Israel.

2.5.3 East European population in Western Europe

Table 2.7 shows that legal residents from most East and Central European countries in Western Europe in 1996 numbered at most a few thousand, in some cases only a few hundred, with one or two specific exceptions. Most regular residents from Eastern Europe are from Yugoslavia, many of long standing as (former) guest workers. Out of 2.889 million East and Central

Immigration to Denmark

Table 2.7 Foreign population in selected European countries, by country of origin, 1996.

(a) Percent of total foreign population from each country of origin

Country of residence

Country of origin	Bel-gium 1996	Den-mark 1996	France 1990	Ger-many 1997	Italy 1996	Nether-lands 1997	Spain 1998	Sweden 1997	Swit-zerland 1997	UK 1996	Total
France	11.2	1.1	...	1.4	2.2	1.6	5.6	0.7	4.1	2.7	2.1
Germany	3.6	4.8	1.4	...	2.9	7.9	8.2	2.6	6.8	2.7	2.1
Greece	2.1	0.3	0.2	5.0	1.0	0.8	0.1	0.9	0.5	1.2	2.4
Ireland	0.4	0.5	0.1	0.2	0.2	0.6	0.5	0.2	0.1	24.1	2.8
Italy	22.8	1.0	7.1	8.2	...	2.5	3.7	0.8	25.8	4.3	8.4
Portugal	2.7	0.2	17.9	1.8	0.4	1.3	5.4	0.3	10.1	1.4	5.5
Spain	5.3	0.6	6.0	1.8	1.0	2.4	...	0.6	7.2	1.8	3.1
UK	2.9	5.3	1.4	1.6	2.0	5.8	11.2	2.2	1.4	...	2.0
Other EU	10.5	7.1	2.4	5.2	4.1	4.9	6.6	4.2	3.7	2.7	4.5
EU Total	61.5	20.9	36.5	25.2	13.9	27.7	41.3	12.5	59.7	40.8	32.9
Finland	0.2	0.9	0.0	0.2	0.1	0.2	0.6	19.6	0.2	0.3	0.8
Fr. Czecho-slovakia	0.1	0.0	0.1	0.4	0.2	0.1	0.1	0.2	0.3	0.3	0.2
Hungary	0.1	0.1	0.1	0.8	0.2	0.2	0.0	0.6	0.3	0.1	0.4
Poland	0.6	2.2	1.3	3.9	1.2	0.8	0.9	3.0	0.3	1.4	2.3
Fr. Yugo. Rep.	0.9	13.5	1.4	17.7	4.5	2.1	0.2	7.0	22.3	0.8	10.2
Russia	0.2	...	0.1	0.7	0.4	0.3	0.3	0.7	0.3	1.0	0.5
Algeria	1.0	0.0	17.2	0.3	0.0	0.2	1.0	...	...	0.3	3.7
Morocco	15.4	1.4	16.3	1.1	10.9	20.4	18.2	...	...	0.4	6.7
Tunisia	0.6	0.0	5.8	0.4	4.1	0.2	0.1	...	...	0.1	1.6
Turkey	9.0	15.0	5.6	28.0	0.4	18.7	0.1	3.6	5.9	2.1	14.8
Iran	0.2	2.9	...	...	...	1.3	0.3	5.2	...	0.9	0.4
India	0.3	0.5	...	...	...	0.4	1.1	...	...	6.5	0.8
Pakistan	0.2	2.8	...	...	...	0.5	0.6	...	...	3.9	0.5
Total above	90.0	60.0	84.4	78.7	35.8	73.0	64.6	52.4	89.2	58.7	76.3
Foreign 1996	100.0	100.0	100.0	100.0	100.0	100.0	100.0	100.0	100.0	100.0	100.0

Pop. 1996
% foreign

** UK data from Labour Force Survey. The LFS cannot accurately record populations less than 10,000.

Most foreign population data relate to 31 December. France (census) February 1990.

Council of Europe data relate to foreign population at 1 January of year stated. OECD data relate to 31 December of year stated (here usually 1993). CoE data are preferred. The totals may differ considerably, and also the former Yugoslav total.

Sources: OECD (1998) table A.1. table B.1.6, Council of Europe (1998).

Table 2.7
continued ...

(b) Distribution of foreign population, thousands

Country of residence

Belgium 1996	Den- mark 1996	France 1990	Ger- many 1997	Italy 1996	Nether- lands 1997	Spain 1998	Sweden 1997	Swit- zerland 1997	UK 1996	Total
101.7	2.6	...	101.8	24.1	10.6	34.3	3.6	56.0	53.0	387.6
32.7	11.4	51.5	...	31.8	53.5	49.9	13.9	93.7	53.0	391.4
19.5	0.6	6.7	362.5	11.5	5.2	0.7	4.5	7.0	23.0	441.2
3.2	1.0	3.3	16.3	1.8	3.9	2.9	0.9	1.3	479.0	513.6
208.2	2.3	253.7	599.4	...	17.3	22.6	4.1	352.7	85.0	1545.3
24.9	0.4	645.6	130.8	3.9	8.8	33.2	1.4	137.8	28.0	1014.9
47.9	1.2	216.0	132.5	11.5	16.6	...	3.0	98.5	35.0	562.3
26.2	12.5	50.1	116.6	22.2	39.3	68.3	11.5	19.8	...	366.5
95.3	16.8	85.0	380.0	45.3	33.1	40.0	22.0	50.5	54.0	821.9
559.6	48.8	1311.9	1839.9	152.1	188.3	251.9	64.9	817.2	810.0	6044.7
1.5	2.1	1.6	15.1	1.1	1.4	3.6	103.1	2.1	5.0	136.6
0.7	0.1	2.0	26.5	2.1	0.5	0.4	1.2	4.1	5.0	42.7
0.9	0.3	2.9	55.7	2.2	1.2	0.3	2.9	3.7	2.0	72.1
5.4	5.3	46.3	283.4	12.8	5.6	5.5	15.9	4.6	27.0	411.8
8.1	32.2	51.7	1296.7	48.8	14.5	1.3	36.6	305.0	16.0	1810.9
2.1	...	4.3	54.7	4.6	2.3	1.7	3.6	4.2	20.0	97.5
9.5	...	619.9	23.1	...	1.1	5.8	...	...	6.0	665.1
140.3	3.3	584.7	82.8	119.5	138.7	111.1	...	...	7.0	1187.4
5.3	...	207.5	28.1	44.8	1.6	0.5	...	...	1.0	288.8
81.7	35.7	201.5	2049.1	3.9	127.0	0.4	18.9	80.2	42.0	2640.4
1.4	7.0	...	...	...	8.6	1.7	27.2	...	17.0	62.9
2.8	1.1	...	...	...	2.5	6.8	...	...	129.0	142.2
1.7	6.7	...	...	...	3.2	3.4	...	...	78.0	93.0
821.0	142.6	3034.3	5755.2	391.9	496.6	394.2	274.3	1221.2	1165.0	13695.8
911.9	237.7	3596.6	7314.0	1095.6	679.9	609.8	526.6	1369.5	1985.0	18326.6
10143.0	5251.0	58265.3	81817.5	57333.0	15493.9	39241.9	8837.5	7062.4	58703.6	342149.1
9.0	4.5	6.2	8.9	1.9	4.4	1.6	6.0	19.4	3.4	5.4

European residents of Austria, Belgium, Denmark, Finland, France and Germany, Italy, Netherlands, Sweden and Switzerland in 1996, 71.3% were from former Yugoslavia (OECD, 1998, Table 1.8).

The overwhelming majority of residents from the East live in Germany; apart from 1,297,000 from former Yugoslavia there are about 280,000 Poles, 100,000 Romanians, and 55,000 from the former Soviet Union (not *Aussiedler*). Poles have been the most active emigrants, although much of it for short-term trading and as seasonal workers. There were already estimated to be 240,000 Poles in Germany by 1990. Hungarians have shown a more modest migratory instinct. Emigration from Hungary, and interest in emigrating among Hungarians, as revealed by opinion polls, has been negligible (Szoke, 1992); Hungary had a relatively liberal exit policy by the 1970s; most who were allowed out as tourists actually went back. Part of the substantial upsurge in labour demand arising from German reunification, now much reduced, was directed to Poland. 271,000 work permits for new arrivals were issued in 1995 (182,000 to Poles) compared with 409,000 in 1992 (OECD, 1997, pp. 104-10). The orientation of work permits and associated training arrangements to the East, including arrangements for 'guest workers' and seasonal workers, evidently owed as much to diplomatic as to economic needs, and was reduced in the light of later German unemployment.

This is not the 1960s when mass low-skill migration was welcome. So far, language problems, lack of hard currency and bridgeheads from previous migration, lack of demand for skills, unfamiliarity with foreign travel and lack of information have kept flows relatively small. Push factors, disparities of income and standards have been less strong than in the south, the prospects for improvement better. For Eastern Europe, now that since 1989 departure is at last possible, would-be emigrants may have missed the boat as far as migration to Western Europe is concerned. Reform has come about thirty years too late.

2.5.4 Eastern Europe as an area of immigration

More interesting is the development of that region into a new area of immigration as well as emigration. The countries of central Europe, Hungary and the Czech Republic in particular, have become attractive to immigrants from further East and from the South; both in their own right as their economies grow and also because of the convenience of their geographical position and of their as yet imperfect border controls for entry to the West. Despite their problems, East and Central European countries became immediately attractive to residents of the former USSR. Much of the initial interest took the form of 'tourism'. As early as 1990 there was an immediate increase in the number of 'tourists' entering Poland; over 8 million from the former USSR in 1991 compared with 3 million in 1989; at least 25,000 are

Table 2.8 Immigrants from former USSR to selected countries, 1985-95.

	Germany All persons gross inflow	Germany Aussiedler	Greece	UK	Sweden	Canada	Poland	Australia	United States	Israel	All countries
1985	1769	460	...	50	143	...	...	240	3521	481	6204
1986	2119	753	...	40	187	190	2588	299	5423	...	...
1987	17433	14488	527	70	280	...	...	290	2384	2172	23156
1988	54725	47572	1365	60	349	...	256	660	2949	2329	62693
1989	121378	98134	6791	20	562	2177	278	1530	11128	12924	156788
1990	192820	147950	13863	50	866	2819	365	1200	25524	184602	422109
1991	195272	147320	11420	140	1552	2415	905	1550	56980	147292	417526
1992	254731	195576	8563	270	...	3157	1087	3320	43614	65093	379835
1993	306404	207347	9639	340	...	4049	833	1820	58571	66145	447801
1994	322900	213214	2360	400	...	...	...	...	63420	68079	457159
1995	310116	209409	...	610	...	...	...	...	...	64847	375573
Total 85-95	1779667	1282223	54528	2050	3939	14617	3724	10800	270679	614263	2754267
Total 90-95	1582243	1120816	45845	1810	2418	12440	3190	7890	248109	596058	2500003

Sources:
Germany: Bundesinstitut für Bevolkerungsforschung, Wiesbaden/Bundesverwaltungsamt, Köln.
SOPEMI Poland, 1994, table 7 (mimeo).
SOPEMI 1993, Greece (mimeo).
SOPEMI Sweden, 1994, table 1, Befolkningsstatistik 1993, Del 2 Inrikes och utrikes flyttningar table 7, table 17 (mimeo).
ECD 1995, SOPEMI Annual Report 1994, table 11.8 excludes 800 privately sponsored and officially recognized refugees. From former Soviet Union to Germany only.
UK Home Office Control of Immigration Statistics,1994, table 6.5 acceptances for settlement.
USA 1994, Statistical Yearbook of the Immigration and Naturalization Service table 3. fiscal year, country of birth.
Australia Overseas Arrivals and Departures, 1993, table 4 (settler arrivals).
Canada Report on the Demogaphic Situation in Canada (various years).
Israel: Statistical Abstract of Israel, table 5.4 (various years). Total includes relatively small numbers of 'potential' immigrants.
Immigrants to Germany only from former Soviet Union, 1992-94.

thought to have become overstayers. Romanian 'tourism' to Poland increased from 19,000 in 1989 to 325,000 in 1990.

Despite some continuing unemployment in Poland, 12,000 work permits were issued in Poland as early as 1992, mostly to nationals of the former Soviet Union, for work in building, industry and agriculture — surprisingly in view of Poland's domestic over-supply. Hungary is the only East European country to report foreign labour to the annual SOPEMI report. It recorded foreign labour inflows declining from 52,000 in 1990 to 15,000 in 1996, and foreign labour declining correspondingly to 19,000 in 1996 (OECD, 1998, table A.2.1., B.2.2).

The downward trend may be correct, even though economic activity is increasing (real GDP had risen to 112 (1989=100) in Poland by 1997, while the Czech Republic had recovered to 98 and Hungary to 90 from much lower levels in the early 1990s (Economic Commission for Europe, 1998, App. Table B.1). The level is probably more accurately described by the informal (and much higher) estimates of officials and academics on the spot. As elsewhere in Eastern Europe, most foreign workers are working illegally in a labour market where the black economy (mostly domestic, of course) may comprise up to 30% of jobs. Even in 1997, registered unemployment in Poland was 10.5%, in Hungary 10.4% and in the Czech republic 5.2%. That in the Russian Federation was comparable — 9% — (Economic Commission for Europe, 1998, App. Table B.6), but the latter figure hides a high level of under-employment.

East European countries are also an important stepping stone for transit migrants from Romania and the former Soviet Union or from China and the Third World aiming to enter Germany (Salt, 1996). As early as 1989, there were 36,000 Romanians living temporarily in Hungary, forcing Hungary to invent a refugee policy and to accede to the Geneva convention. These arrivals were still quite modest by Western standards (18,283 refugees from all origins in 1990) and immediately fell to low numbers after the departure of Ceaucescu. It seems that the Czech Republic became a net importer of people as early as 1991. By 1996 the foreign population of the two members of the Central European groups which had joined the OECD — the Czech Republic and Hungary — had risen to 199,000 and 143,000 comprising 1.9% and 1.4% of their populations respectively. (Other sources give different data: 153,000 permanent foreign residents registered in the Czech Republic and 65,000 in Hungary in 1996) (Table 2.9). Many others are present in an irregular or illegal position. This migration only partly reflects the economic revival in those countries. Of the Czech total for example, 50,000 come from the neighbouring Slovak Republic, part of the same country until 1992. In Hungary, 62,000 foreign residents have Romanian citizenship; many are Hungarian ethnic migrants from the Transylvanian region of Romania. The majority of other legally resident foreigners come from Eastern Europe and the former Soviet Union. Only a small proportion of the whole — 15,000 in the case of Hungary — come from EU countries (mostly from Germany) but this nonetheless represents a large increase on the previously non-existent totals. The Czech Republic now has about 10,000 US citizens, mostly in Prague.

Table 2.9 Foreign residents in Hungary and Czech Republic, 1996.

	Country of residence			
	Hungary		Czech Republic	
Country of origin	Thousands	Percent of foreign population	Thousands	Percent of foreign population
France	0.6	0.4	...	...
Germany	8.3	5.8	5.9	3.0
Greece	1.8	1.3	...	...
Ireland	0.1	0.0	...	...
Italy	0.6	0.4	...	...
Slovak Republic	3.7	2.6	50.3	25.3
Bulgaria	1.5		...	...
Poland	4.3	3.0	24.5	12.3
Romania	61.6	43.2	...	...
Fr. Yugoslav Rep.	14.9	10.5	...	...
Fr. USSR	16.1	11.3	53.0	26.7
Vietnam	1.6	1.1	17.6	8.9
China	...	...	4.8	2.4
United States	2.4	1.7	10.1	5.1
Total above	117.4	82.4	166.2	83.7
Foreign 1996	142.5	100.0	198.6	100.0
Population 1996	10193.0	...	10315.0	...
% foreign	1.4	...	1.9	...

Notes: ... indicates no data. 0.0 indicates less than 0.05%.
Sources: OECD (1998) table A.1, table B.1.6, Council of Europe 1998.

2.5.5 Transit migration and movement from the East and South

Soon after the collapse of communist rule with its fierce controls on entry and exit, movements began of an unexpected and almost unprecedented kind; 'transit' movement both from Eastern Europe and from outside Europe into the Eastern and Central European countries on their way to the West, particularly to Germany. Eastern Europe seemed an easy point of entry to third world migrants in search of any European country which they could enter, illegally, as asylum-claimants, or in any other way. These movements include Iraqis, Indians, Pakistanis, Chinese, Vietnamese and many others. The judgement of the would-be transit migrants was at first quite correct. Movement into and through the countries of Eastern and Central Europe was very easy in the early 1990s. More recently, preferred transit points are reported to change as border control policy tightens. Poland and the Czech Republic are favoured

Table 2.10. Estimated transit migration in selected East and Central European countries, 1993, in thousands.

Country	Transit migrants (1000s)
Bulgaria	30-50
Czech Republic	100-140
Poland	100
Russian Federation	500

Source: International Migration Bulletin No 4, May 1994, p. 10.

because of their border with Germany, Bulgaria and Hungary. Even the Russian Federation (Ivanova, 1996) receives transit migrants hoping to enter Europe via Austria or Greece. The Slovak Republic has become popular following tightening on the Austro-Hungarian frontier, and the Baltic States as a route to Scandinavia, not only for Russians but also to immigrants from the Middle East and Asia entering via Russia. (OECD, 1998 p. 50). Salt (1997) identifies five routes for transit migrants and illegal immigrants linking the South and East with the West from the Baltic down to the Mediterranean. Increasingly this movement is turning into a movement of *de facto* settlement.

Although the policies to moderate irregular immigration described in Chapter 3 are by no means completely effective, they have meant that more would-be migrants are turned away from Western countries of destination or removed from them through bilateral arrangements and end up back in the Central European states. They may then find themselves stuck. Central European countries in turn have improved their own security arrangements, not just to protect their own immediate interests but also to prepare for EU entry, where they would be expected to improve their outer border arrangements in order to join the Schengen arrangements, which requires participant EU member states to remove border controls between each other while imposing uniform controls on movement from outside the EU.

New regulations have been put in place in a number of Central European countries to control movement from the CIS, 'Commonwealth of Independent States: former republics of the Soviet Union' (Eyal, 1991), from the poorer areas of Eastern Europe (Bulgaria and Romania) and of third world asylum-seekers and illegal immigrants. Attitudes to ethnic repatriation in Eastern Europe are complex; some countries accept the return of former emigrant populations, others prefer them to remain where they are (Brubaker 1992). These problems are discussed further in Chapter 3. But until migration regulations become properly implemented, data will remain patchy.

Table 2.11 Summary of gross and net migration flows to and from the Russian Federation, 1989-95.

	Immigrants in 1000's			Emigrants in 1000's			Net Migration in 1000's		Refugees in 1000's	
Year	UN ECE	Acad. Sci	GKS	UN ECE	Acad. Sci	GKS	UN ECE	Acad Sci	GKS	UN ECE
1989	...	854	...	...	692	...	...	163	...	...
1990	...	913	...	...	626	...	...	287	...	...
1991	...	692	...	...	587	...	...	104	...	...
1992	646	926	...	710	570	...	−65	356	...	...
1993	923	923	...	484	379	...	440	544	...	288
1994	1147	1146	1146	337	232	232	810	915	915	253
1995	842	842	842	340	229	229	502	612	612	272

Note: Goskomstat data refer only to migration relating to CIS and Baltic States, up to 1993 inclusive. UN ECE data (also from Goskomsat) include migration flows to countries outside former Soviet Union (almost all emigration).
Negative indicates net loss.
UN ECE figures only available for 6 months in 1992; totals have been doubled.
Sources: UN ECE from Goskomstat, T. Frejka personal communication.
Academy of Sciences A. Vishnevsky personal communication.
Goskomstat A. Volkov personal communication.
GKS: Goskomstat.

2.5.6 The former Soviet Union — new area of immigration

The most dramatic change of all turned the Russian Federation for a time into Europe's leading country of immigration (IOM, 1996), even though it is not yet an attractive place for economic migrants and has no tradition of asylum (Chesnais, 1991). Most of the recorded migration is of persons of Russian nationality (in the former Soviet sense) who have moved back from the former Soviet Republics to the Russian Federation. These ethnic return migrants, in many cases the descendants of original Russian emigrants, are part of a population of about 25 million Russians living in the non-Russian Republics at the time of the 1989 census. In a 1991 survey, 37% intended to migrate to Russia. In 1991 migration was already responsible for 43% of population growth in the Russian Federation which by May 1992 had 315,000 official refugees, mostly fleeing inter-ethnic conflicts (Requent, 1992). Since 1990 their position has been insecure and threatened as former political, cultural and economic privileges have been lost (Brubaker, 1992). Some, notably those from the Baltic states, were expected to look westwards for their final destination (Vishnevsky and Zayonchkovskaya, 1992) but that has not materialized to any great extent despite the new, awkward foreign status which Russian residents now have there following changes in citizenship law.

The migration flow from Russia to the outer Republics had already reversed as early as the 1970s. But return greatly accelerated after 1990. 5.4 million people, mostly ethnic Russians, left the Republics of the former Soviet Union from 1990 to 1995 to settle in Russia (a net balance of 2.2 million), particularly from Kazakhstan and Uzbekistan (De Tinguey, 1997). A summary of statistics from 1989-95, showing some disparities between sources, is given in Table 2.11.

Net migration to the Russian Federation had risen from 163,000 in 1989 to a peak of 915,000 in 1994 (gross inflow of 1.15 million), declining to 612,000 in 1995. Most of these were ethnic Russian migrants. There is also labour migration between the Russian Federation, the Ukraine and the other European Republics. On top of this were 272,000 refugees. Throughout the former Soviet Union, as elsewhere in the former communist countries, ethnic migration is predominant, involving also Ukrainians, Tatars and others seeking out old homelands. Russia is also becoming a vehicle for transit migration for Afghans, Somalis, Kurds, Vietnamese and Chinese heading for the West. Pressure on the long Chinese border is difficult to control; Chinese residents were variously estimated at between 200,000 and 800,000 in 1995.

2.6 Components of migration streams to the West

2.6.1 Labour migration

International labour migration has proceeded for centuries, often without any formal arrangement. Organized labour migration mostly of 'guest workers' was, however, at the core of the migration process into Western Europe from the European fringes and beyond in the 1960s. As noted above, there was little movement between East and West. While the days of mass low-skill legal labour migration into Europe are generally thought to be over, general labour migration did, however, increase from the 1980s to the early 1990s. That is rather a puzzle, as there were in mid-1991 about 12 million unemployed in the EU alone (8.7% of the labour force), about 35% of them under age 25 and disproportionately unskilled. The rate of unemployment has increased until about 1997. At least 1.5 million of the unemployed are themselves immigrants. It was noted above that in the mid-1990s there was little general demand in the depressed economy for ordinary skills, although the willingness to work for low wages in unsatisfactory work conditions of third world immigrant labour, especially illegal immigrants, is attractive to some employers on both sides of the Atlantic.

Instead, much of the recent 'official' labour migration within and into Europe has been 'high-level manpower' of persons with managerial or professional qualifications (especially in finance and engineering) and to a lesser extent, with high-level manual skills (Salt, 1992). Professional and managerial workers accounted for about 80% of the long-term work permits for the UK (work permits are not needed for EU workers). A high proportion of these work permits are issued to nationals of the USA and Japan. Much of this movement is between the component companies of the same large firm (confusingly called 'inter-company transfers') — at least 40% of work-permit entrants to the UK in 1990, for example (Salt 1992). But 30% of new permanent immigrant workers to France in the early 1990s were unskilled; 25% of newly registering foreign workers in the UK came to work in services, especially in low-skill jobs in hotels and catering. Most of these, however, were from the EU (Salt, 1995) and did not require work permits.

With few exceptions, however, foreign labour inflows have fallen since 1992 (Table 2.5), especially sharply in the two countries which still recruit guest workers (Austria and Switzerland). Given the economic recession and high unemployment facing most European countries in the mid-1990s, such a reduction should have been general. The growth in the Italian foreign workforce therefore seems difficult to understand, given high unemployment there. However, as in Spain, much of the new supply of foreign labour on the labour market is illegal and is not recorded by official data. Regular foreign workers, except for those under foreign labour contracts, for the most part impose the same immediate costs on employers as domestic labour.

With respect to immigrant labour from Poland and elsewhere, Germany, as noted, is a special case where foreign policy considerations may outweigh economic ones. In the 1990s the German government expanded the concept of temporary work into a new form of temporary guest worker programme (Werner 1996). This was partly to supply the need for building workers in the reconstruction of East Germany and Berlin, now a declining demand. But it was also advanced for political reasons; it recognized the difficulty of controlling immigration; it was devised instead to channel it and manage it. It also served to train workers from sending countries to help their development and hence reduce migration pressures at source. Finally it was an act of political solidarity to help newly-liberated Central and East European countries and to promote German economic and foreign policy aims in the area. Whether the new 'temporary' guest workers will prove to be less permanent than the previous wave remains to be seen.

2.6.2 Participation rates and unemployment among foreigners

The foreign labour force tends to have high unemployment and low levels of workforce participation. Among foreign men, labour force participation rates (proportion of the working age population in work or unemployed but seeking work) is in most countries lower than that of nationals. This is despite the somewhat younger average age of the foreign population of working age. Exceptions are Italy and Spain where a high proportion of the foreign population — workers or otherwise — are present illegally. In the case of Austria the foreign workforce is specifically recruited on a guest-worker basis. Among women, again with those three exceptions, the participation rates are proportionately even lower. This is partly due to the large family size of immigrants and the social impediments to working outside the home which affect Muslim women. In these respects, Europe has imported third world dependency problems along with its foreign population.

Typically the unemployment rate of foreigners is between two and three times the host country average. In the Netherlands foreign unemployment is over four times the national average, and it is about three times higher in Denmark, Belgium and Sweden. Among Turks and Moroccans in the Netherlands unemployment in the 1990s has been over 40%, over three times that of Dutch nationals. Only in Spain, Italy and Luxemburg was it less than 50% higher in the mid-1990s (OECD, 1998, chart 1.10). Among women the position is more moderate, as Table 2.12 shows. But in only one country listed (Spain) was unemployment among foreign women lower than that of nationals.

In the 1960s and 1970s, foreign unemployment was typically lower than among nationals, at a time when unemployment was typically relatively low in any case. A higher proportion of the foreign population then had been recruited as guest workers to specific jobs or to specific industries. The guest workers did not, on the whole, return home when their jobs disappeared through the modernization of the economy. Because of their concentration in industry they suffered disproportionate job losses. Their relatively low level of skills did not suit them to the new demands of the labour market. Subsequent immigration of adult men has been less oriented to specific employment, arising from spouse migration, regularization of illegal immigrants, settlement of successful asylum-claimants and other non-economic processes. Discrimination undoubtedly played a particular part at least in earlier years. Before the acceptance of 'integration' notions it was often the policy to give preference to the needs of the domestic labour force. But integration policy, which makes compulsory the competition between foreigners and nationals, has not had much of an impact yet. However, foreigners born in the host country often, but not in every country, have higher levels of workforce participation and lower levels of unemployment than those born overseas. (OECD, 1998, table 1.5).

2.6.3 Family reunion and marriage migration

Most migrants to Europe in the 1990s are not labour migrants. Under the influence of economic models, immigration tends to be thought of primarily as labour migration in the late 1990s. It is nothing of the sort, and appreciation of this fact is essential to understanding the dynamics of migration into rich countries from poor ones. Most non-refugee streams have their origins in labour or at least economic migration, usually of men. But they often then

Table 2.12 Workforce participation and unemployment rates among the foreign population, selected countries around 1995.

Participation rate

Country	Men			Women		
	Nationals	*Foreigners*	*Foreign as % of national*	*Nationals*	*Foreigners*	*Foreign as % of national*
Austria	81.3	86.1	105.9	62.9	64.5	102.5
Belgium	73.1	68.9	94.3	53.2	38.1	71.6
Denmark	86.7	78.7	90.8	74.3	48.3	65.0
France	75.2	76.3	101.5	61.8	46.8	75.7
Germany	80.4	79.3	98.6	62.8	50.8	80.9
Italy	73.5	84.7	115.2	42.9	49.8	116.1
Netherlands	81.7	64.1	78.5	59.4	39.8	67.0
Spain	74.9	85.1	113.6	45.3	48.6	107.3
Sweden	84.5	69.7	82.5	80.0	60.2	75.3
United Kingdom	85.2	76.5	89.8	67.4	56.1	83.2

Unemployment rate

	Men			Women		
	Nationals	*Foreigners*	*Foreign as % of national*	*Nationals*	*Foreigners*	*Foreign as % of national*
Austria	3.7	6.2	167.6	4.6	7.8	169.6
Belgium	6.0	19.8	330.0	11.0	31.5	286.4
Denmark	5.4	16.2	300.0	8.4	...	...
France	9.2	20.2	219.6	13.6	24.4	179.4
Germany	6.1	15.1	247.5	9.2	14.8	160.9
Italy	9.2	...	...	16.2	22.6	139.5
Netherlands	5.3	23.1	435.8	8.2	24.3	296.3
Spain	18.0	20.7	115.0	30.3	27.0	89.1
Sweden	8.1	23.5	290.1	7.0	15.6	222.9
United Kingdom	9.8	16.4	167.3	6.7	11.7	174.6

Source: Selected data from OECD 1998 table 1.5 page 35.

acquire their own dynamic, being made continuous, at least in democracies, more by the rights and demands of the settled population of immigrant origin. This is particularly so in the case of migration from undeveloped societies with higher fertility, extended families and extensive kinship connections. In recent decades probably 80% of regular migration to Europe has been the migration of dependants, especially spouses and children (Widgren, 1994). For example family migration comprised 90% of regular gross inflows into Belgium and West Germany in 1988, 70% into France and

55% into Switzerland (Salt, 1991). The *Gastarbeiter* were supposed to return home after their jobs ended, as they are forced to from (e.g.) Arab states. But the immigrants in Europe were reluctant to return; political pressure and humanitarian considerations made it difficult for Western governments to enforce their original policy. Further family reunification follows the admission of refugees and any legalization of illegal immigrants, so new streams are continually being created. These streams are an externality of the macro-economic response to wage differentials in neoclassical economics, one with which neoclassical theory cannot easily cope.

Only a few countries provide data to show the relative size of the different components of migration. In France in the early 1990s, for example (Table 2.13), only 7% of regular immigrants from the Maghreb/Middle East were labour migrants. This may be compared to 5.1% of those to Belgium in 1995. Germany and Switzerland, which still recruit guest workers had higher figures: 23% and 34% respectively (OECD, 1997). Of regular immigrants from the Maghreb/Middle East to France in 1994, 55% were the dependants of persons already settled in France, a further 28% were the spouses of French citizens. Of the latter 49% in 1995 (smaller absolute numbers) were from Africa — it is not stated from which part (OECD, 1997, p. 98).

As in other countries, such as the United Kingdom and the Netherlands, traditional family reunification for some immigrant populations is being replaced by spouse migration (Coleman, 1995c; Schoorl, 1997). One kind of chain migration replaces another. This is particularly prevalent among Asian immigrants from cultures where arranged marriages are normal. The attractions of such marriages for persons in sending countries are considerable. Judgements of the European Court of Human Rights ensure that such a marriage gives to spouses or fiancés of either sex the right to enter the European country of residence of their partner. Almost invariably the 'reunification' takes place in the richer, more attractive country.

There are exceptions in countries with a more recent pattern of immigration, for example Italy. There, 55% of lawful foreign residents in 1995 were given their residence permits on grounds of work. 19% were given for reasons of family reunification (up from 13% in 1990) of which about 45% were from Africa, mostly from the Maghreb (OECD, 1997, p. 120). However, in Italy and in Spain such statistical comparisons are of only limited value because of the high proportion of immigrants who are present illegally and because large-scale foreign immigration is in a much less mature stage.

The importation of marriage partners into France is powerfully influenced by the needs of the immigrant population in France itself, not directly by pull factors from the French labour market. However push factors from the poor living conditions of the Maghreb are likely also to be a major factor, creating a demand for emigration which marriage arrangements can help to facilitate. Routine data often do not show the community which spouse migrants are

Table 2.13. Foreign migration flows of Middle East / North African origin to France, 1994.

	Permanent worker	Family reunifi- cation	Spouse of French citizen	Parent of French child	Refugee	Depen- dant of refugee	Non- salaried worker	Other	Total
Origin									
Europe	11940	1537	1497	126	1584	108	77	102	16971
Turkey	152	3265	261	12	687	243	2	33	4655
Lebanon	420	257	105	15	12	4	5	42	860
Algeria	527	2885	4240	0	28	10	762	245	8697
Morocco	407	5737	1361	145	11	2	24	196	7883
Tunisia	144	1182	748	54	4	2	9	48	2191
Other Asia	1306	1973	1183	51	3310	229	34	186	8272
Other Africa	986	2223	2204	925	940	107	186	332	7903
Other	2467	1587	1546	421	449	71	105	24	6670
Total	18349	20646	13145	1749	7025	776	1204	1208	64102
Subtotal T, L, A, M, T	1650	13326	6715	226	742	261	802	564	24286
Percent in each migrant category	6.8	54.9	27.6	0.9	3.1	1.1	3.3	2.3	100.0

Source: Tribalat, M. (1996). *Chronique de l'Immigration. Population*, 51(1) p. 144, table 1.

joining. However, if all the marriage migrants to France in 1994 were marrying into the immigrant communities (it is probably no more than half), then network migration of various kinds (family reunification, dependants, and spouses) would have accounted for 83% of all legal migration into France in 1994.

In this form of migration, males are increasingly important. In France for example, where previously all spouse migration was of females, in 1994 35% of Turks entering under this heading were males, as were 29% of Moroccans and 20% of Algerians and Tunisians (Tribalat, 1996). On the other hand, while unmarried Algerian immigrants in France especially were particularly prone to choose spouses born in Algeria (overall, only 27% in a sample married a spouse born in France), this proportion marrying a spouse living in France has increased with more recent immigrants and among those who arrived as children themselves (Tribalat, 1996, pp. 170-91). Marriage outside the group among young immigrant Turks in France is almost unknown; their marriages appear to be more severely regulated even than in rural Turkey (Tribalat, 1997, p. 201). Other categories are relatively trivial. Of course illegal migrants, to be considered later, are predominantly males, driven much more by better-ment considerations.

2.6.4 Asylum-seekers

Demand for asylum was relatively infrequent in the 1970s. Countries could maintain generous asylum policies without suffering major adverse con-sequences. Most claimants came from behind the Iron Curtain, most claims were granted.

Since the 1980s all that has changed. From the mid-1980s up to 1992, the number of asylum applicants to Europe dramatically increased and the coun-tries of origin greatly diversified. From approximately 156,000 in 1980 (an in-crease mainly from Iran), claims fell to 73,000 in 1983 and then increased rapidly from the late 1980s to reach 694,000 in the peak year of 1992 (Table 2.6). A substantial proportion of these asylum-seekers then came from three countries: Yugoslavia (37%), Romania (17%) and Turkey (5%), and the re-mainder, especially in more recent years, from developing countries. From 1980 to 1997, about 5 million claims were made. Most of the claimants are as mentioned earlier still believed to be in Europe even though most claims have been rejected. Applicants also bring with them considerable flows of depen-dants. For the most part these are included in the totals given above and in table 2.6.

Asylum and refugee policy in the West is based on the 1951 Geneva Con-vention Relating to the Status of Refugees. The convention formalized, with the changes following from the 1967 New York Protocol Relating to the Status of Refugees, the legal status of refugees. The aim was, and remains, to protect the victims of political, religious and other kinds of persecution and to ensure that migration restrictions do not cause loss of life or suffering of the kind seen during the Second World War. By the late 1990s, most Eastern European countries had joined those of Western Europe in acceding to this convention. A number of international agreements within and beyond the EU (see Chapter 3) have attempted to harmonize the criteria for the recognition of asylum-claimants and the procedures for dealing with their claims. 'De facto' recognition or the grant of 'exceptional leave to remain' can also be given, on 'humanitarian' grounds, or to those whom it is in practice difficult to send back, because they have established themselves in the new country or because of the general situation in the country of origin. Such persons normally enjoy the privileges of permanent residence at once or eventually, including family reunification. In addition, 'Temporary special protection' outside the Conven-tion and outside ordinary asylum statistics has been given to persons dis-placed by conflict in former Yugoslavia, at the request of UNHCR in 1992 (Inter-Governmental Consultations, 1995). This was to ensure that the urgent need to looking after several hundred thousand persons displaced by fighting would not be impeded by the usual formalities of asylum-claiming.

On top of this, most Western countries have signed the European Convention on Human Rights, backed by a European Court of Human Rights in Strasbourg, which guaranteed the 'human rights' of all people in signatory states, including refugees. Western countries have accordingly, it could be said, committed themselves to internationally-enforceable undertakings to accept a form of permanent immigration the volume of which is outside their control. In 1951, the chief humanitarian concern was the displaced people of Europe and the need to find a place of safety for those fleeing tyranny. Western countries had little difficulty in accepting the plausibility of persecution in the Iron Curtain countries. Except at time of rebellion or other periods of unrest (1953, 1956, 1968, 1981-85), the number of claimants was relatively small, thanks, no doubt, to the efficiency of communist security systems. Acceptance rates were high. The majority of claimants, especially those from East Germany, went to West Germany. While the justification for asylum claims from Eastern Europe has now disappeared, those streams have been replaced by others from a quite unexpected origin, mostly from the third world.

For over a decade, these asylum flows have dominated policy-making on migration in Western Europe, and increasingly in the South and East as well. Since the mid-1990s , the overlapping processes of illegal entry or overstaying, described below, has gained increasing attention as asylum has been brought under some degree of control. Some gained entry ostensibly for short-stay visits, others arrived illegally. Asylum-seekers made up about half of the gross inflows into France, Sweden and Germany around that time. Although many claims come from countries with troubled or violent politics (Sri Lanka, Lebanon, Turkey, Ethiopia, Somalia, Algeria, Zaire, Nigeria) the very high proportion of asylum claims which are rejected as Convention refugees (over 90% in most Western countries) shows that most of the claimants cannot show they were persecuted on a personal basis. For example, of 559,054 asylum claims in 12 European countries in 1994, only 46,091 (8.2%) were granted Convention refugee status, although another 39,494 were given a lesser status which still allows them to remain legally (Inter-Governmental consultations 1995, p. 311)

Apart from the Yugoslav emergency, dealt with under 'temporary protection' measures, the rate of increase in claims seems out of proportion to changes in political situations. To a considerable extent it appears to reflect the rapid spread of information about the benefits of asylum-claiming. The preference for particular countries, especially Germany before 1993, and the switching of claims from one country to another in response to changes in rules and practice reflects a well developed information flow. For example, in 1997 and 1998 within a few days of the broadcast of television programmes in the Czech Republic and in Romania describing the ease of entry and of application for asylum in Canada and the UK, large numbers of Czech and Romanian gypsies had presented themselves at ports of entry. In the 1990s, the United Nations High Commission for Refugees, recognizing the importance of information flow, mounted a campaign designed to moderate flows from Albania (IOM/UN HCR, 1992). These processes generate asylum claims from countries with which the receiving countries have had no previous connection. In 1990 Poles were the most numerous asylum seekers in Spain (40% of the total) and in the 1990s the UK enjoyed an influx of Zairians, Angolans and Algerians as well as the usual applications from persons from Sri Lanka, Uganda and Ethiopia.

Generous policies and attractive economies turn certain countries into favoured destinations. On a per capita basis Sweden and Switzerland have attracted the most applications, followed by Belgium and West Germany. But in absolute terms Germany takes up to 60% of Europe's asylum-claimants (32% in 1987). Germany was particularly attractive because until 1993, political refugees had a legally enforceable claim for asylum; with no room for discretion. Those granted asylum (8% in 1988) were granted unlimited residence, and access to integration programmes. Many vanished while awaiting their rejection. Much of the flow, of people and of information, is in the hands of illegal immigrant traffickers and those who provide forged documentation and legends for the claimants to use, including agencies in the receiving countries.

In the UK in 1994, for example, only 4% of applications were granted. Many applicants apply to several different countries (using different names) and it is clear that many are well informed in advance about the mechanisms of asylum application and welfare in the different European countries. When their applications are refused (which can take years), or well beforehand, the asylum-claimants disappear, some to take up illegal employment. Few are known to leave Europe (Inter-Governmental Consultations on Asylum, 1993).

By the early 1990s it was apparent that most asylum claims were judged to be unfounded by the administrative, legal and appeal systems of most Western countries. It had become the general impression among informed observers and authorities that claims were destroying the privileged position of refugees, seriously undermining the aims of immigration law, provoking violent responses in some host countries. The process was certainly imposing huge costs on those countries in processing claims and supporting the claimants. For example, it was estimated that the asylum system in six countries in 1994 (not including Germany) cost $2.67 billion in 1994, or $9500 for each claimant in the system (Jandle, 1995, p. 13). The most likely explanation of the reduction of claims since 1992 is the urgent revision of constitutions, laws and procedures since then (Bosswick, 1994; Guendelsberger, 1994). Surprisingly, the UK with its reputation (not deserved; Coleman, 1997) for effective immigration control has failed the most spectacularly to limit claims, thanks in part to an almost unlimited and publicly paid system of appeals. Immigrant and civil rights pressure groups, and the churches, have been prominent in pressing for arrangements to facilitate asylum claims and appeals, and for the material support of asylum-claimants.

Illegal immigration has attracted more attention in the mid-1990s than previously. It is generally believed to have risen as easier opportunities for asylum-claiming have been moderated. It is difficult to assess its scale, especially flows rather than stocks. In 1990 there may have been 2 million illegal immigrants in Western Europe, plus 500,000 persons refused asylum and whose presence has not been accepted *de facto* on 'humanitarian' grounds (Böhning, 1992). There may be at least 500,000 in Eastern Europe. In the West, most of the illegals appear to be concentrated on the pressure points of Europe's boundaries: in the East (Austria and Germany) and the South (Italy, Spain, Portugal and Greece). Of the 2.7 million foreign population of the latter countries, about half (say 1.3 million) are believed to be illegal immigrants (Salt, 1991). Southern Europe and the US appear to share some similar pressures favouring illegal immigrants; including the desire of some employers to recruit cheap low-skill labour in the face of high domestic costs of employment and easy access to illegal flows.

Other minimal indications come from apprehensions and deportations. In the UK for example in 1997, 19,830 persons were subject to action as illegal entrants, almost ten times the number ten years earlier. Estimates of the UK total of illegals have never been published but European comparisons suggest it is unlikely to be less than 100,000. Estimates of annual flows into Western Europe as a whole, based on these and other considerations, have been about 350,000 per year, about the same as to the US (Widgren, 1994) and the stock between 3.5-5 million, again about the same order of magnitude as in the US. Illegal immigration, particularly the growing trade in trafficking illegal immigrants (International Organization for Migration, 1994) has become a highly organized multi-billion dollar business with legal as well as illegal connections (Salt and Stein, 1997).

2.6.5 Ethnic return migrants

Immigration to Europe by persons from third-world countries of non-European ethnic and racial origin attracts most attention from the media and politics. But another feature of migration in the 20th century has been the return to European countries of people of European origin, many of whom were born outside Europe and whose ancestors may not have lived there for generations.

Of course return migration is a natural complement of any migration stream; of the 54 million Europeans who left Europe between 1815 and 1930, a third may have returned (Baines, 1991). But this ethnic return migration has

specific 20th century elements to it: The consequences of the end of empires
and the return of imperial proconsuls, administrators and the populations
which grew around them or which were encouraged or forced to move by
them. These were numerically trivial in the case of the UK, important in the
case of the French and Portuguese settlers driven out of Algeria, Angola and
Mozambique in the 1960s and 1970s. These involved the return of over 2
million people. It is the dominant component of immigration to the Russian
Federation today, involving perhaps the movement of 5 million people since
1991. This is but one manifestation of a more general process of ethnic migration, often linked to refugee movement.

The end of communist controls has generally unfrozen a process of ethnic
migration set in train by the end of the first and especially the second world
wars, whereby the imperial ethnic mosaic of Eastern Europe is rearranging
itself more on the lines of ethnic nation-states, many of which had never previously existed as independent entities. These movements remain important
in overall migration trends. In Eastern Europe the development of nation
states has been impeded; national boundaries have not evolved gradually over
time by interaction between neighbouring independent states but have been
imposed and fixed by multinational empires (Ottoman, Austro-Hungarian,
Russian and Soviet) or invented by international treaties or deals (Vienna, Berlin, Versailles and Yalta) which in varying degrees ignored ethnic groups and
impeded migration. All these are now unravelling and populations are rearranging themselves, or being rearranged by force, on ethnic lines.

The rise of democratic politics paradoxically puts a premium on counting
populations according to their ethnic interests and may exacerbate the process
(Coleman, 1997). The dismantling of former Yugoslavia has provoked a movement of several million people, not just the well-known refugee movements
of Bosnians out of Yugoslavia as a whole, but also of large numbers of Croats
and Serbs and others from former minority areas. On a somewhat smaller and
much more peaceful scale, large numbers of Poles still live outside the revised
borders of Poland, many ethnic Hungarians still live in Romania. The rights
of these, especially the latter, have been the focus of internal and international
disputes, as was noted earlier. The countries concerned have not actively promoted the return of these populations, preferring to seek to safeguard their
rights *in situ* (see Chapter 3).

The ethnic return migrants who return now to Greece or Germany are very
seldom those who left but their descendants, who may no longer speak their
homeland's language and whose culture may now seem quaint or rustic. The
migration may be encouraged by the pulls of policy (e.g. in Germany, Israel)
which gives citizenship to those who can demonstrate an ancestral connection
with the host country. In processes often affecting the same people, language
and other cultural and social policy in new nations may make the position
of long-standing ethnic minorities impossible (Germans and Russians from

Central Asia, Turks from Bulgaria, and in the 1920s Greeks from Asia Minor).

The return of the Jewish diaspora to Israel is the best known example. As it primarily involves migration from the former Soviet Union to Israel and to the US, it will not be considered further here. The Russian return migration, as noted earlier, has been on such a scale as temporarily to reverse population growth in some of the Central Asian Republics in the mid-1990s. The potential for further movement remains very large, given the existence of at least 20 million Russians in these Republics. West Germany encouraged the return of German populations from East Germany and the descendants of those who, since the middle ages, have spread over Eastern Europe and Russia, some recruited by Russian and other rulers to stimulate economic development. Germany also offered a refuge to persecuted or displaced Germans, especially after the severe truncation of German territory and further by the division of Germany in 1945. During the Cold War and especially following the Berlin Wall in 1961, however, this migration fell to relatively low levels.

It became a flood in the late 1980s as the Soviet empire and its emigration restrictions began to collapse. The *Übersiedler* from East Germany were joined by a growing number of *Aussiedler* from German populations further east (344,000 and 377,000 respectively in 1989). *Übersiedler* migration has by definition stopped. *Aussiedler* migration has stabilised at around 200,000 per year, partly through a moderation of political enthusiasm in Germany. The ethnic Germans have by no means escaped to a trouble-free life in the West. They are difficult to integrate into the labour market and the younger generation is torn between two worlds (Koller, 1996). Ethnic German migration has been a major component of overall migration to Germany, and in some ways to Europe, since 1989. But it is nonetheless finite. At the 1989 Soviet census, 2.04 million persons of German 'nationality' were enumerated. At present rates the *Aussiedler* will be exhausted in a few years as the ancient Eastern European German populations are finally extinguished, at least of their willing emigrants.

Millions of Italians emigrated to Latin America from the late 19th century, and in the 1950s and 1960s to Northwestern Europe. Many of the latter immigrants have now returned. Some of the former — or their descendants — are joining them. Italian return migration policies are given added point by Italy's forecast population decline. Greece welcomes the return of people of Greek origin ('Pontic Greeks') from populations settled in the Crimea (14,000 in 1990), Bulgaria and elsewhere in the East. There is also unfinished business in Africa. About a third of the 3.5 million white population of South Africa is of British origin. Perhaps 800,000 might be able to claim 'patrial' immigration status, and thereby claim right of abode. The most surprising of such movements was the unwilling return of over 340,000 Turks from Bulgaria to Turkey from 1989 under pressure from a (former) official Bulgarian policy of forced assimilation, a movement which continued until the mid-1990s. That

movement perhaps belonged to the same category of ethnic population exchanges between Greece and Turkey in the 1920s. Today, in Turkey and elsewhere in the Middle East, political and social pressures are finally extinguish-
ing many ancient minority cultures, including most of the ancient Christian
populations of the Middle East (Dalrymple, 1997) which in the more remote
past comprised the majority of the population. Most of their surviving
members find refuge in the United States rather than in Europe.

2.7 Demographic patterns of immigrant populations

As many immigrants to Europe in the post-war period have come from poor
countries, either on Europe's fringe or outside Europe altogether, it is not
surprising that they should bring with them demographic differences. These
take the form of preferences and behaviour typical of populations at an earlier
stage of the demographic transition. These are shown in preferences for larger
family size and for sons, unfamiliarity with family planning (IPPF, 1992),
preferences for arranged marriages only with categories of people rigidly specified by religion, race, caste or kin, a preference for living in co-residential
often complex extended family households (Murphy, 1996) and for the pri-
macy of kin contacts and obligations typical of small-scale societies. Many of
these preferences could only be manifested, of course, once the original male
immigrants had been joined by their families, so that communities of immigrant origin could start to develop. Early populations of male immigrants
often had quite high frequencies of inter-ethnic unions.

Typically such communities choose to live in close physical proximity to
preserve a way of life as close as possible to that in the country of origin, and
to protect their members from undesirable influences from the new country
(White, 1993; Coleman, 1995a; Peach, 1996), sojourn in which was often
originally assumed to be temporary. Some of the most important aspects of
the new demographic regimes thereby introduced to Europe are the influence
of extended families, the practice of early and universal marriage (Berrington,
1996) allied especially in the case of Muslims to a specified and restricted role
for women. In Islamic tradition, chastity is firmly linked with family honour,
marriages should not be left to chance and should be arranged as soon as possible, women's involvement in activities outside the home, such as work, are
to be minimized. Preferences such as these have helped to ensure the rapid
growth of immigrant populations through high levels of natural increase and
by maintaining immigration through the large size of dependent families and
the desire to recruit spouses from abroad. Demographic data on trends in
birth and marriage patterns of immigrant populations not only tell us about
their growth rate and future size. They are also invaluable as signposts to the
extent, if any, of social change, integration and assimilation (through data on

fertility and intermarriage (Coleman, 1994)) and of the welfare of immigrants (through data on mortality and morbidity).

2.7.1 Trends in mortality and fertility

Little need be said about trends in mortality. Immigrant populations from outside Europe typically come from a more severe risk environment. In the country of origin they suffer infant and overall mortality rates substantially higher than those of European populations. Once in the host country, however, with its advanced level of public health, housing and medical services, mortality among immigrant populations drops at once to a level usually much closer to that of the host society, although in many groups still slightly higher and with characteristically different patterns of cause of death (Balarajan & Bulusu, 1990; Harding and Maxwell, 1997). Such convergence is helped by the fact that immigrants tend to be a self-selected health group. Higher infant mortality rates are still seen in some (but not all) immigrant groups (Balarajan & Raleigh, 1990). These reflect higher level of child-bearing, younger motherhood among Asians and Muslims in general, low levels of literacy and education, especially among women. Muslim women in particular may be reluctant to take part in routine ante-natal procedures. In some specific groups infant survival is affected by risk factors particular to those groups. Thus in the UK almost 50% of births to women born in the West Indies are illegitimate. The Pakistanis in Britain, who favour close consanguineous marriages, thereby incur higher risks from inbreeding and in the UK have the highest level of infant mortality of any immigrant group (Bittles and Roberts, 1992).

Not surprisingly immigrant populations in the West often show rapid social change. In most immigrant populations in Europe there have been some declines in fertility from initially high levels. Statistics need a little care in interpretation. Naturalization will, other things being equal, tend to remove the more acculturated members of the immigrant population, and therefore those likely to have lower fertility, from statistical view unless there are special surveys of immigrants (Tribalat, Garson, Moulier-Boutang, & Silberman, 1991) or unless the 'ethnic minority' concept is used in official statistics (Coleman & Salt, 1996). However on the other hand the process of naturalization leads to considerable underestimates of the numbers of births to mothers of immigrant origin, and tends artificially to suppress or even reverse the generally upward trends of the number and proportion of such births compared with national totals. Births to foreign women (continental Europe) or foreign-born women (UK) have comprised about 10-13% of all births in Western Europe since the late 1970s, almost double the proportion of foreigners in the population. These figures, however, mean little, and trends in them actively misleading, except in those cases (e.g. Germany and Switzerland) where naturalization is slow. They are shown in the table (Table 2.14) with this important caveat.

Table 2.14 Proportion of births to foreigners, selected countries, 1980, 1990 and 1996.

Country	1980	1990	1996
Belgium	15.5	…	7.8
France	10.2	10.7	10.1
Germany	10.9	11.7	13.3
Netherlands	7.5	6.8	6.1
Sweden	10.2	10.2	13.0
Switzerland	15.3	15.4	22.8
England and Wales	13.6	11.7	12.6

Note: Data for England and Wales refer to births to immigrant women only, most of whom are not 'foreigners'.
Sources: OECD, 1998, chart 1.7, page 26; OECD, 1992, table I.2 p. 19.

The birth rates of most Southern European foreigners (Spanish, Portuguese, Yugoslavs) in the Netherlands, Germany, France, Sweden and elsewhere have fallen to about the same level as that of the host society, and often lower, as is indeed the case in many of those sending countries themselves. In France the Total Fertility Rate (TFR) of non-EU foreigners fell from 4.1 to 3.4 from 1981/82 to 1989/90, compared with a decline from 1.84 to 1.71 for French citizens (INSEE, 1992). The experience with non-European populations is more mixed. The fertility of some West Indian immigrant populations (in the UK and Netherlands) had fallen to almost the same average as that of the host population by the end of the 1980s, as had the birth rates of some non-Muslim Asian populations (East African Asians in the UK; Haskey, 1992; OPCS, 1992). On the other hand, Muslims from Turkey (TFR = 2.5-3.5), North Africa (4-5) and South Asia (5) have shown the least decline in various European countries. Indeed in the mid-1980s the TFR of Turks in the Netherlands and in Germany temporarily increased; from about 2.5 to 3 in the latter case (OECD, 1991). In France, according to the Enquête Famille of 1982, the TFR of women of Moroccan nationality had remained unchanged at about 6 since 1960, while that of Algerians had fallen from a peak of 9 to about 5 by the end of the 1980s (Tribalat, Garson et al., 1991). The data from continental Europe exclude the fertility of persons of foreign origin who have naturalized. Their fertility could reasonably be expected to be lower than that of foreigners who have not naturalized.

Part of the reason for the persistent high level of fertility in some groups is the continuing recruitment to such populations, through marriage migration and other processes, of women from the sending countries who may be illiterate and unfamiliar with family planning. Otherwise, adoption of family

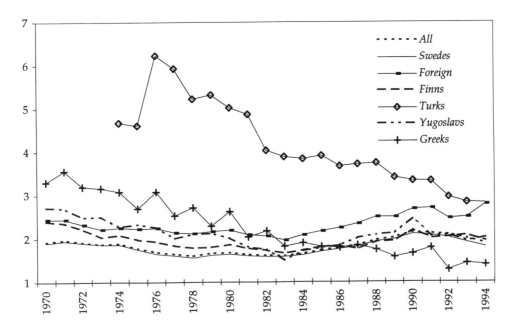

Figure 2.1. Fertility of foreign populations in Sweden (by nationality).
Source: Appendix Table 2.2.

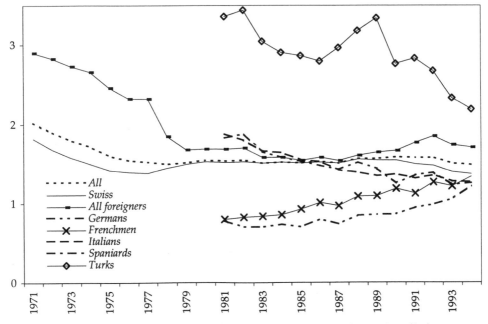

Figure 2.2. Fertility of foreign populations in Switzerland (by nationality).
Source: Appendix Table 2.2.

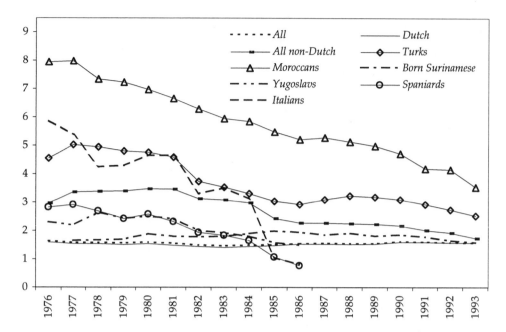

Figure 2.3 Fertility of foreign populations in the Netherlands (by nationality or birthplace).
Source: Appendix Table 2.2.

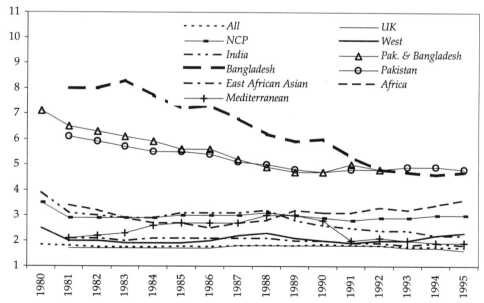

Figure 2.4. Fertility of foreign populations in England and Wales (birthplace or mother).
Source: Appendix Table 2.2.

Table 2.15. Proportion of all marriages which are mixed according to nationality in selected European countries 1975-96.

Year	Belgium	France	Germany	Netherlands	Norway	Portugal	Switzerland
1975	...	...	7.00	...	...	...	16.8
1976	10.30	...	...	...	...	...	...
1977	10.30	....	...	...	...	...	...
1978	10.10	...	...	5.91	...	...	...
1979	10.20	...	...	6.73	...	...	...
1980	10.50	6.2	7.70	7.02	...	...	...
1981	10.10	...	...	7.24	...	...	17.72
1982	9.90	...	...	6.72	...	...	18.40
1983	10.40	...	...	6.70	...	...	19.24
1984	10.25	7.6	...	6.86	...	...	19.59
1985	9.70	7.9	7.05	6.32	13.2	1.4	19.28
1986	9.91	8.8	7.39	6.69	...	...	19.48
1987	9.97	8.0	7.82	6.81	...	...	20.76
1988	10.33	8.2	8.16	8.18	15.7	...	20.72
1989	10.10	9.4	9.00	9.35	...	...	22.66
1990	10.64	10.6	9.60	10.81	...	...	23.00
1991	11.23	11.8	9.68	...	16.9	1.8	27.34
1992	11.39	11.4	10.57	...	...	...	23.33
1993	11.84	...	11.31	...	...	2.4	24.75
1994	...	...	12.10	...	...	...	...
1995	...	...	12.74	...	...	...	...
1996	...	...	13.47	...	...	...	...

Note: Most of the 'percent of mixed marriages' data are are calculated by dividing the total number of marriages involving only one nationality by the total of all marriages, including unmixed foreign marriages.

Sources: INSEE, OECD, Grünheid and Mammey, 1997.

Mouvement de la Population en Suisse table 23, Muus 1991, Council of Europe.

planning is more likely with longer residence in the host country: Studies which can distinguish the length of residence in the receiving countries of immigrant women usually show that longer residence is associated with lower fertility. The data in Figure 2.1-2.4 (see also Appendix Table 2.1), however, refer to all foreign or immigrant women regardless of length of residence. With the few exceptions noted above, most immigrant populations have not yet completely adopted European fertility norms. Some may never do so. Persistent cultural preferences, segregation and differences in socio-economic status may prevent that happening. In the US, the TFR of Chinese and Japanese, and of Cuban immigrants, has been consistently lower than that of the US average for many decades, and that of US blacks (who are not immigrants) consistently higher, while still following the same trends as the majority. Hispanic fertility, although higher than average, is converging somewhat.

Through the combined effects of higher fertility, youthful age structure and immigration, immigrant populations are increasing much faster than host populations. In Britain in 1986-8, for example, there were about 45,000 births to ethnic minority women born outside the UK (irrespective of nationality) and an additional 12,000 births to women of New Commonwealth ethnic origin themselves born in the UK. That, on being rounded up, represented a natural increase of 58,000 and, with net migration then (under-) estimated at 16,000, a net population growth of 74,000 or 3% per year. New Commonwealth population growth at that time varied from 1.5% per year (West Indian) and 6% per year (Bangladeshi) compared with 0.1% for the whole population (Haskey, 1992).

2.7.2 Intermarriage

Convergence of fertility may merely indicate economic integration and some degree of modernization. That could co-exist with substantial social or geographical segregation and isolation. For example, European regional minorities with separatist leanings: Flemings and Walloons, Scots, Catalans and Basques do not have radically different birth rates from the majority population of their respective countries, although such a contrast still exists in Northern Ireland (Compton, 1996). Intermarriage is a more decisive measure. It indicates social contact, although it does not indicate which group, if either, 'captures' the spouse or the children. It is a severe test of social change. In most third world immigrant groups (Asians, not West Indian) marriage is traditionally not a free choice of independent adults but arranged by parents at a young age. Intermarriage may also encounter opposition from white parents. Interpretation of intermarriage data, especially the absence of intermarriage, needs to be qualified by knowledge of culture, the timetable of immigration, residential and other segregation, socio-economic position, etc., of each group.

Intermarriage is proceeding faster than might be expected in some immigrant populations, including some which in economic terms are far from perfectly integrated. However the usual data available from European countries based on citizenship can be misleading. Marriages in the country of origin may not be recorded; what may appear to be inter-group marriages (between partners of different nationality) may simply be between partners of the same national/ethnic origin, one of whom has naturalized or been born in the host country, the other not. For what they are worth, some of these data are given in Table 2.15. They show only very modest trends in intermarriage up to the late 1980s, with some increase since. Some increase in this statistic would be expected simply from the increase in immigration to Western

Table 2.16. Inter-ethnic unions. All married and cohabiting men and women, resident population. Great Britain, 1991.

	White	Black Carib- bean	Black African	Black Other	Indian	Paki- stani	Bang- ladeshi	Chinese	Other Asian	Other	Total
					Ethnic group of female partner						
White	126,150	102	41	63	71	10	0	79	148	139	126,803
Black Caribbean	225	559	8	10	4	2	0	2	3	12	865
Black African	48	16	208	4	2	1	0	0	0	2	281
Black Other	76	3	2	62	1	0	0	0	2	1	147
Indian	134	2	4	1	1,762	18	0	5	4	5	1,935
Pakistani	42	0	0	1	6	775	0	0	4	3	831
Bangladeshi	7	0	2	0	4	1	217	0	0	2	233
Chinese	34	0	0	0	2	0	0	234	0	0	270
Other Asian	55	4	1	1	4	4	1	2	296	6	374
Other	218	2	1	2	7	4	0	2	5	191	432
Total	126,989	728	267	144	1,863	815	218	324	462	361	132,171

Note: The percentage of all marriages which are mixed according to nationality can be calculated in the following way: Total number of marriages where partners have different nationality divided by total number of marriages of all kinds. (I.e. marriages where partners have different nationality plus marriages where partners have the same nationality).

Sources: Berrington (1996) table 7.9, p. 199. Data from 1991 Census One Per Cent Households SAR. Crown copyright.

Europe since the mid-1980s. The data do not tell us whether the propensity to marry outside the group is changing.

A more refined measure of marriage between different groups can be gained from surveys which differentiate people by their birthplace as well as by their nationality, and also in those countries where ethnic minority statistics are collected (Table 2.16). The former data show that levels of inter-marriage between Southern European populations and the host society in the Netherlands and France are very high (up to 80% of recent unions being with spouses from the host population) although the Portuguese appear to have the lowest level of intermarriage. Data on current unions (marriages and co-habitations) from the Labour Force Survey in Britain have shown that since around 1980 up to 40% of West Indians born in the UK have white partners as do high proportions of Antilleans in the Netherlands and young Mag-hrebians in France (Coleman, 1992). Data from the 1991 British Census appear to confirm the impression from the earlier data that more recent unions (with men aged 16-34) are more likely to be inter-ethnic than earlier ones (with men aged 35-59).

For example 40% of West Indian men in the younger group in Britain had white partners in 1991 compared with 22% of the older group, and 19% of younger compared with 13 % of older Africans (Berrington, 1996). These high levels and apparently rising trends are not universal. In the Netherlands and Britain, Asians and North African Muslims and Turks have low levels of inter-marriage, and in Britain there was little upward trend evident in the data relating to Indian men, for example.

These figures do not differentiate between marriages occurring in the country of origin (likely to be ethnically homogeneous) and those occurring in the host countries (the only situation where a mixed union is really possible). Unions between members of different non-white ethnic groups are less frequent than expected by chance (for example West Indians and Africans in Britain; Coleman, 1992). Cultural attitudes to mixed marriage obviously influence these patterns. So do the size and concentration of immigrant groups. The numerically larger they become, and the more geographically segregated and concentrated they are, the less likely they are to generate large numbers of mixed unions (Coleman, 1995a).

2.7.3 Populations of mixed origins and the future

The mixed-origin offspring of these unions are becoming numerically significant, although they are invisible to statistics based on criteria of nationality or birthplace. Since 1981 the Labour Force Survey (LFS) in England and Wales has asked a question on ethnic origin which allows people to identify themselves as being of mixed ethnic origins of various kinds. Following pressure from ethnic groups (persons of mixed origin do not comprise a recognized group for the purposes of receiving subsidies), this category was dropped from the 1991 UK census, although totals can be reconstructed from other categories. These data together show that there were about 300,000 people of mixed ethnic origin in GB around 1991. Over 70% of them were born in the UK. They comprised about 20% of the ethnic minority population in the 0-4 age group, which suggests a high level of inter-ethnic union. The future size and self-identification of these groups, whether they identify with the immigrant or host parent group or neither, has important implications for integration and assimilation. In England and Wales the majority (who are of mixed white/West Indian origin) form unions with whites (Coleman, 1992; Berrington, 1996).

If these trends in immigration and fertility differentials continue then the proportion of people in European countries of immigrant origin will continue to increase. Here the better data are those relating to ethnic minority status, as opposed to the less useful data on citizenship from continental European countries with higher naturalization rates. The author knows only of projections of population by ethnic or foreign origin for Great Britain, the United

States, Germany and France. Even while convergence is in progress, fertility differentials can change numbers by an order of magnitude and hence the ethnic and nationality structure of the host country, especially of its urban areas. For example in the UK, the non-European ethnic minority population, probably less than 30,000 in 1951, had increased through immigration and differential fertility to 3.1 million in 1991 and can scarcely fail to reach 6 million or 10% of the population in the next couple of decades even on the most conservative assumptions (Coleman, 1995b). A recent medium-variant projection for Germany suggests a foreign population of 12% by 2020, although in these models the rate of naturalization as well as of immigration is a crucial variable (Grünheid and Mammey, 1997). The French projections referred to above likewise depend very much on the assumptions about the rate and the significance of naturalization.

Demographic inertia will ensure considerable increase in immigrant populations because of the youthful age structure, irrespective of what happens to the birth rate, just as in third world countries which have not completed the demographic transition. Unless net immigration from those sending countries ceases, and convergence in fertility is completed — which do not seem very likely at present — then populations of wholly or partly immigrant origin in Europe will go on increasing indefinitely (Feichtinger & Steinmann, 1990) and may become a majority in due course (Steinmann & Jäger, 1997). Likewise, in the US non-Hispanic whites will cease to be a majority in the country by about 2050 on current trends compared with 74% in 1995 (US Bureau of the Census, 1993).

2.8 Conclusions

This second chapter has described recent population movements to Europe and some aspects of the diverse immigrant populations which they have already generated. In doing so it attempts to evaluate the consequences of this migration, to see how it relates to European demographic or labour force needs and its effects upon the ethnic and demographic future of Europe's populations.

First it is important to be reminded of the weakness of much data on migration, although the quality and coverage has improved substantially in recent years thanks in part to the efforts of Eurostat and of the OECD. In addition, non-demographic processes such as naturalization can give rise to misleading impressions as to the growth (or lack of it) of foreign populations in Europe. All this means that the details of international comparisons must always be cautious and qualified, especially as regards net as opposed to gross flows.

International migration into Europe was at a relatively low level in the late 1970s and early 1980s. From the mid-1980s however a substantial increase in migration into Western Europe of most kinds, both regular and illegal, has taken place. Although this appears to have peaked in 1992, it is still proceeding at a substantial level. Despite attempts to moderate the flows, regular movement into Western Europe is still more numerous than that to the United States, which considers itself to be a 'country of immigration'.

At the same time, migration between the countries of the EU declined during most of the 1980s and has only revived to a modest extent since, despite the removal of all formal barriers to migration and employment in the EU area. A further surprise has been the relatively moderate level of immigration from most of the former communist countries of Central and Eastern Europe and of the former Soviet Union into most Western countries since 1989. There have, however, been large-scale movements of Poles into Germany, partly facilitated by a revival of 'temporary' guest-worker schemes.

During the 1990s these Eastern European countries have experienced novel patterns of immigration themselves. Part of this is transit migration, of persons from the poorer parts of Eastern Europe and the former Soviet Union, and also from China, Vietnam, North Africa and elsewhere, attempting to enter Western Europe through poorly-guarded frontiers. Many have failed in this attempt and may become permanent residents of Central or Eastern European countries. Much migration within this eastern region is of an ethnic character, the most notable being the movement of some millions of persons of Russian nationality back to the Russian Federation from other former Republics of the Soviet Union, especially from Central Asia.

Only a small part of the migration into Western Europe is formal labour migration under work permit. A high proportion of such work permit migration is of highly skilled persons. There is also some demand for less skilled service jobs, although some of this is met by illegal immigration, an attractive option to some employers because of high social protection costs in many Western countries. The greater part of regular immigration to Western Europe is of dependants and spouses. As immigrant populations of non-European origin become more numerous, migration of new spouses of both sexes to satisfy the demands of arranged marriage are becoming numerically more important. A high proportion of the regular migration both within the Eastern European countries and between them and Western Europe is ethnic in nature as old multicultural empires and societies have disintegrated. The German *Aussiedler* are the most numerous in this category.

Asylum-claiming has become prominent in migration streams only since the early 1980s. Formerly most claimants came from communist Eastern Europe (almost all to Germany) and most claims were accepted. Now most claimants to the West as a whole come from an increasing variety of third world countries and most claims are not accepted although most claimants are believed to remain in Europe anyway, remaining, as many arrived, in illegal circumstances. Numbers of asylum claims came close to equalling regular inflows in the peak year of 1992 (640,000), although in most countries they have now fallen back to lower levels. Although data are inevitably poor, international organizations now believe that illegal immigration is increasing to very high levels — perhaps 350,000 persons per year, facilitated by a large illegal trafficking industry.

More than 20 million foreign residents now live lawfully in Western European countries, about 10 million of them from non-European countries. This has created a new variety in the demographic regimes in Europe. Although immigrant populations are undergoing social change (at different paces depending on their origin, social situation and level of segregation) most preserve higher fertility than the host populations. This, together with a youthful age structure and continued immigration, means that their numbers are growing considerably faster than those of the host populations.

References

Baines, D. (1991). *Emigration from Europe 1815-1930*. London: Macmillan.

Balarajan, R., & Raleigh, V.S. (1990). Variation in perinatal, neonatal, postneonatal and infant mortality by mothers' place of birth, 1982-85. In M. Britton (Ed.), *Mortality and Geography: a review in the mid-1980s. Series DS No. 9.*, 123-37. London: HMSO.

Balarajan, R., & Bulusu, L. (1990). Mortality among Immigrants in England and Wales 1979-83. In M. Britton (Ed.), *Mortality and Geography. A review in the mid-1980s England and Wales. Series DS no. 9*, 103-21. London: HMSO.

Berrington, A. (1996). Marriage patterns and inter-ethnic unions. In D.A. Coleman & J. Salt Eds.), *Ethnicity in the 1991 Census. Volume 1: Demographic characteristics of the ethnic minority populations*, 178-212. London: HMSO.

Bittles, A. and D.F. Roberts (Eds.), (1992). *Minority Populations: Genetics, Demography and Health*. London: Macmillan.

Böhning, W.R. (1972). *The Migration of Workers in the United Kingdom and the European Community*. Oxford, Oxford University Press for the Institute of Race Relations.

Böhning, W.R. (1979). International Migration and the international economic order. *Journal of International Affairs*, 33(2), 187-200.

Böhning, W.R. (1992). *International Migration to Western Europe: what to do? Mass Migration in Europe: Implications in East and West*. Vienna.

Borjas, G.J. (1989). Economic Theory and International Migration. *International Migration Review*, 23(3), 457-86.

Bosswick, W. (1994). Asylum Policy and Migration in Germany. In F. Heckmann & W. Bosswick (Eds.), *Migration Policies: a comparative perspective*, 285-316. Bamberg: European Forum for Migration Studies.

Bourcier de Carbon, P. and P. Chaunu (1986). Un Génocide Statistique: on recherche 1,893,000 étrangers disparus dans l'ordinateur de l'INED. *Histoire, Économie et Société*, 1/1986, 159-68.

Brubaker, W.R. (1992). Citizenship Struggles in Soviet Successor States. *International Migration Review*, 26(2), 269-91.

Cagiano de Azevedo, R. (1995). *The International Migration Process and its Susceptibility to Policy Measures*. In Voets, S., Schoorl, J. and Bruijn, B. de (eds) Demographic Consequences of International Migration. The Hague, NIDI, pp 345-72.

Castles, S. and Kosak G. (1973). *Immigrant Workers and Class Structure in Western Europe.* London: Oxford University Press.

Castles, I. (1991). *Multicultural Australia.* Canberra: Australian Bureau of Statistics.

Castles, S., Booth, H., & Wallace, T. (1984). *Here for Good. Western Europe's New Ethnic Minorities.* London: Pluto Press.

Champion, A.G. (1994). International Migration and Demographic Change in the Developed World. *Urban Studies*, 31(4/5), 653-77.

Chesnais, J-C (1991). *The USSR Emigration: Past, Present and Future.* International Conference on Migration. Paris: OECD.

Compton, P. (1996). Indigenous and Older Minorities. In D.A. Coleman & J. Salt (Eds.), *Ethnicity in the 1991 Census Volume 1: Demographic characteristics of the ethnic minority populations*, 243-82. London: HMSO.

Coleman, D.A. (1987). United Kingdom statistics on immigration: development and limitations. *International Migration Review*, 21, 1138-69.

Coleman, D.A. (1992). Ethnic Intermarriage. In Bittles, A. and D.F. Roberts, (Eds.), *Minority Populations: Genetics, Demography and Health*, 208-40. London: Macmillan.

Coleman, D.A. (1992). *Immigration to the UK: a changing balance? Mass Migration to Europe.* Vienna: IAS/IIASA.

Coleman, D.A. (1993a). The World on the Move? International Migration in 1992. In *UN FPA/UN ECE/Council of Europe European Population Conference March 1993*. Geneva: United Nations.

Coleman, D.A. (1993b). Contrasting age-structure differences of Western Europe and of Eastern Europe and the former Soviet Union: demographic curiosity or labour resource? *Population and Development Review*, 19(3), 523-56.

Coleman, D.A. (1994). Trends in fertility and intermarriage among immigrant populations in Western Europe as measures of integration. *Journal of Biosocial Science*, 26(1), 107-36.

Coleman, D.A. (1995c). Spouse Migration from the Indian subcontinent to the UK: a permanent migration stream? *People and Place*, 3(1), 1-8.

Coleman, D.A. (1995a). The geographical concentration of immigrant and ethnic minorities. In S. Voets, J. Schoorl, & B. de Bruijn (Eds.), *The Demographic Consequences of International Migration*, 225-60. The Hague: Netherlands Interdisciplinary Demograpic Institute (NIDI).

Coleman, D.A. (1995b). International Migration: demographic and socio-economic consequences in the UK and Europe. *International Migration Review*, 29(1), 155-206.

Coleman, D.A., & Salt, J. (1996). The ethnic group question in the 1991 Census: a new landmark in British social statistics. In D.A. Coleman & J. Salt (Eds.), *Ethnicity in the 1991 Census. Volume One Demographic characteristics of the ethnic minority populations*, 1-32. London: HMSO.

Coleman, D.A. (1997). UK Immigration Policy: 'Firm but Fair', and Failing? *Policy Studies*, 17(3), 195-213.

Council of Europe (1998). *Recent Demographic Trends in Europe.* Strasbourg: Council of Europe.

Courbage, Y. (1995). *Results of the survey on statistical information sources concerning national minorities in Europe. Paper prepared for the third meeting of the Group of*

Specialists on the Demographic Situation of National Minorities (POS-S-MIN). Strasbourg: Council of Europe.

Cross, M. (1989). Migrants and the New Minorities in Europe. *International Review of Comparative Public Policy volume 1*, 153-78. Greenwich: JAI Press.

Cross, M. (Ed.). (1992). *Ethnic Minorities and Cultural Change in Europe and N America.* Cambridge: Cambridge University Press.

Dalrymple, W. (1997). *From the Holy Mountain: A Journey in the Shadow of Byzantium.* London: HarperCollins.

De Tinguey, A. (1997). *Repatriation of Persons following the political changes in Central and Eastern Europe.* Strasbourg: Council of Europe.

Department of Employment (1991). *Labour Market and Skills Trends 1992-93.* Moorsfoot, Sheffield: Department of Employment (UK).

Department of Statistics (1993). *New Zealand Standard Classification of Ethnicity.* Wellington: Department of Statistics, New Zealand.

EC Commission (1991). *Employment in Europe 1991.* Luxemburg: EC Commission, DG Employment, Industrial Relations and Social Affairs.

Economic Commission for Europe (1998). *Economic Survey of Europe 1998.* New York and Geneva: United Nations.

Eurostat (1988). *Demographic and Labour Force Analysis based on Eurostat Data Banks.* Luxemburg: Publishing Office of the European Communities.

Eurostat (1991). *Demographic Statistics 1991.* Luxemburg: Eurostat.

Eurostat (1991). *Labour Force Survey: results 1989.* Luxemburg: EC.

Eurostat (1997). *Demographic Statistics 1997.* Luxemburg: Office for Official Publications of the European Communities.

Faßmann, H., & Münz, R. (1992). Patterns and Trends of International Migration in Western Europe. *Population and Development Review*, 18(3), 457-81.

Feichtinger, G., & Steinmann, G. (1990). *Immigration into a below replacement population. Reproduction by immigration — the case of Germany.*

Freeman, G.S. (1994). Can Liberal States control Unwanted Migration? *Annals of the American Association for Political and Social Sciences* (534), 17-30.

Grubel, H.G. (1977). *International Economics.* Irwin, Homewood, Illinois.

Grünheid, E., & Mammey, U. (1997). Bericht 1997 über die demographischen Lage in Deutschland. *Zeitschrift für Bevölkerungswissenschaft*, 22(4), 377-80.

Guendelsberger, J. (1994). New Limits on Asylum in France: Expediency versus Principle. *American University Journal of International Law and Policy* (Spring 1994).

Hammar, T. (1989). Comparing European and North American International Migration. *International Migration Review*, 23(3), 631-38.

Harding, S., & Maxwell, R. (1997). Differences in Mortality of Migrants. In F. Drever & M. Whitehead (Eds.), *Health Inequalities Decennial Supplement. Series DS No 15*, 108-21. London: The Stationery Office.

Haskey, J. (1992). Demographic Characteristics of the Ethnic Minority Populations of Great Britain. In Bittles, A. and D.F. Roberts (Eds.), *Minority Populations: Genetics, Demography and Health*, 182-207. London: Macmillan.

Haut Conseil à l'Integration (1991). *Pour un modèle français d'integration, Premier Rapport Annuel.* Paris, La Documentation Française.

Home Office (1991). *Immigration and Nationality Department: a report on the work of the Department.* London, Home Office.

Höhn, C. (1987). Population Policies in Advanced Societies: pronatalist and migration strategies. *European Journal of Population*, 3, 459-81.

Höhn, C., U. Mammey, et al. (1990). Bericht 1990 zur demographischen Lage: Trends in beiden Teilen Deutschlands und Ausländer in der Bundesrepublik Deutschland. *Zeitschrift für Bevölkerungswissenschaft*, 16, 135-205.

Hollifield, J.F. (1992). *Immigrants, Minorities and States: the political economy of postwar Europe*. Cambridge, Massachusetts: Harvard University Press.

Hönekopp, E. (1997). Labour Migration to Germany from Central and Eastern Europe — Old and New Trends. *IAB Labour Market Research Topics*, 23, 25.

Institute for Employment Research (1991). *Review of the Economy and Employment 1991*. Moorsfoot, Sheffield: Department of Employment (UK).

International Migration Review (1987). *International Migration Review 21; Special Issue on Immigration Data*. Staten Island, New York: International Migration Review.

International Organization for Migration (1997). *CIS Migration Report 1996*. Geneva: International Organization for Migration.

International Planned Parenthood Federation (IPPF) (1992). Family Planing in a Multicultural Society. *Planned Parenthood in Europe* 21(3), (whole issue pp. 35).

InterGovernmental Consultations on Asylum (1993). *Return of Rejected Asylum Seekers. Working Paper submitted by the Secretariat for the Inter-Governmental consultations to the meeting on Return and Readmission, Nyon 16-17 September 1993*. Geneva: Inter Governmental Consultations on Asylum.

InterGovernmental Consultations on Asylum (1995a). *Illegal Aliens: A Preliminary Study*. Geneva: Intergovernmental Consultations on Asylum.

InterGovernmental Consultations on Asylum (1995b). *Report on Temporary Protection in States in Europe, North America and Australia*. Geneva: Intergovernmental Consultations on Asylum, Refugee and Migration Policies.

IOM/UNHCR (1992). *Migration Information Programme for Albania*, 24. Geneva: Joint IOM/HCR Migration Information Programme Unit.

ISOPLAN (1989). Report to the EC Commission. In *OECD Working Party on Migration*, Saarbrucken: Ivanova, T. (1996). Transit Migration in Russia. *Naselenye i Obshestvo* (No 14, October 1996), 1-2.

Jandl, M. (1995). *Structure and Costs of the Asylum Systems in Seven European Countries*. Vienna: International Centre for Migration Policy Development.

Kalibova, K. (1996). Population Census and Ethnicity. *Acta Universitatis Carolinae. Geographica*, Prague (1-2).

Koller, B. (1996). Social and Occupational Integration of Immigrants of German Origin *(Aussiedler)* in Germany. In M. Kaiser, Z. Khakimov, & J. Kozhomuratova (Eds.), *Migration of Labour*, 121-36. Bishkek: German Technical Co-operation Agency.

Korcelli, P. (1992). International Migrations in Europe: Polish Perspectives for the 1990s. *International Migration Review*, 26(2), 292-304.

Kosinski, L. (1970). *The Population of Europe*. London, Longman.

Kravdal, Ø. (1992). The Weak Impact of Female Labour Force Participation on Norwegian Third Birth Rates. *European Journal of Population 8*, 3, 247-64.

Kubat, D. (1984). *The Politics of Return: international return migration in Europe*. New York: Center for Migration Studies.

Kuijsten, A. (1995). The Impact of migration streams on the size and structure of the Dutch population. In S. Voets, J. Schoorl, & B. deBruijn (Eds.), *The Demographic Con-*

sequences of International Migration, 283-306). The Hague: Netherlands Interdisciplinary Demographic Institute.

Kupiszewski, M. (1996). Extra-Union Migration: The East-West Perspective. In P. Rees, J. Stillwell, A. Convey, & M. Kupiszewski (Eds.), *Population Migration in the European Union*, 13-37. Chichester: Wiley.

Kühlewind, G. (1995). Gainful Employment and the Inter-Generational Conflict. *IAB Labour Market Research Topics*, 10, 17.

Le Bras, H. (1997). Dix ans de perspectives de la population étrangère: une perspective. *Population*, 52(1), 103-34.

Lebon, A. (1989). *Immigrés et Etrangers en France. Tendances 1988/1989 (SOPEMI Report for France)*. Paris: OECD.

Lesthaeghe, R., Page, H. and J. Surkyn (1988). *Are Immigrants substitutes for Births?* Free University, Brussels, InterUniversity Programme in Demography, IPD-Working Paper 1988/3.

Livi-Bacci, M. (1991). *South/North Migration: a comparative approach to North American and European experiences*. International Conference on Migration, Rome: OECD.

Lutz, W. (1992). The Future of International Migration. Chapter 4 from the group of Consultants on Europe's Population. Strasbourg, Council of Europe, 3-22.

Macura, M. (1974). Politiques de population dans les pays socialistes d'Europe. *Population et Famille*, 32, 29-52.

Mammey, U. (1990). 35 Jahre Ausländer in der Bundesrepublik Deutschland — die demographische Entwicklung. *Zeitschrift für Bevölkerungswissenschaft*, 2. Ausländer in der Bundesrepublik Deutschland.

Martin, P.L. (1991). *The Unfinished Story: Turkish labour migration to Western Europe*. Geneva: International Labour Office.

Muus, P.J. (1991). *Migration, Minorities and Policy in the Netherlands: recent trends and Developments. (Netherlands SOPEMI report 1991)*. Amsterdam: Dept. of Human Geography, University of Amsterdam.

Münz, R. (Ed.), (1995). Where did they all come from? In European Association for Population Studies, *Evolution or Revolution in European Population? European Population Conference Milan 1995*, 95-53. Milan: Franco Angeli.

Murphy, M. and Berrington, A. (1993). Constructing period parity progression ratios from household survey data. In Ni Bhrolchain, M (Ed.), *New Persectives on Fertility in Britain*. London: HMSO, 17-32.

Murphy, M. (1996). Household and Family Structure among Ethnic Minority Groups. In D.A. Coleman & J. Salt (Eds.), *Ethnicity in the 1991 Census. Volume 1: Demographic Characteristics of the Ethnic Minority Populations*, 213-42). London: HMSO.

Ni Bhrolchain, M. (1987). Period Parity Progression Ratios and Birth Intervals in England and Wales 1941-1971: a synthetic life table analysis. *Population Studies*, 41, 103-26.

O'Brien, P. (1992). German-Polish Migration: the elusive search for a German nation-state. *International Migration Review*, 26(2), 373-87.

OECD (1991). *Migration: The Demographic Aspects*. Paris: OECD.

OECD (1997). *Trends in International Migration. SOPEMI Annual Report 1996*. Paris: OECD.

OECD (1998). *Trends in International Migration. Annual Report 1998 edition*. Paris: OECD.

Okolski, M. (1991). *Migratory movements from countries of Central and Eastern Europe*.

Conference of Ministers on the movement of persons coming from Central and Eastern European countries, Vienna, Council of Europe.

ONS (1997). *International Migration 1995 Series MN No 22.* London: The Stationery Office.

OPCS (1992). *International Migration 1990.* London: HMSO.

Owen, D. (1996). Size, structure and growth of the ethnic minority populations. In D. Coleman & J. Salt (Eds.), *Ethnicity in the 1991 Census. Volume 1: The Demographic Characteristics of the Ethnic Minority Populations,* 80-123. London: HMSO.

Peach, G.C.K. (1981). Ins and Outs of Home Office and IPS immigration data. *New Community,* 9, 117-19.

Peach, G.C.K. (1996). The Meaning of Segregation. *Planning Practice and Research,* 11(2), 137-50.

Poulain, M. (1993). Confrontation des Statistiques de Migrations Intra-Européennes: Vers plus d' Harmonisation? *European Journal of Population,* 9(4), 353-81.

Poulain, M. (1995). Towards a Harmonization of Migration Statistics within the European Community. In S. Voets, J. Schoorl, & B. de Bruijn (Eds.), *The Demographic Consequences of International Migration,* 11-28. The Hague: NIDI.

Poulain, M. (1996). Migration flows between the countries of the European Union. In P. Rees, J. Stillwell, A. Convey, & M. Kupiszewski (Eds.), *Population Migration in the European Union,* 51-65. Chichester: John Wiley.

Rallu, J.-L. and L. Toulemon (1993). Les mesures de la fécondité transversale. Application à la France de 1946 à 1989. *Population.* 48, 2, 369-404.

Redei, M. (1990). The Lost Future and the accessible possibilities. In J. Schoorl & S. Voets (Eds.), *Demographic Consequences of International Migration.* Wassenaar: NIAS.

Rees, P., Stillwell, J. and Convey, A. (1992). Intra-Community Migration and its Impact on the Demographic Structure at the Regional Level. In *Human Resources in Europe at the Dawn of the 21st Century.* Luxemburg: Eurostat.

Reinans, S.A. and T. Hammar (1995). *Changes of citizenship among immigrant populations.* In S. Voets, J. Schoorl, & B. de Bruijn (Eds.), *The Demographic Consequences of International Migration,* 177-206. The Hague: NIDI.

Requent, T. (1992). *Migration situation in Russia.* The Population of the former USSR in the 21st century. Amsterdam, Royal Netherlands Academy of Arts and Sciences.

Rhein, T. (1995). The European Monetary Union: Possible Consequences for Employment and Earnings. *IAB Labour Market Research Topics,* 14, 13.

Rhode, B. (1991). East-West Migration/Brain Drain. COST Social Sciences. Brussels, EC Commission.

Rudolph, H. (1994). Dynamics of Immigration in a Non-Immigrant Country: Germany. In Fassmann, H. and Münz, R. (eds) *European Migration in the late Twentieth Century. Historical Patterns, Actual Trends and Social Implications.* Aldershot, Edward Elgar pp. 113-26.

Salt, J. (1991). *Immigration to Europe.* Luxembourg: EC.

Salt, J. (1992). Migration Processes among the Highly Skilled in Europe. *International Migration Review,* 26(2) (Special Issue; the New Europe and International Migration), 484-505.

Salt, J. (1995). Foreign Workers in the UK Labour Market. *Department of Employment Gazette,* 251-67.

Salt, J. (1996a). Immigration and Ethnic Group. In D.A. Coleman & J. Salt (Eds.),

Ethnicity in the 1991 Census. Volume 1 Demographic Characteristics of the Ethnic Minority Populations, 124-50. London: HMSO.

Salt, J. (1996b). International Migration in Central and Eastern Europe. *New Community*, 22(3), 513-529.

Salt, J. (1996c). *Current Trends in International Migration in Europe*. Strasbourg: Council of Europe.

Salt, J. (1997). *Current Trends in International Migration in Europe. Consultant's Report to the Council of Europe November 1997*. Strasbourg: Council of Europe.

Salt, J., & Clout, H. (Eds.). (1976). *Migration in Post-War Europe*. Oxford: Oxford University Press.

Salt, J., Singleton, A., & Hogarth, J. (1993). *Europe's International Migrants. Data Sources, patterns and trends*. London: HMSO.

Salt, J., & Stein, J. (1997). Migration as a Business: the case of Trafficking. *International Migration*, 35(4).

Schoorl, J. (1997). Migration from Africa and Eastern Mediterranean Countries to Western Europe. In Council of Europe (Ed.), *Mediterranean Conference on Population, Migration and Development*, 123-210. Strasbourg: Council of Europe.

Sexton, J.J. (1994). *A Review of Irish External Migration, Past and Present*. Dublin: Economic and Social Research Institute (ESRI).

Stark, O. (1991). *The Migration of Labor*. Cambridge, Basil Blackwell.

Statistics Canada, & US Department of Commerce (1993). *Challenges of Measuring an Ethnic World: Science. politics and reality*. Washington: US GPO.

Steinmann, G., & Jäger, M. (1997). How Many Immigrants Can a Society Integrate? In *23rd General conference of the IUSSP, Peking 1997*, 17. Liege, IUSSP.

Stola, D. (1992). Forced Migrations in Central European History. *International Migration Review*, 26(2), 324-41.'

Straubhaar, T. (1992). Allocational and Distributional Aspects of Future Immigration to Western Europe. *International Migration Review*, 26(2), 462-83.

Szoke, L. (1992). Hungarian Perspectives on Emigration and Immigration in the New European Architecture. *International Migration Review*, 26(2), 305-23.

Tribalat, M. (1996). Chronique de l'immigration. *Population*, 51(1), 141-91.

Tribalat, M. (1997). Chronique de l'immigration. *Population*, 52(1), 163-220.

Tribalat, M., Garson, J.-P., Moulier-Boutang, Y., & Silberman, R. (1991). *Cent Ans d'Immigration: Etrangers d'Hier, Français d'Aujoud'hui*. Paris: Presses Universitaires de France.

Tribalat, M. (1997). Une surprenante Réécriture de l'histoire. *Population*, 52(1), 137-48.

UN ECE (1991). *Economic Survey of Europe in 1990-1991*. New York, United Nations Economic Commission for Europe.

United Nations (1982). *International Migration Policies and Programmes: a World Survey*. New York: United Nations.

US Bureau of the Census (1993). *Population Projections of the United States, by Age, Sex, Race and Hispanic Origin: 1993 to 2050. Current Population Reports P25-1104*. Washington DC: US Government Printing Office.

van Imhoff, E., & Keilman, N. (1996). The Impact of Future International Migration on Household Composition and Social Security in the Netherlands. In S. Voets, J. Schoorl, & B. de Bruijn (Eds.), *Demographic Consequences of International Migration*, 307-24. The Hague: Netherlands Interdisciplinary Demographic Institute.

van de Kaa, D. (1993). *European migration at the end of history*. In Blum, A. and Rallu, J-L. (eds) European Population Volume 2: Demographic Dynamics. Proceedings of the European Population Conference, Paris 1991. London, Schulibbey. pp 77-109

Vishnevsky, A. and Zayonchkovskaya, Z. (1992). *Emigration from the USSR: the Fourth Wave*. Mass Migration in Europe: Contrasts in East and West. Vienna: IIASA.

Wattelar, C. and G. Roumans (1990). Immigration, factor of population equilibrium? Some simulations. In *Migration: Demographic Aspects* Paris: OECD.

Werner, H. (1996). Temporary Migration of Foreign Workers: illustrated with Special Regard to East-West Migrations. *IAB Labour Market Research Topics*, 18, 35.

White, P. (1993). Immigrants and the Social Geography of European Cities. In R. King (Ed.), *Mass Migration in Europe: the legacy and the future*, 65-82. London: Belhaven.

Widgren, J. (1994). *The Key to Europe: a comparative analysis of entry and asylum policies in Western countries*. Stockholm: Fritzes.

Woolf, H. (1991). *Labour Needs in Europe*. European Population Conference. Paris.

Zimmerman, K. F. and T. Straubhaar (1991). *Migration and the European Community*. The Economics of Migration, London, Centre for Economic Policy Research.

Zlotnik, H., & Hovy, B. (1995). Changing migration flows: what the data reveal. In S. Voets, J. Schoorl, & B. de Bruijn (Eds.), *The Demographic Consequences of International Migration*, 59-96. The Hague: NIDI.

CHAPTER 3

Migration Policies

David Coleman

3.1 The Policy Challenge

The following chapter describes and analyzes the policies on migration and integration which have arisen in response to the migration flows and the immigrant populations described in earlier chapters. It discusses the aims of the policies, insofar as these can be discerned, and some of the legislation which has followed them. It focuses on three major components of migration policy: 'Regular' migration, including labour migration and dependants, irregular and illegal immigration and asylum-claiming, and integration policy directed towards foreign populations. A comprehensive treatment is impossible in one chapter. The United Nations (1998), the Inter-Governmental Consultations (1995a, b) and the OECD (1998) have issued general reviews.

National attitudes and policies to migration and the integration of foreign populations differ considerably. Many have changed in response to new migratory pressures, or to changes in government. Not all countries have a very clear strategy. Very often the different elements of policy affecting migration are not part of an overall plan but have developed at different times as migration and immigrant populations have themselves developed, ending up as a collection of individual ad hoc policies. Hence their effects may not be mutually supportive. Common EU policy is replacing this diversity, however.

3.2 Conflicting aims and diverse responses

The diversity of migration patterns described in earlier chapters, and their capacity to change rapidly over time, provokes a similar diversity in the elements of migration policy. There are also divergent national aims — not necessarily contradictory — in national policy in Europe and other developed countries.

Generally speaking, after the end of communism, Eastern as well as Western countries in Europe want their borders to be open to the movement of their own citizens, to tourists and students, to workers entering freely under treaty or under individual work permit and to spouses and dependants.

They wish to be seen to be open to refugees although they are sometimes alarmed at the consequences. At the same time most governments and important sections of public opinion do not want their societies rapidly transformed in unlooked-for manner by different cultures, languages and customs. Neither do they want their economies and infrastructures overloaded by the needs for integration, housing, education and job creation created by large immigrant or asylum-claimant flows. Whether these concerns can be translated into effective polices depends upon many factors, including the stability and efficiency of the national political system and its agencies: Here there are long-standing differences between European countries, for example between France and Italy (Papademetriou and Hamilton, 1996).

Immigration policies are also obliged to serve foreign policy ends as well as domestic ones (Hammar, 1992) or to respond to conflicting domestic pressure groups. Foreign Offices may claim that cultivating good relations with sending countries is more important than domestic demands for control, or that removing illegal immigrants might prejudice the national 'human rights' image on the international stage. National statements provided for international consumption, for example those presented to the 1995 Cairo Conference on Population and Development and the European Population Conference in 1993 (United Nations et al., 1994), are sometimes ambiguous, opaque or anodyne, citing in vague terms the need to evolve in response to challenges, to serve the country's needs, or to diminish migratory pressures. Some official statements bid for the moral high ground rather than specifying national interest, with much emphasis on the need to respect 'human rights' and 'encourage peace'. Thus we are told that 'Immigration has helped to shape the values that unite Canadians by reinforcing respect for human diversity and human rights, values which have always characterized Canada.' Others assert bluntly that large-scale immigration is not wanted.

There is nearly universal support for the principle of protecting refugees, and widespread support for strategies to reduce emigration pressures at source through aid. Existing immigrant populations and their pressure groups may also need to be appeased, especially those who are enfranchised. Because interest groups and pressure groups favouring immigration tend to be more focused than the wider public, it may be difficult in democracies to limit immigration effectively once it has started, given continuing emigration pressure (Freeman, 1994). Immigration issues, therefore are often contentious.

The major policy divide in the Western countries is that between the USA and Canada on the one hand, and most of the European countries on the other. The former countries see themselves as having been created through immigration. Important strands of political and academic opinion regard immigration as a major component of labour force and population growth, with positive effects upon the economy; an essential guarantor of reliable labour supply and the maintenance of demand (Simon 1989, Papademetriou and

Yale-Loehr, 1996). When North Americans talk of immigration policy they usually have in mind proposals to select migration streams the large size of which is taken for granted. Congressional pressures in the 1990s for a more restrictive approach better focused on economic needs, however, shows that this view, more consensual in the 1970s and 1980s, is now moving closer to that of Europe's.

In European countries migration policy is based on quite different premises. European countries more or less consider themselves to be full and finished. They are not in search of a new ethnic identity, do not regard ethnic diversity as an advantage, and see mass migration as exacerbating existing problems of employment, housing and poverty and especially of social cohesion where mass migration from non-European countries is concerned. There is in general no overarching assumption that labour force growth or population growth through immigration is to be welcomed, although there has been some recent discussion of positive aspects (Spencer, 1994). The future role of immigration as Europe's low birth rates produce fewer young workers for the future has also attracted attention (Coleman, 1992). Domestic political opinion, while sympathetic to the plight of genuine refugees and opposed to discrimination against foreigners, is mostly opposed to continued large-scale immigration. Governments and established political parties have been shaken by the rise of minor political parties hostile to continued immigration and to the foreign presence, and to outbreaks of violence, and have changed policy direction accordingly. Hence immigration policy in Europe typically refers to a set of measures for control, based on the basic aims of limiting the size and composition of potential flows, although without any desire or expectation that immigration can or should be stopped altogether, and increasingly within an EU framework.

Instead, European governments regard some level of immigration and emigration as a normal part of an open society. It is imbalance in the numerical and ethnic composition of net flows which causes concern. European governments permit migration related to the defined needs of the labour market through work permit systems, support free movement within the EU, and accept (with some qualifications) old obligations to family reunification, to spouse migration and to international conventions on refugees.

Even this, however, by itself permits levels of migration considered excessive. So a number of recent legislative acts have been directed to making these rights more conditional. Otherwise, attitudes are restrictive and have become more so in recent years in response to increased migratory pressures. Essentially the concerns are about migration from poor, non-European countries because that is where most of the additional and almost all the irregular flows originate.

As might be expected, there is a major difference between the countries of 'Western' Europe in the political sense, now mostly in the EU, and the former communist countries of Eastern Europe (see Frejka, 1996; IOM, 1997; ICMPD, 1997). The Western countries have long traditions of immigration, integration and asylum policy to build on, even if these have had to be revised quickly in response to recent pressures. The Eastern European countries, on the other hand, having dropped their previous highly restrictive controls on entry and exit from the communist era, found themselves open to a mobile world which did not take long to see them as a convenient stepping stone to the West and then an attractive destination in its own right. Hence they must now reconstruct immigration controls, albeit on more liberal lines, and address such novelties as integration and asylum questions.

While they have the opportunity to avoid making the mistakes of their Western neighbours they do not seem to be taking their chance. In many countries reasonably effective policies are only now emerging almost a decade after the end of the old regime, and the countries concerned have consequently acquired large numbers of transit migrants and illegals. Anxious to ally themselves with the West, to join the Council of Europe and to apply for EU membership, and no doubt also motivated by humanitarian concerns, they have hastened to sign international conventions on asylum and foreigners rights which are prerequisites for such membership. But in doing so they have opened up for themselves new avenues of potential permanent migration which can hardly be welcome.

For example, the Polish Parliament, after years of argument, only finally replaced its old 1963 Aliens Act with a modern new Aliens Law to restrain unwanted immigration in June 1997. The Czech Republic was still preparing such legislation in 1997. Romania still has a very relaxed policy, perhaps confident that its economic situation will prevent it acquiring a large foreign population. Nonetheless its Government was in 1997 working on legislation resembling that in EU countries — an obvious prerequisite for EU entry for which it is now an applicant. Other East European countries, disturbed by immigration flows, have tightened the selection criteria for work permits so as to require special skills or educational backgrounds (Bulgaria 1996) or to refuse entry to foreign workers if the domestic labour situation requires it (Slovakia 1995, Hungary 1996). The Baltic States, with a special problem of a large foreign (Russian) population acquired through a policy of Russification in the Soviet period, only welcome ethnic return migrants.

3.2.1 Types of migration and types of control

As noted earlier, migration policies are somewhat compartmentalized and fragmented as they have responded to evolving patterns of migration. As migratory movements fall into various categories — permanent or temporary stay, primary (new head of household) or secondary (dependant) nature, regular or irregular character and so on — so also do migration policies, or at least the specifics of legislation. Policies intended to regulate flows fall into three categories: To (re)define the conditions under which foreigners can lawfully enter and remain in the country; revision of law and administration relating to asylum-claiming; and last the reinforcement of measures at the border and within the country to combat illegal immigration.

One of the major policy problems is trying to ensure that 'temporary' migrants actually leave. Attempts to ensure that temporary migration remains temporary requires a rather special national political system. No European country will be as tough as are the Gulf States on their foreign workers. The Swiss and Austrians have managed to preserve a special place in the European system. But in Germany and elsewhere, the millions of 'guest workers' of the 1960s showed that there are few things more permanent than 'temporary' labour migrants. In other cases, such as the UK, workers enter for up to four years under a work permit, with a possible option to stay permanently, and may then be allowed to settle if they wish. Increasingly, yet others enter on some temporary pretext and 'switch' — through marriage, asylum-claiming or illegal overstaying — to a more permanent category of residence.

On the other hand, migration assumed to be permanent, family formation and reunification migration, may not be. In the 'countries of immigration' labour and family migrants are often formally described and recorded as arriving for 'permanent settlement'. But even in the latter case, the expectation of 'permanent residence' or 'settlement' may not be realized. Many eventually return to their homelands; perhaps a third of the 54 million Europeans who migrated to the New World in the 19th century did so. Although the US does not keep emigration statistics, it is believed that the volume of outward migration today is about a third of that of inward migration.

Partly in response to fraudulent claims, some countries' control systems (e.g. UK) have almost done away with 'permanent' immigration on arrival , instead accepting most intended immigrants provisionally, and then giving them the right of permanent residence only after the passage of time or the fulfilment of some condition. Thus much immigration which is likely to be permanent is not recognized as permanent at the time of the arrival of the immigrant (this also applies to the US). In the UK for example, almost all 'acceptances for settlement' in recent years (57% in 1983, 96% in 1997) have been of persons earlier admitted to the country for a limited or probationary period (Home Office, 1998 p. 96) as workers or intended spouses.

Aware of the popularity of marriages arranged for the purpose of immigration, some countries make permanent entry for purposes of marriage dependent upon the marriage taking place in a certain time, and of the marriage lasting for a certain time. Persons admitted for marriage must marry within a year, and as spouses must wait a probationary year before being accepted for settlement in the UK. Probably the most 'permanent' migrants are the ethnic return migrants; *Aussiedler* to Germany, Russians moving from the 'near abroad' to the Russian Federation described below. Whatever the problems they may encounter in their old 'homeland' (Koller, 1994), few return to the troubled areas of their former residence and few are likely to.

In Eastern Europe two characteristic forms of temporary migration have become prominent since 1990: The short range and temporary movements of cross-border commuters, labour tourists and petty traders, sometimes described as 'incomplete migrants' (Salt, 1998). A potentially more permanent category are the transit migrants; persons moving from the less developed east of Europe and from Asia and North Africa with the aim of settling (usually illegally or as asylum-claimants) in Western Europe. Some succeed and stay only briefly in Eastern and Central Europe, others are sent back and may become long-term settlers in countries which they originally intended merely to pass through but which may in any case be becoming more attractive places in which to remain.

3.3 The expansion of frontiers

One of the salient features of West European migration policy in the last 30 years has been the increasing importance of free travel areas. Effectively, migration policy relating to a high proportion of the citizens of other European countries has been abandoned; that is, devolved to the individual. In the EU, policy on control of movement into this free circulation space is becoming a community competence since the 1997 Amsterdam Treaty, and is passing out of the hands of national governments, both in respect of asylum and of regular migration (Guild, 1998; Lahav, 1998).

Citizens of member states of free travel areas (EU, the former EFTA, Common Nordic Labour Market, EEA) and their dependants have unqualified right of entry to other member states and can live indefinitely and seek work there. With the EU, this principle represents a substantial abandonment of national control over borders in respect of citizens of other EU states, the number of which has grown from the original six to fifteen, with others in the wings (Slovenia, the Czech Republic, Hungary, Slovakia, Bulgaria, Lithuania and Romania).

In the EU, migration is affected by all three 'pillars' of community action. The first pillar refers to community-wide institutional arrangements legally binding on member states — entitled *directives and regulations* — which are normally adopted by the EU Council. Freedom of movement for EU citizens within the EU area comes under this pillar, policed by the European Court of Justice. The other two 'pillars' are inter-governmental and deal, for example, with forced migration and immigration from outside the EU. Deliberations under the third pillar leads to *joint positions* and the *conventions*, discussed below (where only conventions need to be ratified, while joint positions can be adopted by unanimous vote within the Council). The European Commission claims further that the Single European Act of 1985 obliges EU member states to grant admission in the sense of border crossing and short-term stay to all legal residents of other member states irrespective of citizenship ('third country' residents). This interpretation is denied by the UK government. The position of Denmark towards this issue has largely been identical to that of the UK. If the 1997 Amsterdam Treaty is fully ratified, then important aspects of migration policy will become part of the 'first pillar'.

The Treaty of Amsterdam introduces a new Title (Illa) on Visas, Asylum, Immigration and other policies relating to the free movement of persons, thus moving them upwards from the inter-governmental third 'pillar' (under Title VI) established by the Maastricht Treaty. Member States, exept those which have opted out in various ways (The United Kingdom and the Republic of Ireland, and Denmark) will within five years surrender their powers to control their own borders, by incorporation of decision-making in those areas into the Community. All checks on persons, EU citizens and otherwise at the internal borders of the Union will then cease. The EU Council will set immigration policy and the standards and procedures for checks on persons at the external borders of the Union, including visas and asylum, temporary protection, burden-sharing and related matters.

Similar arrangements apply to the member states of the European Free Trade Area (EFTA) and the Nordic Treaty, all of whose members also belong to the EU or to EFTA. In 1993 the EU countries and EFTA, except for Switzerland which voted not to join, created the European Economic Area (EEA) whereby these privileges of entry, residence and work are shared between all states. Freedom to move and work now applies between 17 (almost all) countries of Western Europe (in the 'political' sense) and will, following successful negotiations with some Eastern European countries, apply to Hungary, the Czech Republic and Poland and no doubt later to others.

Countries which join the EU must change their immigration legislation to fit EU policy, including the adoption of the 'Schengen' principles (see below). Austria, for example, which joined in 1995 naturally had to exclude EU citizens from its quotas on residence and visas and work permits. Switzerland, although outside the EU, has been paving the way for membership by replacing its labour migration policy based on 'three circles' of priority with one which differentiates between EU and non-EU citizens. Most of the restrictions on international movement described below will not apply between these states. The absence of such barriers increasingly differentiates the relations between the Western European countries from those in the rest of the world. The North American Free Trade Area (NAFTA), which includes the US, Canada and Mexico, does not confer easier rights of movement on people, only on goods.

3.3.1 Schengen and the Amsterdam Treaty

In addition, the Schengen Agreement (Convention on the Application of the Schengen Agreement, 19 June 1990) was intended further to speed up trade and travel following an inter-governmental initiative by Germany, France and Benelux in 1985.

Citizens of participating states (All EU member states except the United Kingdom and Ireland, plus association with Iceland and Norway) no longer have to show passports or other documentation for movement for any purpose between the territories of the contracting states, while uniform procedures of control will be applied at the external borders, supported by other checks within the national territories. 'Schengenland' is not yet co-terminous with the EU. The Schengen scheme, at least in theory, requires physical segregation of travellers at airports into 'Schengen' and 'non-Schengen' entry streams. It was to have come into effect on 1 December 1993 but implementation was repeatedly delayed until 26 March 1995. Greece and Italy, together with Austria, did not join the workings of the Zone until 1997. Reservations about operating the agreement have been expressed by France, notably through fears concerning the circulation of drugs. That has twice delayed its implementation by six months and induced it to re-establish some border controls. A Draft convention of EC member states on the crossing of external borders, prepared in 1991 by the Ad Hoc Group on Immigration, resembles the 1990 Schengen accord on external borders. Among other provisions it defined crossing points, criteria for admission of third country nationals and harmonizes visa policies and other matters.

Eventually, the 1997 Amsterdam Treaty integrated the Schengen Agreement into EU law, for the time being under Title VI. All future EU member states must adhere to the Schengen principles, improving the security of external borders, ratifying the right to claim asylum and endorsing various rights for foreign residents, and correspondingly removing controls with other EU countries. This is without prejudice to the EU member states which are not part of the Schengen arrangements. Collective arrangements have already been agreed with Eastern European countries, whereby members of the 'Visegrad group' (Poland, Hungary, the Czech Republic and Slovakia) together with Slovenia, no longer need visas for short (three-month) visits to the EU or to the Schengen area. These countries are all likely to be member states of the EU in the near future and as long ago as 1991 concluded a 'Europe Agreement' with the EU relating among many other matters to the movement of labour.

3.3.2 Policy instruments — hierarchy of barriers

No country allows people to arrive and stay without justification or documentation, although in the early 1990s some of the Eastern European countries were not far from that position, more by default than design. In Europe, few countries allow entry for the immediate purpose of permanent or indefinite settlement unless the migrant has some ancient or ethnic or citizenship connection, or is a spouse or dependant of someone already settled. Those entering as recognized workers or who have been accepted as a refugee are not normally granted long-term residence unless they have been resident for some time.

Nine industrial countries have maintained some kind of quota on admissions, in recent years. When countries are attempting to minimize flows, they tend not to have quotas for permanent migration unless they have made unavoidable commitments which cannot be absorbed all at once. Otherwise migration pressures will turn the quotas into minima. Quotas are nonetheless urged by some who consider that 'management' of unwanted migration streams is all that can be expected.

'Immigration' countries do not have this problem and may use quotas as a convenient mechanism for managing flows and, at least in theory, adjusting them annually to changing economic circumstances. Of the nine countries which have quotas, the US and Canada are 'immigration' countries which apply quotas to their overall inflow as described in detail below. The seven European countries with quotas apply them only to specific components of migration streams, e.g. Austria's annual quota of work and of residence permits, and others maintained by Estonia, Germany, Italy, Norway and Turkey. Despite talk of 'quota zéro' by the French former Interior Minister, M. Pasqua, no formal quota system was established in France. The Italian quota, established by the 1990 'Martelli' law, was set at zero for new residence permits from 1991-94 except for individual workers specified by employers unable to find suitable Italian labour for family reunification and temporary admission for humanitarian reasons. Nonetheless, these amounted to 50,000 per year on average and in any case illegal immigration into Italy is easy. In the UK a quota only applies to a small immigration stream (< 1000/yr) of African Asians without personal UK connections who were given British passports in East Africa at the time that independence was granted to new African states. A broader quota to moderate the inflows of dependants from Asia was promised in the 1970s but never implemented.

These regulations can change fast: In November 1993, Spain introduced quotas for new immigrant workers; in July 1995, Russia agreed quotas of immigrants from Kirghizstan, mostly of persons of Russian origin, to protect ethnic Russians and minimize forcible relocation.

The mechanisms of control into European countries have been in existence for about 80 years, since the end of the First World War. Before that time, international movement, at least between European countries outside Russia was remarkably free; passports were voluntary documents (Fussell, 1980;

Hammar, 1992) and some countries hardly maintained any system of border control. This was possible because the level of movement was low and usually unproblematic. Entitlements (e.g. welfare) arising purely from residence were modest as were the rights expected by and granted to immigrants. In some countries before the First World War, e.g. Germany, labour migration was needed and welcomed for the expansion of industry. All that changed in the 1920s when the beginnings of the familiar apparatus of control were set in place: Visas for entry, work permits for work, residence permits or formal acceptance for permanent residence.

As regards border controls, the world is polarizing. The universal requirement when attempting to enter a country legally was usually to show a valid passport and/or visa. As noted above, citizens of member states of the Nordic countries, the EU and EFTA have for some time not needed visas to enter each other's territory. The creation of the European Economic Area (EEA) expanded this zone of relatively visa-free movement to all member states of the above collectivities, except Switzerland which opted not to join. The Schengen ideal is for passports also to be redundant for movement between member states. Increasingly, for citizens of member states of the EU, displaying a passport is only needed in order to show that one is not needed.

Elsewhere, including between the EU and the outside world, visa demands have become more severe, a response to the increased pressures of asylum-claiming and illegal overstaying. Visas are extending the barriers of control into the sending country from which the pressures emanate, where facts about applicants can be checked in ways impossible at ports of entry in the receiving countries. Such pressure, aided by international agreements, have produced a degree of visa harmonization between the Western European countries. The joint visa list of the EU states imposed visa requirement on travellers from 73 of the 183 non-EU states. At the EU Justice and Home Affairs Council meeting on 25 September 1995, a list of 101 countries was agreed whose nationals must have visas to enter EU countries.

Under carriers' liability legislation, adopted by many countries, airlines are liable to penalties if they accept as passengers persons who cannot provide correct documentation; such passengers may have to be returned at the airline's expense. Some countries station immigration officers at overseas airports to ensure that documentation is correctly checked. In November 1995, EU countries agreed to impose an additional requirement for airport transit visas on nationals of ten countries from which many asylum claims originated (Afghanistan, Ethiopia, Eritrea, Ghana, Iraq, Iran, Nigeria, Somalia, Sri Lanka and Zaire).

We are moving towards a uniform pan-European entry visa regime, where all visas must be issued at embassies before departure, and where 'problem countries' will be identified. The imposition of a visa in respect of a particular country can have sensitive domestic and foreign policy implications. There was considerable opposition to the imposition by the UK of visa requirements on Commonwealth countries for the first time in 1985, to limit asylum-claiming from such countries as Ghana and Sri Lanka. By 1994 a high proportion of New Commonwealth countries were on the visa list. Visa regimes can change at short notice. Germany's on/off visa requirements on Poland reflected its incompatible desires to control irregular migration from Poland and develop good relations with it, complicated by its Schengen membership which would then allow the Poles free movement within most of the EU. In the Netherlands, since May 1994, foreigners from non-EU countries who require a visa must apply for an Authorization for Provisional Stay *(Machtiging tot Voorlopig Verbliff* or MVV) at a Dutch embassy or consulate in their own countries, although that requirement was legally challenged and somewhat relaxed (Muus, 1995).

Policy on former Yugoslavia is mixed: In 1996 none of the EU and EFTA states applied visa restrictions to Slovenia, and 15 did not apply them to Croatia, but all (except Austria and Italy, which had no visa restrictions to the whole of former Yugoslavia) had visa restrictions for Bosnia-Herzegovina. In that year, out of the 22 countries for which data were available, only three did not require any sort of visa for any purpose at the time of the enquiry. These were all states of the former Soviet Union or countries in Eastern Europe, whose immigration policies and laws are still in a state of flux (Lithuania, Russia, Bulgaria). Other countries (e.g. Hungary, Romania) require a visa even for tourism and short stays; elsewhere visas are needed for work or other temporary or permanent residence.

3.4 Categories of acceptance

(i) *Spouses, dependants or family members*

With varying degrees of reluctance, all Western European counties accept the principle of family reunification, albeit with some restrictions. It is accepted as a principle and enshrined in immigration law in all the EU countries, in Canada, the US and in most of the others. In the EU, family reunification extends to all persons legally resident in the country, irrespective of citizenship but with other restrictions. In other countries, the right of entry often applies only to dependants or spouses of citizens (e.g. Bulgaria). Family reunification or spouse migration would normally not be regarded as problematic between countries where the migration could be expected to be roughly reciprocal. It raises difficulties when it becomes part of immigration pressure processes between poor and rich countries.

Under such circumstances the movement is only one-way. Fraudulent applications and marriages arranged for immigration purposes might become common, those who enter illegally and then claim asylum or are granted leave to remain under amnesties also become eligible; the practice of constrained marital choice and arranged marriage common in many non-European populations guarantees further movement. This way the migration of dependants and spouses, once assumed to be limited, becomes perpetual. It is helpful to distinguish the immigration of existing spouses (usually wives) and dependant children of established immigrants (family reunification migration) from the immigration of new spouses or fiancé(e)s, of either sex, of the younger generation of immigrant communities (family formation or spouse migration). Family migration has been the biggest component of legal migration to Europe for some time. The marriage dimension is replacing dependant migration. In the late 1970s and early 1980s, family reconstitution was by far the most important component. Its initial rise and then slow decline over time, as the families of remaining guest workers came to join them, was the main reason why overall immigration to Europe first increased by the later 1970s and then declined again until the early 1980s. In recent years, new family formation streams are growing and eclipsing the numbers entering for reunification in some countries, e.g. the Netherlands (Muus, 1991) and the UK (Coleman, 1995).

Many sending countries have defective or non-existent registration systems, and fraudulent applications are frequently made and are difficult to check. Consequently some receiving countries require detailed evidence to show that dependants are indeed related as claimed. In response to this problem, especially in respect of applications for 'entry clearance' (a visa certifying dependant status) from the Indian subcontinent, the UK became the first country in the world to institute compulsory DNA tests to ascertain that the child is related to the parents as claimed.

Spouses or dependants are often only admitted under conditions. As well as the probationary period for spouses, a number of countries also require a sponsor to be nominated to ensure that adequate accommodation is available (sometimes, as in Italy, this must be private, not state-subsidized accommodation) and that the spouse or dependants can live an independent life without recourse to public funds (as in Germany). These requirements have in general been tightened in recent years.

In the Swiss system, where there is much emphasis on annual, seasonal and short-term contracts for trade and tourism, family reunification has only been possible for permanent resident and annual workers, not seasonal or short-term workers. However seasonal status can eventually be changed to annual, with a corresponding increase in entitlement to reunion. Generally in Western Europe, family reunification is available to the immediate family dependants of any person lawfully resident in the country (worker, student, accepted refugee), with some qualifications. For example, the person whose family is entering usually has to be lawfully resident and, in the case of Germany, holding an employment permit.

Entitlement to family reunion may not be immediate (in Germany it ceased to be so from 1 April 1979), and dependants may not have immediate access to the labour market (as in Germany from 25 September 1981). In some cases, e.g. the UK, persons who have established their status to the satisfaction of consular officials abroad, and been given 'entry clearance' certificates, are then admitted for settlement. In France, however, permanent residence was only granted after 10 years' residence, and since 1993 that has no longer been automatic. As noted later, families of persons accepted as refugees are usually admitted. In Israel (since 1970), unqualified entry to relatives only applies to relatives of Jews.

Those desiring entry on family or dependant grounds must show that they have suitable resources (Netherlands, France) and/or access to housing (Spain, UK) for their care without dependency on the tax-payer. Guest workers were initially meant to be an exception to this principle, possibly more because it was assumed that they would depart rather than because it was seriously supposed that they could be excluded from a general entitlement. In fact, in Germany little thought was given at the time to the long-term consequences of this opportunistic labour policy (German Federal Ministry of the Interior, 1993). Official opposition began to be revived following the proposals of the Federal/Länder Commission on immigration policy (28 February 1977). In Switzerland it was supposed that such restrictions could be maintained, given the substantially seasonal nature of the migration and the privileged access to Swiss nationality. This was abandoned in 1996 (partly to facilitate harmonization of Swiss practice with that of the EU countries, which it was supposed that Switzerland was to join). Family reunion, reluctantly accepted as inevitable by the guest worker countries of Europe in the 1970s, has turned from a flow which was not meant to happen into a major stream.

Family reunion policy has come under closer scrutiny in a number of countries. Welfare costs provoke concern as continuing primary immigration or amnesties continue to add recruits to streams whose disappearance has been long promised. For example, the 'Zero Immigration Package' adopted by the incoming Gaullist government of 1993 introduced stricter rules on family reunification. By the Act of 24 August 1993 the waiting time for an immigrant's close relatives was extended from one to two years. The obligation to guarantee financial support was made more stringent. The person requesting reunification of his family has to be resident continuously in France for two years, not one. Permanent residence permits would no longer be issued after 10 years. Among other measures, it was then intended to end the possibility of uniting families altogether, after a period of time (Widgren, 1994b, p. 31). Similar reforms were introduced into the Netherlands in 1993.

Germany has also tightened up its measures on family reunification. The Act amending The Aliens Law of 9 July 1990 (Section 17) required that dependants of foreigners can only enter if they are joining a foreign resident who has a residence permit or right of unlimited residence, if the living space is acceptable and if maintenance is assured from the employment or personal assets (not state assistance) of the foreigner concerned. The one-year waiting period for spouses, however, has been abolished. The UK Immigration Act 1988 required that all immigrants, including those previously exempted by section 1(5) of the 1971 Immigration Act, show that adequate accommodation was available for their families before reunification could take place. The application of a final time limit for the entry of dependants had been considered in the 1970s. The same government, frustrated by the seemingly unending flows arising from this commitment, had, after an official report (Home Office, 1977), promised to introduce a register of dependants during the 1979 election. No action was ever taken. In Germany, the maximum age of children who could enter as dependants was lowered to 16 and other measures proposed to limit spouses joining second-generation foreigners, on 2 Dec 1981.

(ii) Spouse migration

Family formation migration refers to new spouses or fiancé(e)s. Almost all countries permit persons who are permanently resident to bring a new spouse to live with them; the principle is enshrined in human rights conventions. Furthermore, at the Copenhagen meeting in June 1993, EC Immigration Ministers agreed a resolution on 'Harmonization of national policies on family reunification'. Although not legally binding, Member States agreed to grant admission to a spouse and unmarried dependant children below age 16 (or 18) subject to such restrictions as visas, waiting times, primary purpose tests, tests of maintenance and housing availability, excluding polygamous spouses. These restrictions apply to families of lawful long-term residents, not necessarily to the Member States' own nationals or to other EU nationals. However some countries which had little experience of immigration until recently have only formalized the entitlement to spouse migration in their own legislation in the last decade; for example in Italy's 'Martelli Act' of 1990.

Most countries, while admitting in general the right for spouses to enter, place conditions on their immigration. Many new spouses are joining partners who come from the new non-European immigrant population or who are the children of immigrants, and the spouses often 'recruited' in the sending countries through traditional arranged marriage systems or through advertisements. This form of immigration, driven by the growing and still youthful age distribution of immigrant-descended populations, is fast displacing family reunification in the Netherlands and the UK (Muus, 1991; Coleman, 1995b) as the single most important component of regular permanent immigration. Because of demographic increase, spouse migration will continue to grow unless practices of partner choice change further to favour European partners or at least those of immigrant origin but who were born in Europe. Mixed marriages (on a citizenship criterion) in some countries are on the increase (OECD, 1994), but elsewhere are showing little upward trend (see Chapter 2). Some countries have tried to limit such migration for some time; for example the German government proposed to limit overseas spouses joining second-generation foreigners as long ago as December 1981.

Previously it was assumed that such new households should be formed in the country of origin of the husband, so that new wives or fiancées may join husbands but husbands might not join wives. However the European Court of Human Rights has deemed otherwise, and countries which are signatories to the European Convention on Human Rights (which includes all EU countries and others) must now allow husbands as well as wives to join their spouses. This is becoming a potent new source of primary migration. In 1985 the UK was obliged by the European Court of Human Rights to change its Immigration Rules in this way, a step followed by a substantial and persistent rise in immigration of husbands and male fiancés.

Such marriages are attractive to potential immigrants, some are believed to be arranged primarily for migration rather than for matrimony. A number are believed to be fraudulent transactions arranged for money. Some countries attempt to counter such abuses. For example until 1998 the UK imposed strict tests of 'primary purpose' on such intending partners of either sex and still admits them for a one-year probationary period only in the first instance. Since the abolition of this 'primary purpose' rule by the new Labour government, spouse migration has increased considerably, from 22,000 to 32,000 from mid 1997 to mid 1998 (Home Office, 1998a). Other countries have adopted similar steps to minimize fraudulent entries based on sham marriages. For example The Netherlands New Aliens Law of 1993 (with effect from 1994) states that marriages between legal residents and persons living abroad cannot be registered without prior consultation and approval by the municipal authorities and the aliens police, and that persons may only be entered in a municipal register if they possess a valid residence permit. Few European countries admit other family members, neither spouses nor dependants. For example Denmark does so only on specific compassionate grounds.

(iii) Nationality/ethnicity

A number of countries in Europe specifically state ethnic origin, national origin or former citizenship as a consideration for permanent admission; usually this carries entitlement to unrestricted entry and to citizenship — an extension of the *ius sanguinis*. These are mostly countries with considerable diasporas of their former citizens (see van Hear, 1998). In some cases the provision exists to prevent unreasonable hardship to former emigrants and their children who departed their homeland in times of easy immigration controls, and who would now be prevented from returning under modern provisions (e.g. UK).

Table 3.1 Persons admitted through an ancestral connection with the country (diaspora return).

Country	Grounds
Estonia	ancestry
Finland	ancestry: Ingrians
Germany	ancestry: *Aussiedler*
Greece	ancestry: 'Pontic' Greeks
Hungary	national origin
Israel	Jews or close relatives
Lithuania	those who have kept right to citizenship
Poland	ancestry
Russia	Russian 'nationality' in former Soviet sense
Turkey	ancestry
Italy	Italian origin
UK	'patrials'; persons with at least one grandparent born in the UK, irrespective of nationality or ethnic origin

Others wish to facilitate the return of former labour migrants (Italy) or deportees and forced migrants from the Soviet period (Estonia).

In the numerically most important case (Germany) the aim is to help the return of people of ancient German origin dispersed throughout Eastern Europe and the former Soviet Union, many of them deported during the Second World War to outlying Soviet Republics from their former Russian 'homelands'. Their position was made difficult after the Second World War, especially in recent years, by the rise of national feeling in newly independent former Soviet Republics. Since 1990 return migration of persons of Russian nationality to the Russian Federation, for similar reasons, has greatly exceeded the flow even of ethnic Germans to Germany.

By contrast, the 'countries of immigration' no longer lay down any ethnic privileges. The US (and Australia and New Zealand) abolished national origin preferences (which mostly worked in favour of European or in the latter cases people of British origin) in 1965. Canada abolished most such preferences in 1962 and finally in 1967 (Hawkins, 1989), having eliminated free entry to British citizens as early as 1946 (unrestricted entry of Canadians to the UK persisted until 1962). The only indirect ethnic/national origin restriction in the US is not part of the preference system, but arises from the rule under the 1990 Immigration Act that no single country must exceed 20,000 visas out of the annual total quota of 270,000 available, and applicants who exceed this quota must be put on a waiting list.

Of the other countries which mention ethnic or national origin as a criterion for entry (Table 3.1), most have had a turbulent history in the 20th century, particularly associated with the consequences of the First and Second World Wars and associated deportations and shifts in national boundaries.

Most of these countries have experienced a change, usually a contraction, of national boundaries (Finland 1945, Germany 1918, 1945, Hungary 1918, Poland 1918, 1945, Russia/Soviet Union 1991, Turkey 1918) which have left minorities of national origin stranded in former national territory which has become part of a foreign country. Many of these have also had substantial populations displaced by war (especially Germany 1945, Greece 1922, Poland 1939-45) or deported (Latvia 1945). In other cases, many citizens fled abroad to avoid new political regimes (Greece 1949, Baltic States 1945, Poland 1945). Change in political circumstances have caused some historical diasporas (Germany, Russia) or populations in ancient homelands (Greece) to become isolated in increasingly unfavourable conditions under alien rule. The special conditions of Israel, which came into existence as a result of the turmoils noted above, are well known.

(iv) Labour migrants

Labour migration from outside EU member states has usually been regulated through the work permit system to respond to the rise and fall of domestic unemployment. Hence rising unemployment in Europe in the 1990s has led to a general downward revision of work permit numbers since the early 1990s. Generally these changes reinforce the so-called 'priority rule'; that is, the expectation that available jobs will be offered first to citizens, legally resident foreigners and (for EU members) citizens of other EU states. Sometimes the law needs to be changed to make it more responsive to such regulation or to fit EU-wide labour market requirements. The Dutch Aliens Employment Act (11 September 1995) and recent legislation in Germany have attempted to limit non-EU labour recruitment, and Austria has reduced its existing quotas. Austria and Switzerland have also modified their labour recruitment and other immigration policies, but that is more in connection with actual or possible future EU membership.

The inflow of highly skilled workers, in relatively small numbers but with high economic potential, is generally seen as a non-problematic and indeed desirable form of labour exchange, without social or political complications. A high proportion of such moves are 'inter-company transfers' arranged by multinational employers. Many countries have facilitated such movement, e.g. Switzerland (1995). The US and Canada have been reorienting their immigration policy towards more skilled migration.

In the case of the EU, entry for work and seeking work, as for all other purposes, is free to citizens of member states without limitation of time. Almost all countries accept labour migrants from other countries under work permit, enabling some adjustment to be made to flows in the light of the unemployment situation. Only the 'countries of immigration' (Canada and the US) now accept regular labour migrants as permanent residents on arrival.

Many countries, however, while admitting labour migrants for a limited period in the first instance, may then permit them to stay permanently once they have completed some years' residence or employment (four years employment in the case of the UK, five years' residence in the case of Belgium and Bulgaria).

In Germany the initial grant of a residence permit (*Aufenthaltserlaubnis*) is limited to one year, subsequently to two years and finally is granted without limitation. Such unlimited residence permits guarantee permanent residence. Foreigners in employment with a residence permit are entitled to an unlimited residence permit (*unbefristete Aufenthaltserlaubnis*) only under certain stricter conditions. Economically inactive foreigners must have their own means of subsistence to gain unlimited residence. Foreigners who have held the *Aufenthaltserlaubnis* for 8 years or the *unbefristete Aufenthaltserlaubnis* for three years are then entitled to the right of unlimited residence (*Aufenthaltsberechtigung*) as long as certain conditions are met.

In the Netherlands the Law on Foreign Labour *(Wet Arbeid Vreemdelingen,* WAV), effective 1 September 1995, which replaced the previous Law on the Employment of Foreign Labour (WABW), requires new non-EU workers to obtain a work permit which is only given if no other permanent legal resident of the Netherlands is available. These permits, for up to three years, are taken primarily by 'non-traditional' applicants (e.g. Americans, Poles, Japanese) and are usually subject to strict conditions on duration of advertisement, non-residence in the country, minimum wage and other aspects of Dutch interest including housing availability. The other route to employment, the 'Declaration' *(Verklaring)* is primarily given to children or partners of legal residents who are already in the country. Regulations relating to them have been changed (see Muus, 1995). Most applicants for this documentation have been people of 'traditional' immigrant origin. Unlike the work permits, applications have increased substantially until 1993. These restrictions are further structured by the Law on Identification of 1 June 1994 which requires job-seekers to identify their nationality and to possess a 'Social-Fiscal' (SOFI) number, for which a valid stay permit is required.

In the countries of immigration, there is a disposition to believe that substantial levels of labour immigration are generally beneficial for the economy (US Dept. of Labor, 1989), and that such positive inward streams only need to be managed in order to maximize the skills and professional level of the immigrants and (in the case of Canada) to adjust the intake each year in relation to the performance of the economy and its position in the economic cycle. In Canada the 'independent' labour migration stream was almost stopped, for example, between 1982 and 1986 during the economic downturn. In Canada independent immigrants are not obliged to have the offer of a job, although to have a job offer enables independent immigrants to by-pass the points system. Instead selection is by the points system. Despite all these complexities, however, employment-based immigration in both countries is only a small proportion of the total, as noted above. On the other hand some of those who enter under family preferences have skills, and there are no restrictions on employment upon those who enter under family (or refugee) preferences.

Work-permit systems, based on individual job applications, do not usually involve quotas, which are based on local or national assessments of labour needs or maxima for absorption. There are at least two exceptions, and both of these still operate guest worker recruitment. One is Austria, where during the 1980s 50-60,000 permits were distributed annually to employers by the government. Under the reformed Austrian legislation from 1991 quotas were established each year after consultation on the basis, as before, of economic need and absorptive capacity for the total foreign worker population, which then determine how many new foreign workers, if any, may be admitted. (Widgren, 1994b p. 26). Quotas were a feature of the guest worker period until 1973. Often these quotas were negotiated between government, employers and trades unions, as in the case of Austria's *'Kontingentesystem'*. In Switzerland quotas of annual, seasonal and short-term workers have for a long time been fixed annually by a similar process of discussion as part of long-term migration and economic planning. The short-term nature of much Swiss labour migration means that it approximates most closely to the 'model' of a guest worker policy. Such quotas have, of course, become progressively overtaken by unplanned and uncontrolled asylum-claimants and illegal immigrants.

Guest worker recruitment ended in 1973 (except in Austria and Switzerland), and specific government legislation on new systems of labour immigration followed shortly after (Germany 1973, Austria 1975).

At the other extreme, since 1975 Norway has operated a more or less 'zero quota' of work permits for persons from outside the Nordic area, except for a small number of outside experts, employees of the oil industry and foreigners already granted residence as refugees or for other reasons. Until 1971, every non-Nordic person offered a job in Norway received a permit almost automatically. The rise of spontaneous immigration from Pakistan, India and Turkey provoked legal changes in 1971 to limit such economic migration on social grounds, because of the limited 'reception' possibilities. The economic crisis of 1973 led to a one-year stop to permits in 1974. In 1975 the regulations were introduced which are still in force in modified form (Widgren, 1994b). Greece, with severe economic problems and a surfeit of illegal immigrants, also declares that it is not a country in need of economic migrants and issues work permits very sparingly (Fakiolas, 1993) and Ireland is also very selective and restrictive (Sexton, 1994).

Labour migration under work permits has increasingly developed as a high-skill professional migration of elites (Salt, 1988; Salt and Ford, 1993), and has been uncontroversial in most European counties in the last decade

(Stalker, 1994). In western Europe, many permit holders move between different components of international companies. Labour demand, current and forecast, is for more educated and skilled technical managerial and professional workers (Department of Employment, 1991; Tessaring, 1993). Few problems are perceived here. Asylum-claiming and illegal immigration, however, create a whole labour market outside the regulated work-permit system. It is these later topics which dominate in the recent legislation listed in this report and in most academic and political commentary. The free movement of labour within the Nordic countries, the EU and now the EEA has likewise given rise to few problems or disputes where the citizens of member states are concerned. Indeed within the EU area, labour migration between EU countries was relatively stagnant or declining over the 1980s, despite the co-existence of some labour shortages and areas of high unemployment. Labour migration between EU countries recovered at the end of the decade (Poulain, 1996) as noted in chapter 2.

Switzerland found its guest worker policy was not sustainable. For decades Switzerland has had by far the highest proportion of foreigners in its population and by the 1970s this *'überfremdung'* was becoming a political issue, quite apart from any economic considerations. The rise of asylum- seeking and illegal immigration has worsened that perception. Switzerland also faced pressure from a different direction. The provisions of the seasonal worker arrangements were not compatible with law in the EC, which Switzerland then looked likely to join and may still do. The radical revision of Swiss immigration law adopted by Parliament in 1991 proposed a unified policy: The ratio of the domestic to the foreign labour force will not be allowed to change further, future foreign labour will be recruited from EEA member states, not from other European countries or countries outside Europe, and the distinctive Swiss seasonal worker system will gradually be abolished. This goes hand in hand with a policy placing more emphasis on integration and easier access to citizenship.

Eastern and Central European countries are having to invent labour migrant policies from scratch, along with the rest of migration policies, especially those countries subject to high levels of illegal immigration or which may be about to experience labour shortages (e.g. the Czech Republic).

Finally, guest workers have recently been reinvented. Switzerland and Austria never gave them up. Germany and a few other countries have re-introduced the concept for workers from Eastern Europe, but under a different name (*Gastarbeitnehmer*). This has followed the new freedom now enjoyed by the former communist countries of Eastern Europe and the opening of the door to Europe's 'natural' labour resource, shut off from Western Europe by the Iron curtain and now — as argued earlier — open probably 30 years too late. Despite the tightening of the immigration restrictions and growing unemployment in Western countries, a number of Eastern European countries

Table 3.2 Guest worker countries.

Host	Main sending countries (dates give year of bilateral agreement)	Quotas for workers?
Former guest worker countries		
Belgium	Italy, Spain, Greece, Morocco and Turkey	No
Denmark	Yugoslavia, Turkey, Pakistan	No
France	Portugal, Spain, Italy, Morocco, Algeria, Tunisia	No
Germany	Italy (1955) Spain, Greece (1960) Turkey (1961) Morocco (1963) Portugal (1964) Tunisia (1965) Yugoslavia (1968)	
Netherlands	Morocco, Turkey	No
Former and current guest worker countries		
Germany	Poland, Hungary other E. Europe	Various (see text)
Austria	Yugoslavia, Italy, Spain, Turkey	Annual (see text)
Switzerland	Italy, Yugoslavia, Portugal, Spain	Annual (see text)
Countries of substantial immigration which did not organize guest worker programmes		
Norway	India, Pakistan, Turkey, (Nordic)	Yes
Sweden	Spain, Yugoslavia, Turkey, (Finland and other Nordic)	No
United Kingdom[1]	India, Pakistan, Bangladesh, West Indies, Africa, Hong Kong, Ireland.	No[2]

1. UK organized temporary labour migration of European displaced persons to help in post-war reconstruction in the late 1940s. Many returned home.
2. Quotas for unskilled workers from the New Commonwealth were established as a transitional arrangement in the 1962 Commonwealth Immigrants Act and abolished in 1971.

(Hungary, Poland, Romania, Russia) proposed in the early 1990s that Western countries take temporary workers, trainees, apprentices on a contract or short-term basis.

Only Germany has made any substantial response, despite the problems of unemployment in the former East Germany after unification in 1990, partly in order to help rebuild East Germany, and in particular the future capital Berlin, partly from foreign policy considerations. Four categories of workers are defined in the new bilateral agreements. Up to the end of 1994, work contracts (*Werkverträge*) operated through subcontractors were limited by national quotas to an average of 41,000 per month for maximum two years, mostly in construction. Guest employees (*Gastarbeitnehmer*) up to about 5,508 placements for one year mostly in construction; seasonal workers (up to three months) with no limit on numbers (mostly Poles); a few staff to care for sick and elderly; cross-border commuters without limit of number or employment (Rudolph & Hillmann, 1995). Amid accusations of unfair competition from trades unions and employers, the quotas have since been cut and agreements

not extended; numbers involved were halved from 1992 to 1994 in a worsening employment situation as Germany entered recession. It is promised that
the new guest workers really will be temporary this time. Initially, some
demand existed for the rebuilding of Berlin and its transformation into the
national capital but demand for the new permits from employers had fallen
by 1995. A summary of the situation is given in table 3.2.

3.5 Irregular migration — asylum policy

Asylum-claimants generally intend to become 'immigrants' in the UN definition of the word, and in many cases clearly wish to have the option of permanent settlement. Most succeed in becoming immigrants in a long-term
sense, as most of the majority of claimants whose claims are rejected are believed to remain in the country concerned. A minority of claimants are recognized as Convention refugees and given leave to settle either at once or
after the passage of time, usually permanently. A larger number are allowed
to remain indefinitely or for a limited time, often on conditional terms, on 'humanitarian' grounds. More asylum-claimants are not recognized as Convention refugees nor allowed to remain on humanitarian or other grounds. Instead most claims are rejected as ill-founded. While firmly endorsing the
principle of asylum, the recent policy proposal from the UK Home Office
notes (1998 b) that 'there is no doubt that the asylum system is being abused
by those seeking to migrate for purely economic reasons. Many claims are
simply a tissue of lies'.

Asylum-claiming is one of a number of options open to illegal immigrants,
who have attracted increasing policy attention, as it is believed that their numbers have increased as other opportunities have been closed off by policy
moves in the 1990s. Information from police, from immigration control, from
international organizations and from academic researchers has persuaded
western policy makers that they now have to counter a new level of well-
funded organizations behind illegal movements. Illegal immigrant trafficking
has rapidly risen to a multi-billion pound activity (IOM 1995, Salt 1997), with,
it seems, the traffickers increasingly influencing where flows will end up. In
the nature of things its significance is hard to establish, but in 1996 it was
estimated that 60% of the illegal entrants to Germany had been brought by
traffickers mostly via and from Eastern Europe (Ternes, 1996 in Salt, 1998, p.
20). In 1996, human trafficking was worth about US $ 7 billion worldwide ac-
cording to the International Organization for Migration.

The rise of asylum-claiming and illegal immigration in the 1980s seemed
to show that the controls imposed by receiving countries over their immigration streams had ceased to be effective. Labour migration is at least no-
minally under the control of work permit, quota or points system and of re-

sponses to demand in the economy and the workforce of the receiving state. Family reconstitution usually occurs in an orderly manner. Asylum-claimants and illegal immigrants and overstayers are in a different category. Flows of asylum-claimants and of genuine refugees, unlike most other migration flows, have nothing to do with demand, unless the weakness or ease of asylum provisions constitutes a form of demand, or at least of attraction. The rapid rate of increase in claims in the last decade from most of the large and growing number of countries from which claimants come cannot easily be accounted for by concomitant changes in push factors, let alone pull factors. The numerous refugees from former Yugoslavia, mostly dealt with under 'special protection' arrangements, are an obvious exception. As Böhning (1980 p. 119) puts it, 'No government articulates a demand for refugees, most want to keep them out, although many accept them'.

During the late 1980s and early 1990s claimants were most attracted to Germany and Sweden, which were known to have, and which had long proclaimed themselves to have, the most open and generous asylum legislation, coupled with buoyant economies. In time asylum-claimants have discovered almost all other European countries, most recently the Republic of Ireland. By the early 1990s, many European countries found themselves receiving as many or more asylum claims as they had regular migrants. This unplanned and expensive inflow was universally unwelcome to governments. The inflow was also, to a certain degree, unwelcome to the greater part of their electorates. However, in most Western countries pro-asylum pressure groups, individuals, churches and NGOs favour them on humanitarian grounds and offer support and protection against removal (for example the Brussels-based Churches Commission for Migrants in Europe). Nonetheless there has been a rapid rise in new administrative procedures to limit duplicate and false asylum claims and to prevent asylum becoming part of the repertoire of economic migrants for entering or staying in the Western countries of their choice. These steps fall under a sequence of checking, validation and removal.

(i) Asylum policies — 'manifestly unfounded' claims

The large numbers of claims made it imperative to distinguish between those which have a case for being well-founded and those which do not qualify after scrutiny or which are 'manifestly unfounded'. The time taken for a review of an asylum claim, traditionally a long-winded expensive semi-judicial process often subject to appeals, makes it unsuitable for the mass-processing of claims. The total cost of the asylum process in Western Europe must have reached well over $10 billion per year in processing and (mostly) welfare: The cost for Germany alone in the year 1993 was estimated to be $9.6 billion (Jandl 1995). The huge backlog of claims caused by the time taken to process each one thoroughly causes injustice to the minority of genuine cases and allows others to prolong their stay at taxpayers' expense, and disappear into the appropriate immigrant community.

Hence national and EU asylum and refugee law increasingly emphasize the need to distinguish 'manifestly unfounded' cases from more serious and genuine cases. (E.g., the 1992 London Resolution on manifestly unfounded applications for asylum.) Towards the implementation of this principle, 'fast-track' asylum procedures, to screen out manifestly unfounded claims, have been implemented in all EU countries, whereby selected claims are not put through the whole procedure (although the UK and the Netherlands adopted this practice as late as 1993). It should be mentioned that this concept and the special procedures for processing this category of applications, are not consequences of recent EC or EU asylum policy harmonization. The category of manifestly unfounded applications was defined and the introduction of special procedures recognized as early as 1982/83 by the UNHCR Executive Committee (Conclusions No. 28 and 30).

(ii) 'Safe countries', 'de facto' status and other concepts

Since the mid-1980s, with few exceptions, West European countries have developed and applied the principle of return to the country of first asylum (i.e. the 'first safe country' which is entered by an asylum-seeker after leaving his/her own country, defined as one which adheres to the 1951 Geneva Convention). However, in 1997 doubts were raised as to the correct interpretation of this concept. Furthermore, applications for asylum by claimants from 'safe countries' themselves are now increasingly likely to be refused *a priori* as they are defined not to generate refugees in the Geneva sense because the rule of law prevails in their home countries. This has applied particularly to claimants from Eastern Europe or claimants who have passed though Eastern European countries now adhering to the Convention. In communist times the likelihood of claimants from Eastern Europe being accepted as refugees in the West was much greater.

In many countries *de facto* refugee status has been given to those who do not qualify as Convention refugees, but whom it is difficult to return to their country of origin for a variety of 'humanitarian' reasons. This can include unrest in the country of origin, but often simply means that the claimant has managed to marry or otherwise settle in, and it would be thought unreasonable to remove him. Governments in liberal democracies are seldom willing to expose themselves to criticism for having refused, or sent back, asylum-claimants whose fate is then outside their control or observation. Furthermore governments do not wish to be blamed for the consequences of mistaken removal and are likely to err on the side of caution. These cases comprise the majority of the 'successful' applicants to Western Europe in recent years. The major part of debate and of European legislative developments have been addressed to them.

The main reason for the exceptional increase in applicants in 1992 was the displacement of people from the former Yugoslavia. Accordingly, many countries have introduced legislation which makes possible a 'temporary protected status' (TPS) as proposed through the Ad Hoc Group at the London and Copenhagen conferences of EU Ministers noted below (see Inter-Governmental Consultations 1995). These initiatives should be seen as a co-ordinated follow-up on the Comprehensive Response to the Humanitarian Crisis in the former Yugoslavia, originally initiated by the UN High Commissioner for Refugees at the decisive meeting held in Geneva on 29 July 1992. They facilitate the temporary stay of refugees from the former Yugoslavia without a long-term economic and political commitment. The benefits to the individual depend upon existing national laws and regulations.

(iii) Removing rejected asylum-seekers

One of the most troublesome problems of immigration in Europe is the difficulty of removing people with no entitlement to be there. These include illegal entrants or overstayers and most numerous of all, asylum-claimants whose claims have been rejected but who remain in the host country. Inevitably it is difficult to be certain about data, but it is thought that at least 80% of rejected claimants do not leave. Only about 5% of rejected claimants are removed or are known to depart voluntarily from some countries (Inter-Governmental Consultations, 1993). A number of factors combine to make removal difficult. Some asylum-claimants destroy their documents, which makes it difficult to repatriate them. Others take advantage of the backlogs of processing to disappear into local immigrant communities, or do so when they learn that their claims have been rejected. Others marry or become parents. Some of these difficulties lead to their being given leave to remain on humanitarian grounds — often because removal is judged impracticable rather than through any justification of claims. It has been easier to return rejected claimants to 'safe third countries' (mostly in Eastern Europe) where they may have previously resided and where they could have claimed asylum (but which were probably less attractive as final destinations). A number of bilateral agreements have been reached in this area, for example in respect of Romanian gypsies in Germany. It is more difficult to remove unsuccessful claimants to countries of origin in the third world.

Since the mid-1980s, many countries have adopted the principle of return to the country of first asylum (a principle made explicit in the Dublin Convention as noted below). This of course is a procedure invoked before the claim is considered. Through legislation in the early 1990s, this principle has become law in Switzerland (1990), France and Germany (1993), the Netherlands and the United Kingdom (1993). Only Germany specifies in its legislation which countries should be defined as 'safe countries', applications from which should not generally be accepted *a priori*. In other countries this is done on a more ad hoc basis.

In addition an increasing number of countries require that asylum-claimants live in specified places or collective accommodation (e.g. Germany) or are confined there (Denmark, Norway) while their cases are being considered. Additionally, those to be deported may be detained until they can be removed (e.g. Germany, Sweden and others). These steps are intended to stop claimants disappearing into immigrant communities when their claims are being processed, and to ensure that they are available for removal if their claims are rejected. Such procedures become more affordable and acceptable when the speed of processing is increased, but otherwise attract criticism from humanitarian pressure groups. This is an expensive option although such residential care, together with faster processing, can replace welfare transfer payments and make longer commitment less likely. For example in Belgium, under proposals introduced in 1995, asylum-seekers must claim asylum on arrival, will not be eligible for welfare, but will instead be cared for in reception centres. In some of these the claimants will be confined until their cases are decided.

(iv) International efforts, agreements and convergence

The large increase in the number of asylum claims has provoked urgent attempts not only to revise national asylum policies but also to harmonize them across Europe.

The first of these attempts to minimize asylum shopping around the EC was set up at a meeting of EC Interior and Justice Ministers as early as October 1986. This meeting created the 'Ad Hoc Group on Immigration', which with its immigration sub-groups has held over 100 meetings per year since. These arrangements were formalized under the Maastricht Treaty (Bunyan & Webber, 1995).

One of the first results of international co-operation has been the agreements to prevent asylum-claimants travelling between countries trying their luck in each. First, countries have agreed to accept each others' asylum decisions (usually negative), so that if a claim is refused in one it will not be considered in another. Second, the EC's Dublin Convention in June 1990 (Convention Determining the State Responsible for Examining Applications for Asylum lodged in one of the Member States of the European Communities) agreed that claimants should be returned to the first country (safe third country or host third country) in which they could have claimed asylum, or had already been granted asylum. The Ministerial meeting in London on 30 November 1992 reaffirmed this principle, together with the adoption of accelerated procedures for dealing with manifestly unfounded applications for asylum. Third, the same meeting agreed to specify countries in which there is no serious risk of persecution. This 'safe country' principle is now widely adopted. Asylum claims from specified countries deemed to observe 'human rights' are considered to be *a priori* manifestly unfounded. For example such a 'white list' was presented after the new UK Immigration and Asylum Act of 1996.

Asylum pressures have also led to increasing convergence or harmonization on practices which work (speeding up processes, fingerprinting, pre-screening and confinement). Particularly open asylum criteria in Sweden and Germany have been abandoned, and restrictions on the privileges of claimants imposed (e.g. the ability to work, in France). The decline in the number of asylum-seekers since 1993, particularly noticeable in Western Europe and Canada, is very likely attributable to their implementation, although no sophisticated methodology exists to test such claims.

Refugees from Yugoslavia presented a special case. Few doubted the horrors from which many were fleeing. The mass of migrants was well in excess of the capacity of asylum systems in Austria and elsewhere to evaluate. Consequently at their Copenhagen meeting in June 1993, EC Ministers agreed guidelines on 'temporary protected status' for people displaced from former Yugoslavia, outside the usual asylum criteria, and also stated their intention to provide relief wherever possible in the region of origin, in safe areas as close as possible to home (IGC 1995). Consequently, most forced migrants from former Yugoslavia after 1992 fall outside the usual asylum statistics and are counted instead under the category of 'temporary protection'.

Agreements within the EC from the Treaty of Rome, the Single European Act, the Maastricht Treaty and the Schengen Agreement have attempted further to harmonize treatment of asylum-claimants and refugees by the member states, and develop information systems and databases. These include the Centre for Information, Discussion and Exchange on the Crossing of Borders and Immigration (CIREFI), the Centre for Information, Discussion and Exchange on Asylum (CIREA) both established by the Ad Hoc Group in 1992, and the Schengen Information System (SIS) in 1990, the lateness of which impeded the implementation of the Schengen agreement. Under the 'third pillar' of the Maastricht treaty a formal structure for inter-governmental consultation concerning migration was set up, and under the Amsterdam treaty the EU will take over responsibility for immigration and asylum policies. But international agreements are not confined to the EU or EEA. The Dublin and Vienna discussions, and the Informal Consultations in Geneva span Europe and beyond. However the only continuing discussions at government level which appear to span major countries in Eastern and Central as well as in Western Europe is the 'Budapest Process', which originated in the Berlin conference of autumn 1991. This is primarily concerned with illegal immigration (UNECE, 1995a).

3.6 Illegal immigration

Illegal immigration and overstaying often, as mentioned earlier, operates in parallel with asylum-claiming.

There have been illegal or irregular migrants in Europe for decades. Many of those who were employed in the 1960s in France and Germany entered illegally, having their position regularized after they had found employment. Few of them seem to have thought of claiming asylum when apprehended or deported. That in itself needs explanation. The partially alternative nature of illegal entry and asylum-claiming is illustrated by the inclination of apprehended illegals or overstayers to claim asylum, and by the relative balance between asylum-claiming and illegal entry. When the latter is easy and/or rewarded with amnesties, as in Southern Europe, asylum-claiming tends to be low. When asylum-claiming becomes harder or less profitable, as in most of Western Europe since 1992, the trend shifts to illegal entry and overstaying, which has become the new big migration challenge (Inter-Governmental Consultations, 1995).

Organized trafficking of illegal immigrants by criminals has, as we touched upon earlier, become a significant problem (International Organization for Migration, 1994). Partly because of the large premiums paid by illegal immigrants (or often put together by their families) and by the returns on their employment, immigrant smuggling has a become a multi-billion dollar international business. Large-scale migration, to the United States and Canada as well as to Europe, of illegal immigrants from China is driven by a potentially limitless supply, apparently encouraged by the Chinese Government (Salt and Stein, 1997). Of course illegal immigration also follows demand, for unregulated labour to do dirty jobs or to evade high employer taxes and other 'social protection' regulations, for prostitution and drug-running, some of it organized by the traffickers themselves. The difficulty of providing statistics to serve as a rational basis for discussing this problem scarcely needs exaggerating.

Most of the EU/EFTA countries, and the trans-Atlantic states, have moved towards stricter measures against illegal immigrants, and against those who assist them. Sanctions against persons in these categories can vary. There are a number of obvious points in the process at which to deter illegal immigration, many of which will also deter asylum-claiming:

1. Requiring document checking before departure by airplane.
2. More effective controls at ports and crossing-places.
3. Deportation of illegal migrants efficiently at an early stage.

4. Detection of illegal immigrants in the host society (identity cards and other devices).
5. Obstacles for illegal immigrants to find work or claim social security (identity cards).
6. Criminal sanctions against the employment of illegal immigrants (employer sanctions).
7. Avoidance of amnesties.
8. Deterrence of illegal immigration or overstaying by ensuring that asylum procedures do not reinforce it; for example by ensuring that asylum claims can only be entertained if made immediately on arrival.
9. Publicity for the response to illegal immigration is known in the sending country.
10. Measures to reduce migration pressures at source (Böhning & Schloeter-Paredes, 1994).

Several countries have used regularization as part of their migration programme, offering amnesties whereby irregular migrants who entered the country before a certain date can regularize their position (see OECD 1998). During the 1980s, Italy, Spain, Sweden, the Netherlands, the USA and France, all carried out regularizations with differing degrees of success. However, regularization does not seem to be a viable long-term solution. The hope of future regularizations may stimulate further irregular migration flows. Amnesties then have to be repeated; in France 1997-98; Italy 1996; Portugal 1996; Spain 1996.

The struggle to control irregular immigration has developed more through the use of stringent deterrent methods such as sanctions against employers etc., and amendments to asylum legislation. It is evident, though, that sanctions against employers are only effective if the fine is very high or if a prison sentence is substituted and the chance of detection is high. Low fines are, to some extent, just a business expense. Employers cannot be expected to distinguish illegal immigrants without an identity card system, and identity documents based on paper or card, as opposed to plastic, appear to be easily forged. Through monitoring the movements of repeated asylum claims it is hoped that an important element of irregular migration flows will be removed. Finally, the right of entry and abode which goes with marriage to a citizen or permanent resident in most countries is being abused to secure entry through bogus marriage. In the Netherlands, for example, it is believed that between 5-10% of all marriages involving a foreign partner (which comprise about 10% of all marriages) are bogus, entered into for purposes of immigration through a transaction often arranged by criminal organizations.

3.7 Integration policies

As immigration flows have increased in volume and diversity, expectations of large-scale repatriation on the part of host societies, and of the 'myth of return' on the part of immigrants have equally faded. The question then arises what to do with large new populations of alien culture and language, numerically dominant in many urban areas to a degree which would have been regarded with incredulity thirty years ago. What to do with these un-expected new populations, which often have different needs, capacities, values and loyalties from the host population and often a very uneasy relationship with them? One response is to encourage repatriation, as Belgium, France, Germany and the Netherlands have attempted and still do attempt in some cases to encourage. Repatriation policies in a slightly different form have been given new prominence by the rise of asylum claims and by the need to remove rejected claimants, as discussed earlier. However, repatriation of regular migrants has not had a major demographic effect and will not be discussed further here.

Instead, given that a substantial part of the foreign presence is now accepted as permanent, more attention has been given to integration policies. These policies are intended in various ways to enable immigrants and their descendants to move freely in the economic and social space of their new country, to alleviate social and cultural and administrative disadvantages, thereby reduce unemployment, housing problems and educational disadvantage, and above all to forestall or to reduce ethnic tensions and discrimination. Control of immigration from non-European countries is regarded as essential for the peaceful integration of those already in the host country. In practice, these policies deal with language abilities, access to jobs, housing, education, legal protection, health care and welfare, and increasingly political rights and naturalization. Some detail of the position in Europe in the early 1990s was given elsewhere (Coleman, 1994).

The question has been given new urgency by the rise of concern about ethnic tensions and by new debates on the place and identity of immigrants in relation to the national population, and indeed on the identity of the nation itself. These problems affect immigrants of all kinds, but tend to be much more acute in respect of large populations of non-European immigrants who are more distinct by religion, language and custom who are visibly identi-fiable. In the early 1980s it was widely supposed that non-European immi-gration was declining and that integration, however defined, was the obvious next step for those who remained after the immigration episode was over. Since the late 1980s, now that it is clear that the immigration episode is not over, as Chapter 2 showed, such discussions have been made more urgent, and perhaps taken a different direction. Now they must proceed in parallel with a revived pace of immigration. This complicates the integration task and threatens to make it a continuous or long-term one, not a one-off operation.

3.7.1 Terms of debate

In the 1990s the debate centres around terms such as pluralism, multi-culturalism, and whether integration should be 'passively facilitated' or 'actively promoted' (Entzinger, 1990).

Integration can mean many things. As a starting point we may define it as the opening of opportunities to immigrants to move freely in the geographical, social and economic space of the country in which they now live, including steps to ensure that they have access to jobs, housing and education on an equal footing with the native population. This follows from considerations of equity and justice towards immigrants, foreigners and minorities and in the self-interest of the host society: Improving and making more effective its reserves of human capital and avoiding the problems of crime and unrest which would arise from a disaffected and poor ethnic underclass.

In the 1990s that is usually taken to be the starting point for debate, and most argument concerns how much further policy should go in meeting immigrant needs, in particular (varying much country by country) in encouraging or facilitating 'multicultural' policies to favour the conservation of the specific ethnic features of the community life of immigrant populations (see Vermuelen, 1997). Proponents of 'multicultural' policies claim that ethnic politics of that kind are essential for the equality of opportunity which integration is meant to achieve, and are best adapted to the new 'Europe of the Regions' with established 'transnational communities' where the nation-state is losing ground. This section considers integration, multicultural and related policies in Europe.

3.7.2 Previous attitudes

Before we do that it is desirable to remind ourselves how far we have come. The notion of 'integration', now consensual among policy makers and international bureaucrats, was in earlier years by no means regarded as the obviously just and fair way to deal with immigrant or foreign populations. The civic rights and welfare states of developed societies represent the inheritance of cumulative investment, indebtedness and commitment over many years by citizens with loyalties and obligations in common. It was not then obvious that all a society's privileges, especially political rights, should immediately be available to newcomers of a potentially temporary nature who had not made that commitment or contribution and who might not share the same values or loyalties. That was one of the axioms behind the guest worker policy.

Insofar as any thought or expectations were directed towards the future of immigrant populations in the 1960s it was one which assumed assimilation or departure. The success or failure of immigration was then based on the ability of a newcomer to adjust, to be accepted by a host society if it chose to, while that host society remained virtually untouched by the process (Heisler, 1992). It was then assumed that citizens should have first priority for employment or housing when this is in short supply; that political participation should follow, not precede, the identification and commitment of immigrants to the new society; that further participation should require the corresponding abandonment of previous commitments and sympathies where these may conflict. If immigrants found that this conflicted with their values or preferences then it seemed natural to remember that they were at liberty, unlike the indigenous population, to return to their original homelands.

Such views received short shrift in the 1980s and early 1990s, and today would increasingly be regarded as 'discriminatory' or even 'racist'. 'Integration' in the 1990s means that natives are expected to compete with foreigners on an equal basis, a notion which is almost universally supported by Western governments. The few remaining obstacles which once offered employment protection to natives (except for labour migrants on certain kinds of work permits) are being dismantled. Nonetheless, the attitudes noted above have not entirely gone away, and as continued immigration has become politically salient, some governments, no doubt, have felt pushed by public opinion into a somewhat less accommodating attitude to the demands of immigrant populations or by groups supporting their demands.

3.7.3 Present practice

Today the prevailing view — following Costa-Lascoux (1990) — may be expressed as follows:

The institutional means for achieving integration have become the same in all European countries: Equal treatment for nationals and immigrants; social policies to help the neediest (in housing, education and training); fighting against discrimination through the use of both legislative means and the increased funding of racial awareness projects; naturalization and participation in local elections.

Change in policy may correspond with the change in nature of migrant flows to Europe, from economic and possibly temporary movements of males to flows of family members for family reunification and family formation which will create immigrant colonies of a distinctive and potentially permanent kind, with policy implications for welfare, housing and education, naturalization and citizenship. Many review articles of these policy developments have been made, and classifications offered (Cross, 1989; Nanton, 1990; Coleman, 1994; Cagiano de Azevedo, et al., 1994), with regular updates in the annual SOPEMI reports (OECD, 1998), which it would be pointless to repeat here in detail. Such policies are still changing. There is no consensus yet on the most appropriate policies to adopt on moral or political grounds, and national practices differ somewhat, although they appear to be converging.

International bodies attempt to persuade national governments to adopt common integration polices on the lines which they advance, on grounds of their interpretation of morality, justice and human rights. These generally favour the interests of immigrants and involve greater public expenditure. For example, the Parliamentary Assembly of the Council of Europe recommended (n. 1206, 4/2/93) that

positive action should be taken in education, urban planning and housing, in order to combat the lack of qualifications of many migrants and the disadvantageous situation they find themselves in, with respect to housing and social welfare facilities.

EU institutions seek more harmonized polices in this, as in other areas of national policy. The EU Consultative Committee on 'Racism and Xenophobia' stated in 1995 that EU powers over member states must be enlarged further to provide for community competence in combating 'racism' and 'xenophobia', an aim encouraged by The Amsterdam Treaty, which has incorporated this aim into the third (inter-governmental) 'pillar' of community action.

The actual legal position of the rights of foreigners in Europe is rather more varied than might be expected in view of the general encouragement to integration and harmonization.

Within the EU itself, citizens of other member states are treated on terms approaching equality with respect to medical treatment, welfare and pension rights, freedom to live and work at will, and the ability to vote in local and EU (but not national) elections, much of which was defined in the Maastricht Treaty of 1993. However, it is more crucial to address the position of non-EU foreigners, as these are more likely to be culturally distinct, poor and un-employed. Generally speaking, even within the EU, non-EU foreigners on work permits have no rights to change their employment without permission although they can set up businesses. Some Western countries maintain considerable restrictions on foreigners working in the government and public service (e.g. Germany); others are more permissive (e.g. the United Kingdom). Most restrictions on residence now apply only to asylum-seekers, although in 1985 Belgium permitted communes which believe that they have as many foreigners as they can absorb to refuse registration to any more, a programme inevitably under pressure from time to time. Germany had a similar policy to prevent particular areas being over-burdened, which now seems to have been abandoned. Problems of concentration of immigrants was addressed in Denmark by legislation in 1994 to allow local authorities to place immigrants in housing developments with few resident foreigners. Further legislation followed in 1998 to encourage a more even distribution of migrants among the municipalities. In the UK attempts by local authorities to moderate the creation of ethnic ghettos were ruled illegal under the Race Relations Acts.

As far as welfare benefits to non-EU citizens are concerned, conditions vary. The Netherlands, Germany and France put no restrictions on the availability of health care to foreigners. As regards pensions, in some countries there is a delay of some years before non-EU immigrants become entitled to full benefits, e.g. 10 years for entitlement to pensions in Denmark and a variable delay in France. In 1998 Denmark introduced a relative reduction in the entitlement of non-EU citizens to certain welfare benefits, compared with that enjoyed by EU citizens. In other EU countries, for example the Netherlands, foreigners are entitled to health, pensions and family allowances on the same basis as Dutch citizens. Rules in Central and Eastern Europe are in some respects more strict, and resemble the position in Western Europe in earlier decades. In some countries there are restrictions, or prohibitions, on owning real estate and land. However in most Eastern European countries, as in the West, permanent residents are eligible for pensions and other welfare benefits. Temporary workers must usually pay for medical care if they are not covered by bilateral agreements, and involvement in elections is strictly reserved for citizens.

3.7.4 Aims of policies

Before the detailed policies can usefully be presented or compared, the aims which they are intended to serve should be made as clear as possible. These are quite varied, and may change over time. Differences in integration policies follow from different perceptions of immigration and their immigrant populations. As Enzinger has noted:

Differences in the degree of cultural and social pluralism that a country wishes to accept also influence the choice of instruments. Should the role of the state be to promote the development of immigrant communities and institutions in increasingly multi-ethnic societies, or should the state facilitate the individual migrant insertions into existing institutions, even if this may imply assimilation? Here, we touch upon the classical Aristotelean dilemma that there is as much injustice in equal treatment of differing cases as there is in differential treatment of equal cases (Entzinger, 1990).

More 'multicultural' policies favour integration into the national society with due concern for the protection and in some cases the preservation through subsidy of the immigrants' own cultural background. That characterises the policies of the United Kingdom, Sweden and the Netherlands (somewhat changing over time), and above all the English-speaking countries abroad. Non-multicultural policies provide assistance in satisfying basic needs, but are neutral towards cultural differences or regard them as an obstacle to assimilation. France is the most striking example of this approach, at least in theory, regarding ethnic and religious divisions as a challenge to national unity and to the equality of all citizens. Naturalization is encouraged in the belief that common citizenship will reduce such divisions (Haut Conseil, 1991). From a somewhat different viewpoint (based more on *ius sanguinis*) Germany, Austria and Switzerland have been reluctant to recognize officially the ethnic pluralism created by their foreign populations.

3.7.5 Legislation

Most European countries have developed new legislation and administrative measures in this area. These fall under three major headings.

The first is to suppress 'xenophobic' actions, sentiments or thoughts, in order to remove provocation, ensure order and create a basic climate of tolerance. This is regarded as the basic pre-conditions for the wider participation of immigrants and foreigners in the society and economy. One approach is to define specifically as illegal words, remarks, speeches and statements, harassment or violence directed against immigrant minorities likely, or intended, to stir up racial hatred. Many such actions, insults or comments would already have fallen foul of existing legislation, some would not. In the Anglo-Saxon countries prohibitions have become interpreted in a very wide sense, encouraging the use of 'politically correct' language. Legislation against racial hatred does not actively promote integration, but is intended to promote the necessary feeling of confidence and security among immigrants, which may be its prerequisite. A recent further step is to declare illegal public statements of belief in certain facts or their absence, for example the belief that the mass murder of Jews in the Second World War did not occur or was exaggerated. Its counterpart is to prevent the publication of statistics and other material which might be interpreted in ways unfavourable to immigrants or ethnic minorities, for example the statistics on the ethnic origin of those committing street offences in the London Metropolitan Police Area, which were published by the Home Office until their suppression in 1989.

The second avenue to integration is to open up those institutions which are insufficiently accessible to migrants, including legislation against discrimination by nationality, birthplace and so on. That means removing any restrictions imposed on immigrants or foreigners concerning their employment or change of employment, or their place of residence. Discrimination against foreigners (or on grounds of ethnic origin) especially in the provision of goods and in services such as education, employment and housing are made illegal.

If, as is often the case, the removal of obstacles does not of itself produce sufficient equality of outcome, a further step is to take various kinds of positive action to enable foreigners or minorities to compete more effectively. The uncontroversial end of this is to provide the tools with which migrants may be able to integrate successfully (notably language and education, for example). Indeed, access to certain benefits by foreigners in Sweden and in the

Netherlands is conditional upon taking appropriate instruction in Swedish or Dutch. Other forms of 'positive action' can include advertisements or training programmes targeted particularly at foreigners or minorities, which may go hand in hand with the formal legal recognition of group rights for specified ethnic minorities, as in the Anglo-Saxon countries and the Netherlands. A further step is to extend particular privileges, in employment and in housing, to foreigners or to members of ethnic minority groups. For example in the UK it is lawful to discriminate in favour of ethnic minorities in respect of certain kinds of job, and to offer publicly-subsidized housing (through 'black housing associations') only to members of specified ethnic or religious minorities.

Some of these steps comprise 'positive discrimination'. The United States is explicit that it follows this principle (called 'affirmative action') through quotas and positive discrimination in employment and education, for example. However this is not without controversy and in recent years has faced increasing legal challenge. Other countries, such as the UK, claim that positive discrimination and quotas are illegal, although the 'positive action' and 'targets' which are officially promoted may not easily be distinguishable from them.

A third approach is that of ethnic pluralism or multiculturalism. This aims to recognize, institutionalize and if necessary subsidize as permanent social divisions specified 'ethnic minorities' or communities of immigrant descent. These policies tend to be the speciality of the Anglo-Saxon world and with some reversals have also been followed in the Netherlands. Some elements of multicultural policy — recognition of group rights or entitlement — can be found in most European countries however, even in France whose official policy has been to oppose this notion as being divisive.

Thanks to their history, the position of the North American countries (which have been something of a model for Britain) is different. In Canada bi-cultural policies are inevitable because of the official status of both English and French languages and the pressure to accommodate Quebecois cultural identity. It has become impossible to deny such privileges to the speakers of other languages of recent immigrant origin; all complicated, as in the US, by the existence of aboriginal minorities whose claims for recognition and the collective redress of ancient wrongs have grown much stronger in the last two decades. In the US the multicultural movement was given its major impetus by the 'civil rights' movement of the 1960s which improved the position of the black (and non-immigrant) minority. The same principles were extended to all minorities, including recent immigrants who in previous decades would have been expected to adopt an American identity. In Canada (and also Australia) multiculturalism remains a specific policy goal; in the US 'diversity' is now officially applauded, although increasingly opposed (especially on the language issue) by states such as California with large immigrant populations.

3.7.6 Citizenship and naturalization

Policy and law on naturalization remain varied, according to different historical migration experiences, national identities and legal traditions. A difference can be discerned between those countries which regard naturalization as a means to integration, offering naturalization on easy terms, at least to some categories of people, by registration on request (UK up to 1983 in respect of Commonwealth Citizens, also in France and Sweden), and those countries which regard it as the end point of acculturation and the acquisition of language and social skills needed for commitment to a new country (Germany, Austria and Switzerland).

On the whole, the experience of the last decade is that those countries which held out for strict conditions on naturalization are modifying their policy (e.g. Germany, Switzerland) and thus coming to resemble rather more the practices of other states. Austria now aims to promote the integration of resident foreigners, with naturalization of integrated foreigners a long-term goal. Movement can be slow, however. A proposal of constitutional revision to allow for easier naturalization of young foreigners in Switzerland, on 12 June 1994, was rejected. Similar convergence through the abandonment of originally restrictive polices can be seen in the changes of attitude towards dual nationality, where some of those countries which once opposed it (Belgium, Netherlands) now permit it.

Most residents of any country acquire its citizenship by birth. But most of their parents are in the nature of things also citizens. The crucial difference is whether citizenship is conferred through birthplace alone (*ius soli*) or whether it is conferred by descent from citizen parents or even by remoter descent, even from outside the national boundaries (*ius sanguinis*). These principles, already alluded to in earlier sections, generate different results for the citizenship of children of foreign parents, or the foreign-born children of parents of a particular ancestry. Some countries adhere to *ius sanguinis* (Sweden, Germany, Switzerland) others to *ius soli* (UK until recently, France, Netherlands, Belgium). Movement here is in both directions. *Ius sanguinis* countries are softening their position on the children of immigrants; some *ius soli* countries (e.g. UK) have slightly restricted the right in relation to foreign parents to those who will reside for some time in the UK, as opposed to shorter-term visitors. Children born of foreign parents on French soil used automatically to acquire French citizenship upon reaching the age of 18, unless they specifically renounced it. However, under the 1993 amendment to French citizenship law (Law no. 93-1417, 30/12 1993, modifying Law no. 45-2658), French citizenship of a child born to foreign parents on French soil has to be applied for. It is no longer automatic. In most countries there is a combination of the two principles, e.g. when a child of a French citizen is born abroad, it is granted French citizenship at birth. For those who migrate after birth, citizenship is either by naturalization or by registration (a formal annotation in a public register that a person is a citizen of a country on request of that individual Reinans & Hammar, 1995).

In all countries, citizenship can be applied for under certain conditions. Residence is a condition in all cases except Hungary. In Canada and the US, naturalization is considered an immigrant's right, given a period of residence (allegiance under an oath in the case of the US) and good conduct, whereas in the West European countries it is still on a discretionary basis. In Greece, naturalization is permitted only under very limited circumstances.

In the former Soviet Baltic Republics and Eastern European countries, citizenship rights extend to those people displaced or deported in the communist period, or in some cases to their descendants. Otherwise, as in Latvia, naturalization is difficult and requires considerable local knowledge (language and culture). There has been much debate over the access of residents of Russian origin to the new citizenship in Latvia and the other Baltic States. Those states have a particular problem because the policy of 'Russification' in the Soviet period has given them large Russian minorities, 48% of the population in the case of Latvia in 1989. Germany offers automatic citizenship to returned *Aussiedler*. Steps have been taken to ease the obstacles in the way of the German-born children of foreign residents acquiring German citizenship.

Naturalization is also usually dependent upon skills such as knowledge of the native language and integration into the cultural norms of that society (a weak requirement in such countries as the UK, a strong one in such countries as Switzerland).

3.8 Conclusions

In almost all the European countries immigration policies and the stated aims behind them indicate strong reservations about high levels of immigration. In almost all cases measures are in hand, or have recently been implemented to reduce immigration flows. Fears of unemployment, of welfare costs, of unhelpful effects of continuing immigration upon the difficult task of integration, political and social friction are all variously mentioned. Public opinion usually has two faces: The first is one of sympathy for individual cases and for the general principle of protecting refugees, particularly where the horrors of conflict can be seen on television in every home. The other is a feeling that immigrants are already too numerous and that many who claim asylum do not deserve it. The exceptions on migration policy are the two transatlantic countries of immigration, the US and Canada. There, official statements still endorse the economic, demographic and cultural benefits of immigration, and positive attitudes to cultural diversity are explicit, although in the US this endorsement has been challenged by various restrictive measures proposed in Congress in the 1990s.

Restriction has been the almost invariable pattern of their legislation history since the 1960s and particularly since the late 1980s, cf. also Appendix Tables 3.1 and 3.2. Generally speaking, European countries attempt to limit immigration to labour migration (usually to specified jobs), family reunification and family formation migration, recognized refugees and returning co-ethnics. With the exception of the last, there are no programmes to encourage settlement, no entitlements for other than immediate relatives and no freedom to settle without meeting one of these criteria. For countries which have no inheritance of guest worker populations (in Southern and Eastern Europe) that makes for small legal streams. In all cases, however, as Chapter 1 showed, irregular or illegal immigration makes the actual flows greater than intended and in some cases these comprise a high proportion of migrants. The policy measures introduced in the late 1980s and in the 1990s are widely believed to have led to the reduction in regular immigration and in asylum claims generally observed since 1992. In the 1990s, many of these measures, especially in visas and asylum, have been co-ordinated by inter-governmental agreements. Following the treaties of Maastricht and Amsterdam, European asylum and immigration policies are becoming a community competence over which most member states are relinquishing control.

The general picture on integration policies is perhaps more complex, but on the whole it is in the direction of greater accommodation towards the needs and demands of immigrant populations. Those countries which practiced the strictest policies on assimilation or return, with the hardest tests for naturalization (e.g. Germany and Switzerland), have ameliorated those policies. Most European countries have introduced 'equal opportunities' legislation, or defined racial offences more specifically (Netherlands, Belgium) and there is increasing EU pressure for conformity in these areas. 'Multicultural' and 'ethnic' notions, formerly anathema, are discussed more frequently in Germany and France. However some of the more extensively developed multicultural programmes targeted at group rights and privileges, in the Netherlands and in Sweden, have been moderated, not least in the light of popular disapproval and the continuing problems of immigration and asylum-claiming.

References

Böhning, W.R. (1980). Guest worker employment, with special reference to the Federal Republic of Germany, France and Switzerland: Lessons for the United States. ILO Document WEP 2-26, June 1980 Geneva: International Labour Office.

Böhning, W.R., & Schloeter-Paredes, M.-L. (Eds.), (1994). *Aid in place of Migration?* Geneva: International Labour Office.

Bunyan, T., & Webber, F. (1995). *Intergovernmental Co-operation on Immigration and Asylum*. Brussels: Churches Commission for Migrants in Europe.

Cagiano de Azevedo, R., Cantore, A., Di Prospero, R., & Sonnino, B. (Eds.). (1994). *Immigrants Integration Polices in Seven European Countries. Final Report*. Rome: Università degli Studi di Roma 'La Sapienza'.

Coleman, D.A. (1992). Does Europe need Immigrants? Population and Workforce projections. *International Migration Review*, 26(2) (Special Issue: The New Europe and International Migration), 413-61.

Coleman, D.A. (1994). Integration and Assimilation Policies in Europe. In M. Macura & D. A. Coleman (Eds.), *International Migration and Integration: Regional Pressures and processes.Economic Studies No 7*. New York and Geneva: United Nations Economic Commission for Europe.

Coleman, D.A. (1995). Spouse Migration from the Indian sub-Continent to the UK: A permanent migration stream? *People and Place*, 3(1), 1-8.

Costa-Lascoux, J. (1990). Citizenships and Discriminations in Europe 'The Integration of Immigrant Minorities in Europe'. In *European Population Conference, 8-9 October, 1990*. Paris.

Cross, M. (1989). Migrants and the New Minorities in Europe. In H. Enzinger & Carter (Eds.), *International Review of Comparative Public Policy volume 1*, 53-178). Greenwich: JAI Press.

Department of Employment (1991). *Labour Market and Skills Trends 1992-93*. Moorsfoot, Sheffield.: Department of Employment (UK).

Entzinger, H. (1990). The Emergence of Integration Policies for Immigrants in Europe. In *International Colloquium 'L'Integration Locale des Immigrés en Europe'*. Paris.

Fakiolas, R. (1993). *1993 SOPEMI Report: Migration from and to Greece*. Mimeo, available from the author.

Freeman, G.S. (1994). Can Liberal States control Unwanted Migration? *Annals of the American Association for Political and Social Sciences* (534), 17-30.

Frejka, T. (Ed.), (1996). *International Migration in Central and Eastern Europe and the Commonwealth of Independent States*. New York and Geneva: United Nations.

Fussell, P. (1980). *Abroad: British Literary Travelling Between the Wars*. Oxford: Oxford University Press.

German Federal Ministry of the Interior (1993). *Survey of the Policy and Law concerning foreigners in the Federal Republic of Germany*. A1-937 020/15 July 1993 Bonn: German Federal Ministry of the Interior.

Guild, E. (1998) *Competence, discretion and third country nationals: the EU's legal struggle with migration*. Journal of Ethnic and Migrations Studies 24,4, 613-25.

Hammar, T. (1992). Law and Policies Regulating Population Movements: A European Perspective. In M.M. Kritz, L.L. Lim, & H. Zlotnik (Eds.), *International Migration Systems: a global approach.*, 245-62. Oxford: Clarendon Press.

Haut Conseil à l'Integration (1991). *Pour un modèle français d'integration, Premier Raport Annuel*. Paris: La Documentation Française.

Hawkins, F. (1989). *Critical Years in Immigration: Canada and Australia compared*. Montreal: McGill-Queen's University Press.

Heisler, B.S. (1992). The Future of Immigrant Incorporation: Which Models? Which Concepts? *In International Migration Review*, 26(2).

Home Office (1977). *A Register of Dependants. Report of the Parliamentary Group on the feasibility and usefulness of a Register of Dependants. Cmnd. 6698*. London: HMSO.

Home Office (1998). Control of Immigration: Statistics United Kingdom, First Half 1998. *Home Office Statistical Bulletin 24/98.*

Home Office (1998a). *Control of Immigration: Statistics United Kingdom 1997 Cm 4033.* London: The Stationery Office.

Home Office (1998b). *Fairer, Faster and Firmer — A Modern Approach to Immigration and Asylum. Cm 4018.* London: The Stationery Office.

Inter-Governmental Consultations (1995a). *Summary description of Asylum Procedures of States in Europe, North America and Australia.* Geneva: Inter-Governmental Consultations on Asylum, Refugee and Migration Policies in Europe, North America and Australia.

Inter-Governmental Consultations (1995b). *Report on Temporary Protection in States in Europe, North America and Australia.* Geneva: Inter-Governmental Consultations on Asylum, Refugee and Migration Policies in Europe, North America and Australia.

Inter-Governmental Consultations on Asylum (1993). *Return of Rejected Asylum Seekers. Working Paper submitted by the Secretariat for the Inter-Governmental Consultations to the Meeting on Return and Readmission, Nyon 16-17 September 1993.* Geneva: Inter-Governmental Consultations on Asylum.

International Centre for Migration Policy Development (1997). *Migration in Central and Eastern Europe.* Vienna: International Centre for Migration Policy Development.

International Organization for Migration (1994). Trafficking in Migrants. 11th International Seminar of the IOM. Geneva: IOM.

International Organization for Migration (1997). *CIS Migration Report 1996.* Geneva: International Organization for Migration.

International Organization for Migration (1995). *Trafficking and Prostitution: the growing exploitation of migrant women from Central and Eastern Europe.* Budapest: Migration Information Programme, International Organization for Migration.

Jacobson, D. (1996). *Rights Across Borders: Immigration and the Decline of Citizenship.* Baltimore: Johns Hopkins University Press.

Jandl, M. (1995). *Structure and Costs of the Asylum systems in Seven European Countries.* Vienna: International Centre for Migration Policy Development.

Koller, B. (1994). Social and Occupational Integration of Immigrants of German Origin in Germany. *IAB Labour Market Research Topics.*

Lahav, G. (1998). *Immigration and the State: the devolution and privatisation of immigration control in the EU.* Journal of Ethnic and Migration Studies 24,4, 675-94.

Muus, P.J. (1991). *Migration, Minorities and Policy in the Netherlands: recent trends and developments. (Netherlands SOPEMI report 1991).* Amsterdam: Department of Human Geography, University of Amsterdam.

Muus, P. (1995). *Migration, Immigrants and Policy in the Netherlands: recent trends and developments. (SOPEMI Netherlands 1995).* Amsterdam: Centre for Migration Research, Department of Human Geography, University of Amsterdam.

Nanton, P. (1990). National Frameworks and the implementation of Local Policies: is a European model of integration identifiable? In *ADRI International Colloquium on the Integration of Immigrant Minorities in Europe.* Paris.

OECD (1994). *Trends in International Migration: Annual Report 1993.* Paris: OECD.

OECD (1998). *Trends in International Migration. Annual Report 1998 edition.* Paris: OECD.

Papademetriou, D.G. (1994). International Migration in North America: Issues, Policies, Implications. In M. Macura & D.A. Coleman (Eds.), *International Migration: Regional*

Processes and Responses. Proceedings of a UN ECE/UN FPA informal Expert Group Meeting on International Migration, 77-107. New York: United Nations.

Papademetriou, D.G. (1996). *Coming Together or Pulling Apart? The European Union's Struggle with Immigration and Asylum*. Washington D.C.: Carnegie Endowment for International Peace.

Papademetriou, D., & Hamilton, K. (1995). *Managing Uncertainty: Regulating Immigration Flows In Advanced Industrial Countries*. Washington D.C.: Carnegie Endowment for International Peace.

Papademetriou. D. and Yale-Loehr, S. (1996). Balancing Interests: Rethinking U.S. Selection of skilled Immigrants. Washington D.C.: Carnegie Endowment for International Peace.

Reinans, S.A., & Hammar, T. (1995). Naturalization: Changes of Citizenship within immigrant populations in Western Europe. In Voets, S., Schoorl. J. & S. Voets (Eds.), *Demographic Consequences of International Migration*. The Hague: Netherlands Interdisciplinary Demographic Institute, 177-206.

Rudolph, H., & Hillmann, F. (1995). Labour Migration between Eastern and Western Europe. *Employment Observatory East Germany* (14 March 1995), 3-7.

Salt, J. (1988). Highly-skilled International Migrants, Careers and Internal Labour Markets. *Geoforum*, 19(4), 387-99.

Salt, J., & Ford, R. (1993). Skilled International Migration to Europe: The shape of things to come? In R. King (Ed.), *Mass Migration in Europe: The legacy and the future*, 293-309. London: Belhaven.

Salt, J., & Stein, J. (1997). Migration as a Business: The case of Trafficking. *International Migration*, 35(4).

Salt, J. (1998). *International Migration in the UN ECE Region: Patterns, Trends, Policies*. London: Migration Research Unit, Dept. of Geography, University College London (mimeo).

Sexton, J.J. (1994). *A Review of Irish External Migration, Past and Present*. Dublin: Economic and Social Research Institute (ESRI).

Simon, J.L. (1989). *The Economic Consequences of Immigration*. Cambridge: Basil Blackwell.

Spencer, S. (ed.) (1994). *Strangers and Citizens: a positive approach to migrants and refugees*. London: Institute for Public Policy Research.

Stalker, P. (1994). *The Work of Strangers: A survey of international labour migration*. Geneva: International Labour Office.

Tessaring, M. (1993). Manpower Requirements by Levels of Qualification in West Germany until 2010. Implications of the 1989 IAB/Prognos projection for the qualification structure of jobs. *IAB Labour Market Research Topics*, 1993(4), 25.

United Nations/Council of Europe (Ed.). (1994). *European Population Conference Proceedings Volume 2*. New York/Strasbourg: United Nations/Council of Europe.

United Nations (1998). *International Migration Policies*. New York: United Nations.

UNECE (1995a). The Budapest Process. *International Migration Bulletin* (7, November 1995), 10-11.

US Dept. of Labor (1989). *The Effects of Immigration on the US Economy and Labor Market*. Washington, D.C.: USGPO.

US Immigration and Naturalization Service (1996). *Immigration to the United States in Fiscal Year 1994*. Washington, D.C., US Government Printing Office.

van Hear, N. (1998). *Modern Diasporas*. London, University College London Press.

Vermuelen, H. (1997). *Immigration Policy for a Multicultural Society: A comparative study of integration, language and religious policy in five Western European countries.* Brussels: Migration Policy Group.

Widgren, J. (1994a). Immigration Policies: a comparative overview. *People and Place*, 2(4), 1-7.

Widgren, J. (1994b). *The Key to Europe: a comparative analysis of entry and asylum policies in Western countries.* Stockholm: Fritzes.

Chapter 4

Migration to and from Denmark during the period 1960-97

Søren Pedersen

4.1 Introduction

Migration between countries is not a new phenomenon. Throughout history there have been significant periods of migration. Since the 16th century most large-scale migrations of populations have been from Europe to North America. It has been estimated that from the 17th century to the start of the Second World War, somewhere in the region of 50 million people emigrated from Europe to North America.

Neither is immigration to Europe and Denmark a new phenomenon restricted to the post-war years. Nevertheless, for most of the 20th century, the number of emigrants exceeded the number of immigrants.

In Denmark, the main source of immigration during the final years of the 19th century was Swedes who had travelled south as seasonal labourers and subsequently settled in the country. Towards the turn of the 19th and during the first years of the 20th century, the majority of immigrants were Jews fleeing, for example, from the pogroms in Russia. During the same period, Poles began arriving in the Danish islands of Lolland and Falster to work in the sugar beet fields. They were also soon dubbed 'roepolakkerne' (*the Beet Poles*). After the Russian Revolution in 1917, immigration was principally once again refugees from Russia. The political circumstances during the 1930s also led to a large influx of refugees from Nazi Germany.

In the first three chapters, David Coleman has dealt with international migration in recent years, with special emphasis on immigration to Europe. The aim of David Coleman's contribution is to place migration to and from Denmark in an international perspective. In this chapter, migration across Danish borders will be placed in the context of contemporary history, with the main emphasis placed on immigration.

Immigration to Denmark since 1960 is dealt with first, in section 4.2, which looks mainly at the most important immigration of that time — that of guest or foreign workers from Turkey, Pakistan and the fomer Yugoslavia, as well as the immigration of refugees during the last 10-15 years. This section also looks at immigration through family reunification. This analysis includes a review of the degree to which family reunification legislation is used to reunite already existing families or to form new families. Section 4.3 invest-igates how successful immigrants are in the labour market by comparing their participation rates and levels of unemployment with those of the entire population. This factor is of great importance for the level of integration in Danish society achieved by immigrants. Finally, section 4.4 comprises a con-clusion of the points raised in the chapter.

4.2 Immigration: 1960-97

This section starts by presenting an overall picture of emigration from and im-migration to Denmark since 1960. As this statistic covers both Danish and foreign nationals, the material also includes an overview of the development in the number of foreign citizens resident in Denmark. Once an immigrant is granted Danish citizenship, he or she will no longer be included in the sta-tistics of immigrants. In order to shed light on the fact that the statistics covering foreign nationals are very much influenced by the different pre-ferences among immigrants from the various countries to apply for Danish ci-tizenship, it is necessary to provide a description of the extent of natu-ralization for immigrants from certain countries.

The sex and age composition of immigrants is then analyzed to evaluate how these factors affect the composition of the population as a whole.

Because of the poor employment situation, a total ban on immigration to Denmark was introduced in 1973. Nevertheless, immigration continued in the form of family reunification and refugees. A more detailed description is therefore supplied of these two types of immigration. Section 4.2.5 concludes with a description of more recent statistics from Statistics Denmark, which at-tempts to take into account some of the conceptual problems which have so far applied to statistics relating to immigrants and their descendants.

As can be seen in Figure 4.1, the period from the conclusion of the Second World War and up to the end of the 1960s was characterized by an extremely modest emigration from and immigration to Denmark. A mere 15,000-35,000, or less than 1% of the population, actually migrated during these years. Until 1959 there was a preponderance of emigrants, while in the period since, with few exceptions, migration has consisted of an influx of immigrants. When interpreting Figure 4.1 it is important to keep in mind that the figures cover both Danish and foreign nationals.

After the Second World War and until the mid-1960s migrants arrived mainly from Norway, Sweden, Great Britain, Germany and the USA. Sim-ilarly, it was to these countries that Danes emigrated (Matthiessen, 1998). It was largely a question of Danes returning home after a period of residence

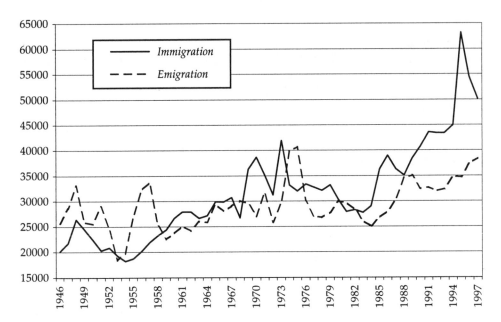

Figure 4.1: Number of migrants to and from Denmark, 1946-97.

Source: Poul Chr. Matthiessen (1998), *Statistics Denmark, Befolkningens bevægelser*, 1994 and *Nyt fra Danmarks Statistik*, no. 46, 1998. (*Vital Statistics*, 1994, and *News from Statistics Denmark*, no. 46, 1998).

abroad; just as emigration mainly consisted of people returning to their respective native countries. To give an example: Of the 26,638 people immigrating to Denmark in 1960, some 26% were Danish citizens (Statistics Denmark, 1961). The destinations of the approximately 23,000 leaving the country the same year were primarily other Nordic countries (approximately 30%) and the USA (almost 9%). Migration during this period was therefore between countries with many common cultural traits.

As a result of the historically high economic growth enjoyed in the 1950s and 1960s, immigration altered in both extent and structure towards the end of the 1960s. On average, gross domestic product (GDP) increased by 5.3% a year in the period 1957-65, and by 4.4% from 1965-70 (Hansen, 1983). Similarly, unemployment, with few exceptions, remained low in the 1960s, averaging between 2% and 4%, which is effectively full employment.

High levels of growth demanded in turn a larger workforce. During the 1960s, employment rose by 20-25,000 a year (*ibid.*). New manpower was provided partly by the post-war baby boom and partly by the increasing participation rate among women.

However, despite these two factors, the available manpower was still insufficient for the demands of the labour market. Denmark, in line with many other West European countries, therefore started importing manpower,

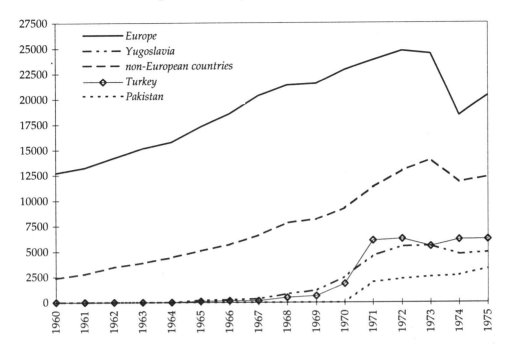

Figure 4.2: The number of foreigners with residence permits, 1960-75.

Note: Until 1965, Yugoslavia and Turkey were included in the figures for Europe. Until 1970, Pakistan was included in the figures for non-European countries. The figures in Figure 4.2 were provided to Statistics Denmark by the Commissioner of Police (Aliens Police). Note too, that these figures do not cover citizens from other Nordic countries. Similarly, as of 1974, children under 16 are not included unless they do not live with those possessing parental custody rights over them. The figures cannot therefore be compared directly with those from Statistics Denmark (see Table 4.1, which includes all foreign citizens).
Source: Statistics Denmark, *Statistical Yearbook 1960-1975* (as supplied by the Commissioner of Police to Statistics Denmark).

primarily from Turkey, former Yugoslavia, and somewhat later, also from Pakistan.

This trend is illustrated in Figure 4.2, which shows the number of foreigners with residence permits in Denmark during the period 1960-75. As can be seen from the figures, which cannot be directly compared with those of Table 4.1 (see note to figure), the number of immigrants from Yugoslavia and Turkey is less than 500 a year between 1965 and 1967 — 1965 being the first year when information is available for these countries. The numbers from these two countries then increase to 5-6,000 in the following years. 1971 is the first year with data for Pakistan, which show that the number of people that obtained residence permits is almost 2,000. This figure increased to just in excess of 3,300 in 1975.

During the 1950s and 1960s, entry and residence in Denmark was regulated according to the Aliens Act of 1952. This legislation provided for wide discretion which could result in ample opportunity for foreigners to move to Denmark, find a job, and receive a work permit after having applied to the regional labour market authorities (see, for example, Andersen, 1979, and Matthiessen, 1998). As a rule (from the mid-1960's), foreigners seeking work were only turned back at the border if they did not have enough money to provide for themselves and for the trip home. Without such funds they could be rejected on the grounds of having insufficient means (Ministry of Labour, 1971). The rules were different for subjects of the Nordic countries, as a 1954 agreement permitted the free movement of labour between these countries. This agreement allowed any citizen of a Nordic country to work and reside in any other Nordic country without the need for a work or residence permit.

At the end of the 1960s, many of those emigrating from Turkey and Yugoslavia spontaneously chose Denmark as their preferred destination. Part of the immigration in 1967 was due to a slowdown in economic activity in the then West Germany, which encouraged foreign workers to look elsewhere, including Denmark. Immigration was not to any great extent based on agreements between Danish companies and placement services in the various countries (Andersen, 1979), though this was occasionally the case (see Bent Jensen's chapter on B&W's engagement of workers from Yugoslavia).

Legislation governing entry to Denmark was changed in May 1969 due to the dramatic increase in the numbers of foreigners in search of work (Ministry of Labour, 1971). As a result of this new legislation, those seeking work could be turned away at the border even though they were in possession of sufficient funds to provide for themselves and pay for a ticket home. If a foreigner declared that he did not wish to seek work, a 'tourist' stamp was entered in his passport and any subsequent application for a work permit rejected without consideration of the employment situation. This new system also led to an increase in the numbers applying for work permits at Danish embassies and consulates abroad.

However, it was soon acknowledged that the new system had obvious defects, and that it worked in a completely arbitrary manner. For example, it was practically impossible to monitor all foreigners entering the country to ascertain whether they wished to work or merely visit as tourists. Two people in exactly the same position and wishing to seek work could therefore be dealt with differently at the border.

It was therefore decided that as of 1 January 1970 it was not enough that foreigners wishing to work in Denmark should apply for a work permit at a Danish embassy or consulate before arriving at the border. An application for a work permit had also to be backed by a promise of work from a Danish employer along with a statement that an unsuccessful attempt had been made in co-operation with the local job centre to take on qualified Danish manpower (Ministry of Labour, 1971). Foreigners that actually found work in Denmark had to become members of unemployment insurance and health insurance funds, and their employers had to ensure that the foreigners respected contractual agreements regarding salary and working conditions.

Despite these moves, immigration to Denmark continued with unabated strength. More and more immigrants sent for relations and friends and, as formulated in a report from the Danish Social Science Research Council (SSF), a form of chain migration became the order of the day (SFF, 1983). A freezing of all first-time applications for work permits was therefore introduced on 5 November 1970, a move that led to an increase in migration to other countries, e.g. Norway (Andersen, 1979). Norway in turn therefore introduced changes to its liberal immigration legislation in July 1971.

The reason for the Danish freeze, which was not total in that dispensation options were available, was a fear that unemployment would increase in excess of seasonal fluctuations in the winter of 1970/71. But increasing social problems also played a role, and there was a desire to win time in which to formulate a clear policy in this area (see also Bent Jensen's chapter). The freeze turned out to be only temporary, in that having discussed the matter with the two sides of industry, the Ministry of Labour after only a very brief period introduced certain exceptions. As shown in by Figure 4.2, immigration also continued despite the freeze.

Up to the oil crisis in autumn 1973, administrative changes to foreigners' ability to enter Denmark were made on an ongoing basis. However, the soaring price of oil at the end of 1973 sent all the Western economies into long-term recession. Unemployment rose rapidly, which led to a government decision to introduce an actual ban on all immigration in November 1973. This meant that residence permits were awarded in only a very few cases, on the basis of employment and commercial interests. Such a political decision was permissible within the framework of the Aliens Act of 1952. The stoppage, however, did not apply to EEC citizens or those from the other Nordic countries.

As regards nationals from other EEC countries, the aliens legislation from 1952 had been altered on Denmark's entry into the EEC to ensure the free movement of labour (Act no. 155 of 21 March 1973).

Nevertheless, as already mentioned, this new administrative move did not lead to a halt in immigration from third-party countries, i.e. those outside the Nordic area, the EEC and North America. Table 4.1 shows the development in the number of foreign citizens resident since 1974, which is the first year for which Statistics Denmark has precise, comprehensive statistics concerning foreign nationals.

When interpreting Table 4.1, note that it includes foreign nationals only, i.e. if a person takes on Danish citizenship, he or she will no longer be included in the statistics. The development in the number of foreign citizens from different countries of origin should therefore be interpreted with a certain degree of caution, in that there is a varying frequency among the different

Table 4.1: Foreign nationals resident in Denmark by citizenship, 1974-98.

	Nordic countries	EU[1]+ North America	former Yugoslavia	Turkey	Pakistan	Other countries	Total third p.	Total
			------ *Third party countries* ----------					
1974	21,774	28,895	6,779	8,138	3,733	20,536	39,186	89,855
1975	21,945	30,683	6,892	8,129	4,982	21,300	41,303	93,931
1976	21,096	29,450	6,396	7,857	5,178	20,877	40,308	90,854
1977	21,419	29,211	6,434	8,628	5,400	20,563	41,025	91,655
1978	21,886	29,605	6,674	10,299	5,557	20,394	42,924	94,415
1979	22,480	30,368	6,966	11,989	5,933	20,531	45,419	98,267
1980	22,608	29,308	7,126	14,086	6,400	20,268	47,880	99,796
1981	22,390	29,379	7,317	15,838	6,598	20,078	49,831	101,600
1982	22,147	28,418	7,402	16,705	6,822	20,420	51,349	101,914
1983	22,201	28,296	7,344	17,240	6,750	21,221	52,555	103,052
1984	22,334	28,424	7,397	17,827	6,659	21,421	53,304	104,062
1985	22,600	29,299	7,617	18,806	6,692	22,712	55,827	107,726
1986	23,023	30,783	7,943	20,408	6,619	28,175	63,145	116,951
1987	23,379	31,924	8,348	22,313	6,590	35,701	72,952	128,255
1988	23,130	32,097	8,799	24,423	6,500	41,228	80,950	136,177
1989	22,977	31,658	9,149	26,072	6,454	45,706	87,381	142,016
1990	23,064	31,829	9,535	27,929	6,285	52,002	95,751	150,644
1991	23,242	33,365	10,039	29,680	6,231	58,084	104,034	160,641
1992	23,512	33,766	10,719	32,018	6,081	63,429	112,247	169,525
1993	23,745	35,196	11,306	33,653	6,259	69,944	121,162	180,103
1994	24,192	37,058	11,618	34,658	6,368	75,120	127,764	189,014
1995	25,387	39,584	11,324	34,967	6,401	79,042	131,734	196,705
1996	27,052	41,057	28,081	35,739	6,552	84,265	154,637	222,746
1997	28,660	43,638	32,184	36,835	6,736	89,642	165,397	237,695
1998	29,927	45,969	33,931	37,519	6,934	95,348	173,732	249,628

Notes: 1974 is the first year for which reliable information is available regarding foreign nationals resident in Denmark. The table includes all foreign citizens registered in the national registration office as living in Denmark.

1. As of 1 January 1981, Greece is included as part of the EU; Portugal and Spain are included in the EU figures as of 1 January 1986. The former East Germany is included in the EU figures as of 1 January 1991, and Austria as of 1 January 1995. Sweden and Finland are included in the figures for the Nordic countries.

Source: Matthiessen, 1998.

nationalities in their desire to apply for Danish citizenship. This point will be dealt with later.

Table 4.1 shows that the number of nationals from former Yugoslavia almost doubled from 1974 to 1995, the civil war in this region having created an extraordinary situation. For the entire period 1974-98, the number of

Pakistani nationals basically doubled, while there was a fivefold increase in the number of Turkish citizens.

That the number of foreign citizens immigrating to Denmark from third-party countries did not decrease as a result of the immigration freeze is due to several factors. First, foreign workers from Turkey, Yugoslavia and Pakistan were not sent home with the onset of the oil crisis, despite the dramatic rise in unemployment figures. Instead, they were gradually awarded permanent residence and work permits (Matthiessen, 1998). The general attitude at the time was that, having invited foreign workers to come to Denmark one could not just deport them when there was insufficient employment (see also Bent Jensen's chapter). This stance was allowed under the 1952 legislation, which was a framework act, and therefore the authorities responsible were at liberty to flesh out the details within the framework.

A second factor was that those guest workers who had been granted permanent residence, now brought their wives and children to Denmark in accordance with family immigration legislation. Legislation governing family reunification gave any foreigner with a residence permit the right to bring his or her spouse and any children under 18 into the country. Family reunification will be dealt with in more depth later in the chapter.

Thirdly, the growth in the number of foreign citizens can be explained by an increase in the number of refugees. The increase in the number of foreign citizens from former Yugoslavia in the period 1995-96, and then up to 1998 is accounted for by refugees from the civil war in the region. In fact, many Yugoslavs arrived on temporary residence permits as early as 1991 and 1992, but they first appear in Table 4.1 on being granted permanent residence during the course of 1995 and 1996 (see later).

Added to the effects of family immigration and refugee immigration is the fact that citizens from third-party countries have a higher fertility rate than the rest of the population. In 1977, women from Turkey, Yugoslavia and Pakistan resident in Denmark gave birth to 4.5, 2.5 and 7 children each respectively, which compares with 1.7 for Danish women. Even though these fertility rates have since fallen, they remain higher than those for Danish women.

The effect immigration has on the composition of the Danish population as a whole, depends, among other factors, on the extent to which immigrants leave the country at a later stage. A significant migration back to their own countries occurs among immigrants from other Nordic countries, EU countries, and from North America. As can be seen from Table 4.2, almost 70% of immigrants from the Nordic countries and the EU who came to Denmark in 1977 left again within five years, a figure that is as high as 87% where North Americans are concerned. The table shows that immigrants with Turkish citizenship are nowhere near as likely to leave again. These figures are, for example, just 14% of those who immigrated in 1977, and 24% and 26% of Yugoslavs and Pakistanis respectively.

Table 4.2: The number of foreign citizens who immigrated in 1977 and 1990, and who left again within five years, 1974-98

Country of origin	1977		1990	
Turkey	14%	(1,846)	10%	(1,155)
Former Yugoslavia	24%	(510)	18%	(681)
Pakistan	26%	(300)	23%	(453)
Asia[1]	31%	(1,466)	19%	(4,660)
North America	87%	(1,838)	85%	(1,739)
EU countries	69%	(4,567)	63%	(3,411)
Nordic countries	69%	(3,047)	68%	(2,705)

Note: The figures in brackets show the total number of immigrants in the year in question.
1. Excluding Pakistan.
Source: Statistics Denmark, Vital Statistics, 1983, and other material from Statistics Denmark.

For all the countries shown in Table 4.2 in the period 1977-90 there was a drop in the number of foreign citizens who returned home within the space of five years. For example, among the Turkish citizens who emigrated to Denmark in 1990, only 10% returned to Turkey within five years. A similar fall is noticeable for people from Yugoslavia, Pakistan and other EU countries, while the drop is not quite so noticeable for North America and the Nordic countries.

As Table 4.1 shows, Turkey is the country with the largest increase in the number of foreign citizens immigrating to Denmark in the period up to 1995. Table 4.2 contributes to an explanation of this increase, in that the table shows that fewer Turkish than Yugoslav and Pakistani citizens return to their native countries. Additionally, second-generation immigrants among Turkish citizens were more prone to utilize the possibilities for family reunification.

4.2.1 Naturalizations

Foreign citizens that have lived permanently in Denmark for at least seven years (six years for refugees from the time they are granted their residence permit) are legally entitled to apply for Danish citizenship. In the case of citizens of other Nordic countries this period is just two years, and four years for those applicants who have been married to a Danish citizen for at least three years. As can been seen from Figure 4.3, the number of naturalizations in the period 1980-90 lies between 3-4,000 a year. This figure rose to over 5,000 in 1991 and remained at that level throughout the 1990s. The increase appears to be due to a change in the composition of immigrants in Denmark. More now come from those countries with a greater disposition for seeking Danish citizenship, e.g. 73 former Iranian citizens were granted Danish citizenship in 1990 compared with 989 in 1991 (see Statistics Denmark, 1998a).

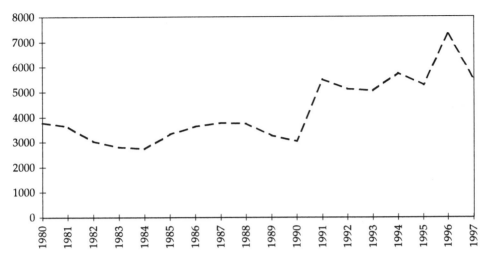

Figure 4.3: Number of naturalizations, 1980-97.

Source: Statistics Denmark, *Statistical News, Population and elections*, various editions.

Turkish citizens do not apply for Danish citizenship to anywhere near the same extent as Pakistanis, for example. During the period 1980-97, for instance, some 6,600 former Turkish citizens were granted Danish citizenship, while almost 6,000 former citizens of Pakistan were given Danish passports during the same period. These figures should be understood in the light of the fact that there are many more of Turkish than Pakistani origin in Denmark.

The greater tendency for Pakistani nationals to seek Danish citizenship is also a contributory cause to there being an apparent proportionately larger increase in the number of Turkish residents in Denmark than Pakistani.

Table 4.3 shows the number of people who were granted Danish citizenship compared with how many were eligible to apply.

The number eligible to apply for Danish citizenship has been found by carrying out a special computer query at Statistics Denmark, where the number of foreign nationals are categorized according to how long they have lived in Denmark.[1] In this way it is possible to approximate how many have the 'right' to be naturalized (potential naturalizations), and how many exercise this 'right' (actual naturalizations).

This type of analysis is also known as 'take-up' analysis, and has previously been used by the Rockwool Foundation Research Unit with regard to housing benefits (see Hans Hansen and Marie Louise Hultin, 1997) and the utilization of the right to periods of leave/sabbaticals (see Peder J. Pedersen and Søren Pedersen, 1998).

---

1. Periods of residence are divided into intervals of less than 2 years, 2-6 years, and 7 or more years.

Table 4.3: The number of people naturalized in 1997 in relation to the number of foreign nationals who as of 1 January 1997 had the 'right' to become naturalized.

	No. naturalized in 1997	Potential naturalizations[1]	Naturalization percentage[2]
Nordic countries[3]	331	24,286	1.4%
EU	322	21,011	1.5%
North America	81	3,144	2.6%
Former Yugoslavia	291	7,373	3.9%
Turkey	1,036	23,165	4.5%
Pakistan	149	4,198	3.5%
Iran	553	3,638	15.2%
Iraq	244	1,364	17.9%
Vietnam	126	2,003	6.3%
Poland	130	2,981	4.4%
Lebanon	160	1,891	8.5%
Somalia	17	460	3.7%

1. For nationals from other Nordic countries, residence in Denmark is stated as more than two years. For all other countries the minimum period of residence is seven years.
2. The naturalization percentage indicates the number of people naturalized in relation to the number of potential naturalizations.
3. Sweden and Finland are included in the figures for the Nordic countries.
Source: Statistics Denmark, *Statistical News, Population and elections 1998:5*, and special computer query from Statistics Denmark.

In the case of nationals from other Nordic countries, the number of naturalizations is seen in relation to the number of citizens who have been in Denmark for two or more years; for all other countries in relation to the number of citizens who have been here for at least seven years. As mentioned above, the figures will not include people who have the 'right' to naturalization sooner if they are married to a Danish citizen (or if they are refugees). It has, however, not been possible to take this factor into account in the figures presented in Table 4.3.

Table 4.3 shows that the naturalization percentage for citizens of Iran and Iraq is significantly higher than among nationals from other countries. Generally speaking, the naturalization percentage is low for citizens of other Nordic countries, the EU and North America (1.5-2.5%), while for Iranian and Iraqi nationals the figure is between 15% and 18%. The percentage for Lebanese and Vietnamese is 6-8%.[2]

2. It should be borne in mind that the naturalization percentages shown in Table 4.3 cannot be directly compared with previous figures relating to the frequency with which people apply for Danish citizenship, as the figures provided in Table 4.3 refer only to a single year.

If a person exchanges his or her original nationality for Danish citizenship it is presumably a sign that the person wishes to continue to live in Denmark. No Danish statistics are available detailing how many of these naturalized persons return to their country of origin. But Swedish data show that 'only' approximately 6% of those naturalized in the period 1967-89 returned to their country of origin (see Lundh and Ohlsson, 1994). Taking up Danish citizenship is, however, no clear indicator as to whether the person in question has become integrated into Danish society. As already mentioned by David Coleman in chapter 2, this requires other forms of analysis. One should nevertheless be aware of the dangers inherent in analyzing the whole scenario of immigration and immigrants purely on the basis of statistics concerning foreign nationals. Statistics Denmark has therefore introduced a second conceptual definition of immigrants and their descendants, a definition that will be considered in more detail later in section 4.2.5.

4.2.2 The composition of immigrants by sex and age

As illustrated in Figure 4.4 there is a considerable difference between the age composition of the population as a whole and that of the immigrant population.

Even though it has not been possible to separate foreign nationals from those immigrating in 1960, it is nevertheless possible to ascribe a certain weight to the figures, as it is unlikely that a significant shift has occurred in the age composition from 1960 to 1997 as regards the mix of immigrants and Danish nationals. There were, for instance, in 1960 relatively larger numbers of young people in the 15-29 age group among immigrants (almost 58%), compared with the entire population (over 20%). Conversely, there were fewer in the 30-59 age group and over-60's among immigrants compared with the entire population. In the case of children under 15, there were relatively more in the population as a whole in 1960 than among immigrants. This picture was different in 1997, where the percentages for this age group were roughly the same. This reflects the fact that the immigration of foreign citizens since the mid-1970s has been mainly in the form of family reunification. Guest workers during the late 1960s were young and of working age, and went on to bring their spouses, children and, in some cases, parents to Denmark.

A second contributory factor to the increasing numbers of children is that since the start of the 1980s refugees have brought their children with them to Denmark.

The increasing number of children and the continued relatively high percentage of immigrants of working age means that, other things being equal, the age composition of the population as a whole is reduced as a result of immigration. The age composition is also influenced, as mentioned above, by

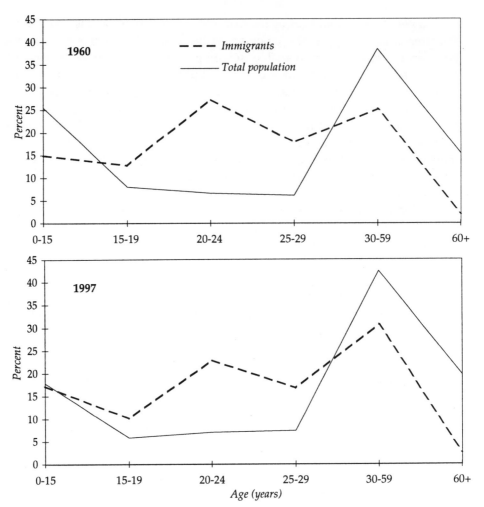

Figure 4.4: Age composition for immigrants and the population as a whole in 1960 and 1997.

Note: Immigrants comprise both Danish and foreign citizens in both 1960 and 1997.
Source: Statistics Denmark, *Statistical Yearbook* 1961 and 1998.

the fact that women from third-party countries have a higher fertility rate than Danish women.

The percentage of women among immigrants with foreign nationalities varies with the type of immigration. As illustrated in Figure 4.5, the percentage of women among immigrants with foreign citizenship fell from 50% during the early 1960s to around 40% by the late 1960s. In this period, as mentioned above, most immigration was labour-oriented, i.e. foreign workers,

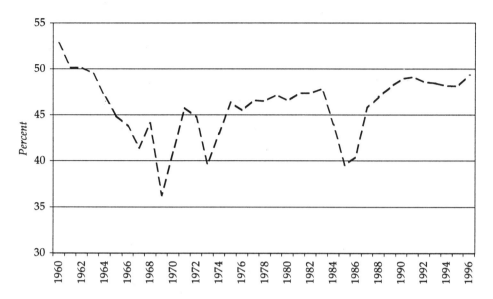

Figure 4.5: Percentage of women among immigrants with foreign citizenship, 1960-96.

Note: The figure for 1970 is interpolated.
Source: Statistics Denmark, *Statistical Yearbook*, various years.

where the demand was especially for male labour (Lundh and Ohlsson, 1994). From 1974 the percentage of women begins to increase again, and reaches 48-49% in the 1990s. This increase is due partly to the increased level of family immigration and partly (since the 1980s) to the increasing number of refugees. To recapitulate, the statistics for the number of foreign citizens in Denmark are affected by the fact that Pakistani nationals are likely to a much greater degree to apply for Danish citizenship than their Turkish counterparts. In the future the number and distribution of foreign nationals will be further influenced by the high naturalization percentages for Iranian and Iraqi nationals (15-18% in 1997).

Immigrants and refugees are generally speaking somewhat younger than the population as a whole. In more recent years there have been just as many female as male immigrants. Female immigrants are, generally speaking, of child-bearing age, and this, combined with the higher rate of fertility of women from third-party countries in particular, means that the population as a whole should become younger.

Despite the immigration freeze introduced in 1973, immigration has continued unabated up to the present time. The next two sections will take a closer look at two specific forms of immigration: refugees and family immigration.

4.2.3 Refugees

As mentioned above, the number of foreigners resident in Denmark has increased partly because of an increasing number of refugees. Section 7(1) of the Danish Aliens Act incorporates the Geneva Convention of 1951 with regard to the definition of refugees who are entitled to asylum. According to the Geneva Convention a refugee is defined as a person who

... owing to well-founded fear of being persecuted for reasons of race, religion, nationality, membership in a particular social group or political opinion, is outside the country of his nationality and is unable, or owing to such fear, is unwilling to avail himself of the protection of that country; or who, not having a nationality and being outside the country of his former habitual residence, is unable or, owing to such fear, is unwilling to return to it (with reference to Langlouis and Tornøe, 1993).

Over and above the terms of the Geneva Convention, Denmark grants asylum under section 7(2) of the Aliens Act to any foreigner

... who is not included under the terms of the Convention relating to the status of refugees of 28 July 1951, but who due to circumstances similar to those laid down in the Convention or due to other weighty reasons ought not to be required to return to his or her country of origin,

This provision covers the concept of *de facto* refugees.

The concept of *de facto* refugees was developed in administrative practice during the mid-1960s and written into the Aliens Act of 1983 (Langlouis and Tornøe, 1993).[3] In the most recent amendment to the Aliens Act, cf. Law no. 473 of 1 July, 1998, section 7(2) has been changed and now reads

... who is not included under the terms of the Convention relating to the status of refugees of 28 July 1951, but who due to circumstances similar to those laid down in the Convention or due to other weighty reasons *that involve a well-founded fear of persecution or similar violations*, ought not to be required to return to his or her country of origin,

The concept of *de facto* refugees was applied especially during the 1960s to defectors from Eastern Europe, inasmuch as they would be subjected to serious punishment if they returned to their countries of origin. Some of the Iranian refugees of the mid-1980s were granted residence permits for similar reasons (see Bent Jensen's chapter). The concept was also applied to young men fleeing because they refused to be drafted for active military service in their countries of origin. The concept of *de facto* refugees is also used in cases

---

3. See later in this chapter for a more in-depth description of the Aliens Act of 1983.

involving 'significant subjective fear', e.g. where a person has been tortured or raped just prior to leaving the country, but where there are no real grounds for concluding that a similar infringement will be repeated should the person return.

Most applications for asylum are from so-called 'spontaneous asylum-seekers', who make their own way to Denmark.

The wording of section 7(2) of the Aliens Act provides only limited guidance as to which groups of people the provision is meant to cover; neither does the preparatory work provide any specific instructions. It has therefore very much been left to the Danish Immigration Service and the Refugee Appeals Board to lay down guidelines for when to advise de facto status (Langlouis and Tornøe, 1993).

As can been seen in Figure 4.6, the number of refugees officially recognized as such in Denmark ranged between 2-3,000 per five-year period from the end of the 1950s to the end of the 1970s. At the end of the 1950s refugees came from Hungary after the unsuccessful rising against the Soviet occupation.

During the 1960s most refugees were defectors from Eastern Europe, while towards the end of the 1960s and early 1970s the influx was primarily from Poland, from where Jews fled from persecution. Jews were given permission by the Polish government to emigrate on condition that they gave up their Polish citizenship (Langlouis and Tornøe, 1993).

From the mid-1970s there were two main streams of refugees: 'boat people' from Vietnam after the communist victory and the defeat of South Vietnam, and Chileans fleeing after Pinochet's coup d'état in 1973. The number of refugees from Vietnam remained at a similar level for every five-year period since, up until the beginning of the 1990s. In the 1980s refugees arrived from Iran and Iraq as a result of the war between these two countries. Other refugee groups were stateless Palestinians and Tamils from Sri Lanka.

In the 1990s refugees have included stateless Palestinians as well as tribal peoples from Somalia and Iraq. The largest refugee group, however, came from Bosnia-Herzegovina, from where in 1995 alone, Denmark granted permanent residence permits to 16,185 people, a figure that constitutes a good 20% of all the refugees who came to Denmark during the period 1956-95.

As can be seen from Figure 4.6, no less than a sixfold increase in the number of refugees occurs from the period 1980-84 to the period 1985-89. This should be considered in the light of the fact that the 1980s witnessed a sharp increase in the number of asylum-seekers to all European countries (see David Coleman, Chapter 2). The figure of 156,000 people seeking asylum in Europe in 1980 rose to over 313,000 in 1989.

Poul Chr. Matthiessen (1998) argues that the influx of refugees in the 1980s and 1990s is due to considerable increases in the populations of the countries they wish to leave, combined with only modest economic growth and

Immigration to Denmark

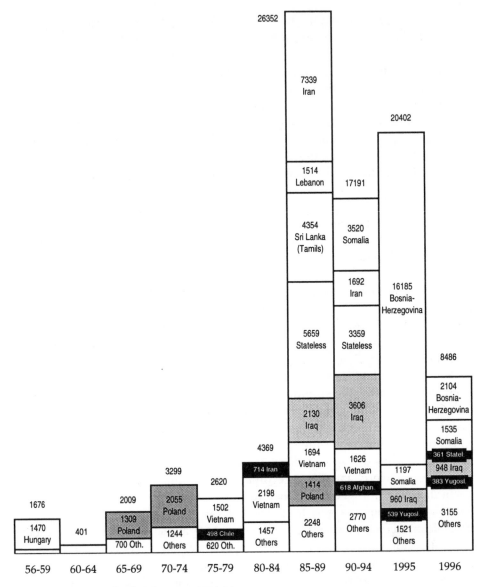

Figure 4.6: Recognized refugees, 1956-96.

Source: The Danish Refugee Council (1996).

considerable political unrest. Added to this, the collapse of the communist system in the former Soviet Union and in Eastern Europe gave rise to great political and economic instability, which in turn led to many ethnic tensions. The veritable flood of refugees was further aided by increasingly cheaper forms of transport and information on radio or television about the standard of living in Western Europe. In Chapter 1, David Coleman also points out that many citizens from third world countries over the years had already come to the West, and so could relay back information about their new homelands to their fellow countrymen as to the conditions in the Western countries, including details of the regulations governing asylum and immigration.

In 1983, only a short time before the sudden increase in the numbers of refugees arriving at Europe's borders, the Danish Parliament passed a new Aliens Act, which replaced the 1952 Act and the various amendments introduced in the interim.

The aim of the new Aliens Act was to improve the legal protection for those foreigners who had already established firm ties with Denmark. In comparison with its predecessor, the Act contained a more precise formulation of the provisions governing expulsion and the granting, extension, discontinuation, etc., of residence permits. In brief, the conditions for turning down applications from foreigners were tightened up.

The 1973 immigration freeze mentioned above was upheld in the 1983 Aliens Act, inasmuch as it was only extremely seldom that residence permits were to be issued to people from third-party countries on the basis of employment and commercial interests.

The legal rights of refugees under the 1983 Act have been described in detail by Christensen *et al.* (1995), and these rights were actually strengthened. The Act introduced an actual legal claim to a residence permit for *de facto* refugees, in that it includes an express provision to grant *de facto* refugees residence permits. Insofar as refugees with Convention status were concerned, access to protection had been available under the 1952 Act, as Denmark, as mentioned above, had bound itself to respect the terms of the Geneva Convention. The 1983 Act went further than its predecessor in that both Convention and *de facto* refugees were ensured a legal right to a residence permit. Not only this, but the procedural safeguards in the asylum procedure were strengthened as well. The Refugee Appeals Board was established to deal with complaints about decisions reached by the Danish Immigration Service, which was the first authority to deal with asylum-seekers. Family reunification for the parents (over 60), children (under 18) and spouses of foreigners was also formulated as a legal claim. The Act also upheld the principle of allowing free access to the Danish asylum procedure. All foreigners arriving in Denmark and seeking asylum were given the possibility of entering the country and staying while their applications were processed, no matter whether they were in possession of a valid passport or visa. The study mentioned above (Christensen, 1995: 237) could conclude that:

Internationally, the 1983 Act drew considerable attention due to its liberal approach to the question of refugees, and with the passing of this new legislation Denmark acquired a reputation for leading the way in providing a humanitarian approach to refugees.

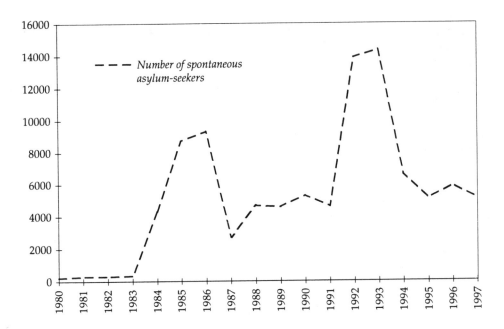

Figure 4.7: Number of spontaneous asylum-seekers, 1980-97.

Note: The figure for 1997 is provisional. The figures for 1980-83 are supplied by the Ministry of the Interior (1994:73). These figures for spontaneous refugees do not include people from former Yugoslavia covered by the law on temporary residence permits unless they also sought asylum at the same time.
Source: *News from Statistics Denmark*, no. 43, 1989, no., 46 1990, and *Statistical News, Population and elections*, 1998:11.

The number of asylum-seekers also rose from 332 in 1983, to 4,312 in 1984, and 8,698 in 1985 (see Figure 4.7). The increase in the number of asylum-seekers led to considerable strain on the Danish Immigration Service and the Refugee Appeals Board. The 'manifestly unfounded' procedure was therefore introduced in 1985 to ease the processing of cases. This amendment to the Act allowed the Danish Immigration Service — after having presented the case to the Danish Refugee Council — to issue a final refusal in asylum cases without asylum-seekers being able to appeal to the Refugee Board. This amendment did not, however, influence rights of *access* to asylum procedures or the *criteria* that applied (*ibid.*).

As shown in Figure 4.7, the numbers of asylum-seekers continued to increase, which resulted in a new amendment being introduced in 1986, limiting the right to enter the country and seek asylum. It now became possible to turn back an asylum-seeker without a valid passport and visa at the border if the person arrived from a country where he or she was considered to be in safety. Furthermore, the possibility was introduced of issuing fines to airlines and other carriers that transported people into the country without valid passports and visas. This amendment led to a fall in the number of spontaneous refugees· in 1987, see Figure 4.7. This was paralleled in the same year by an increase in the numbers seeking asylum from abroad (almost 5,000). However, those seeking asylum from abroad were seldom issued with a residence permit. Therefore very few people from this group ever arrived in Denmark, which means that they are less interesting statistically (Statistics Denmark, 1998b), and as such are not included in Figure 4.7.

The number of asylum-seekers remained basically constant (approximately 5,000) from 1988 to 1991. The major increase in the years 1991-92 and 1993 was due first and foremost to the civil war in former Yugoslavia. As mentioned above, many asylum-seekers from this area were granted permanent residence permits in 1995.

Since then various steps have been taken to tighten up the provisions of the Aliens Act (Kjær, 1995). In 1992 it became possible to take fingerprints and wider-ranging provisions were made available for detaining asylum-seekers whose applications had been turned down. In 1994 it was made more difficult to remain in the country after receiving a rejection, the problem being that, after such a rejection, many attempted to seek residence permits for humanitarian reasons or, alternatively, complained to the ombudsman. Until the 1994 amendment these asylum-seekers were permitted to stay in the country while their application for residence permits on humanitarian grounds or their complaint to the ombudsman was processed, despite their normal obligation to leave the country as a result of the rejection of their application for asylum. This amendment provided a much wider range of possibilities for expelling asylum-seekers whilst their humanitarian-based application or complaint to the ombudsman was being processed. The amendment was introduced in reaction to the time it was taking to process cases, which according to Kjær (1995) was as much as two years.

In the case of refugees from former Yugoslavia, it should be noted that a law was passed in 1992 granting temporary residence permits to people in this special emergency situation, as agreed with the UN High Commissioner for Refugees. In addition, temporary residence permits were issued to spontaneous refugees who had arrived *before* December 1992. Immediate family members were also granted temporary residence permits. In 1993 temporary residence permits were issued to spontaneous refugees who had arrived *after* 1 December 1992, and to members of their immediate families. It was possible to suspend processing such cases for a maximum period of two years. Furthermore, an agreement providing the right to screen people in the immediate region of origin was drawn up with a view to providing protection where this was felt to be necessary (Ministry of the Interior, 1996). When the initial two-year deadline expired at the end of 1994 the great majority were approved as refugees in accordance with section 7 of the Aliens Act (Kjær,

1995). In January 1995 a new Act was passed giving people from former Yugoslavia with temporary residence permits permanent residence if they were still considered to have a need for asylum. This, as mentioned above, is clearly evident from Figure 4.6.

Generally speaking, approximately 50% of all application from asylum-seekers were turned down in the first instance in the period 1990-93 (Danish Immigration Service, 1998).[4] In 1994 the refusal percentage rose to approximately 70%, before falling to 57% in 1995 and 33% in 1996. Provisional figures for 1998 point towards a rejection percentage of about 42%, which represents a fall of 4% points compared with 1997. According to the Danish Immigration Service fluctuations in the rejection percentage reflect more the nationality of those seeking asylum at any one time than any changes in the practices followed in processing applications. If, for example, in a given period, there is a large number of asylum-seekers from countries for whom asylum is practically never granted, then the refusal percentage will, quite naturally, increase.

To summarize, it can be concluded that the number of refugees increased fivefold in the five-year periods from the mid-1980s compared with previous periods. This increase in the number of refugees coincided with the adoption of a new Aliens Act (1983) which was seen by many as being very liberal. The increase in the number of refugees triggered a political reaction, with a majority in the Danish Parliament agreeing to introduce restrictions in the provisions of the legislation, first in 1986. These amendments are clearly reflected in the number of asylum-seekers, which fell immediately (1987) and has remained at the same level ever since. The Aliens Act was made further restrictive in the 1990s. This new round of restrictive measures did not, however, affect those fleeing from war-stricken former Yugoslavia, who were granted permanent residence in 1995. The number of refugees from former Yugoslavia was considerable, constituting 20% of all the refugees accepted by Denmark since 1956.

4.2.4 Family reunification[5]

The Aliens Act of 1983, which has been dealt with in depth by Langlouis and Tornøe (1993), contains, as already mentioned, a legal right to family reunification under section 9 (1).

---

4. As mentioned above, it is the Danish Immigration Service that processes applications in the first instance. Those who are turned down here can appeal the decision and be granted asylum by the Refugee Board, a fact which the figures here do not take into consideration.
5. The term 'family reunification' used here covers both reunification of existing families and the formation of new ones.

Nevertheless, certain conditions have to be met. For example, parents who are to be brought to Denmark must be over 60 years of age. Furthermore, the parents of immigrants must not have any other children in their home country.[6] Refugees in Denmark are in this respect placed on an equal footing with a Danish or Nordic citizen, for which reason there is no proviso that parents are not allowed to have other children in the home country. When amending the Aliens Act in 1992 a provision was introduced which stated that in the case of family reunification for parents of immigrants (legally speaking this applies to people who are neither EU citizens, Danish citizens, Nordic citizens, nor refugees) certain conditions must be met regarding the obligation and ability of the immigrants to maintain their parents. In the case of Danish and Nordic citizens and refugees, the original Act of 1983 *could* be used to demand as a condition for granting a residence permit that those resident in Denmark would provide for their parents. Such a family reunification *could* after the amendment in 1992 also be made conditional on such an ability being substantiated. In 1998 this demand was further tightened up, in that those resident in Denmark must as the principal rule substantiate their ability to provide for their parents. In addition, the enforcement of the maintenance demand was tightened in 1992 and in 1998.

To receive a residence permit for a foreign spouse or cohabitant in Denmark requires that the person is over 18 and that both live at the same address. In the case of cohabitants, it is required that the couple has lived together for a protracted period (typically at least 1½-2 years). A 1992 amendment to the Aliens Act made it an additional requirement that the person already living in Denmark if not being a Danish citizen, Nordic citizen, or a a refugee, must have stayed legally in Denmark for more than five years. The five-year limit for immigrants was introduced to combat *pro forma* marriages in which, to obtain a residence permit, a foreigner is married to a person living in the country, and is later divorced, perhaps in order to enter into a marriage with a person from his or her home country.

Residence permits can also be issued to minors (i.e. children under 18 years of age), if the child lives with one of the holders of parental custody. While children live with their parents they are not required to have their own residence permit. If, for example, a foreign child arrives in Denmark in accordance with the legislation governing family reunification and as such lives with one of the people holding parental custody rights, but shortly afterwards moves from the shared address, the child might be refused permission to

6. This rule has applied since 1992 and marks a clampdown compared with the original formulation in the 1983 legislation, where it was also a condition for refusing family reunification that any children in the native country could provide for the parents. By the 1998 amendment to the Aliens Act the legal right of family reunification for parents of immigrants was repealed.

Table 4.4: Notified residence permits, 1988-97.

	1988	1989	1990	1991	1992	1993	1994	1995	1996	1997[1]
Refugees	3,905	4,452	3,044	4,014	3,807	3,424	2,818	20,347	8,717	5,954
Family reunification	7,560	7,559	8,444	7,872	8,517	8,091	5,033	6,017	6,327	8,727
EU/EC residence permit	3,375	2,541	1,846	1,670	2,280	2,825	4,342	3,780	5,887	5,861
Due to employment	3,142	2,733	2,790	2,395	2,439	2,058	2,124	2,232	2,750	2,958
Other forms	3,852	4,041	4,602	5,056	4,780	4,273	4,967	5,193	6,251	6,707
Total	21,833	22,211	20,154	21,652	21,397	17,613	20,268	37,879	32,332	29,040
Family reunification as a % of all residence permits	34.6	38.0	39.1	39.3	37.8	28.6	29.7	16.7	27.0	26.0

1. Provisional figure.
Source: *News from Statistics Denmark no. 46 1990*, and *Statistical News, Population and elections 1998:11*.

reside in the home country. It should also be noted that the regulations governing family reunification with minors do not apply if the child has established his or her own family in the home country.

Just as with the regulations governing family reunification with parents, the rules applying to family reunification with spouses and children were tightened in 1992 as regards the financial position of those family members already living in Denmark. The obligation to provide for these family members was in itself not new (Vedsted-Hansen, 1997), in that this followed current legislation concerning both private and public maintenance responsibilities (*ibid.*). It became *possible* to require that the person living in Denmark provide for his or her spouse or cohabitant and, where relevant, children and substantiate his or her ability to do so. In the 1998 amendment to the Aliens Act this financial demand was repealed with respect to Danish citizens, Nordic citizens and refugees. For immigrants living in Denmark, it is still, however, the principal rule that they must substantiate their ability to provide for their spouse or cohabitant. As a further tightening in the 1998 amendment an immigrant must have stayed in Denmark for at least 6 years in order to be able to be reunified with his or her spouse or cohabitant.

All family reunification regulations represent exceptions to the immigration freeze introduced in 1973, and have been introduced on humanitarian grounds.

A statistical record of just how many foreigners are granted residence permits in Denmark as a result of family reunification legislation was started in 1988. Apart from in 1995, the number of immigrants entering the country in accordance with the legislation governing family reunification in every year since 1988 has constituted the largest part of the notified residence permits issued, followed in second place by the allocation of refugee status. As can be seen in Table 4.4, the annual number of residence permits issued due to family reunification totalled approximately 7-8,000 in the period 1988-92, or about 40% of the total number of residence permits issued in this period.

From 1992-93 the number fell to about 5,000 and the share of the total notified residence permits to just less than 29%. This fall was caused by the introduction of the more restrictive regulations described above, i.e. the five-year 'wait' for immigrants and the ability to provide for family members.

The low share of the total number of notified residence permits issued on grounds of family reunification, especially in 1995 is, as described above, due to the many refugees from former Yugoslavia who were granted permanent residence that year. From 1994 the number of residence permits issued as a result of family reunification increases, though still, with the exception of 1996, below the level in 1992, (Statistics Denmark, 1996, 1997b).

Note that the figures for notified residence permits are not directly comparable with immigrant statistics for the same period, partly because there might be a time gap from a permit being granted to the actual immigration taking place, and partly because some residence permits are never taken up. A residence permit is sometimes not used if a person has already received a residence permit in accordance with a different provision of the Aliens Act (Statistics Denmark, 1998b).

It is very difficult to predict the quantitative effects on immigration with respect to family reunification due to the 1998 amendment to the Aliens Act. Many things indicate, however, that the effects will be fairly modest. Partly the legal right to family reunification is repealed, but instead it is now possible to give a residence permit by discretion in each case. This, however, only affects a small group, namely parents of resident immigrants. Partly there have been introduced regulations in order to avoid giving residence permits to arranged or pro-forma marriages, but the quantitative effects of these are of course difficult to predict. Finally the rules concerning obligation to provide for spouses for Danish citizens, Nordic citizens and refugees have been changed, but this is to some extent merely a formalized legal adjustment in accordance with earlier practice (Vedsted-Hansen, 1997) so the quantitative effect of this will hardly become particularly big.

Granting family reunification on humanitarian grounds was introduced originally to facilitate the reuniting of already existing families. Until now, however, it has been uncertain to what degree the regulations governing family reunification have been used for *reunifying* existing families or for the *formation* of new ones. The Rockwool Foundation Research Unit has therefore asked Statistics Denmark to run a special query through their computers with a view to shedding light on this matter for people who have immigrated to Denmark since 1 January 1976. No precise immigration dates are available for people immigrating prior to this date.

The query was based on the definition of immigrant used by Statistics

Denmark (of this, more later). The information for married immigrants also includes data concerning date of marriage and a number of family-related facts about the spouse. It is therefore possible to compare the immigration date and the marriage date for all existing marriages among immigrants who have arrived in Denmark since 1 January 1976.

As can be seen in Table 4.5, 35.7% of all married men were married within a year prior to or after their immigration to Denmark. For married women this figure is even higher: all of 52.2%.

Among married men there is a considerable difference between the different countries of origin as to the percentage of men who are married less than a year before or after immigrating. The percentage is as high as 64.2% for Pakistani men, and 45% for Turkish men. The percentage of married men from Germany and Great Britain is much lower: Around 30%, and for men from other Nordic countries, approximately 25%.

For married women there is also a big difference between country of origin and whether they were married less than a year prior to or after immigrating. The highest figure is for Thai women, of whom 87.3% of all married women are married within a year prior to or after immigration; the next highest figure is for married women from Poland. For married Turkish and Pakistani women the percentage was 55.0% and 56.8% respectively. For married women from Somalia and former Yugoslavia the figure drops to 35.1% and 29.9% respectively.

If we take all immigrants, then the family reunification legislation is used in connection with a marriage in over 44% of cases to form a new family. Among Turkish immigrants the family reunification regulations are used in over half of the cases among those married to form a new family (50.9%), while for married Pakistanis the figure is 59.7%.

It is too early to say whether the lower percentages for both men and women from former Yugoslavia and Somalia reflect a different trend in the formation of families than, for example, people from Turkey and Pakistan, or whether it is because immigrants from Somalia and former Yugoslavia have not yet lived in Denmark long enough for them to marry people from their respective native countries. Former Yugoslavia is included here because according to Jensen (1998) it is estimated that as many as two thirds of the refugees from this area are Muslim.

In a research study from 1989 of young (18-25-year-olds), second generation immigrants (also called descendants, see below), Kirsten Just Jeppesen has discovered that 95% of those married or engaged and who have Turkey as their country of origin, are married or engaged to a fellow countryman. For Pakistanis, the corresponding figure is 90%, while the figure for those from former Yugoslavia is decidedly lower: Approximately 70%. Most descendants are married or engaged to a countryman who, when the match

Table 4.5: Married immigrants, categorized according to entry date and marriage date. Status as of 1/1-1998.[1]

	Married more than a year before/after immigration to DK		Married less than a year before/after immigration to DK		Percentage who are married less than a year before/after immigration		
							Men and
	Men	Women	Men	Women	Men	Women	women
Nordic countries	1,326	1,405	435	599	24.7%	29.9%	27.5%
Germany	1,348	1,092	585	755	30.3%	40.9%	35.4%
Great Britain	1,841	827	888	624	32.5%	43.0%	36.2%
Poland	309	479	206	1,594	40.0%	76.9%	69.6%
Turkey	3,356	3,637	2,795	4,446	45.0%	55.0%	50.9%
Former Yugoslavia	4,800	4,790	1,752	2,046	26.7%	29.9%	28.4%
Pakistan	388	733	695	965	64.2%	56.8%	59.7%
Iran	1,338	870	692	870	34.1%	50.0%	41.4%
Vietnam	556	559	281	667	33.6%	54.4%	46.0%
Jordan	63	55	83	105	56.8%	65.5%	61.4%
Somalia	1,569	1,396	717	754	31.4%	35.1%	33.2%
Thailand	28	244	71	1,680	71.7%	87.3%	86.6%
Other	15,706	11,262	8,898	14,707	36.2%	56.6%	46.7%
Total	32,628	27,349	18,098	29,812	35.7%	52.2%	44.4%

1. Includes immigrants who have entered Denmark after 1.1.1976.
Source: Special query at Statistics Denmark.

is arranged or the engagement announced, still live in their country of origin. For descendants originating from Turkey and Pakistan this applies to 75-87%, while the proportion of Yugoslav men and women is 47% and 63% respectively.

In conclusion it can be said that the Aliens Act of 1983 introduced a legal claim to family reunification. During the period 1988-92, 7-8,000 residence permits a year were issued in accordance with the provisions governing family reunification. This is the equivalent of almost 40% of all allocated residence permits during this period and represents the largest share of all residence permits. Later, more stringent provisions were introduced for family reunification, including the possibility of requiring that immigrants living in Denmark supply proof of their ability to provide for children, parents and spouses they wished to bring to the country. This resulted in a fall in the number of residence permits issued on the grounds of family reunification. Turkish and Pakistani immigrants are especially likely to use the regulations governing family reunification to form a new family. For Turkish immigrants these provisions are used in over half of the cases to bring a spouse to

Denmark, while the corresponding figure for Pakistanis is almost 60%. This figure is significantly lower for immigrants arriving from other Nordic countries, Germany and Great Britain.

4.2.5 The definition of immigrants and descendants of immigrants

As pointed out by David Coleman in Chapter 2, and as is clear from the above, statistics regarding immigrants and numbers of foreign citizens, etc., are not always as clear as they might appear at first sight, e.g. not all immigrants are necessarily foreigners, just as not all foreigners are necessarily immigrants.

Matthiessen (1998) describes how the demarcation of the immigrant population is primarily of a legal nature, with the main emphasis placed on people with foreign citizenship. This is, however, not appropriate if, for example, you wish to shed light on the degree to which immigrants have become integrated in Danish society. If an immigrant changes nationality and becomes Danish, he or she will no longer appear in the statistics covering foreign citizens. But a Danish passport does not necessarily mean that a person is better integrated in Danish society. Since at the same time, as has been mentioned above, there are differences in the propensity of different nationals to apply for Danish citizenship, merely studying those registered as foreign citizens will give a distorted picture of the real numbers of various national groups in Denmark.

In an attempt to compile better statistics within this field, Statistics Denmark took up an idea first used in Norway and, parallel with other statistics, introduced a new set of statistics in 1991 dealing with the immigrant population. Statistics Denmark categorized the immigrant population as either *immigrants* or *descendants*:

- Immigrants are people born outside Denmark, whose parents are both foreigners or born outside Denmark. If both parents are unknown and the person is born abroad, such a person is also defined as an immigrant.[7]
- Descendants are defined as people born in Denmark of parents who either are immigrants or themselves descendants. If a person is born in Denmark, but both parents are unknown and the person is a foreign citizen, he or she is also defined as a descendant.[8]

In the case of each person included in the statistics, information is gathered from the Central Population Register regarding place of birth and nationality,

---

7. A person born outside Denmark where one parent is unknown and the other is not Danish is also defined as an immigrant.
8. A person born in Denmark where one parent is unknown and the other is not Danish is also defined as a descendant.

as well as the same information about parents in order to categorize people as immigrants, descendants or 'other'.[9] Statistics Denmark has thereby attempted to classify the immigrant population according to origin and not merely nationality and country of birth. When Statistics Denmark carried out the new categorization for the first time in 1991, figures dating back to 1980 were published at the same time (Pedersen, 1991).

The figures are shown in Table 4.6 and compared with the number of foreign citizens. As can be seen, there are more immigrants than foreign citizens, in that the definition of immigrant is independent of whether a person holds Danish citizenship. All told, immigrants and descendants comprised 6.6% of the entire population in 1998, as opposed to a figure of 4.7% for foreign nationals. As pointed out by Matthiessen (1998) the new definition means that immigrants and descendants of the immigrant population from less developed countries[10] totalled 183,319 on 1 January 1998 (see *Statistical ten-year review 1998* from Statistics Denmark) while the corresponding number of foreign citizens from the same countries totalled 132,548.[11] Close to 53% of all immigrants and descendants originate from less developed countries.

In other words, according to the new definition, there are over 50,000 more immigrants and descendants from the less developed countries than if one studies the figures for foreign citizens alone.

Statistics Denmark has also calculated the fertility rate of immigrants and descendants from more and less developed countries respectively. During the period 1993-96, the average fertility rate for immigrants and descendants from the more developed countries was 1.7 live births per woman, which is on a par with the level for the entire population which is 1.8. For immigrants and descendants from less developed countries the fertility rate was higher, i.e. 3.2 on average during the same period, though with a tendency to fall (from 3.4 in 1993 to 3.1 in 1996).

Based on the assumption that the net migration to Denmark from less developed countries will remain at approximately 7,000 a year in the ensuing years (equal to an estimate of net immigration in 1997), and that the fertility rate will fall from the 1997 rate of 3.2 to 2.1 in 2020, and that mortality rates remain the same for the entire population, Statistics Denmark has made a

9. The 'other' category used by Statistics Denmark refers to all those who cannot be categorized as being either immigrants or descendants. The more idiomatic 'Danes' will be used for the rest of this chapter.
10. Statistics Denmark respects the UN definitions, see Statistics Denmark, *Statistical News, Population and elections*, 1997:16. The more developed countries comprise Europe excluding Turkey, Cyprus, Azerbaijan, Uzbekistan, Kazakhstan, Turkmenistan, Kirghizia, Tadzhikistan, Georgia, and Armenia. The USA, Canada, Japan, Australia and New Zealand are also included in the UN definition of the more developed countries. The less developed countries embrace all other countries.
11. See Statistics Denmark, *Statistical News, Population and elections*, 1998:5.

Table 4.6: Immigrants and descendants, 1980-98.

	Foreign citizens	Immigrants	Descendants	Immigrants and descendants as a % of entire population	Foreign citizens as a % of entire population
1980	99,796	134,705	18,253	3.0%	1.9%
1981	101,600	136,229	19,423	3.0%	2.0%
1982	101,914	136,411	20,554	3.1%	2.0%
1983	103,052	136,976	21,552	3.1%	2.0%
1984	104,062	137,541	22,278	3.1%	2.0%
1985	107,726	140,566	23,360	3.2%	2.1%
1986	116,951	149,476	24,439	3.4%	2.3%
1987	128,255	160,358	26,203	3.6%	2.5%
1988	136,177	167,837	28,369	3.8%	2.7%
1989	142,016	173,576	30,527	4.0%	2.8%
1990	150,644	181,109	33,462	4.2%	2.9%
1991	160,641	189,649	36,553	4.4%	3.1%
1992	169,525	198,898	40,343	4.6%	3.3%
1993	180,103	208,865	44,507	4.9%	3.5%
1994	189,014	217,154	48,915	5.1%	3.6%
1995	196,705	224,995	53,464	5.3%	3.8%
1996	222,746	249,885	58,838	5.9%	4.2%
1997	237,695	265,794	64,498	6.3%	4.2%
1998	249,628	276,781	70,252	6.6%	4.7%

Note: The figures shown for the period 1980-98 for immigrants and descendants are the revised figures, see Statistics Denmark, *Statistical News, Population and elections*, 1997:16. The figures for 1981-84 and 1986-87 are provided by Statistics Denmark, but have never previously been published.
Source: Statistics Denmark, *Statistical ten-year review*, 1998 (for the years 1988-98). *Statistical News, Population and elections*, 1997:16 (for the years 1980 and 1985).

population forecast for the number of immigrants and descendants in 2020.[12]

According to this population forecast, immigrants and descendants from less developed countries in Denmark in 2020 will total 438,000 people, or 7.9% of the population. Currently, as mentioned above, they comprise 183,000, or 3.5% of the population. The number of immigrants and descendants from less developed countries will therefore more than double during the course of the next 25 years. For immigrants and descendants from the more developed countries, the population forecast shows that they will grow from 3.1% of the population in 1998 to 5.2% of the population in 2020.

12. See Statistics Denmark, *Statistical News, Population and elections*, 1997:11.

4.3 Labour market conditions

As has been shown in Eskild Wadensjö's chapter on the socio-economic con-sequences of immigration, the position of immigrants in the labour market is of decisive importance when influencing public finances.

At the end of the 1960s and the start of the 1970s, the labour force par-ticipation rate for immigrants was relatively high.[13] The primary reason that these immigrants came to the country was to work. There are no Danish figures for the number of foreign citizens in the workforce prior to 1981, but Swedish figures show that the labour force participation rate among foreigners during the 1960s was actually 20% higher than that for the entire population (Lundh and Ohlsson, 1994).

It is actually possible to find the number of foreign citizens aged 16-66 in the workforce for the first years of the 1980s for particular nationalities. But, unfortunately, it is not possible from the statistics available to the general pub-lic to separate the total number of foreign citizens in precisely this age group (16-66). That it is possible for the 15-64 age group is precisely the reason why this age demarcation is used as the denominator when measuring the par-ticipation rate. The aberration this leads to in relation to a completely correct calculation of labour participation rates must be seen as being minimal, as there are not many foreign citizens in Denmark in the 65-66 age group, though of course any minor fluctuation in developments over a period of time should be interpreted with caution.

As can be seen from Figure 4.8, the participation rate for the entire pop-ulation is around 80% throughout the entire period, with a slight tendency to fall towards the end of the 1980s.[14] The participation rate for foreign citizens, inasmuch as it could be measured, has developed in a clearly different manner.

The participation rate for both Turks and Pakistanis has throughout the en-tire period in question been lower than for the population as a whole. In 1981 it was between 74% and 75% for these two nationalities, while the national average was close to 79%. During the early 1980s their participation rate was on a par with the level for citizens from the EU and Nordic countries. Since then it has fallen to just over 56% for Turkish nationals and almost 49% for Pakistanis in 1997. The corresponding participation rate for the entire pop-ulation is 77%, and approximately 66-67% for citizens from Nordic countries

---

13. The labour force participation rate measures the participation of a given age group in the workforce, i.e. employed and unemployed in relation to everyone in this age group.
14. The participation rate for the entire population is given as the number of people in the workforce between the ages of 16 and 66 in relation to the number of people in the entire population within the same age group. Statistics Denmark, *Statistical ten-year review* (1991, 1994 and 1998).

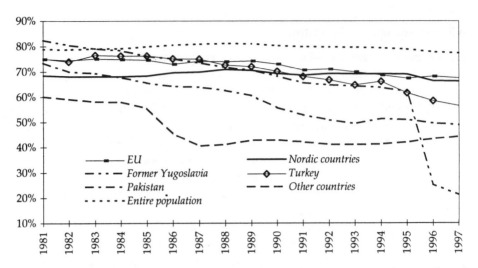

Figure 4.8: The labour force participation rate for foreign citizens from selected countries and for the entire population, 1981-97.

Note: Spain and Portugal are included in figures for the EU as of 1.1.1986. Sweden and Finland are included as a part of the Nordic region until 1995 and after that in the EU. Austria is included in the EU from 1995.
Source: The figures for the workforce in the 16-66 age group are taken from Statistics Denmark's Municipal Statistical Database (RAS34), the participation rate for the entire population from the *Statistical ten-year review 1998, 1994* and *1991*; data on the number of foreign citizens between the ages of 15 and 64 is likewise from the Municipal Statistical Database at Statistics Denmark.

and from the EU. The fall in the participation rate for Pakistanis occurs because the number of Pakistanis in the workforce has remained basically stable, while the number of Pakistani nationals has increased. Where Turkish nationals are concerned, the number in work has increased, but not enough to compensate for the increase in the numbers arriving from Turkey.[15]

Clearly then, the fall in the labour force participation rate for Turkish and Pakistani nationals is due to the continued intake of immigrants as a result of the regulations governing family reunification. When, for example, a new spouse moves to Denmark, it will naturally take some time before this person has obtained sufficient knowledge of the Danish language and of Danish society to participate in the workforce — either as employed or unemployed. The same pattern is evident for citizens of former Yugoslavia. It is, however,

15. Note that the tendency for Pakistanis to a much greater extent than Turks to apply for Danish citizenship will somewhat blur the picture here. Pakistanis who have been granted Danish nationality will typically have lived in Denmark long enough to have presumably achieved a closer affiliation to the labour market. When they take up Danish citizenship they will therefore no longer appear in the group of Pakistani nationals represented in the statistics. The fall in the participation rate for Pakistanis will therefore be overestimated.

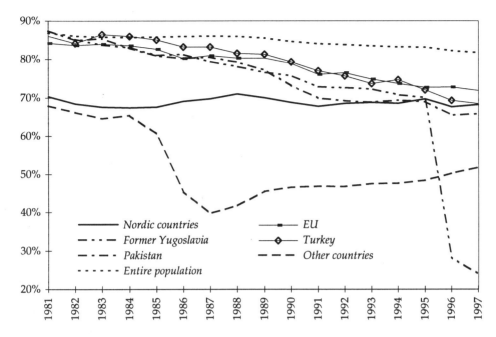

Figure 4.9: The labour force participation rate for male foreign citizens from selected countries and for the entire male population, 1981-97.

Note: See comments to Figure 4.8.

interesting to note that the participation rate for former Yugoslavs in 1981 and 1982 was actually higher than for the population as a whole. The extremely rapid fall in the participation rate for citizens of former Yugoslavia after 1995 is of course due to the previously mentioned rapid increase in the number of refugees fleeing from the civil war in that region.

The group 'Other countries', which cannot be subdivided any further for the period in question, is an extremely mixed group and includes citizens from the new refugee countries of the 1980s as well as the USA, Canada, Australia, New Zealand, etc. The participation rate for these 'Other countries' fell dramatically after 1984.

This is due to the relatively large increase in the number of refugees from countries such as Iran, Iraq, Vietnam, Lebanon and Sri Lanka (see also Figure 4.6), in that it is not completely unrealistic to assume that the participation rate for citizens from countries such as the USA, Canada, Australia and New Zealand is basically the same as that for the overall Danish population.

If the participation rate for men is examined, Figure 4.9 shows that the rate for the entire male population fell by over 5% points from 1981 to 1997. The same trend applies to all men from the various countries and groups of countries. However, the fall is greater for foreign citizens.

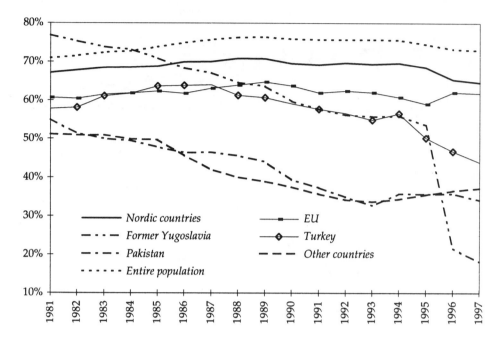

Figure 4.10: The labour force participation rate for female foreign citizens from se-lected countries and for the entire female population, 1981-97.

Note: See comments on Figure 4.8.

Generally speaking the negative development in the participation rate for men from Turkey, Pakistan and former Yugoslavia is similar to that for male nationals from the EU countries. It should be noted, however, that citizens from former Yugoslavia saw their participation rate fall especially rapidly from 1995 to 1997 due to the large influx of fellow countrymen as refugees in the 1990s.

It is also worth commenting on the fact that in the early 1980s the par-ticipation rate for Pakistani, Turkish and Yugoslav men was actually on a par with that for the entire population and in fact during certain years actually exceeded that of the male population as a whole. It was first during the mid-1980s that the participation rate fell noticeably below that for the male pop-ulation as a whole.

The labour force participation rate for women is shown in Figure 4.10. As can be seen, the participation rate for the entire female population is higher than that for all the other countries and groups of countries, barring the relatively unimportant exception in the early 1980s where, for example, women from former Yugoslavia had a higher participation rate than women in the population as a whole.

The development in the participation rate for women from EU and Nordic

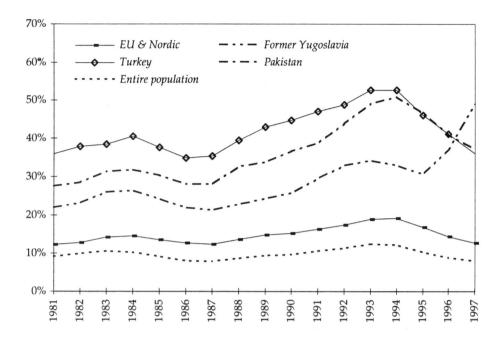

Figure 4.11: The average unemployment rates for foreign citizens from selected countries and for the entire population, 1981-97.

Note: The unemployment percentages are calculated as an average of the number of unemployed in relation to the workforce. The figures for the 'EU & Nordic' group cover the Nordic region for the years 1981-83 only. There are no published data for other countries for the whole period other than those shown in the figure.
Source: Statistics Denmark, *Statistical News, Labour Market 1983-1998* and *Statistics Denmark, Statistical News, Unemployment 1981-1983.*

countries is basically the same as that for the entire female population, although the actual level is slightly lower. The participation rate for women from former Yugoslavia, Turkey and Pakistan has, on the other hand, fallen throughout the period and is now approximately 44% for Turkish women and 34% for Pakistani women. By comparison, the participation rate for the entire female population was approximately 73% in 1997.

Where unemployment is concerned, up until 1993 the Turkish population had by far the highest unemployment figures (see Figure 4.11). In the early 1980s unemployment among Turkish nationals was approximately 40% of the workforce, a figure that rose to 50% in 1992 and 1993. From around 1994 their unemployment figures fell to 36%, which is comparable to the development for Pakistanis during the same period.

Unemployment among former Yugoslavs was somewhat lower up until 1995, any fluctuations basically following the same pattern as seen for Turkish and Pakistani nationals during the same period. From 1995 unemployment among Yugoslavs rose dramatically, which was not surprising after the huge influx of refugees from the civil war in former Yugoslavia, discussed above.

Unemployment as a percentage of the workforce among Nordic and EU citizens shadows that of the population as a whole, though 3-4% points higher. Part of the explanation for the higher levels of unemployment among foreign nationals might be that they are, generally speaking, younger than the population as a whole. Up until the 1996 budget, which introduced changes aimed at greatly reducing effect on unemployment among the under 25s, unemployment among young people was higher than that for the entire population. However, Hummelgaard *et al.* (1995) have studied unemployment in the period 1984-91 among refugees and immigrants in the 30-34 age group and compared it with that among 30-34-year-olds in the population as a whole. The analysis concluded that even though refugees and immigrants are, generally speaking, younger than the entire population, the difference is a modest one and as such is not of decisive importance when attempting to explain the high unemployment among foreign citizens.

The more pronounced increase in unemployment among Turkish, Pakistani and former Yugoslavs after 1987 appear to be due to the continued influx of new immigrants due to family reunification and because of the issuing in 1995 of permanent residence permits to more than 16,000 Bosnians. These new immigrants had, for example, a poorer knowledge of Danish than those who had been in the country considerably longer.

But, as can be seen in Figure 4.11, when employment figures fall for the population as a whole, they also fall for citizens from other countries. There is therefore nothing that appears to indicate that foreign citizens 'miss out' on upturns in the economy – they certainly did not during the mid-1980s and in the 1990s. But it is also quite clear that during recessions and periods of rising unemployment for the population as a whole, unemployment increases relatively more dramatically among Turkish, Pakistani and former Yugoslavs.

The relative importance for integration of a knowledge of Danish and the economic climate in Denmark at the time of arrival — as well as other conditions such as their experience of discrimination, or the financial incentives proffered to refugees and other immigrants to take up a job — cannot be analyzed satisfactorily on the basis of current data.

The importance of language skills for access to the labour market can be indirectly seen from the fact that the longer immigrants have been in Denmark, the greater their participation rate (as of 1 January 1997). And among those who are already a part of the labour market there is a clear trend that the longer they have been here, the greater the number employed. This applies both to immigrants from the more and less developed countries (see Statistics Denmark, 1998c). More than 60% of the immigrants from the less developed countries who have been in Denmark for more than ten years are now part of the labour force. For those who have been in the country for between five and ten years, the figure is just 40%. Among all immigrants from the less developed countries, approximately 43% of them were part of the workforce in 1997. Hummelgaard et al. could show a similar result for the period 1981-91: The longer the period of residence in Denmark, the lower the risk of being unemployed. One must assume that over and above language skills, the opportunities to learn a trade in Denmark also play a role as regards stronger links to the labour market.

An extremely important explanatory variable for success in the labour market is education. Generally speaking, the educational skills of immigrants are poorly covered by the Danish public records. Among employed immigrants, information about educational background is unavailable for some 50%. This compares with 4% for the population as a whole. A Norwegian survey which shed light on the educational background of immigrants by asking them, documented that, generally speaking, their level of education was lower than that of the population as a whole (Blom and Ritland, 1997).

A new Danish study shows that, as regards vocational courses, there has been an increase in enrolment of immigrants and their descendants by all of 51% from 1980 to 1994 (University of Copenhagen, 1998), while the corresponding enrolment for the entire population has increased by 42% (Statistics Denmark, *Statistical Yearbook* 1982 and 1996). In vocational courses, the percentage of places taken up by immigrants and descendants therefore increased from 1.6% in 1980 to 4.0% in 1994. For courses of further and higher education, the picture is just the opposite, the increase being 59% for immigrants and their descendants (University of Copenhagen, 1998) as opposed to 76% for the entire population. The immigrants' and descendants' share of places in courses of further and higher education therefore dropped from 5.1% in 1980 to 4.7% in 1994.

The study carried out by the University of Copenhagen also shows that, when following the class of immigrants and their descendants who matriculated in 1986, generally speaking fewer of them than for the population as a whole had completed their training/course of education 8-10 years later. For the entire population, 60% of those who matriculate have completed a course of further education after ten years, compared with just under 40% after eight years among immigrants and the descendants of immigrants.

As regards descendants, there is nothing to suggest that they should not end up with as good an education as the population as a whole (Hummelgaard *et al.*). Among the 20-24-year-olds there are more descendants of immigrants without qualifications than among the entire population. The opposite, however, is the case for the 30-34-year-olds. This study also shows that there are relatively more descendants of immigrants in the process of completing a course of further education than among the population as a whole. Conversely, there are relatively more among the native population who have taken or who are taking a vocational education.

Table 4.7: The percentage of a year starting an upper secondary education, a two-year course leading to a Higher Preparatory Examination, or an adult upper-secondary level course as of 1 October 1980, 1990 and 1997, grouped by immigrants or descendants of immigrants from selected countries.[1]

	Men			Women			All		
	1980	*1990*	*1997*	*1980*	*1990*	*1997*	*1980*	*1990*	*1997*
	--*Frequency*---								
Total, immigrants and descendants	**25.4**	**29.7**	**26.0**	**33.8**	**30.0**	**38.4**	**29.3**	**29.8**	**32.1**
Of which:									
Turkey	1.9	10.5	15.4	0.0	14.1	28.0	1.1	12.5	21.7
Former Yugoslavia	13.2	17.9	16.1	13.0	19.9	28.4	13.3	18.5	22.2
Vietnam	11.1	38.1	27.3	3.8	37.3	42.0	9.2	37.7	33.7
Poland	26.4	51.3	48.8	91.3	68.3	58.1	55.9	59.4	54.7
Iran	..	58.7	52.5	..	71.8	79.3	..	63.3	65.3
Iraq	...	16.7	16.0	...	24.4	51.3	...	21.2	31.8
Pakistan	15.7	33.0	37.6	12.0	32.3	40.9	14.4	32.9	39.4
Entire population	29.4	32.0	32.2	44.5	50.0	55.0	37.0	41.0	43.6

Notes: The figures can be compared, for example, with those in Table 11, page 27 in Statistics Denmark's *Statistical News, Education and culture*, 1997:3. '..' Available information is not conclusive. '...' Data not available.

1. The percentage in the table presents the total of the percentages of the 16, 17, 18-year-olds, etc., up to and including those 39-year-olds starting on such a course of education. The percentage can, therefore, theoretically be above 100%.

Source: Special query at Statistics Denmark and Statistics Denmark, *Statistical News, Education and culture*, 1992:3.4

The Rockwool Foundation Research Unit has asked Statistics Denmark to carry out a special query run on their computers to ascertain how large a percentage of any particular year of young immigrants and descendants of immigrants starts an upper secondary education or prepare for a Higher Preparatory Examination in the years 1980, 1990 and 1997. The results are shown in Table 4.7.

Since 1980 there has been an increase in the percentage of the population as a whole starting an upper secondary education. The period has also seen an increasing percentage for immigrants and descendants, but not as high as that for the entire population. This applies to both men and women. As can also be deduced from the table, the percentage for immigrants and descendants together for all the years is less than for the population as a whole. In

1997, the percentage was thus 43.6% for the entire population against 32.1% for immigrants and descendants. As will also appear, there are rather big differences between immigrants and descendants from different countries. For example, Iranians are the group of whom most start on a course of higher education in 1990 and 1997, e.g. more than 65% in 1997, which is significantly higher than for the population as a whole. The percentage for immigrants and descendants from Poland is also rather high, i.e. almost 55% in 1997. The lowest share for all the years is that for immigrants and descendants from Turkey, just as that for immigrants and descendants from former Yugoslavia is generally relatively low. Finally, it is worth noting that since 1980 a heavily increasing share of immigrants and descendants from Pakistan has started an upper secondary education, i.e. from 14.4% in 1980 to 39.4% in 1997.

In a Dutch survey, Kee (1994) analyzed the importance of an education gained in their native countries for how well immigrants succeed in the labour market, and compared this with how well they did in courses of education taken in Holland. The result of this survey showed that immigrants were much more successful if they had taken courses of education or training in Holland. Unfortunately, the type of survey carried out by Kee requires a level of knowledge about educational standards in immigrants' native countries that is not currently available in Denmark. A closer study of the correlation between the educational status of immigrants and their affiliation to the labour market must therefore await the results of new research.

In an analysis of the socio-economic consequences of immigration, Christensen (1998) points out that one of the possible explanations for the higher levels of unemployment among foreign nationals could be that many refugees and immigrants lack financial incentives to find a job. The combination of cash benefits and supplementary benefits means, for example, that a married couple with three children, living in rented accommodation and both receiving cash benefits, would basically gain nothing, from a purely financial point of view, if one of them took an unskilled job paid at DKK 180,000 (EURO 24,200) a year, as cash benefits, free childcare and rent support benefits would be cut in line with earned income.

It is perhaps worth noting that the higher rate of unemployment and the lower participation rate are significant reasons why more than 75% of immigrants from the less developed countries in 1996 received transfer income in the form of unemployment benefit, sick pay, maternity pay, cash benefits, early retirement pensions, old age pensions, etc. By comparison, just over 50% of Danes and immigrants from the more developed countries received transfers the same year. Immigrants from the less developed countries receive on average a larger amount in transfers than the population as a whole, which is mainly due to their receiving such benefits for longer periods than Danes (Statistics Denmark, 1998c).

Table 4.8: Employed wage earners as of 1 January 1997, percent.

	Immigrants from the less developed countries	Denmark
Top management and top-paid salaried employees	8.0%	15.0%
Salaried employees at a medium level	6.6%	16.0%
Salaried employees at a basic level	40.0%	48.0%
Other wage earners	45.4%	20.9%
Total	100.0%	100.0%

Source: Statistics Denmark (1998c: 52).

Women have a higher rate of unemployment than men.[16] This applies to all countries and groups of countries, with the exception of the Nordic and EU countries. In 1993 and 1994, for example, unemployment among Pakistani and Turkish women was in excess of 60%, as opposed to 45% for men from both countries. For women from the EU and Nordic countries, unemployment was lower than for men every year except 1985, 1986 and 1997.

The relatively pessimistic picture that emerges from this statistical review of the level of integration of immigrants in the Danish labour market in the period 1981-97 does however have positive aspects. For example, one of the main political goals concerning the labour market – that of encouraging the growth of new, small companies – has been tackled with a much better degree of success by immigrants than the rest of the population, inasmuch as it is often immigrants from the less developed countries rather than those from the more developed countries or Danes who start their own businesses. As of 1 January 1997 over 16% of immigrants from the less developed countries who were in employment were self-employed, compared with 10% and 8% of immigrants from the more developed countries and Danes respectively. Immigrants from the less developed countries are to be found as self-employed within commerce and the hotel and catering trades, where all of 70.8% of the self-employed have placed their businesses, compared with just 17.3% of self-employed Danes (Statistics Denmark, 1998c).

The socio-economic status of immigrants from the less developed countries who actually do become wage earners is slightly weaker than that of Danes, but without the situation in any way being an expression of a proletarianization of this group of the population (see Table 4.8).

In conclusion, it can be said of the development in the affiliation of immigrants to the labour market that when the first guest workers came to the country in the 1960s they enjoyed a higher participation rate than Danes. Un-

16. Cf. Statistics Denmark, *Statistical News, Labour Market 1983-1998* and *Statistics Denmark, Statistical News, Unemployment 1981-1983.*

employment was not a problem at that time. This pattern changed in the 1970s. Though their participation rate remained high, the rate of unemployment among immigrants began to increase more rapidly than that of Danes. This situation deteriorated still further in the 1980s, which to begin with had a relatively high participation rate but which gradually fell during the course of the decade. At the same time, rates of unemployment among immigrants increased, which was due to a changed pattern of immigration, with larger numbers of refugees and a significant element of family reunification.

As regards the level of education of immigrants and its importance for their integration into the labour market, it is difficult to reach many conclusions before further research has shed new light in this area. Norwegian studies appear to indicate that the level of education among immigrants is low er than that found among the rest of the population. Furthermore, a Dutch study has shown that courses of education taken in Holland were more likely to improve the chances of finding employment that an education taken in the immigrant's native country. Since 1980, the proportion of places in vocational courses in Denmark held by immigrants and descendants of immigrants has increased, while their share of further and higher educational places has fallen.

One important political goal – increasing the number of self-employed – has been an especially successful area for immigrants from the less developed countries. No less than 16% of all working immigrants are self-employed, compared with just 8% of Danes in work. Recent Danish research appears to draw the conclusion that there is no noticeable difference in the educational qualifications of descendants of immigrants and the population as a whole.

4.4 Summary

Immigration into Denmark since 1960 began as a form of manpower migration from Turkey, former Yugoslavia and Pakistan. With the onset of the oil crisis in autumn of 1973 the Danish government decided to implement a freeze on this labour-based migration. This move did not, however, slow down the rate of immigration. Instead, immigration took on a different composition on the grounds of family reunification and refugees. During the 1970s the first guest workers began to receive permanent work and residence permits, and went on to bring their families to Denmark. This process of family reunification (both reunification of existing families and the formation of new ones) continued throughout the 1980s and 1990s. In the mid-1980s immigration began to be very much influenced by an influx of refugees, mainly due to the Iran-Iraq war, but also by stateless Palestinians and Tamils from Sri Lanka. The civil war in former Yugoslavia brought the refugees of the 1990s. Indeed, the number of refugees from former Yugoslavia constitutes approximately 20% of all the refugees accepted by Denmark since 1956.

During the 1960s, immigrants were mostly men who came to work. But with the advent of family reunification and refugees, a more even balance between the sexes was achieved. Immigrants are, generally speaking, somewhat younger than the population as a whole.

From 1960 to 1984 Denmark accepted an average of 1,000 refugees a year. This figure increased more than fivefold during the period 1985-89. During the 1990s Denmark has accepted four to five times as many refugees a year as during the period 1960-84. The increasing number of refugees during the 1980s was not a phenomenon restricted to Denmark, but reflected a general increase in the number of refugees on a global scale. However, at the same time the Danish Parliament introduced a new Aliens Act (1983) that was seen by many as being very liberal. The number of spontaneous refugees also increased dramatically during the years 1984-86, which led to a huge administrative burden on those authorities charged with processing the many applications for asylum. Restrictive amendments were therefore introduced to the Aliens Act, both in 1985 and 1986, and these led to a fall in the number of asylum-seekers in subsequent years. Later, further restrictive amendments were made to the aliens legislation, among other reasons, to limit the time it takes to process applications and to combat of pro forma marriages.

The regulations governing family reunification were not affected by the 1973 immigration freeze. Apart from 1995, family reunification has represented the largest percentage of all notified residence permits during the period 1988-97. The exception in 1995 was due to the granting of permanent residence permits to more than 16,000 refugees from former Yugoslavia. If one takes all married immigrants who have successfully applied for family reunification, more than 44% of them have done so to form a new family, i.e. to bring a spouse to Denmark. Among married Turkish immigrants, the regulations governing family reunification have been used by more than half (50.9%) of them to form new families; the percentages for married Jordanians and Pakistanis are even higher – 61.4% and 59.7% respectively.

During the 1960s, when the first guest workers arrived in the country, they had a higher labour force participation rate than Danes. At that time unemployment was not a problem either for immigrants or Danes. This pattern, however, changed in the 1970s as the recession deepened. The participation rate among immigrants remained high, but unemployment began to rise more among immigrants than among Danes. Conditions deteriorated still further in the 1980s, which in the early years still witnessed a relatively high participation rate among immigrants. But during the course of the decade their participation rate continued to fall. At the same time the rate of unemployment rose still further. This can be explained partly by the change in the pattern of immigration, which now saw more refugees and higher levels of family reunification, and partly by fundamental structural changes in the entire economy, which brought in its wake an increased demand for highly qualified labour. The demand for people who can take low-paid jobs, an area previously dominated by immigrants, has therefore been reduced significantly.

One important political goal – increasing the number of self-employed — has been an especially successful area for immigrants from the less developed countries. No less than 16% of all working immigrants are self-employed, compared with just 8% of Danes in work. Recent research appears to draw the conclusion that there is no noticeable difference in the educational quali-fications of descendants of immigrants and that of the population as a whole.

All in all, the period under analysis saw during its first decade, the 1960s, guest workers come to Denmark looking for work. Immigration continued despite a freeze implemented in 1973 and various restrictive amendments made to the Aliens Act in the following years. What might have been seen as an expected improvement in the level of integration of immigrants due to the policies followed by successive governments and a period of relative pro-sperity has been undermined by a renewed round of immigration in the form of family reunification and refugees. However, a wider and better knowledge of the correlation between the integration of immigrants into society and their involvement in the labour market must await the findings of new research.

References

Act no. 473 of 1 July (1998). *Lov om ændring af udlændingeloven og straffeloven*. Copen-hagen.

Andersen, K. (1979). *Gæstearbejder — Udlænding — Indvandrer — Dansker. Migration til Danmark i 1968-78*.

Blom, S. and Ritland, A.A. (1997). 'Trang økonomi, men færre enn antatt opplever diskriminering'. In *Samfundsspeilet*, 1/97.

Christensen, L. (1998). 'Immigration, arbejdsmarkedet og de offentlige finanser i Dan-mark'. In *Indvandringens økonomiske konsekvenser i Skandinavien*. Esbjerg.

Christensen, L.B., N.H. Christensen, G. Homann, L. Johannesen, E.B. Jørgensen, K.U. Kjær, M. Kjærum, N. Lassen, J. Vedsted-Hansen, (1995). *Udlændingeret*. Copenhagen.

Danish Immigration Service, *Årsberetning 1998*, Copenhagen, 1998.

Danish Refugee Council (1996). *Flygtninge tal. Statistik om asylsøgere og flygtninge i Danmark og Verden*. Copenhagen.

Danish Social Science Research Council (SSF) (1983). *Indvandrerforskning i Danmark. Rapport fra udvalget vedrørende indvandrerforskning*. Copenhagen.

Hansen, H. and Hultin, M.L. (1997). *Aktuelle og potentielle modtagere af velfærdsydelser med hovedvægt på boligstøtten 1987-1992*. Copenhagen.

Hansen, Sv. Aa (1983). *Økonomisk vækst i Danmark. Bind II: 1914-1983*. Copenhagen.

Hummelgaard, H., L. Husted, A. Holm, M. Baadsgaard and B. Olrik (1995). *Etniske mi-noriteter, integration og mobilitet*. Copenhagen.

Jensen, H. (1998). 'Hvad er det for en skole?! Midlertidighed og bosniske børns skolegang'. In J. Schwartz (ed.), *Et midlertidigt liv: Bosniske flygtninge i de nordiske lande*. Nordisk Ministerråd.

Jeppesen, K.J. (1989). *Unge indvandrere — En undersøgelse af andengeneration fra*

Jugoslavien, Tyrkiet og Pakistan. National Institute of Social Research, report no. 89:6. Copenhagen.

Kee, P. (1994). Native-immigrant employment differentials in The Netherlands: the role of assimilation and discrimination. In *International Review of Applied Economics*, vol. 8, no. 2, 1994.

Kjær, K.U. (1995). Historik: 'Oversigt over udviklingen i den danske asylprocedure', kapitel 10 in L.B. Christensen et al., *Udlændingeret.* Copenhagen.

Ministry of the Interior (1996). *Statistik om udlændinge 1994,* Copenhagen.

Ministry of the Interior (1996). *Udlændinge '96. En talmæssig belysning af udlændinge i Danmark.* Copenhagen.

Ministry of Labour (1971). *Betænkning om udenlandske arbejderes forhold i Danmark,* White Paper, no. 589. Copenhagen.

Langlouis, H. and C. Tornøe (1993). *Udlændingeloven.* Copenhagen.

Lundh, C. and R. Ohlsson (1994). *Från arbetskraftsimport till flyktinginvandring.* Stockholm.

Matthiessen, P. Chr. (1998). *Befolkning og samfund.* Copenhagen.

Pedersen, L. (1991). *Indvandrere og deres efterkommere i Danmark.* Danmarks Statistik, Statistiske undersøgelser, nr. 43. Copenhagen.

Pedersen, P.J. and S. Pedersen (1998). 'Arbejdsmarkedspolitik, arbejdsløshed og beskæftigelsesopsving'. In N. Smith (ed.), *Arbejde, incitamenter og ledighed,* Aarhus.

Statistics Denmark (1961). *Statistisk årbog 1961.* Copenhagen.

Statistics Denmark (1982). *Statistisk årbog 1982.* Copenhagen.

Statistics Denmark (1997). *Statistisk årbog 1996.* Copenhagen.

Statistics Denmark (1985). *Befolkningens bevægelser 1983.* Copenhagen.

Statistics Denmark (1996). *Befolkningens bevægelser 1994.* Copenhagen.

Statistics Denmark (1997a). *Befolkningens bevægelser 1995.* Copenhagen.

Statistics Denmark (1983-98). *Statistiske Efterretninger, Arbejdsmarked.* Copenhagen.

Statistics Denmark (1997). *Statistiske Efterretninger, Uddannelse og kultur 1997:3.* Copenhagen.

Statistics Denmark (1981-83). *Statistiske Meddelelser, Arbejdsløsheden.* Copenhagen.

Statistics Denmark (1996). *Statistiske Efterretninger. Population and elections 1996:11.* Copenhagen.

Statistics Denmark (1997b). *Statistiske Efterretninger. Population and elections 1997:8.* Copenhagen.

Statistics Denmark (1997). *Statistiske Efterretninger. Befolkning og valg 1997:16.* Copenhagen.

Statistics Denmark (1998a). *Statistiske Efterretninger. Befolkning og valg 1998:5.* Copenhagen.

Statistics Denmark (1998b). *Statistiske Efterretninger. Befolkning og valg 1998:11.* Copenhagen.

Statistics Denmark (1998c). *Indvandrere i Danmark.* Copenhagen.

Statistics Denmark (1998). *Nyt fra Danmarks Statistik nr. 46 1998.* Copenhagen.

Statistics Denmark (1998). *Statistisk tiårsoversigt 1998.* Copenhagen.

University of Copenhagen (1998). *Indvandrere i det danske uddannelsessystem — en deskriptiv analyse af perioden 1980-1994.* Copenhagen.

Vedsted-Hansen, J. (1997). 'Forsørgelseskrav i familiesammenføringssager'. *Juristen,* no. 10.

CHAPTER 5

Thirty years of press debate on 'the foreigners' in Denmark

Part I: Migrant and guest workers, 1963-80

Bent Jensen

5.1 Introduction

Søren Pedersen's contribution to this book gives a detailed description of the number of foreigners who came to Denmark from the beginning of the 1960s to the present day, their legal basis for entry, their attachment to the labour market and many other factors connected with these migrations. This and the following chapter will discuss the popular view of these 'foreigners' in some of the major Danish dailies: How did the debate on this increasingly visible element in Danes' everyday life — at least in some parts of the country — develop? And how did the political comments in the press change in the period from the mid-1960s to the mid-1990s as the nature of immigration changed? This chapter deals with the debate on labour force migrations in the 1960s and 1970s, while the next chapter discusses the debate from the beginning of the 1980s.

5.2 Choice of newspapers

Generally speaking, the newspapers selected for the study reflect as far as possible the main viewpoints of the entire political spectrum over the past 40 years. While it is true that, in the 1960s and 1970s, most Danish newspapers abandoned their traditional status as party newspapers in favour of a more non-partisan status, editorial traditions, and thus also general ideological directions, still make the choice of newspaper on the basis of political affiliation relevant.

The four old parties — the Conservative (K), the Liberal (V) (in Danish Venstre)[1], Social-Liberal (R) and Social Democratic (S) parties — each had their

---

1. The Danish political party 'Venstre' is often called the 'Liberal' party in English, but their views should not be confused with those of the modern British Liberal-Democrat Party. The Danish party is on the right wing politically, standing for classical Liberal principles and agricultural interests.

own nationwide network of papers, while the fifth big party in this period, the Socialist People's Party, failed to establish a viable paper, much less an actual press (the most the party managed was to sustain the *minavisen/ Socialistisk Dagblad* (Socialist Daily) between 1970 and 1982).

The biggest national papers from the Conservative, Social-Liberal and Social Democratic press respectively have been chosen for this analysis: *Berlingske Tidende* (independent Conservative), *Politiken* (Social-Liberal/independent social liberal) and *Aktuelt* (Social Democratic). Since the Liberal party hasn't been permanently represented by a fully national paper since 1905, we have chosen the Liberal-affiliated provincial newspaper which has had the biggest impact on the debate in the period: *Vestkysten*. *Jyllands-Posten* is also included as the (often) leading mouthpiece of the ideological right, and, in addition, *Information* (independent), which, since 1945, has often broken new ground and generally taken a leading part in the public debate on principles. Finally, *Ekstra Bladet* has also been selected as a representative of the tabloid press, since this type of newspaper must also be included in order to get a complete picture of how the public's image of foreigners was shaped via the 'fourth estate' (see appendix 5.1 for a further description of these papers, which has been written with the assistance of Jette Drachmann Søllinge, press historian).

5.3 The opening debate: Economic boom and labour shortages

Towards the end of the 1950s, somewhat delayed, the long economic boom which all western countries were experiencing in this period finally came to Denmark. From being relatively high during the early post-war years, unemployment had fallen to historically low levels by the beginning of the 1960s. Since practically all the remaining unemployment could be considered as either seasonal or caused by job changes, in reality there was now full employment, the result of which was a wage-price spiral. Consumption took off and the balance of payments was in chronic deficit for most of the rest of the 1960s.

The Social Democratic/Social-Liberal government which came to power in 1962 under Jens Otto Krag (S) was quick to consider how such a situation — which, though not unfavourable, clearly demanded swift and firm action — could be resolved. The government was especially concerned about looming labour shortages in the crucial export industries. Among the initiatives taken in the early 1960s to slow consumption and take the steam out of economic activity was the so-called 'construction stop' and the introduction of purchase tax in 1962. But perhaps the pressure could also be eased by the addition of extra labour in the form of foreign workers?

In the 1950s, stories about 'foreigners' in the Danish press concerned refugees from the communist countries of Eastern Europe, mostly Hungarian refugees in 1956/57, but occasionally also groups of Russian, and especially Polish, defectors. It was therefore something of a volte-face on foreigners that Erik Eriksen, the former Liberal prime minister, speaking about the situation in the construction industry at a meeting in December 1963, said:

(...) here too we must tread the path of liberty. Personally, I would think that, if the construction industry cannot find the labour it needs at home, then the obvious solution would be to import it from abroad.[2]

Reports of labour shortages continued throughout spring 1964, which must have kept Eriksen's remarks in people's minds — including in government circles.[3] On June 29 1964, Hilmar Baunsgaard (R), the Minister of Trade, kicked off the debate in earnest with an article in *Aktuelt* headlined: 'Foreign labour?' This was probably nothing more than a political feeler put out to assess the mood of union members in a trade union movement that had traditionally been relatively hostile to foreign workers:[4]

All the indications are that Denmark will have a labour problem for a long time to come. There are two ways of solving this — either by limiting production and work to the productive capacity of existing manpower or by obtaining extra manpower. If we choose the latter, we can stabilize growth at a higher level than by choosing the former. To the extent we cover our need for more labour by importing foreign workers, we create higher economic activity and higher production. Other countries, e.g. Sweden, Switzerland and Germany, have created higher growth and welfare for themselves by this means. Denmark has now reached the point where we also have to include this option in our considerations.

That Baunsgaard had hit home became clear the same evening, in an interview with Kjeld Philip (R), the Minister of Economic Affairs, in *Berlingske Aftenavis* (Berlingske evening paper). Philip, though broadly in agreement, was more cautious than his cabinet and party colleague:

2. Quoted from Avisårbogen 1963 (The Danish parallel to 'Keesing's Contemporary Archives').
3. In June 1964, in response to the increasing shortage of labour, the government decided to increase the labour force by stopping military (re)call-ups and speeding up air force demobilization. Other initiatives included a recommendation to municipalities to postpone repair and maintenance work. The situation *was* taken extremely seriously.
4. For trade unions and workers' attitudes to Swedish workers who immigrated to Denmark in the second half of the nineteenth century and Polish workers who came from the end of the nineteenth century up to 1930, see Willerslev (1983) and Nellemann (1981). As a rule, leading social democrats tried to show solidarity with the foreign workers, while the man on the factory floor was more reserved.

I agree with the Minister of Trade that we should seriously consider the possibility of foreign labour. Getting construction and investment started again would make us all richer. However, I do not feel we should rush into things. Even if we opened the doors today, it would hardly be likely to lead to much immigration in the coming months. The employment situation is too tight all over Europe for that (*Berlingske Aftenavis*, June 29 1964).

In a freelance article in *Politiken* the following day, Harald R. Martinsen[5] cited a number of West European countries that had had extremely good experiences with the use of foreign workers. Denmark, he observed, hadn't even taken the smallest step. The trade unions were directly opposed, and neither the government, employers nor the press had examined the possibility, even though it stared them in the face. Martinsen mentioned Switzerland, 'where immigration has played a clear and convincing role in ensuring steady and continuous economic growth'. Danish workers had nothing to fear from foreigners who, on the contrary, had turned 'the Swiss worker into a specialist, foreman, the man who drives the tractor — while the foreigner does the more physically demanding work'. And he echoed the view which, at this time, was prevalent in Western Europe:

As regards recession, the Swiss feel very reassured about the presence of foreigners. They can always send them home before unemployment hits the Swiss themselves. This is perhaps a cynical way of thinking, but it is nonetheless rational (*Politiken*, June 30 1964).

Aktuelt returned to the topic on the same day in interviews with leading unionists. Viggo Wivel, general secretary of DASF (the Danish General Union of Unskilled and Semi-skilled Labourers),[6] observed in a comment that the situation was hardly so serious that it warranted an infusion of foreign labour — besides, who could say how long the good times would last? — and Edith Olsen, Kvindeligt Arbejderforbund (Women Workers' union in Denmark), was directly opposed. Hans Rasmussen, general secretary of the Smiths' Union, also had strong reservations, because he didn't believe there were enough unemployed workers in Europe: 'There's only Spain, Greece or Turkey. These are people with a completely different way of life — and where are they supposed to live?' But the smiths' strong man could at least suggest alter-

5. Harald R. Martinsen, 1900-81, a journalist at *Politiken* in the 1920s and now, among other things, publisher of '*Martinsens Informationsbreve*' (Martinsen's Newsletter) (from 1939). In 1973, he co-authored (together with Christian Estrup) the book 'Fremmedarbejderne som faktor i dansk økonomi' (Migrant workers as a factor in the Danish economy).

6. In 1973, the union changed its name to *Specialarbejderforbundet i Danmark (SID)* (The Danish General Union of Semi-skilled Workers).

natives in Denmark, Danish housewives in particular. Furthermore, he pointed out, firms should use a larger part of their profits on investments in labour-saving technology rather than paying big dividends. But Rasmussen had nothing against contacts with foreigners as such; it furthered international understanding. Like the unions, Kaj Bundvad (S), Minister of Social Affairs and acting Minister of Labour, was sceptical and, according to reports in *Aktuelt*, claimed that the labour market was already sufficiently liberalized.[7]

In *Ekstra Bladet*, the issue was commented on in a leader on June 30 1964. Although the paper wasn't directly opposed in principle, in practice the editor did not believe that the Danish labour market could attract enough foreign workers. The labour shortage would therefore have to be solved at home, e.g. by easing the rules for joint taxation of married couples, which made it economically unattractive for married women to work. The debate also provoked a number of readers letters, one of which had the following comment: 'I read the following headline — "Skilled foreign workers are welcome" — with horror'. The reader justified the outrage by the housing shortage in the 1960s:

If the rumours are true, flats and homes are being found for both foreign workers and refugees, but I fail to understand how the government can even think of making the housing problem worse. For the homeless, this is adding insult to injury.

There were also leaders about foreign workers in *Information* — June 30 and July 1 1964 — and, like *Aktuelt* and *Ekstra Bladet*, reactions here were negative too. What the country needed most was investments in labour-saving machines and incentive pay systems.[8] An article by Professor Jørgen Gelting (D.Sc. (Econ)) also failed to endorse the idea. Gelting remarked instead on un-exploited reserves of labour in Greenland (a Danish protectorate).

7. Statute no. 224, June 6 1952 on foreigners' entry to Denmark constituted the then current legal basis for the possibilities of foreigners to live and work in Denmark. In accordance with the law, it was the Minister of Justice who decided the procedure for considering applications for residence and work permits. There was a different procedure for Nordic citizens, however, an agreement from 1954 having established a common Scandinavian labour market, cf. Søren Pedersen (1999). Sweden had already in 1943 given citizens from the other Nordic countries the right to work in the country without a work permit, cf. Karen Andersen, 1979, p. 9.

8. 'What an idea! Incentive pay systems can give 10-20% higher production without the need for more labour' (*Information*, July 1 1964). This figure was based on information from Verner Smith, LO's (Danish Confederation of Trade Unions) time studies expert. Since the early 1950s, the trade union movement had actively supported the rationalization of Danish industry, including work/time studies (Henrik S. Nissen, 1991, p. 45), while various Social Democratic governments had introduced tax policies favourable to technological innovation in Danish industry.

Berlingske Tidende in many ways was just as dubious about Baunsgaard's feeler. On July 1 1964, the paper printed Hans Rasmussen's (general secretary of the Smiths' Union) views on the proposal's lack of realism, which were repeated in a leader the following day, despite the fact that, in principle, the paper was a firm supporter of a liberalized labour market. A few days later, the paper observed that:

If you want foreign labour today, then, in reality, you have to go outside Europe, and much of what is available is unskilled, where the only possibilities for employment are in the coal mining and iron industries.

In some countries, e.g. Belgium, there had also been considerable adjustment difficulties. A report from Switzerland the next day was also equivocal. While these foreigners — 'migrant workers or guest workers, as they tend to be called today' — had undeniably contributed to increased wealth, there were signs of lower productivity and a decline in traditional Swiss quality. In addition, there were problems with migrant ghettos and a dichotomous labour market, in which foreigners were given the worst and most dangerous jobs. Finally, Italian workers in particular were migratory workers, who went where the best paid jobs were to be found. In this way, even guest workers could create inflation.

An article in *Jyllands-Posten* on July 1 1964 discussed the seriousness of the labour situation in more general terms, and reported the start of a debate on the use of foreign labour. According to the article, the debate was part of the political manoeuvrings between the coalition parties, with social democratic ministers supporting the idea and the Social Democratic party, and especially the unions, being more reserved. Responding to, for example, Kaj Bundvad's and some trade unionists' arguments that the Aliens Act was already flexible enough, the paper pointed out that, on the contrary, the unemployment insurance funds were too slow in answering requests for work permits forwarded by the Aliens Authorities. Put another way: A liberalisation was needed!

Vestkysten took the issue up in an article on June 30 1964, which was otherwise about the acute labour shortage in the slaughterhouses, and in a leader on July 1 which described the proposal as a Social-Liberal attempt to cover up the government's lack of control over the economy. The leader drew attention to union reservations and confirmed that there was little possibility of finding large numbers of foreign workers at the moment. The two sides of industry would therefore have to concentrate on breaking down rigid demarcation lines instead, while the government needed to introduce policies designed to control costs which didn't worsen the export industries' competitiveness further. The paper rounded off on July 2 1964 with the announcement of a new estimate for work permits for foreigners from countries outside

Scandinavia. The first Italians had entered the country, albeit in modest numbers, only 337 permits being issued to this nationality.[9]

5.4 The pork glut in 1965: A job for Spanish workers?

The chapter by Søren Pedersen shows that much immigrant labour in the 1960s from so-called third countries,[10] i.e. primarily Yugoslavs and Turks and, around 1970, also Pakistanis, was spontaneous.[11] Trade organizations or large firms did, however, make some attempts to recruit foreigners systematically. In 1965, workers were needed to help with an overflow of pork at the slaughterhouses, and this attempt to hire foreigners was followed closely in the press, even though the plans came to nothing, both because of developments in the industry itself and due to the introduction of various emergency measures, e.g. the sale of cheap pork to Folkekirkens Nødhjælp (DanChurchAid).

On July 24 1965, *Aktuelt* revealed that the slaughterhouse workers' union had approved a trial import of foreign labour, the industry being notoriously undermanned. A condition of their approval was that the foreign workers had to join the union and be given the same pay and working conditions as Danish workers. The president of the meat industries confirmed to the paper that this would be a temporary measure only. The article expressed doubts about the plan's feasibility, however, and a few days later the newspaper commented in a leader that:

Large numbers of foreign workers should not be brought into the country before all domestic labour reserves have been exhausted, e.g. through rationalizations and higher labour market mobility. In truth, labour shortage precipitated rationalization, while sufficient labour postponed it (*Aktuelt*, July 27 1965).

9. The Social-Liberal's leader was undismayed, however, despite widespread opposition in parts of the press and the trade union movement. An article in *Politiken* on July 31 1964 quoted Baunsgaard from a speech in which he had criticized union opposition to foreign workers. At the same time, he emphasized that the labour shortage was a long-term problem which had the biggest implications for production, and with it prosperity.

10. Defined as countries outside Scandinavia, the EU and North America.

11. For example, many years later, Dusan Jovanovic, a Serbian guest worker, told *Politiken* how he came to Denmark: 'Dusan grew up on his parent's small 24-acre farm, where they raised livestock, and produced maize, alfalfa, corn and wine. They were poor. He found work at a co-operative contracting firm and was sent to Austria for three months to learn about landscape gardening. "In the train, I met some countrymen who were on their way to jobs in Denmark. I joined in their conversation and noticed their fine clothes, and, full of dreams about getting rich, decided to go to Denmark. I wanted to earn enough to buy a small lorry and start my own haulage firm back home"' (*Politiken*, December 12 1994).

On July 27 1965, *Aktuelt* also reported a disagreement between the slaughter-houses and the union. The employers now wanted 2000 men, not the 100 which the article claimed the union had agreed to. The paper also reported that the employers would ask Erling Dinesen (S), the Minister of Labour, for clarification on the conditions for a possible import of foreign labour. Asked by *Aktuelt* for his comments on this, the minister said that:

In principle, the government's position on the question of foreign labour is that the labour market should be as free as possible. We already have a free Nordic labour market, and the question of the free movement of labour in the European labour market will be discussed in connection with a widening of co-operation between 'the 6' and 'the 7'.

Notwithstanding, Dinesen did not directly support the use of foreign labour. Migrant labour led to greatly increased costs in the form of education and training and increased housing construction, and there had been considerable problems in other countries after guest workers had sent for the rest of their family. The minister therefore found it easier, cheaper and quicker to solve the problem through rationalization and planning.

The results of the negotiations between the employers and the minister appeared in *Aktuelt* on July 29 1965. The industry had assured the minister that only between 100 and 200 Spaniards were involved, and that they would have the same pay and working conditions as Danish workers. Under these conditions, the minister could see little problem in granting residence and work permits. He would therefore inform the Minister of Justice, and the labour minister would help with the solution of various social problems. Frands Petersen, acting general secretary of the Danish Confederation of Trade Unions (LO), said that, though his organisation would not stand in the way of the hardest-hit sectors, it didn't mean that LO would let foreign workers jump the queue for housing: 'We can't spare housing for migrant labour, so the only solution is to accommodate them in some kind of camp'.

In *Politiken*'s coverage of the plan, the paper stressed the fact that there actually was wide agreement between the employers and the slaughterhouse workers' union, and that the slaughterhouses were indeed prepared to limit the initial introduction of foreign labour to those places where the need was greatest. On July 29 1965, it was announced that: 'The ministry has no ob-jections to the import of labour'. In its account of the negotiations, *Politiken* emphasized that the two sides were ready and willing to solve any problem that might occur, pointing out at the same time that a bigger labour force would enable production in the canning industry to be increased by 15-20%. LO's reservations were not mentioned.

Berlingske Tidende's story on July 23 1965 described how the pork surplus had grown to 21,000 tons. All storage space in Denmark being full to capacity, the industry had been forced to find cold stores in Sweden and central Germany. On July 24 1965, it was reported that the two sides of the meat industry had reached agreement that, as a temporary measure, employers could import foreign labour to help alleviate the problem. The article mentioned that, as there was insufficient labour in neighbouring countries, it would have to come from southern Europe: 'This immediately creates bigger problems, both as regards language, food habits, housing, etc., and at the same time makes it much more difficult to limit to a short period'. It was thus 'highly questionable whether the initiative would have much effect'.

This rather negative attitude, which fully reflected the paper's position the previous summer, was somewhat softened over the following days. On July 25 the paper pointed out that the industry could increase exports by 15-20% if it had more labour, and J. Jensen, the union's general secretary, was quoted as saying: 'Danish workers have no objection to the import of foreign labour', though he also added that there were problems involved with using foreign labour, of course. Jensen stressed that these workers should have the same working conditions as Danish workers.

On July 27 1965, the paper again reported that the employers and unions seemed to have reached agreement about a trial scheme. In a statement to the paper, the president of the Meat Industry's Producers' Association said:

Since Spanish workers are not as skilled as Danish slaughterhouse workers, they are likely to be given less skilled jobs, thus freeing Danish labour for the more demanding work.

However, the article ended by reiterating the labour minister's reservations. On the 29th, it was finally established that: 'The import of labour will not create problems'. According to *Berlingske Tidende*, the labour minister had guaranteed that there would be no formal obstacles to the import of foreign workers. The minister was also reported to be 'very positive about the plans'.

Vestkysten carried an article on the difficulties of the meat industry on July 23 1965, but could already report the next day: 'Spanish workers to start on pork glut'. Judging by statements by the producers' association, the Spanish workers could start arriving very soon indeed. *Vestkysten* estimated that about 2500 workers would be needed, and, like *Politiken* and *Berlingske Tidende*, thought that production could be increased by up to 20%. On the 27th, the paper revealed that: 'Turkish labour was also available'. At the same time as the negotiations were taking place in the Ministry of Labour, the Turkish government had made a request for work permits for Turkish workers. The request was passed on to the Danish Employers' Confederation (DA) for comment, whose director, Arne Lund, said that the confederation had no objection to the use of foreign labour. The article was quick to point out the effect this request would have on the domestic debate, since it had often been claimed that foreign labour was impossible to find. In fact, however, several European countries had 'long since taken in Turkish workers. Germany, for example, already has 100,000 Turks'. On September 8 1965, *Vestkysten* could report that the Spanish authorities had approved the recruitment of workers, and that hiring would begin soon.

On July 24 1965, *Jyllands-Posten* quoted the president of the Meat Industry's Producers' Association as saying that the industry had a chronic shortage of labour, and that the use of foreign workers was a possible solution. The previous day, the paper had quoted the liberal paper, *Vejle Amts Folkeblad*, as saying that Sweden, which already employed a great many foreigners, was considering letting in even more migrant workers, a proposition 'which was widely supported'. Possible reservations about the slaughterhouses' plan were mentioned on July 24 and 27 but in its subsequent coverage of the story, the paper focused on the industry's expectations regarding foreign workers, including the fact that any increase in production could be exported, spearheading what was likely to be a lasting market expansion.

The producers' association president gave an outline of the situation in an interview in *Information* on July 23 while on the 26th the paper interviewed Erling Dinesen, who referred to the considerable problems which foreign workers cause. In an interview in *Information* on July 27 1965, Thomas Nielsen, secretary of the LO, said that: 'There's no need for foreign labour'. The LO stressed once again the need for investment and further training, and pointed out that the import of foreign workers neither could nor should solve the problems. Those foreigners who did come should receive the same pay and conditions as Danish workers. The same day, the paper carried what was perhaps the first Danish interview with a guest worker, a Spanish slaughterhouse worker, who had a real success story to tell: In Spain he was paid DKK 170 per fortnight for a 14-hour day and a 6-day week, whereas in Denmark he was paid DKK 600 a week for considerably shorter hours. He also had a place to live and had met a Danish girl, and was also learning the language. He had had a friendly reception everywhere, and had joined the union.

On July 28 1965, *Information* carried an article describing the experiences of the widespread use of foreign workers in West Germany. West German recruiters and public authorities had already hired the first million workers from 'the poorest corners of Europe — Portugal, Spain, Yugoslavia, southern Italy, Greece and Turkey'. According to *Information*, foreign workers were mostly given those jobs German workers didn't want themselves. But the paper also pointed out that the foreigners also had access to the West German social system: 'A Spanish bricklayer working at Quickborn near Hamburg, who had 12 children in his home country, could collect DEM 400 a month in child support! A gang of Turkish workers on a section of the Duisburg-Düsseldorf railway received a total of DEM 1240 in child support a month ...'.

In other words, the exclusivity of the welfare state — in the sense of its benefits being reserved for the country's own citizens — was hardly likely to continue in the face of the widespread use of foreign labour. The paper also reported dissatisfaction among German workers, arising from the fact that foreign workers were often given long-term contracts, which in some cases had led to the dismissal of German workers during a recession. But the foreigners themselves also had trouble adjusting, and at work could often hear comments that they were 'dirty and lazy'. However, there were no serious social problems, such as those in large English cities at the time, nor was there any increase in crime.

Ekstra Bladet started its — likewise extensive — coverage of the possible use of foreign labour to cope with the pork glut with an article on July 22 1965, in which Erling Dinesen repeated his reservations about the plan. Niels Westerby, a MP, was also interviewed, though his views were rather different: 'we should do everything possible to bring foreign labour into the country, especially to the construction industry'.[12] The liberal politician stressed that all foreigners should be required to join a union to avoid undercutting Danish workers. Westerby, while acknowledging the fact that the impact of foreign labour should not be allowed to delay much-needed rationalizations, also insisted that there were industries which suffered from chronic labour bottle-necks, and that, here, the use of foreign labour was an obvious solution. At the same time, this use of foreign labour could dampen inflationary pressures, and thereby prevent a potential deterioration in competitiveness which, in the longer term, could lead to rising unemployment in Denmark.

On July 28 1965, *Ekstra Bladet* reported from Spain that it was a 'Good idea to send Spanish labour to Denmark'. According to the article, the Spanish workers were sober-minded, hard-working people who would probably find it easy to integrate into Danish society. On the 29th, the paper reported that negotiations in the ministry appeared to be nearing concrete results, though it would clearly be a makeshift solution, and involve only a limited number of workers. Another article on the same day gave a general account of Spanish labour migration in Europe, noting that the Spanish government would probably demand social security guarantees from the Danish government.

5.5 On a broad front: The employers wanted foreign labour

The views of the meat industry in the above debate were clear — it was obvious that the industry wanted to go even further than the political and union climate was prepared to tolerate, and, from September 1965 at least, employers

12. Niels Westerby, Member of Parliament in the period 1964-68, first as a Liberal MP and, from 1965, as a member of the newly formed Liberal Centre party.

on a broad front started arguing more forcefully for the use of foreign workers.

On September 2 1965, *Politiken* reprinted a leader from the DA's trade paper, *Arbejdsgiveren* (The Employer), which thundered that another summer of acute labour shortages had again made the situation urgent. The DA demanded an easing in the administration of the Aliens Act. The *Politiken* article ended with the following quotation from 'Arbejdsgiveren':

The crucial thing from an employer's point of view is to be able to obtain the necessary labour and utilize costly machinery. It is much easier to maintain a stable and high employment rate if, through more flexible rules for the use of foreign labour, the bottle-necks in production and employment, all too common now, can be avoided (*Politiken*, September 2 1965).

Workers again voiced their opposition, and, as before, unskilled workers were the most vociferous. At the DASF congress in September 1965, Viggo Wivel repeated the union's opposition to the use of migrant workers, which was now strengthened by the argument that winter unemployment had still not been eliminated. Before the union would even consider the use of foreign workers, therefore, employers would first have to spread the workload evenly throughout the year. The general secretary also pointed out that the foreigners could give social problems.[13] However, the main argument was as before: 'The employment of Danish workers can be pushed into the background, and we must therefore clearly signal our opposition' (*Berlingske Tidende*, September 7 1965).

Aktuelt's angle on the DASF congress was: 'Say no to mass immigration':

The mass immigration of foreign labour means that employers must guarantee foreign workers contracts of six months to a year — which is not unreasonable from the workers' point of view — which can mean layoffs if production falls, and since the foreign workers are guaranteed work for a specific period, the only workers who can be laid off are Danish ones.

The union could under no circumstances accept this 'discrimination'.

On the political front, in December 1965, the Liberal party once again entered the fray, when Henry Christensen (V) proposed a relaxation of the rules for employment of foreign labour during parliamentary negotiations on a new indirect-tax package.[14]

That the debate was now finally under way, and with the lines clearly drawn on all sides, can be seen from Avisårbogen's index for this period: In 1965 a new entry appeared: *Labour, foreign*.

13. *Berlingske Tidende*, *Politiken* and *Ekstra Bladet*, September 7 1965.
14. Cf. Avisårbogen for 1965.

5.6 The first foreign workers arrive:
The debate from 1967 up to the ban on immigration in 1970

The previous section shows that, though there had indeed been a debate on foreigners in the press from summer 1964, the discussion — despite the clear positions of politicians and industry and union organizations — was somewhat surreal: In the event, hardly any had yet arrived. This changed towards the end of the 1960s, however, as immigration picked up speed.

The arrival of greater numbers of foreigners, together with the fact that the demand for labour during a thundering economic boom was still not satisfied, probably explains why Thomas Nielsen — now general secretary of the LO — in *Aktuelt* on September 24 1967 subtly changed his previous statements. On the face of it, there was no change from July 1965: All foreigners should receive the same pay and conditions as Danish workers. This was an absolute and unchanging demand throughout the period — as it had been since the late 1890s, when Polish migrant workers flooded into the country.[15] The LO thus wanted regulations against abuse, and, under current rules, employers in areas covered by collective agreements would already be in violation of the agreement if they failed to pay foreign workers the same as Danish workers.

Under these conditions, however, Thomas Nielsen was more open to the possibility of labour migration than previously: 'I see nothing wrong in Danish workers going abroad for further training or other reasons, and, by the same token, I see nothing wrong in foreign labour coming to Denmark'.[16]

Ekstra Bladet enlarged on this in a leader the following day, though in another tone to begin with:

Foreign labour is clearly unpopular in Denmark — among wage earners at least. People can put up with workers from other Nordic countries coming to Denmark, which they have a perfect right to do under the terms of the Nordic common labour market. But there is little enthusiasm for those who come from further afield — e.g. Germany or Italy[17] (*Ekstra Bladet*, September 25 1967).

Ekstra Bladet adopted Thomas Nielsen's standpoint, however. Some migration could therefore be allowed, on condition that everybody received the same pay and conditions. The leader thus called for a revision of legislation to 'prevent foreigners acting as scabs. And the relevant bodies in the labour market

15. In the 1880s, when the union movement was facing an influx of Swedish labour, the demand had been that jobs — at least in public works — should be reserved for Danish workers.
16. *Aktuelt*'s, *Ekstra Bladet*'s and, in some cases, also *Politiken*'s coverage of foreign workers in the period 1967-70 has been analyzed by Jørgen Würtz Sørensen (1988a). Some of his results have been incorporated in the present account.
17. Quoted from the above-mentioned analysis.

could do this themselves'. By this means, the issue could also be taken out of politicians' hands and the usual Danish tedious bureaucracy reduced.

As mentioned above, the LO had implied that there were already large numbers of migrant workers in the country, which was confirmed in an article in *Ekstra Bladet* later that autumn, which disclosed that, according to the Aliens Authorities, Denmark had become a magnet for migrant workers. An employee at the Aliens Authorities was quoted as saying:

> So popular unfortunately that, in some cases, foreigners think that the streets are paved with gold and that jobs grow on trees. This is far from the case, and Danish workers are getting fed up with foreigners skipping the country after they have worked here a year and have to start paying tax (*Ekstra Bladet*, October 21 1967).

The gist of *Ekstra Bladet*'s story was that 'incipient unemployment, fraudulent assignment of work and increasing criminality among foreigners' would induce the police to introduce tougher border controls. The fear was also that foreigners would cost the state dearly if the authorities had to pay for sending them back home.

At the same time, readers letters, especially in *Ekstra Bladet*, but also partly in *Aktuelt*, grew harsher in tone, presumably influenced by the increasing references to southern men in newspaper crime reports. One of the observers of press history in this period, Jørgen Würtz Sørensen, notes that some of these letters were not far off what has been interpreted as racism: 'Apart from unemployment, crime, the housing shortage and Danes' right to their own country, one other factor became a recurring theme in the debate from the beginning, namely foreign workers'/southern men's relation to women. This had partly to do with the fact that a lot of Danish women fell for 'southern-looking' men, and partly to do with the way they treated women, and with it their whole perception of the relationship between the sexes'.[18]

March 1968 saw the first question about foreign workers in parliament (Folketinget). It was put to Lauge Dahlgaard, the Social-Liberal labour minister, by Gunhild Due, of the Socialist People's Party (SF), who wanted social counselling to be available for foreign workers too.[19] Influenced by growing unemployment in 1968, the trade union movement, and especially DASF, were still active voices in the debate, their main concern being to ensure that immigration was regulated. According to Højsteen (1992), of all the unions, DASF was the one most affected by competition for jobs and which pushed the hardest for an administrative tightening of work permit regulations, in which they actually succeeded in May 1969, cf. Søren Pedersen (1999). In 1968,

18. Jørgen Würtz Sørensen, 1998a, p. 19.
19. Ibid., p.13.

Aktuelt also began to probe into the problem of unscrupulous Turks who swindled unsuspecting countrymen out of large sums of money and lured them to Denmark with promises of work contracts and permits.[20] It was clear that immigration now was dominated by Turkish workers.[21]

At the same time as the rules were tightened in May 1969 — e.g. foreigners suspected of seeking work were turned away at the border, even if they had money both to support themselves and for a return ticket[22] — a more general debate flared up after the first violent confrontation between Danes and foreign workers. Confrontation is perhaps too strong a word; it was an unmotivated attack by some rockers on a house where a group of Turks were living.

Würtz Sørensen (1988a) relates that the incident led to an outcry in the press. *Aktuelt* carried the story on May 12 1969 and again the following day on the front page, followed up by a full-page article inside: 'This is why they were beaten up: The Turks are stealing our jobs', and 'Why didn't the police intervene?'[23] (both on May 13 1969). Witnesses said they 'were shocked by apparent police passivity' at what the paper described as 'the attack by a gang of leather-jacketed bullies'. The Turks themselves were described as peaceful and much liked at their workplace. In its coverage of the case, *Berlingske Tidende* also reported the rockers' claim that 'the Turks had been bothering some girls we knew' (*Berlingske Tidende*, May 13 1969)

Like *Aktuelt*, *Information* also lambasted the police for intervening too late and, in a leader, maintained that Denmark now had a 'pariah caste' (May 17 1969). The paper also predicted an 'outbreak' of xenophobia if unemployment were to continue over a longer period. In response to the attack, *Ekstra Bladet* carried articles describing the difficult position of foreigners, with many small and non-unionized employers paying non-union rates, and landlords charging sky-high rents.

Information's leader on May 17 1969 echoed the call for a *real immigrant policy* made by *Politiken* — also in a leader — three days earlier:

20. Ibid., p. 16.
21. 'Turks are willing to work for a wage that is very low by Danish standards. They live in huts, tents, in miserable lodgings, and their living expenses are therefore ludicrously low by Danish standards. Foreigners who work for low wages are a growing problem for DASF, 40,000 of whose members are currently out of work. On principle, therefore, they now refuse to approve work permits as long as there are Danes who are unemployed', *Aktuelt*, April 2 1968, quoted here from Würtz Sørensen (1988a), p. 17.
22. If a foreigner stated that he wasn't seeking work he could still enter the country, and 'tourist' was stamped on his passport. If he later applied for a work permit, it was rejected without consideration to the employment situation, cf. Søren Pedersen, 1999.
23. Which they did the following day, locking up 10 of the 'wild angels', cf. *Aktuelt*, May 14 1969. Five more Angels were arrested, but released again.

Whereas OECD says that, for a job to go to a foreigner, it must be vacant for a month, Denmark only requires it to be vacant for a week. There can be no doubt that this particular openness gives some people in this country the distinct impression that we are more tolerant than others. But since this openness hasn't been followed up by any coherent policy on foreign workers, such easy access to the Danish labour market has ended up doing immigrants more harm than good. There is no doubt that the almost informal immigration of labour has turned Denmark into a country where migrants are guaranteed to get stuck with the worst-paid jobs, which nurtures the feelings of those who see immigrants as pariahs, and to become easy victims of housing speculators and employers who couldn't care a fig about the agreement on equal wages for Danes and foreigners (*Politiken*, May 14 1969).

The features in *Aktuelt* followed suit with a call for government regulation of immigration, based on the Swedish model.[24] Policy makers in Sweden had drawn up rules for how many foreign workers were needed and then given the job of recruitment to the Swedish consulates. It was the responsibility of the consulates, which thus functioned as recruitment offices, to check whether immigrants were guaranteed a job and accommodation, on reasonable terms, before they emigrated. In June 1969, the then Liberal/Conservative/Social-Liberal government appointed a committee under the labour minister, Lauge Dahlgaard (R), chaired by N. Elkær-Hansen, a chief county administrative officer, charged with drawing up new rules for the issuing of work permits. The committee included representatives from various ministries and the DA and LO.

In 1969, the labour shortage led to a new attempt — this time followed closely by the press — to recruit large numbers of foreign workers, namely B&W's (Burmeister & Wain, a major shipyard) employment of Yugoslav workers in July 1969. Before going ahead, B&W had both advised the Minister of Labour of its intentions and reached agreement with the LO on the terms of employment; among other things, B&W was to provide accommodation for the workers, the number of which was strictly fixed. And the Yugoslavs also had to join the union.[25]

The issue was now as topical as it had ever been, and, based on a Reuter's telegram from Belgrade, both *Berlingske Tidende* and *Information* carried almost identical articles about the Yugoslav workers on July 31 and August 1 1969 respectively. The articles revealed that there were at least 400,000 Yugoslavs in W. Europe, and that this 'brawn drain' was causing a problem in the donor country. What was interesting as far as the domestic debate was concerned was the claim that 'the majority go back home', which confirmed the common belief that the Yugoslavs and Turks only came for short periods.

Non-organized immigration accelerated up to 1970, and the unions and

24. See, for example, *Aktuelt*'s leader on June 11 1969.
25. Würtz Sørensen, 1988a, p. 36.

social democratic press dealt with many cases of poor wages and working conditions, which led to fresh calls for tighter regulations. *Ekstra Bladet* continued to cover guest workers' living conditions in articles criticizing their housing conditions, contributions describing incompatibilities between Danes and foreigners began to appear again, and the papers started writing about foreigners' social problems. Many letters to the editor now revealed a first-hand knowledge of foreigners, which, however — as Würtz Sørensen (1988a) observes — didn't necessarily mean that they were friendlier in tone. Some contributions warned against racism, several writers even fulminating that 'we Danes should be ashamed of ourselves'.

On January 1 1970, stricter rules for work permits came into effect, which meant that a work permit could no longer be granted during a stay in Denmark, cf. Søren Pedersen's chapter. Job-seekers now had to apply for a work permit at one of the Danish Representations abroad, and applications had to be accompanied by a written offer of a job from a Danish employer, together with a letter certifying that no qualified Danes could be found for the job. Permits were issued for a period of six months, but could be renewed.[26] According to Højsteen (1992), the rules were designed to create a balance between supply and demand, and also ensure that foreign workers went back home again. Despite the new rules, however, the debate rolled on, and there was a growing realization that something had to be done to ensure orderly conditions.

5.7 A stop for immigration in 1970 and 1973

On October 26 1970, *Berlingske Tidende* carried a background article on guest workers and at the same time published a Gallup poll on peoples' attitudes to them. The article quoted experts as saying that, given present population trends, 10,000 extra workers a year would be needed, and that more than 50,000 were needed at the moment. The Minister of Labour, Lauge Dahlgaard, warned that Danes would have to get used to immigration, even though he acknowledged that there was a problem with guest workers. The article emphasized that different interest groups had different views of the matter:

Symptomatically, the differences in opinion are reflected in employers' criticism of the insufficient and unqualified supply of new labour, while, on the other side, workers' views are reflected in the former Social Democratic labour minister's call for a temporary stop for immigration and his reasons for this, namely social and human considerations for foreign workers (*Berlingske Tidende*, October 26 1970).

The Gallup survey confirmed this: Many workers and — less predictably —

26. Signe Højsteen, 1992, p. 31.

an even greater number of farmers failed to see the point of importing foreign labour, while the great majority of white-collar workers and businessmen regarded foreign workers as an economic gain for the country. Overall, a majority of 46% did not think it benefited the country, 34% saw it as a gain, while 20% were undecided. Politically, only the conservative voters were overwhelmingly in favour, while a majority of the other parties' voters disapproved. On the question of whether foreigners depressed wages, workers, especially unskilled workers, were more uneasy than others.

On October 27 1970, the Social Democratic party, prompted by increasing social problems and incipient unemployment among guest workers, proposed a motion in parliament for a temporary stop for guest workers.

On precisely the same day, *Information* carried a Ritzau telegram which confirmed the rising unemployment and alleged that many employers enticed foreigners to Denmark with promises of jobs which failed to materialize once they arrived. This piece of information came from an assistant police commissioner at the Central Aliens Police, who also said that once foreign workers arrived in the country, they stayed.

Berlingske Tidende on October 27 countered some of the charges in an interview with a head of department at the DA who explained that it could take between four and ten weeks for a Turkish worker to arrive at a factory after he had been offered a job. Firms that couldn't wait that long were therefore forced to hire someone else.

Jyllands-Posten also carried a story about rising unemployment on October 27 1970, in which it was mentioned that the government was considering a proposal for further restrictions on guest workers coming to Denmark. Elkær-Hansen commented that, as a result of the regulatory system introduced on January 1 1970, guest workers were piling up in Hamburg waiting to come into the country, and 'it has cost them a lot just to get this far'. The government's solution to this was to propose that work permits only be issued in guest workers' own country, i.e. as in the Swedish arrangement.

Vestkysten carried a more detailed account of the labour minister's deliberations, which, he claimed, should 'make the temporary stop proposed by the Social Democratic party unnecessary' (October 28 1970). The idea was that employers 'could 'order' the guest workers they needed via Denmark's representatives in the countries concerned, who would co-operate with local employment services'. That foreign workers were no longer exclusively flocking to the cities, but had also settled in *Vestkysten*'s rural hinterland was evident from another article the same day about Danish lessons for Turkish guest workers at a local brickyard, which they 'followed attentively'. However, a letter to the editor in the paper the same day — 'No to foreign workers — an open letter to the Minister of Justice' — showed that some of *Vestkysten*'s readers were also against foreigners. The letter was an angry response to the minister's bill on race discrimination. In the writer's opinion:

If the bill is passed, it will be a criminal offence to do something so fundamental and necessary as to fight to preserve Denmark as an independent country with an ethnically homogeneous population, a common culture and a common religion.

The reader also claimed that an alliance of 'employers, various influential persons and leftist intellectuals' were advocating 'lifting practically all restrictions on immigrant workers', but that 'the Danish people as a whole, and working-class people affected by immigrant workers in particular' were increasingly opposed. In the reader's view, none of the political parties were aware of this opposition to guest workers, and this had resulted in a political vacuum — a claim which has since been documented by research:[27] 'At the moment, ordinary voters who want to voice their concern over this issue have no political party they can turn to'.[28]

An article in *Berlingske Tidende* on October 28 1970 — 'No reason for stop' — can also be seen as a contribution to the ongoing debate. This was an interview with professor Ernst Schellenberg, a leading German social democratic politician with an interest in social welfare, who maintained that German industry could absorb a lot more foreigners than it had up to now. He went on to say that many had settled down and brought their families to Germany. Yes, this could tax the school system and lengthen the housing list, but so far it had not led to rising unemployment. The message to Danish readers was that there were no large groups of guest workers on their way from Germany to Denmark at the moment. The same day, *Berlingske Tidende* also reported that the labour minister had announced a ceiling on the number of guest workers for the coming months. The minister reiterated, however, that in fact guest workers were an economic gain for the country. They produced for DKK 1.5 billion annually, only cost DKK 500 million in wages, and paid about DKK 150 million in taxes.

On October 28 1970, *Jyllands-Posten* reprinted a leader from the liberal newspaper *Frederiksborg Amts Avis* as a direct contribution to the debate, the paper having commented on the prospect of tighter restrictions in the following way: 'There is nothing in the job situation that warrants putting up a

27. Jørgen Goul Andersen et al. (1992, p. 171): 'It is debatable whether attitudes to immigrants affect party choice (see, for example, Tonsgaard, 1989), and it is generally accepted that attitudes to the EC do not. But in the case of political mistrust, the effect of the two sets of attitudes is just as strong as the effect of party-political polarization and right-left polarization combined'.
28. The reader perceived the bill as a general threat to freedom of speech, which was also the theme of an article by Søren Krarup in *Jyllands-Posten* on November 8 1970: 'Freedom of speech is being subjected to just such an amputation now. By means of law, the authorities are trying to deny citizens the right to harbour certain sympathies and express certain antipathies, and hereby give legal form to a particular philosophy of life'.

'No admittance' sign at the border! And this would also be a strange back-drop for an almost unanimous parliamentary resolution to apply for member-ship of the EC, whose goal is precisely to eliminate such restrictions on the free flow of labour'.

On November 5 1970, *Berlingske Tidende* quoted a just-published DASF report again deploring the lack of policy in the area. The union proposed a number of new regulations, e.g. that immigration should be limited to fewer countries, that immigrants should not make up more than 25% of any one occupational group in a firm, that work permits should only be issued in the country of origin, and that employers should keep wagebooks so that the payment of wages could be checked. The unions also stepped up demands that all guest workers should be unionized.[29]

The Social Democratic party's proposal for a temporary stop for first-time work permits came into effect on November 6 1970:

As of midnight there has been a temporary ban on all further entry of foreign labour. This is a temporary measure and is for the coming winter period only (...). The reason given for the ban is the fear of unemployment over and above normal seasonal un-employment in the coming months (*Information*, November 6 1970).

It transpired that both the DA and the LO had taken part in the negotiations at the ministry.

Berlingske Tidende stressed the fact that the DA had reservations about the initiative. However, firms with a desperate need for manpower could be granted exemption.[30] The then general secretary of DASF, Anker Jørgensen, was quoted as saying that the stop for issuing first-time work permits was a significant concession to the trade union movement and the Social Democratic

---

29. For a fuller account, see Signe Højsteen, 1992, p. 38.
30. On December 28 1970, the Ministry of Labour and the two sides of industry agreed that the following foreigners would be exempt from the ban: Foreign workers seeking work in Denmark due to a special connection to the country, e.g. Danish-born, married to a Dane, or living with a spouse, parents or children who were legally resident in Denmark. Finally, foreigners whose case would not have been submitted to the labour market authorities under previous practice, e.g. because they had a particular qualification or occupation, cf. Karen Andersen, 1979, p. 17. The same source also mentions that employers could apply for work permits for groups of 10 or more foreign workers if they were crucial for production, and that individuals could get a work permit if they had qualifications or skills which weren't available in Denmark. In addition, foreigners could get work permits for jobs that were necessary for the continued employment of a relatively large number of Danes. Applications for exemption could only be granted if suitable Danish labour or suitable foreign labour already legally resident in Denmark were unavailable.

party, and that the way was now open for the solution of guest workers' social problems.[31]

Jyllands-Posten (November 6, 1970) also saw the stop as a concession to the LO, while *Vestkysten* the same day gave ample space to Lauge Dahlgaard (R) in an interview:

The impact of foreign labour has grown to such proportions — about 1000 a month — that, with the onset of the winter season, when we know with certainty that un-employment among Danish workers will increase, we had to take some sort of action to limit the number of guest workers,

The minister also stressed that it was an administrative decision, 'which really has nothing to do with either the Social Democratic party's desire for an immediate stop to guest workers or the extensive demands made in DASF's report'. Moreover, the minister drew attention to the possibilities for exemption, which were added as a concession to industry. According to the minister, the opposition had demanded a total stop for new immigrants. The minister added that the government had secured acceptance of the initiative from the guest workers' organization.

Ekstra Bladet ran a series of articles in autumn 1970, which, among other things, attacked housing speculators who exploited guest workers and, not pulling any punches, the paper deplored what it regarded as generally racist behaviour among Danes.[32] On October 29 the paper turned to foreigners' social position: 'These people find themselves in the same situation that Danish workers found themselves in around the turn of the century. They have been let down by the government, the social authorities, the employers and the unions'. Through interviews with foreign workers, the paper de-scribed how they had usually borrowed money for the journey, that unem-ployment meant they couldn't pay this back, and that in this way they were forced to stay in Denmark. The Turks now unveiled plans to form a union of foreign workers, since 'Danish unions haven't done anything for us'. The paper's report on the entry ban under the heading 'Gate slammed shut on guest workers' on November 6 was therefore completely in accordance with the editorial spirit. The article reported that the employers had been extremely

31. Clearly, in autumn 1970, guest workers had won a prominent place in *Berlingske Tidende*'s editorial pages. Other articles from this period dealt with problems with health checks of guest workers (October 29) and swindles involving false job offers from Danish firms (November 11 and December 17).

32. See, for example, the articles 'DKK 600 deposit for a bed in a mini-ghetto' (October 27), 'Why do we treat guest workers so shoddily?' (October 29), 'Danes reveal their true colours to guest workers' (November 10), 'Making fortunes from mini-ghettos for foreigners', and 'Guest workers complain to minister over bad treatment' (November 13 1970).

critical, while Anker Jørgensen referred to the DASF report, which described the situation as chaotic. Accordingly, social democrats were determined that parliament discuss the issue in the form of a general debate on foreign workers.

The debate was held on November 10 1970 and it was reported in *Berlingske Tidende* on the day after. Here, it was emphasized that the stop in itself had not led to disagreement between the government and the opposition, but that the Social Democratic party had criticized the government for its last-minute attempts to formulate a policy in the area.

Jyllands-Posten attached equal importance to the political agreement, but stressed that the minister had declared that the 'curb' would be softened by various possibilities for exemption.

In similar vein, *Information*'s report noted that the parties' spokesmen had been satisfied with the temporary halt to immigration, which now gave politicians a good chance to sort things out. According to *Information*, Finn Christensen, the social democratic spokesman, had referred to a KFUK (YWCA) poll of guest workers in Roskilde which showed that many were leading a miserable existence at the railway station and in stairways. Palle Simonsen (K) maintained that it was becoming a problem to ensure that laws and regulations were being kept. Svend Kjær Rasmussen, of the Left-Wing Socialist Party (VS), went furthest in the criticism, accusing the government of deliberately trying to stir up racial discrimination in order to disunite wage earners.

Politiken's report complained that the debate had been too brief, but, like the other papers, emphasized the fact that all parties were otherwise in agreement. There was perhaps more focus on Finn Christensen's criticism in *Politiken*, and the left wing's criticism was also clearly reflected:

Svend Kjær Rasmussen (VS) put the blame for the problem squarely on employers' greed, while Hanne Reintoft (Communist Party) called for more regional development instead of the concentration of industry in the metropolitan area. Then fewer guest workers would be needed.

In an interview the same day, the president of the 'Yugoslav Association' regretted that the interest had come four years too late.

Vestkysten quoted Palle Simonsen as saying that, though the Conservatives regarded the ban as a sensible measure, it should not be allowed to aggravate the labour situation in industry for longer than strictly necessary. Robert Christensen (V) also found the ban correct, since it meant that conditions for the guest workers could be improved. According to the report, the Left-Wing Socialists demanded a complete stop without exemptions so as not to divide the labour movement.

On December 12 1970, *Berlingske Tidende* reported the labour minister's statement to parliament. The minister wanted guest workers to play a complementary role in the economy. On the one hand, he said, we should not import so many unskilled workers to low-wage jobs that structural adjustment, including investments in new technology, ground to a halt. But, on the other hand,

We should not allow labour shortages to continue for so long that bottlenecks become permanent and viable export industries get into difficulties. The supply of foreign labour should at all times be regulated accordingly.

Politiken and *Jyllands-Posten* adopted the same angle in their articles 'Guest workers can also be a hindrance' and 'Rationalization can be hampered by low-wage guest workers'. *Vestkysten* concurred that 'Guest workers are the most mobile', though the point here was that there 'shouldn't be unrestricted access for foreign labour, but the labour shortages shouldn't be allowed to continue either'. The paper thus made it quite clear that the trend in population probably made some continued immigration inevitable.

On December 17 1970, *Berlingske Tidende* recapitulated parliament's debate on the minister's statement. The emphasis was again on the political consensus. Finn Christensen (S) interpreted the statement as a guarantee that 'the situation prior to the stop for work permits for foreign workers will not be allowed to arise again'. Palle Simonsen accepted the goal of a balanced immigration so that structural rationalizations were not delayed. The guest worker problem should therefore be included as an important part of general labour market policy. Robert Christensen (V) adopted a positive tone: 'Denmark was lucky to have guest workers, but he stressed that it was necessary to control the numbers, that there should be a balance'. *Politiken* quoted the minister as saying that the temporary ban should be a model for fixed rules for immigration according to the needs of the labour market.

In the event, however, the temporary stop didn't do much to dampen immigration either.[33] And then there was also illegal immigration to contend with, which, according to the rumours circulating at the end of the 1960s, was considerable.[34]

In the spring of 1973, faced with a continued shortage of labour, especially in the metal industries, the DA negotiated a quota scheme with the Social Democratic government under Anker Jørgensen and with the unions. *Politiken*

33. At the time of the next ban on further immigration in 1973, there were approximately 40,000 citizens from third world countries in Denmark, cf. Togeby, 1998, p. 1140. In 1967 there had been about 10,000 officially registered third world citizens (ibid.).

34. 'It is, of course, impossible to determine the precise number of 'illegal' foreign workers, but according to sources in union and political circles at the beginning of 1968, there were about 12,000 foreign workers in Denmark without work permits' (Würtz Sørensen, 1988a, p. 13).

reported this on June 30, disclosing that, up to now, 2,000 new work permits had been granted. Only firms which belonged to an employer's organization or were bound by a collective agreement could be considered.

When the first oil crisis broke out a few months later, in autumn 1973, and market conditions took a sudden turn for the worse, the unions renewed their demands for another stop, this time made to Anker Jørgensen's government. Towards the end of November 1973, all the papers were full of alarming articles on the oil shortage. The examples are numerous, but the following front-page headlines reflect the prevailing mood quite well: 'Denmark on Arab "black list"', 'Danger of further oil cuts', 'New oil intervention imminent', and 'Thousands of Danes' jobs in danger'.

On November 24 1973, *Aktuelt* reported that oil supplies had run down faster than expected. Supplies to industry now had to be cut by 25%, and this physical constraint on production led to widespread fears of rising unemployment. In a splash article on November 25 1973, the paper wrote that 'Tens of thousands risk losing their jobs'. According to the article, the situation could quickly get out of hand, but, on November 28 1973, the paper's headlines proclaimed: 'Government saves employment: Speedy action to avoid crisis'. DASF worried that up to 20,000 of its members might become redundant in the plastics industry alone, which fully 'justified a stop for foreign workers'. It was also predicted that thousands of foreign workers already in the country risked being sent home. The article continued inside the paper: 'The oil crisis can force the repatriation of foreign workers'. According to the paper's information, an immediate stop to the import of foreign labour could be expected any day, and, in the longer term, the residence permits of established foreign workers were in danger of being revoked. The seriousness of the situation was again underlined in a front-page headline the following day: 'Shop stewards: Our worst fears are being confirmed'.

On November 30, *Aktuelt* reported an 'Immediate stop for foreign workers. In addition, foreign workers who already have a work permit will be sent home when it expires, unless the employment situation improves considerably'. According to the paper, the stop for foreign workers had been agreed at a meeting between the unions and employers, labour minister Erling Dinesen (S) and trade minister Erling Jensen (S) the previous day:

The decision was taken as a result of the worsening employment situation in the wake of the oil crisis, which threatened large numbers of firms with falling production, or at worst closure, due to dwindling oil supplies.

The unions were reported as being satisfied with the negotiations:

The government has agreed to our request. It doesn't solve all the problems, of course, but it does address some of our concerns on the employment of foreign workers.

Like *Aktuelt*, *Jyllands-Posten* focused on the 'immediate effect' of the stop. Again like *Aktuelt*, the paper mentioned that, at the same time, residence permits for foreign workers already working in Denmark would 'in principle' not be renewed.

On November 25 1973, *Politiken* carried a report about 'Police raids on illegal guest workers'. While this was not linked directly to the oil crisis, the paper mentioned that so far that year, over 200 illegal migrant workers had been found and subsequently deported. The same day, the paper quoted Hans Nielsen, spokesman for the employers' association in the plastic industry, as predicting that guest workers would be fired first, which seemed to be confirmed by yet another article on November 28 1973: 'The LO wants ban on guest workers':

'It would be disastrous for both the Danish labour market and the guest workers themselves if they came to Denmark at a time of large-scale redundancies due to the energy crisis,

said Inga Olsen, LO. Arne Lund, director of the DA, sounded a more cautious note, however: 'Let us see how bad it gets first'. On November 29 1973, *Politiken* reported that the three main unions involved wanted a ban on guest workers. The three unions, which for the time being only wanted a temporary ban, were: the Women Workers' Union in Denmark, the Danish Metal Workers' Union, and DASF. And now the employers also dropped their objections: 'This is inherent to the whole guest workers policy, they say'.

Ekstra Bladet's front-page headline on November 28 1973 predicted 'Over 100,000 will lose their jobs'. Employers regarded the situation as 'extremely serious', and inside the paper, Anker Jørgensen was quoted as saying at an election meeting before the general election in December 1973 that 'it is necessary to limit the intake of foreign workers, and if things get worse, we will also have to consider shorter working hours. The latter is not something we relish doing, ended the prime minister'. In the leader on the same day, the paper recalled the 'spectre' of the 1930s, when 'unemployment was a stark reality in thousands of Danish homes'. If such a situation arose again, 'one way (of solving it could) be to reduce the number of foreign workers, and another to reduce working hours — though neither is ideal'. On November 29 the paper reported that a number of unions had demanded that LO general secretary Thomas Nielsen 'take immediate steps to reintroduce the ban on guest workers'. Jørgen Sønder, section head at the Ministry of Labour, was quoted as saying: 'Guest workers who have a job and a valid residence permit will not be affected. But if they lose their job, and Danish labour is available, then the employer who brought them here will have to pay to send them home'. On November 30 1973, *Ekstra Bladet* also reported a 'Stop for guest workers'.

Like the papers mentioned above, *Vestkysten* also carried articles describing the serious energy problems and the spillover effects on employment. On November 29 1973, it wrote that 'three unions want a ban on foreign labour due to the threat of unemployment'. On December 1 1973, the paper further reported that the union movement in Esbjerg would insist that, irrespective of their contractual rights, foreign workers should be laid off before Danish workers. This did not include workers from EC countries, however:

John Leo Thomsen, head of the workers' local joint organization said that the situation had been discussed and that the general feeling was that Danish labour should be guaranteed employment as long as possible. This meant that foreign labour must be laid off first. Those on 3-month contracts should be sent home with pay for the period in which they were promised work, said Leo Thomsen.

Asked who was to pay for this, he replied: 'The employers, there's no one else as far as we can see'.

On November 24 1973, *Berlingske Tidende* sent a report on a German stop for guest workers from Bonn. Influenced by the worsening energy situation, the federal government had announced an immediate stop to the recruitment of guest workers from countries outside the EC. On November 28 1973, the paper reported that a stop could be expected in Denmark too, and on November 30 1973 announced: 'Guest workers must go home'. This was also commented on in a short leader the same day: 'Oil and pain: Guest workers become the first scapegoats of the oil crisis. However, this is hardly likely to cushion the effects of energy shortages on employment'.

Information also deplored the consequences for foreigners. On November 28 1973, the paper quoted labour minister Erling Dinesen (S) as saying that it could become necessary to decree a stop for guest workers. On December 1 1973 — the day after the ban on guest workers was imposed — the paper observed:

The possible shortage of oil in Danish industry is already wrecking normal industrial relations. Collective agreements are being suspended. Occupational health and safety legislation is being disregarded. Mass layoffs are being announced. Foreign workers are being openly declared unwanted. Firms are closing down. These are some of the more extreme examples of the effect of the energy crisis.

Under the sub-headline 'Xenophobia', the paper noted that:

Foreign workers in Denmark will bear most of the brunt, either through layoffs and re-patriation or because they push Danish workers out. Earlier in the week, the LO called for a ban on foreign workers on account of the oil crisis.

K.S. Blunch, president of the Association of Employment Service Heads in Denmark, was quoted as supporting the ban, since, he said, the rules governing the employment of foreign workers meant that Danish workers risked being laid off before foreign workers. Firms were legally obliged to employ foreign workers for at least three months after they start work in the firm.

5.8 Guest workers and recession

In June 1974, Kaj Westergård, an economic statistics expert at the Ministry of Labour, proposed a new solution to the migrant worker issue. The oil crisis had worsened the balance of payments deficit, and the headline of Westergård's article in *Aktuelt* on June 17 was characteristic of the period: 'Might currency considerations make immigrants preferable to migrant workers?'

Westergård based his article on the just-published Perspektivplan II (Perspective Plan II), which predicted continued labour shortages in the export industries. Unemployment was therefore no more of a spectre than that:

Those firms which produce the goods and services that help ease our trade deficit with the rest of the world must expect a drain on their manpower. It is therefore not surprising that it is precisely from this quarter that the most eager calls to plug the 'holes' with foreign labour come.

Westergård noted that there was still no clear picture of the economic effects of immigration. However, the results of a study by the West German central bank had important implications for the balance of payments:

The primary goal of migrant workers in western countries is to earn money to support family and relations in the home country. Only foreign workers who have brought their families here, and who have lived and worked in the west for many years, have savings on a level with those of the native population. But savings are often high even among these, because the obligation to support others usually extends far beyond the nuclear family (*Aktuelt*, June 17 1974).

Foreign workers thus created a form of capital flight, and the downward pressure this exerts on the balance of payments might therefore be reason enough to warrant a continued stop for immigration in favour of a determined effort to 'integrate the migrant worker and his family'.[35] The word 'integration' had thus entered the debate, though clearly from the point of view of the needs of the receiving country.

Unemployment continued to increase, however, soon especially among foreigners, and the nature of the problem changed.[36] In March 1976, *Berlingske*

---

35. See Ingrid Henriksen (1985) for estimates of how much the various immigrant groups send home to their country of origin.
36. According to Hammer (1976), unemployment among Danish and foreign members of SID went more or less hand in hand in 1974 and up to early spring 1975. For the rest of 1975, unemployment among foreign SID members was considerably higher.

Tidende ran a series of articles on the deteriorating situation for foreigners under the title 'Danes of a sort too'.[37]

On June 17 1976, the paper printed an article entitled: 'The saddest of the sad queues — unemployment hits our migrant workers the hardest'. The emphasis was on the exposed position of migrant workers, which the article illustrated by the case of a job centre in Tøndergade, in the Vesterbro part of Copenhagen. Among SID's 6,000 foreign members, 2,100 were out of work, corresponding to a jobless rate of 35%, against an average unemployment of 25% for the union as a whole. *Berlingske Tidende* continued:

> The migrant worker came to Denmark to earn money and save up so that he could return home to a better life. This was his only reason for leaving family, friends and place of birth. Without work it must seem pointless to endure a socially desperate existence in a country whose language he perhaps doesn't even like. But he cannot return empty-handed to derision — and perhaps debt — either. So rather wait and hope in the saddest of the sad queues in Tøndergade.

This empathy with migrants' situation also characterized articles on problems with the reunification of migrant workers' families, on their children's difficulties at school, and on the cultural conflicts they were faced with.[38] The paper stressed society's obligation to integrate the children, and Danes were exhorted to show more tolerance, whether foreign workers stayed in the country or returned home.

Other articles around this time in the main conservative newspaper indicated that the probability was that the migrants would be *staying*. On March 20 1976 the paper cited a just-published report from Statistics Denmark on the number of foreign citizens. This showed that, while a lot of single men had returned, this was offset by 'a corresponding influx of women and children. This implies that the social problems associated with migrant workers' stay in this country will increase'. The nature of international migrations was thus changing, towards a higher degree of family reunification.

On March 23 1976, it was reported that, influenced by economic conditions, the EC was rethinking its immigrant policy. More precisely, the EC was re-negotiating a 1970 agreement on the gradual free movement of labour between Turkey and the EC, due to be implemented between 1976 and 1980.

37. According to a Vilstrup survey, among Danes themselves, 'an absolute majority were opposed to Denmark accepting any more refugees and against accepting any more immigrant workers as long as there were unemployed Danish workers' (quoted from *Fyns Tidende*, March 15 1976). As can be seen from Søren Pedersen (1999), most refugees at that time came from Chile and Vietnam.
38. A Ministry of Education circular in 1970 confirmed that migrant workers' children had to attend school if they were expected to be in the country at least six months, cf. *Berlingske Tidende*, November 6 1970.

Faced with an estimated one million potential Turkish immigrants, the EC was digging its heels in.

The general debate on immigrants intensified towards the end of the 1970s — influenced partly by the increase in family reunifications.[39] The questions being asked now were: Should migrant workers be sent home or be allowed to stay? Should they be given the right to vote in local elections, and how much should they be allowed to deduct in tax for money sent to the family in the home country (deductions under so-called 'family support contracts')?

A new party, the Progress Party (Z), stormed into parliament in the 'Landslide Election' in 1973, and towards the end of the 1970s was venturing its views on immigration, 'which found great sympathy in large sections of the population, but which had not previously been represented in parliament' (Højsteen, 1992). Conservative politicians were also making sporadic attacks on immigrants, with a number of critical articles in *Jyllands-Posten* in particular. In one such article on July 21 1979, for example, the Conservative politician Ib Stetter criticized the Liberal/Social Democratic coalition government for its lack of policy on immigrant workers and refugees, observing at the same time that 'there were numerous problems in absorbing people of a foreign culture into our society'. On August 3 1979, Ib Stetter wrote in the same paper that The Danish Conservative Party would demand the immediate expulsion of all foreigners — including those with Danish citizenship — involved in drug-related crimes: 'They must not be given the chance to poison our society ever again. They should be deported irrespective of family ties'.

In the middle of September, the paper also reported news that the government was going to 'Put a stop to immigrant workers' abuse of tax allowances' (September 15 1979). Anders Andersen, the Liberal Minister of Taxation, announced that, in the coming parliamentary session, the government would crack down on the unintended use of these deduction possibilities. The paper reported:

It appears that many immigrant workers abuse the right to deduct money sent home to support their family from the amount of tax due. In many cases, this money is deposited in an account which the immigrant worker withdraws himself when he leaves Denmark (*Jyllands-Posten*, September 15 1979).

In autumn 1979, *Jyllands-Posten* also conducted a reader debate through the letters to the editor columns, 'where many readers called for immigrant workers to be sent home from economic motives' (Højsteen, 1992, p. 58). To judge from a study carried out by Ole Hammer involving selected papers in 1982 and 1984, this would be a recurring theme in the debate conducted

---

39. See Søren Pedersen, 1999, for figures.

through letters to the editors of many of the Danish dailies in coming years.[40]

On November 21 1979, the papers reported a parliamentary debate on immigrant policy, initiated by a question from the Left-Wing Socialist Party, perhaps as a reaction to the sharper tone in the immigrant worker debate.[41] The debate on the question coincided with the announcement by the new Social Democratic government, on taking office on November 6 1979, of an overall review of immigrants' conditions, including the right to vote in local elections. The prime minister, Anker Jørgensen, had also promised that the government — now a Social Democratic minority government — would continue efforts to revise the rules on immigrants' tax allowances.

Politiken wrote that, during the debate on November 20 1979, the government had confirmed that the notified changes in the election act would be introduced in a bill. Anker Jørgensen also stuck to the decision to limit the tax allowances, among other reasons because, he said, many Danes found it hard to see the fairness in the scheme, and that this growing dissatisfaction could develop into a general antipathy towards guest workers. And while the prime minister rejected any thought of a separate immigration ministry, he vowed to do everything possible to further immigrant integration.

In fact, according to *Politiken*, all parties — apart from The Danish Conservative Party and the Progress Party — acknowledged that Denmark had a responsibility towards guest workers. Several party spokesmen spoke out against 'the attempts in recent years to whip up hatred against immigrant workers, based on incorrect and undocumented information about abuses of the social system, criminality, etc.'

Completely unperturbed, the spokesman for the Progress Party demanded that work permits for unemployed immigrants should no longer be renewed.

Information's coverage of the debate, together with *Aktuelt*'s, cf. below, was probably the most extensive, consisting of a leader and a front-page article. The leader heaped abuse on the Progress Party in particular:

(...) Ole Pilgaard Andersen, spokesman for the Progress Party, emphatically denied that his party supported a smear campaign against immigrant workers — but on the other hand, foreign workers' *exploitation of our social system* ought to be looked into, and something should also be done about *all these marriages of convenience* between Danes

---

40. Hammer, 1984, p. 7. Another result of the study was that the papers analysed 'generally had a positive attitude to immigrants (...). The negative attitudes are first and foremost reflected in the letters to the editor, where there is a certain predominance of negative attitudes'. Hammer also noted that the papers mainly cover problem areas such as crime and racial discrimination, which gives immigrants a 'problem image', while their situation vis-à-vis the labour market is glossed over.

41. The question was formulated as follows: 'What does the government have to say about the situation of immigrants' families and other foreigners, and what does the government propose to do about it?'

and immigrant workers, not to mention all the *foreigners who enter the country on a false passport, large numbers of whom lived in Christiania* (an 'alternative' community on a former military base in Copenhagen). When Preben Wilhjelm (VS) later demanded documentation for these allegations, Pilgaard could only lamely reply that 'it was evident from numerous other debates' and 'it had also been mentioned in the press' (*Information*, November 21 1979).

The leader was also scathing about the views of the parties of the right, Peter Brixtofte (V) and Hagen Hagensen (K) having supported demands for an overhaul of the family support contract system of tax allowances, which the two politicians believed were being abused. Hagensen also fell into disfavour in the paper for his insistence on knowledge of Danish as a condition for being able to vote in local elections.

Nonetheless, the paper could with satisfaction note positive expressions of sympathy from almost all parties except the Progress Party. But would these count for anything in the real world? Hardly:

The only concrete result so far is a report on foreigners' legal status, a proposal on foreigners' right to vote in local elections, and a proposal to limit the use of family support contracts. Plus, of course, sympathy and good intentions. But it is doubtful whether this will lead to anything (*Information*, November 21 1979).

Like *Information*, *Ekstra Bladet* was also highly critical of possible clampdowns. Among other things, the paper had quoted Bernhard Baunsgaard (R) as describing the action against the tax allowance as 'petty': 'It was we who asked them (the foreigners) to come. They must be allowed to support their families, otherwise we risk destroying their family patterns' (November 21 1979). Preben Wilhjelm was quoted for bringing immigrants' legal position up:

By making their stay here a matter for the police, we automatically criminalize immigrants. The right-wing smear campaign has toughened the police's expulsion policy, and this has increased uncertainty among immigrant workers.

Aktuelt stressed the general agreement: 'The debate showed that a very large majority in Parliament, with the Progress Party as almost the only exception, stands behind a common desire to improve things for immigrants'. Commenting on the prime minister's statement, the paper mentioned that he had referred to a partial paper from the 1977 Aliens Act Commission on administrative guidelines for residence and work permits and for procedure in deportation cases. Anker Jørgensen was also quoted as saying that, though the ban on further immigration would be upheld, he wanted to liberalize conditions for those immigrants already in the country. Professor Ole Espersen, the Social Democratic chairman of the parliamentary law committee, was quoted for drawing attention to immigrants' economic and cultural importance, and Peter Brixtofte (V) for having warned against using the group as a football for party-political interests. Brixtofte also

strongly dissociated himself from highly discriminatory remarks from members of the Progress Party and from Ib Stetter's especially injudicious remarks on immigrants and drug-related crime.

In its article 'Immigrant children often end up as losers' on the same day, the paper stressed the need for an overall immigrant policy.

Jyllands-Posten reported on the debate in an article entitled 'Guest workers get the right to vote' (November 21 1979). The paper stressed that all the party spokesmen agreed that the situation for the over 50,000 immigrants from Pakistan, Yugoslavia and Turkey was serious. The paper also noted that a 'very large majority' agreed that 'Denmark should be ashamed that it is precisely this small section of the population that has the biggest problems as regards unemployment, education, housing and well-being'. According to *Jyllands-Posten*, the debate had on the whole revealed a willingness to ensure that Denmark adopted a more humane immigrant policy in future. Peter Brixtofte (V) was quoted as saying that the goal for a revised immigrant policy should be both to integrate the immigrants and to ensure the preservation of their cultural background. The main impression the article gave was one of general sympathy, and that, supported by the political consensus in the House, the government already had new legislative initiatives under preparation. *Jyllands-Posten* thus showed towards the end of this article that it did not fully support the view of either the majority of its readers in the paper's letters-to-the-editor debate or the contributions of right-wing politicians earlier in the autumn.

Berlingske Tidende reported on the government's policy statement on immigrant integration and a statement from the prime minister that 'these groups have nothing to fear for their future'. The paper made no mention of right-wing criticism during the debate, focusing instead on Preben Wilhjelm, who, according to *Berlingske Tidende*, had said

that these foreigners had been enticed here at a time when private capital needed them — that they had never had decent conditions, that these conditions had deteriorated, and that their legal situation had to all intents and purposes worsened.

Summing up, *Berlingske Tidende* said that the debate had been broad and far-reaching, and that most of the parties had adopted the government's position. On November 22 1979, the paper printed an interview with Hagen Hagensen, in which he reiterated his deprecatory views on changes in the election act. Furthermore, in Hagensen's opinion, current rules requiring that a foreigner must have lived in Denmark for seven years before qualifying for Danish citizenship were too lax.

The headline in *Vestkysten* was 'Basic agreement on guest workers', which was also the main theme of the article, though it also included 'several highly critical statements'. The Liberal line was put by Peter Brixtofte, who maintained that an immigrant policy is not just a matter of money or political decisions: 'What matters most is people's attitudes. This is a challenge which the Liberal party hopes the Danish population wants to meet'.

A new parliamentary debate in November 1980 fanned the flames of the immigration issue again. The same occurred in spring 1981, when the then Minister of Housing, Erling Olsen (S), outlined ideas for special immigrant towns or quarters, which residents themselves could plan. *Ekstra Bladet* commented on the proposal in a leader on March 21 1981, in which it stressed that 'there can be no doubt that Erling Olsen means well'. But the paper warned against trying to solve immigrants' problems by segregating them in special quarters. On the contrary, they should be solved by forcing social housing out into 'the large Green Belt, where municipalities have up to now blithely turned their backs on the country's social problems'. The leader also pointed out that the educational situation for immigrant children was 'a ticking bomb'.

5.9 Summary of the debate from the beginning of the 1960s up to around 1980

It appears from the above account that the debate on the use of foreign labour started in summer 1964 in an article in *Aktuelt* written by the then Social-Liberal trade minister Hilmar Baunsgaard. At this early stage the argumentation was not overwhelmingly sophisticated, it merely being maintained that an influx of migrant workers in a situation of chronic labour shortage could increase the country's wealth. This was an apt comment on the spirit of the times, namely a preoccupation with — neatly captured by a Social Democratic election slogan — 'making good times better'. In the minister's view, the only alternative to the use of foreign labour was economic stagnation.

With the exception of *Politiken* and *Jyllands-Posten*, however, Hilmar Baunsgaard's proposals for the use of foreign labour met with resounding criticism in the other papers. In *Aktuelt*, but also in *Berlingske Tidende*, *Information* and *Vestkysten*, it was the opposition of the trade union movement that received the most attention. The unions and Social Democratic politicians thus embarked on a course they were to hold for the rest of the 1960s: They would at any time prefer investments in new technology — also to maintain the country's competitiveness — to the import of southern European workers, who would increase pressure on wages and preserve outdated production forms and systems. At the same time, it was pointed out that the spectre of unemployment was always present, and that there were still unexploited reserves of labour in Denmark among married women. *Information* presented similar views, with a focus on technological modernisation rather than the import of unskilled workers, finding support for these views in parts of economic theory.

Another feature of this first debate was that several papers sent reports from Germany and Switzerland on the effects there of the presence of large groups of immigrant workers. It is also worth noting that the debate had hardly got underway before the first letters to the editor appeared, almost spontaneously, and with a hostile tendency which struck the tone in hundreds of later letters.

By the following year, when the debate on labour problems in the meat industry broke out, the right-wing papers had worked out a clearer position. All the right-wing papers now accepted that the use of foreign labour could ease industry bottlenecks, dampen inflation and facilitate desirable market expansions. In this connection, *Vestkysten* and *Jyllands-Posten* were perhaps also influenced by the fact that there were clear agricultural interests at stake. *Aktuelt* and *Information* were largely unsympathetic to this, while the tabloid *Ekstra Bladet* was reconsidering its views on the use of foreign labour.

In the years up to 1970, these positions remained more or less unchanged, though union views vacillated according to the risk of unemployment, i.e. the economic situation. Thus, in 1967, one could be forgiven for thinking that unemployment was a thing of the past, and Thomas Nielsen, the LO general secretary, was able to sound more accommodating in *Aktuelt* than two years previously. But when trade conditions briefly worsened in 1968, at the same time as immigration increased, union attitudes once more hardened, especially among unskilled workers, who wanted a total ban on immigration. Towards the end of the 1960s, union arguments in *Aktuelt* and the other papers also focused more on the increasing social problems among immigrant workers, prompting both *Aktuelt*, *Information* and *Politiken* to call on the government to formulate an actual immigrant policy.

The pressure culminated in autumn 1970, and resulted in the first temporary stop for first-time work permits for foreigners. It now also appeared from the newspaper debate that a majority of the population was sceptical about continued unregulated immigration, and that the political establishment was in fact agreed that the rules should be tightened, thereby giving politicians a chance to formulate a clearer, more coherent policy. Disagreement now centred on the length and degree of the ban, with the conservative and liberal papers — and also *Ekstra Bladet* — arguing for a more flexible stop as a safety valve for continued labour shortages in certain industries and parts of the country.

When the oil crisis broke out in autumn 1973, the fronts had softened further — the majority of the papers were now agreed that the ban should be total, at least for a while, even though *Information* and *Berlingske Tidende* more than implied that guest workers had become scapegoats in a game that the Danish government was finding it extremely hard to control. For its part, the trade union movement felt that their fears of the 1960s had now been confirmed.

In the following years the focus shifted to the importance of immigrants for the ever-depressed balance of payments and to immigrants' social problems.

With the change in the nature of migration up through the 1970s from labour migrations to family reunification, and with the subsequent increased recourse to the welfare system, the debate changed tack again towards the end of the period, though the new theme had already been touched on relatively early in the debate, e.g. in reports on the situation of immigrant workers in central Europe.

A contributing factor in this was also that the political vacuum for opposition to immigration, which a reader had drawn attention to in *Vestkysten* in 1970, had now been filled by the appearance of the Progress Party. Some Conservative politicians — perhaps especially articulated in *Jyllands-Posten* — now adopted a much harder line on the earlier guest workers and their families than they had before the worsening in trade conditions.

On a more general note, the papers and a majority of the political parties still affected a sympathetic understanding of the situation — at least as far as editorial opinions were concerned. Letters to the editor were another matter. This view is clearly supported by the reports of the debate during a parliamentary hearing in 1979, which was intensively covered by the media. But politicians also failed to formulate an actual immigrant policy on this occasion too.

References

See the combined bibliography for chapters 5 and 6 at the end of chapter 6.

CHAPTER 6

Thirty years of press debate on 'the foreigners' in Denmark

Part II: The debate on asylum-seekers

Bent Jensen

6.1 Introduction

Until the middle of the 1980s, the dominant topic in the debate on foreign immigrants was 'guest workers'. The number of refugees had remained relatively small until that time, and the source of the refugees had continued to
be primarily Eastern Europe, though with the addition from the mid-1970s of
Vietnamese boat people and refugees from Chile in the wake of the 1973
military coup. However, the pattern of the debate altered from the mid-1980s,
as a consequence of the increase in the number of refugees seeking asylum in
Denmark.[1]

---

1. The fact that the guest worker theme was the main one in the debate up until the
   mid-1980s does not necessarily mean that there was no discussion in the 1960s and
   1970s about the acceptance of refugees. The press commented from time to time on
   defectors from Eastern Europe, and in several cases it performed its function as 'the
   fourth estate' by questioning the fairness of a number of cases of expulsion of asylum-seekers from among these people. For example, *Politiken* commented in June
   1965 on the decision of the Aliens' Authorities to refuse asylum to some Hungarians
   and referred to 'the fate that is certain to await them as suspected defectors'. The
   paper commented: 'This hardening of attitude towards people who wish to flee the
   communist states has taken place without the knowledge or approval of the elected
   authorities; but what is most distressing is the shock which this new policy has
   given to the East Europeans, who believed that they could simply choose to live in
   a democratic country' (*Politiken*, June 10 1965). The paper then posed the question
   to the Head of the Aliens' Authorities as to whether 'it is no longer regarded as a
   human right of Eastern European citizens to seek political asylum in Denmark?'
   According to the paper, the basis for the decision had been an over-literal
   interpretation of legislation from 1961, which laid down that to be granted political
   asylum a person must have suffered political persecution in their home country.
   Thus it was no longer enough — as had been the previous practice — that 'refugees
   state that they find the political situation in their home country insupportable, and

As already described in Chapter 5, the Danish Parliament had set up a committee on refugees in 1977. One of the tasks of this committee was to draft more detailed administrative procedures for notification of the granting of residence and work permits and for handling expulsion orders, these procedures to be used at least until a new law on aliens was passed. This resulted in a report on administrative procedures in 1979 and a further report in 1982 which included a proposal for a new legislation concerning aliens.

In drafting the proposed new government legislation, the Minister of Justice, Erik Ninn-Hansen (Conservative[2]), based his proposals on the views of the majority on the committee. The opposition proposed a number of amendments, drafted by the future ombudsman, Hans Gammeltoft-Hansen, among others; these amendments were based on the views of the minority of the committee.[3] Among other things, the minority wanted to give foreigners already in Denmark greater opportunities to bring dependants into the country (family reunification).

In 1983, between the first and second readings of the bill, Erik Ninn-Hansen stated in *Jyllands-Posten* his belief that the welfare system made residence in Denmark an attractive goal for people in poor countries. The new law, then, should be formulated in such a restrictive manner that Denmark, with its population of only five million, could remain a 'nation-state in the future'. In addition, one should consider the foreigners themselves:

Until now, we have not had any serious problems. But we know that if it is possible to find a scapegoat for one's frustrations, most people are ready to do just that. It is easy to make foreigners scapegoats for problems, because they are often different in appearance and culture. There is thus a future risk of social unrest occurring which is directed against foreigners. That would be fundamentally unfair.[4]

In other words, he said, it would be dangerous if foreigners with the right to reside in Denmark were granted large-scale rights to bring other members of their families into the country. He claimed that he was motivated in saying this by the need to safeguard the civil rights of those immigrants already resident in Denmark.

Despite the minister's reservations, the final negotiations over the law saw a compromise on the issue between government and opposition, with the Progress Party (Z) distancing itself utterly from the legislation. In the debate the party said that the views of the majority in parliament were in conflict with the will of the Danish people; during the coming year, according to

that consequently they have good ground to fear that their democratic attitudes may in the future lead to trouble from the government'.
2. The government at the time was a centre-right coalition.
3. See Gaasholt and Togeby, 1996, p. 28.
4. *Jyllands-Posten*, April 10 1983.

Gaasholt and Lise Togeby, this became 'a central argument of the Progress Party'.[5] One of the central areas of the 1983 legislation was an improvement in the rights of refugees. Refugees for whom Denmark was the first country in which they had sought asylum were to have a legal claim to such asylum, and a number of safeguards were included in the process of handling applications for asylum. Any foreigner who sought asylum at the Danish border now had the right to enter Denmark and to remain in the country while the application was processed. The newly-established Directorate for Aliens (Direktoratet for Udlændinge) took over the processing of asylum applications from the Aliens' Authorities of the police (fremmedpolitiet). Any disputes could be brought before the Refugee Board (flygtningenævnet), also a newly-established body, which comprised three officials from the Ministries of Foreign Affairs, Social Affairs and Justice, two representatives from the Danish Refugee Council (Dansk Flygtningehjælp) and one representative from the General Council of the Danish Bar and Law Society (Advokatrådet). With the introduction of the revised law Denmark gained an international reputation, in the words of a legal commentator, 'for taking the lead in operating a humanitarian refugee policy'.[6]

As will be seen from the following, the act provoked violent debate in the years succeeding its passage. This debate has continued right up until the present day. However, since it is difficult to distinguish and analyse current trends in opinion in present-day newspaper writing, this chapter will only cover the period up until the end of 1994.

6.2 'The Queen told us off': The debate after the new aliens' law came into force, 1984-85

In the summer of 1984, when the influx of refugees was still modest in scale, the majority of Danish newspapers were still in favour of the new law.[7] In the late summer and autumn of that year, however, newspaper comment began to reflect a sometimes high level of dissatisfaction with the increasing number of refugees, and in many cases a feeling of clear hostility towards them. The signs of what was to come were already present in the summer of 1984, when the number of Iranian asylum-seekers increased from 64 in June to 201 in July.[8]

Conservative politicians began to suggest that a revision of the 1983 Act

5. Gaasholt and Togeby, 1996, p. 28.
6. Lone B. Christensen *et al.*, p. 237.
7. Nykøbing Falster, Juelsminde and Randers were the first towns to provide homes for Iranian refugees. The local newspapers in these areas were all very positive towards the Iranians, using phrases such as 'our young refugees' (*Lolland Falster Folketidende* August 23 1984, quoted in Peter Tygesen, 1985).
8. Ibid.

was needed — a view which appeared to find an echo in several newspaper reports. For example, on August 13 1984, *B.T.*[9] reported that among the 're-fugees' there were a large number of guest workers from West Germany whose residence permits had expired. On the same day, the newspaper published an interview with Liberal MP Svend Heiselberg,[10] in which he said that:

We must try to hold back this mass invasion by Iranian refugees. I fear we shall soon see 25-30 thousand Iranians living in Denmark and creating an Islamic revolution.

In August, many papers published a report from the Ritzau news agency that described how 'floods' of refugees were being attracted to the country by the new law.

On September 24 1984, *B.T.* published an interview with the Minister of Justice, Erik Ninn-Hansen, who by this time had begun to argue consistently and continuously against the legislation on aliens; and on September 26 *Jyllands-Posten* wrote that 'the reality is that Denmark is open to anyone who asks for political asylum'. The next day, the paper published the results of a survey by Observa: 'Every second voter would say "no" to an increase in the number of refugees.' Fewer than one in ten believed that Denmark accepted too few refugees, and those who expressed this opinion were generally on the political left. In a lead article published the same day, the paper demanded that the authorities should ensure that refugees had genuinely fled spontaneously

That is, that they are people from areas where their lives or their freedom are endangered on political, religious or other grounds. It's not the idea that we should take planeloads of people who could live in perfect safety in their home countries, even if their material standard of living might be low.

However, the leader did maintain that 'genuine' refugees should definitely be accepted. On September 29 1984, *Vestkysten* published an article on the situation in Sweden which could be seen as an indirect contribution to the debate in Denmark. 'The Lebanese are flooding into Sweden', the paper said, but the Swedish government had recently decided to harden its attitude towards Lebanese asylum seekers, who 'can now be returned to Lebanon'.

The dividing line between *genuine refugees* and *economic migrants* was emphasized on September 30 1984 by *Berlingske Tidende*, which quoted an official

9. An evening paper.
10. As mentioned in Chapter 5 The Danish political party 'Venstre' is often called the 'Liberal' party in English, but their views should not be confused with those of the modern British Liberal-Democrat party. The Danish party is on the right wing politically, standing for classical Liberal principles and agricultural interests.

from the Directorate for Aliens as saying: 'A number of economic migrants have concealed themselves among the refugees, using forged passports as a means of obtaining a new refugee identity.' The paper also published that day an interview with an Iranian, who stated that the differences in the laws of the various European countries were significant:

So they come first to Denmark, and take the temperature of the water. The news spreads very rapidly: no-one has been thrown out, it's safe, and so many more follow.

In October 1984, the Minister of Justice once again perceived a link between the new law and the flow of refugees; on October 10, *Berlingske Tidende* quoted from Ninn-Hansen's written statement to parliament, released in advance of the parliamentary debate on the new law concerning aliens, as follows:

I warned Denmark against undertaking an obligation which is disproportionate in international terms and which at the national level it does not have the capacity to fulfil.

Politiken reported the debate on the law under the headline 'Majority for a mild law on refugees — government proposal gets a rough ride'.[11] It was clear that a parliamentary majority made up by the Social Democrats, the Social Liberals and two left-wing parties wanted to retain the existing law, though the Liberal MP Bjørn Elmquist had warned against leaving it unchanged when other countries failed to live up to their obligations. Later that autumn, the Conservatives reiterated their belief in the need for restrictions; and there was a constant flow of objections to the refugee policy from the Progress Party, as expressed for example at its national congress in September 1984.

By the end of the year the debate had become so generally intense that Queen Margrethe took up the topic in her traditional New Year broadcast, a point which was extensively reported in the press. One other factor causing the debate to heat up in January and to continue with great intensity throughout the year was presumably the increasing number of asylum seekers now arriving not only from Iran but also from Iraq, Lebanon and Sri Lanka.

The intensity of the debate, and the fact that it involved points of fundamental principle for the parties, interest groups and others involved, is discussed in sections 6.2.1 to 6.2.3 below describing the commentaries in *Berlingske Tidende*, *Jyllands-Posten* and *Vestkysten* in 1985; these three newspapers were in general especially critical of the 1983 Act. Sections 6.2.4 to 6.2.7 describe the progress of the debate as expressed in the other papers.

11. *Politiken*, October 17 1984.

6.2.1. The debate in *Berlingske Tidende* in 1985

Berlingske Tidende published around 50 items concerning foreigners in January 1985, including pieces related to the Queen's New Year message; the front page headline on January 1 was 'The Queen told us off'. The paper published the full text of the Queen's speech. This is what she had to say about refugees and guest workers:

On the one hand, we are proud that refugees choose to come to our little paradise; but when we see them getting confused over our way of living and our language, then feelings of hospitality are forgotten all too quickly, and disappointment sets in on both sides. There are others, too, that have had the same experience, namely guest workers and their families. Now times are a little harder than they were when many of them came here; and things are often especially difficult for those who are not from families that have lived here for generations, and who therefore find it harder to adapt to the changing times. Then we come along with our so-called 'Danish humour' and our 'smart' comments. And so we begin to treat them coldly; and then it is not so far from that to harassment and worse — and, we should be ashamed of that.

The further coverage of the subject in January can be divided into two categories. First, there were more wide-ranging commentaries on Denmark's obligations towards refugees; the debate on a revision of the law had again become a concrete issue, largely on the initiative of Erik Ninn-Hansen. Second, news items on asylum-seekers continued to be published.

The majority of the more general items expressed significantly more sympathy for the refugees than had been the trend during the autumn of 1984. For example, the actor Erik Wedersøe penned a passionate defence of the refugees headed 'Unbelievably cold hostility', and Professor Jørgen Grønnegård Christensen declared that politicians should not give in to popular opinion, but should instead 'clearly and unequivocally state that this is an obligation that we have already undertaken'.[12]

While the editorial coverage stressed that refugees should integrate into Danish society, the majority of letters to the editor expressed their opposition, saying that the foreigners only came to take advantage of the Danish welfare system.

The news coverage of asylum cases focused on Iranians; two Iranians were refused asylum in an appeal to the Refugee Board. Since the cases would set a precedent, they aroused considerable interest. News of the refusal to grant asylum was published on January 11, and the next day the Iranians who were threatened with expulsion were quoted as saying 'We would rather be killed here than in Iran, because in Iran we will be tortured first', and 'Through this decision, the Danish people have condemned us to hell.' The chairman of the

---

12. *Berlingske Tidende*, January 13 and 20 1985.

Refugee Council, Professor Thor A. Bak, expressed his 'amazement' at the decisions in the two cases.

On January 12, the news focused on the Iranians threatened with expulsion. The next day there was a different viewpoint, with an assistant commissioner from the national police headquarters expressing his views. He pointed out that Denmark had consistently observed the terms of the Geneva Convention, and would certainly never send a person to his/her death. The assistant commissioner added that many refugees left Denmark voluntarily for such reasons as: 'It's too cold here, or the climate is too dry. The family's not well, and cigarettes are too dear.' According to this official, many of those in the country were economic migrants.

On January 14 1985 the Minister of Justice was quoted as saying that 'the Iranians must leave'. The Danish Refugee Council would have urged the Minister to grant the two Iranians temporary residence permits, but Ninn-Hansen pointed out that under the new law he no longer had that power. The article also stated that the Ombudsman would like to determine whether there had been any errors in the Refugee Board procedure. The next day the paper announced that 'the two Iranians are to have another chance'. The Ombudsman had criticized the Refugee Board for undue haste, and had requested a new assessment of the case. Bernhard Baunsgaard (Social Liberal) proclaimed that 'more people must be employed to handle asylum cases quickly but thoroughly, and the Minister of Justice must immediately apply for the necessary funding for this.'

On January 15, *Berlingske Tidende* surveyed the effect the Queen's message had had on the reporting of *B.T.* and *Ekstra Bladet*. *Berlingske Tidende* claimed that the two papers had backed the tenor of the speech in their editorials, but that the flood of letters received from readers were mainly against the Queen. There had been over 80 items on the subject in the two papers in the first week of January, and 'if the readers' letters in these two big evening papers are regarded as a reflection of the nation's views, then it seems clear that the Danes are deeply divided on the issues of refugees and foreign workers.' The article presented the trend evident in the readers' letters, and concluded: 'A dip into the mailbox reveals a mixture of racism, self-righteousness and understanding.' The views of the Liberal party on refugees were also expressed in an article on January 15 which reported an interview with the Foreign Minister, Uffe Ellemann-Jensen. The Minister emphasized Denmark's responsibility, but at the same time suggested that a clearer distinction could be made in the legislation between 'genuine and phoney refugees'. It was the use of precisely this type of argument that was the basis of a criticism of the government put forward in the same article by the sociologist Jacques Blum, who claimed that the Government was largely responsible for the fact that the debate had become so violent because they had made 'the refugee case into a question of economics — and of whether a refugee was "genuine" or not'.

That, he said, 'is the application of a double standard. It means that people have been prejudged.' An almost identical view was put forward by Thor A. Bak of the Refugee Council when on January 18 he commented on the Government's policy that

they are whipping up public opinion against people in need ... it is primarily the politicians, and especially Minister of Justice Erik Ninn-Hansen, who are using the refugee issue as ammunition in a fight between Government and Opposition.

An answer from Ninn-Hansen was published in *Berlingske Tidende* the next day. He began by stating his opinion that some of the refugees were *not* genuine. The current expulsion cases had caused the flood of refugees to fall off, and 'I think it's also time that we said that people can't just come to Denmark to study.' In more general terms, the need continued for the government to keep the flow of refugees under control and also to prevent young Iranians from coming to Denmark because they had been refused entry to Tehran University:

That will lead to refugee status being used to get around the ban on immigration — a ban which has been applied rigidly during the processing of the new law on aliens.

The Iranians continued to fill *Berlingske Tidende*'s columns throughout the winter and spring, in part because of a hunger strike which some of them started at the end of January. In mid-March the influx of refugees was undiminished, and on March 13 1985 the paper published an article entitled 'Tougher controls on refugees'. It seemed that several right-wing politicians had been joined by a spokesman for the Social Democrats, the former Minister of Justice Ole Espersen, in agreeing to the idea of making admission harder by giving 'extended powers to the Chairman of the Refugee Board' to refuse entry to people if it was clear that they were not refugees — though with the provision that the rules regarding residence permits should be relaxed at the same time. On the tougher controls, Espersen was quoted as saying:

We naturally do not want to see people who are quite obviously not refugees staying in Denmark for months while their cases are processed. However, we would like to see the Chairman of the Refugee Board working in co-operation with a representative of the Refugee Council.

The paper concluded that the law probably would be changed.

On March 20 1985 *Berlingske Tidende* announced that the negotiations between the Government and the Social Democrats had broken down, and that the Social Democrats, Social-Liberals and two left-wing parties had tabled a proposal to give the Minister of Justice increased powers to grant temporary residence permits on humanitarian grounds in cases where asylum-seekers were denied refugee status by the Refugee Board. It was proposed that one possible reason for granting a temporary residence permit could be 'the degree of fear that a foreigner appears to display at the prospect of being sent home'. The Opposition further proposed that the Chairman of the Refugee Board, acting together with a representative from the Refugee Council, should be empowered in appeal cases to reject manifestly groundless applications for asylum. It was apparent that the Government would press ahead with its own proposal that this power be given to the Chairman of the Refugee Board acting alone, but it was still hoped that a compromise could be found. On March 23 the paper quoted a warning from Bjørn Elmquist (V) concerning the political pressure that might be applied to a minister of justice if he were empowered to grant residence permits on humanitarian grounds; nevertheless, on the same day the paper suggested that both sides were still seeking a compromise as a conclusion to the negotiations.

At the end of May 1985 the final details were settled. On June 1, under the headline 'Sharp attack on the Progress Party', *Berlingske Tidende* published details of the negotiations, which had ended in a broad compromise the previous day, though with the Progress Party being excluded. The result was an alteration to the powers of the Minister of Justice to grant temporary residence permits, and a decision that a three-man committee consisting of the Chairman of the Refugee Board, a representative from the Refugee Council and a ministerial official would have the power to reject manifestly unfounded cases. The Progress Party came under heavy attack during the debate from more or less all the other parties. For example, the leader of the Centre Democratic Party, Erhard Jakobsen, was quoted as describing the attitude of the Progress Party as being incredibly callous. For her part the Progress Party leader, Pia Kjærsgaard, said that the law was 'an attack on the Danish people'.

Despite the change in the law, the debate kept going and indeed reached a new peak on July 27, when during a town fête some residents of Kalundborg attacked a group of Iranians who had been quartered in a local hotel. The attack made the front page of *Berlingske Tidende* on July 28, and there was comprehensive coverage on the inside pages, including reports on the way politicians distanced themselves from the attack. Uffe Ellemann-Jensen (V) described the episode as 'a stain on Denmark's name'. Bernhard Baunsgaard said it was the most dangerous threat to Danish culture since the thirties, while Torben Lund (Social Democrat) called the attack scandalous. When interviewed, some of the rioters explained that they had made the attack because 'they take our jobs and our girls'.

The attacks on the hotel continued the next night, causing politicians to make further efforts to disassociate themselves. On July 29 Ellemann-Jensen called for a broad popular debate on the matter; it was his belief that tougher laws alone could not provide a solution. Only the Progress Party remained apart from the general consensus. Pia Kjærsgaard expressed the view that the violence could also be seen as 'an expression of the animosity which the people feel towards the Government's policy on refugees'. In a leader that day, the paper maintained the view that:

It is perfectly permissible to express varying opinions on Danish policy on refugees …, but under no circumstances is it acceptable that the presence of refugees in the country should lead to campaigns of a racist nature, such as we have seen recently. And it would of course be completely unacceptable if such campaigns should lead to actual attacks on and violence towards the refugees themselves.

In *Berlingske Tidende* on August 8 1985 it was reported that the flood of refugees continued unabated; the paper described how an entire Lebanese family of 40 people, including babes in arms and the very elderly, had asked for asylum. According to this conservative paper, a further revision of the law was called for. The debate continued throughout the autumn, and the end of 1985 saw a further tightening of the law. The parliamentary negotiations were described in *Berlingske Tidende* on December 11. It was stated that the negotiations had centred on the concept of 'manifestly unfounded applications for asylum'. The most significant change to the law was that it was no longer possible to appeal against refusal of asylum to the Refugee Board if the Directorate for Aliens and the Refugee Council were in agreement that the case was unfounded. According to the paper, the reason for the change was the long processing time for cases and the prospect of reaching a figure of 10,000 asylum-seekers in 1985. The Government and the Social Democrats backed the compromise, and even the Progress Party voted for it, since the party saw it as a small step in the right direction. The Social Liberals, The Socialist People's Party and the Left-wing Socialists voted against the change. During the debate, these three parties had described the changes as an attack on the security of asylum-seekers, and they had demanded a definition of 'a clearly groundless application'. The parties supporting the compromise had, however, argued that the essential guarantees of security remained intact.

6.2.2 *Jyllands-Posten*

Jyllands-Posten printed the whole of the Queen's message on January 1 1985, and produced an approving leader on January 3, which also warned that 'We must not make "the foreigners" into scapegoats. When all's said and done, it's not their fault that we have been living beyond our means for many years.'

In the days that followed, the paper published many articles on the problems of finding places for refugees to live in towns and villages around Denmark. The Social Democrat mayors of Kolding and Vejle were particularly strongly opposed to the Refugee Council's plans to quarter large groups of

Iranians in their towns. The mayors were dissatisfied with the plans to house the asylum-seekers right in the centres of the towns,[13] and in Vejle there was also resentment at the unwelcome costs of providing services such as education for the asylum-seekers. The Major of Vejle was also quoted as saying: 'The rules that apply to everybody else must also be respected by the Refugee Council. We will not tolerate the establishment of a state within the state.' A businessman from the town centre told the paper that no-one dared to criticize the plans for Vejle openly after the Queen's New Year speech.

On January 7 1985, *Jyllands-Posten* reported that the National Association of Local Authorities in Denmark wanted to take up the matter. The chairman of the association, Mayor Evan Jensen (V) of Lejre, was quoted as saying that 'the state should provide extra grants for local authorities which accept large numbers of refugees'. The next day, *Jyllands-Posten* reported that the Minister for Home Affairs, Britta Schall Holberg (V), was willing to consider amending the state grants to local authorities so that those with large refugee centres would be compensated through this system. However, the minister did not think that she could get more money in total for the local authorities, only that the available funds could be redistributed. At the same time, Bjørn Elmquist (V) warned that the local authorities should be very cautious in this area and not start making offers of Danish language teaching or other means to help refugees to integrate when they were only being given temporary accommodation and had not yet been granted asylum. The Social Democrats, in contrast, as reported in the paper on January 9, wanted to apply pressure on the government to pay the extra costs involved to the host authorities.

The issue of refugees thus became a question of economics in the debate in *Jyllands-Posten*, and on January 10 the leader was indeed headed 'Refugees and the economy'. The editorial maintained that since the granting of refugee status was a state responsibility, the state, and not the local authorities, should bear the costs involved. Furthermore, it was Parliament that had passed the 1983 Act, which had 'clearly led to a veritable invasion of refugees'. On January 12 it was estimated that the increasing number of refugees would eventually cost the local authorities forty to fifty million DKK (Euro 5.4-6.7 million). Once again, the National Association of Local Authorities stressed that the state should bear these costs:

It was Parliament which drafted and passed the Aliens Act. It is Parliament and the state who determine how many refugees are allowed into the country. The local authorities have no influence on this. The state has the authority, and it is a good principle that whoever has the authority should also foot the bill,

---

13. Among the reasons for this was the fear the mayors had that there would be disorder in the towns when residents let their hair down at weekends.

said Evan Jensen (V), Chairman of the National Association of Local Authorities.

Throughout the rest of January, the newspaper wrote about the fate of the Iranians, both in its news reporting and in major news background articles. For example, the journalist Erik Thomle described life in the reception camp at Koldkær, situated at the mouth of the Limfjord.[14] Thomle had earlier been 'the first Danish journalist' to describe the organized — and very expensive — escape route from Iran to Denmark. In the report on the reception camp, he quoted an Iranian who said that the migrant-smugglers had promised him that there would be free education and DKK 10,000 (Euro 1,350) a month waiting for him on arrival in 'the land of joy'. Now, it seemed, there was cold comfort indeed for those waiting at Koldkær (appropriately enough, a literally translation of Koldkær is 'cold pond'). An article that appeared on January 17 under the headline 'Refugees accepted' suggested that the refugees had found a welcome with some local communities; however, on January 29 the paper reported this same refugee group as being affected by a widespread fear of the consequences of expulsion from Denmark. The group's spokesman explained that 'two Iranians who left Denmark in October last year to return to Tehran have been hanged'. He said that just the act of applying for asylum was considered sufficient grounds for executing Iranians.

Towards the middle of the month, *Jyllands-Posten* printed various items of news which could be interpreted as indicating a view that the law was perhaps too liberal, and that not all refugees could be regarded as genuine. For example Claus Tornøe, Head of the Directorate for Aliens, was quoted as saying that 85% of all asylum-seekers were granted refugee status; and in the same article the view was expressed that it was the 1983 legislation which had 'opened the way for the flood of refugees'.[15] The paper also published an interview with the UN High Commissioner for refugees, Poul Hartling, who said:

Let me make it clear that not all refugee cases are equally straightforward. They can be full of tricks ... It's really not always true that people are in danger. Often, they just want to be in some other place than where they are. And so they invent a story that they are refugees who are in danger. We see cases where the people are actually just adventurers who want to see something of the world.

On Iranian refugees, Poul Hartling said that they first came to Turkey and sought asylum, 'and some of them are granted it', but 'then maybe some of them hear that if they pay some money they can get to Belgium, Germany or Denmark. That's something they do at their own risk.'[16]

14. *Jyllands-Posten*, January 13 1985.
15. *Jyllands-Posten*, January 13 1985.
16. *Jyllands-Posten*, January 16 1985.

In a leader following the publication of this article, the paper wrote that

only a tiny handful of right-wing extremists want to see Denmark close its doors on refugees. The vast majority believe that we should fulfil our international obligations and accept people who have been persecuted and terrorized in their own countries. Let that be our irrevocable principle!'[17]

However, 'only the blind' would claim that a flood

of the proportions we have seen in the past couple of months would not lead to problems... And when someone with the authority of Poul Hartling, the High Commissioner for Refugees, says that refugees often invent stories to the effect that they are in danger, just to get to some other country, attracted there by that country's social welfare system and educational and work opportunities — then it is reasonable to ask whether we should indeed let in all and sundry.

The paper proposed that the liberal law, which made it impossible to refuse entry to asylum-seekers at the border, should be retained; but that all refugees should have their cases investigated as soon as they came into the country, and those found to be economic migrants should be expelled as quickly as possible. The paper also wrote on January 17 that neither the Social Democrats nor the Socialist People's Party were prepared to see the law made tougher. As the paper put it:

Neither the former Minister of Justice Ole Espersen (Social Democrat) nor the Socialist People's Party's legal affairs spokesman Leif Hermann are concerned about the fact that the majority in Parliament would apparently not vote in accordance with the views of the people on the new, liberal law on refugees.

On January 20 the paper printed an article about how the Danish Red Cross and the Refugee Council had written the text for a guide to asylum; this guide would state more clearly not only what rights the Danish Aliens Act gave to asylum-seekers, but also what rights it did *not* give. The General Secretary of the Refugee Council was quoted as saying that he foresaw that

a clear statement of the situation in Denmark will be reported back to those Iranians who have plans to travel to here, and this will stem the flow. It will form a counterweight to the high hopes given to the Iranians by the people who sell organized refugee journeys.

The guide, said the General Secretary, 'would really be a warning'.
    The paper published a number of major contributions to the debate in the course of January 1985, including a series of articles on the theme of im-

17. *Jyllands-Posten*, January 17 1985.

migration. In one article, the Minister for Home Affairs, Britta Schall Holberg (V), noted that integration of foreigners

is the continuation of a long historical tradition ... . It's no exaggeration to say that to a large extent the Denmark we know today has been built and developed by immigrants and their descendants.[18]

In order to solve the current problems of integration, the Minister proposed increased co-operation with immigrant organizations. However, she also noted that 'it will be necessary for the immigrants to recognise that there may be elements of their cultures that cannot be continued in Denmark', even though she hastened to add that 'naturally, I think that immigrants should be able to maintain their own culture and traditions to the greatest extent possible'. More concretely, the Minister pointed to the importance of competence in the Danish language as a precondition for successful integration.

A more unusual contribution was published on January 26. This was an article in which Søren Krarup, a pastor, discussed 'the so-called immigrants'. Concerning popular opinion among the Danish people, he wrote:

The strong reactions from the populace are nothing other than a genuine protest against the lies. At the same time, the views expressed by the authorities are the product of either fear or hypocrisy, preventing the truth being told. People are scared. People have been scared off from making their opinions known by a campaign which is an equal mixture of Salvation Army admonitions and sunday-school unction.[19]

In his article, the pastor metaphorically described Denmark as 'a home': 'An old nation state is exactly like a home. Here the family — the populace — can find sanctuary and companionship.' However, the politicians were turning this home into a 'public hostel'. In particular, Danish identity was under threat from the current immigration of Muslims:

If too many Mohammedans come in to Christian Denmark, which isn't just an empty spot on the map, then a desperate and explosive situation will be created — because talk of *the integration of peoples is built on a misrepresentation of reality.*

Other, mutually opposed, contributions to the debate were published under titles such as 'We must distinguish between refugees and immigrants', 'Ma-

18. *Jyllands-Posten*, January 22 1985.
19. In the following year, a *Jyllands-Posten* reader objected to the fact that Søren Krarup so often referred to the views of the silent majority, saying that 'He clothes the silent majority in the colours of the loud-voiced minority' (October 19 1986).

dame Justice must find things strange in Denmark' and 'Parliament forgot to listen to the voice of the people'.[20] This last article was written by Knud Lind, a former Progress Party Member of Parliament, who was putting forward the party's increasingly familiar argument that the parliament which had passed the legislation on aliens — 'by 155 votes for and 12 against' — was in conflict with the will of the people. On January 30 1985, *Jyllands-Posten* published an article entitled 'Immigrants in our national heritage', written by the Chairman of the UN Association Executive Committee, Bent Østergaard, which suggested that the Danish identity had been formed as a product of waves of immigration. In other words, the debate also concerned Denmark's national identity, and the issue of whether this identity was compatible with foreign cultures.

In the view of the paper, as expressed on March 20 1985, the situation was 'still a couple of steps away from consensus on the refugee law'. In its coverage of the parliamentary negotiations, the newspaper emphasized that the Government and the Opposition were trying to find a compromise solution. The negotiations had temporarily broken down because of the Government's desire that the Chairman of the Refugee Board acting alone should have the authority to carry out the urgent processing of manifestly unfounded asylum applications. However, 'the Social-Liberal Bernhard Baunsgaard completely rejected the model proposed by the Government parties; he had once called this procedure a court martial'. It was therefore predicted that the Government and the Social Democrats would find a compromise solution. On June 1, the paper described the result of the efforts to find common ground:

It was the most emotionally charged debate of the day. The duelling was particularly intense between Bernard Baunsgaard, the leading campaigner for the refugees, and Pia Kjærsgaard of the Progress Party. Baunsgaard almost flew up to the rostrum when Pia Kjærsgaard claimed that the Progress Party would be looking after Denmark's interests by putting a stop to the flood of refugees.

In a commentary headed 'Faster processing of asylum cases' published on December 12 1985, *Jyllands-Posten* discussed the compromise between the Government and the Social Democrats; a satisfied Erik Ninn-Hansen estimated that in the future, the processing of each case would take around 14 days.

6.2.3 *Vestkysten*

A number of contradictory threads can be traced in *Vestkysten*'s coverage of the topic in January 1985. On January 1, the paper printed the text of the Queen's speech under the headline 'Congratulations to the Queen', the jour-

---

20. *Jyllands-Posten*, January 21 1985 and (for the last two articles) January 29 1985.

nalist Søren Bloch built on the content of the speech in a background article entitled 'Danish racists' hardening view: Immigrants are primitive, stupid, naive and idle. Snide Danes make life tough for immigrants'.[21]

Later in the month there were a number of items defending the refugees and their rights, including a letter to the editor from Søren Nørgård Sørensen, MP (Social Democrat), who claimed that Denmark accepted very few refugees, even though 'it would be a little too much to suggest, as Flemming Behrendt, the chief information officer for the Danish Refugee Council, has done, that Denmark's quota of refugees should be raised to 30,000'. In articles such as 'Refugees complain about their interpreters', 'Rejected Iranians given extended time limit' and 'Police chief accused of being racist', the paper presented information about the plight of the Iranian refugees, with representatives of the Refugee Council being given plenty of space.[22] A Social Democrat demand for a hearing on refugees in Parliament was reported on January 31, together with the information that Denmark had not taken in an especially large number of refugees. The paper's coverage of the reception of a group of refugees in Ribe County also displayed a positive tone throughout, as shown for example in articles about how staff from the Refugee Council made advance preparations for the reception of refugees.

However, in parallel with these items there were other trends in the paper. For example, on January 16 an article based on a Ritzau agency report quoted from *Jyllands-Posten*'s interview with Poul Hartling under the headline 'Extensive trickery in refugee cases'. On the same day, in an article headed 'Danish farmers fear Iranians', the paper quoted the Chairman of the Agricultural Cooperative Association in Ribe County as saying that he would like to see a law requiring that buildings on land bought and added to a farm should be demolished if they were not sold again within a year. He said, 'When refugees can be housed in the Grand Hotel in Vejle, without the municipal authority being aware that this is going on, it doesn't take much imagination to see what disused farm buildings could be used for', and one didn't want Iranians as neighbours. In a leader, the editors stated their belief that one could readily accept Poul Hartling's statements at face value:

High Commissioner for Refugees Poul Hartling is a nice man who expresses himself politely. When he says that 'Refugee cases are not always straightforward. They can be full of tricks,' this can be translated into straight Danish as meaning that refugees are often full of lies.

The leader concluded:

There is absolutely no reason to start teaching the basics of the difficult Danish

21. *Vestkysten*, January 5 1985.
22. *Vestkysten*, January 14 and 15 1985.

language to Iranians while it is still undecided as to whether the people concerned are to be integrated into society.[23]

A letter to the editor commented on 'an unmanageable law on refugees': 'Now people must tell their politicians what to do. Or else Denmark will find herself getting into a tragic state of utter confusion' (January 16 1985).

In July 1985, the paper reported from Kalundborg that the Union of Immigrant Associations had requested that an effort should be made on all sides to enable Danes and foreigners to live in peaceful coexistence. On July 31 there was a report of a meeting of the Parliamentary Legal Committee at which, according to the Prime Minister, Poul Schlüter (K), there had been general agreement to 'support the line advocated by the Government — namely, to ensure that refugees can live here with us in safety'. Among the Government's plans was one for an information campaign on 'the real situation of refugees' since there was 'in certain circles, for example, a totally exaggerated conception of how much financial support refugees receive from the state'. Bjørn Elmquist (V) was quoted as saying that it was necessary to spread the refugees around the country more widely, so that they could be more quickly absorbed into local society. There were reports from Ribe County on various initiatives to counter racism, and from Varde came the claim that 'Race riots in Varde would be quite impossible!'. The leader of the local refugee group had said that 'It could hardly happen here. The West Jutlanders are such level-headed people.'

6.2.4 *Politiken*

If we turn now to consider the other papers, we find that *Politiken*'s coverage of the Queen's New Year message was marked by the same acquiescence as the conservative and liberal papers. Later in January, *Politiken* took a special interest in the Iranian asylum-seekers, as evidenced by a number of leaders in the course of the month. These leaders argued against the wish of the conservatives to tighten the law. According to *Politiken*, the 1983 Act did no more than embody international agreements and what normal propriety demanded.

In one such leader, published on January 28, the paper concluded that the investigation by the authorities of the refugees' backgrounds was a deception, since the claim made by refugees that they risked death if they were returned to Iran could simply not be checked.[24] The Danish people therefore simply had to adjust to the fact that there was a new element of 3,000 Iranians in

---

23. *Vestkysten*, January 17 1985.
24. See also the leaders 'Myths of Escape' (January 2 1985), 'New Year words. Two speeches by the Queen' (January 3 1985) and 'Refugees. Society must pay' (January 10 1985).

their society. According to the leader, these people were as culturally alien to Danish society as it was possible to imagine. The majority were Shiites, the product of a society 'which has for centuries trained its members in religious intolerance and belief in their superiority over the rest of the Muslim world'. The leader-writer therefore indicated the necessity for extra tolerance. People had to recognise that they should not expect the Iranians to become Danish overnight. A successful, understanding policy of integration could, however, be expected to produce the result that the next generation would be able to speak Danish, and that 'their grandchildren will also be Danish in mentality'.

In the regular news coverage, and also in many other contributions to the debate, the Iranians' case was constantly defended in *Politiken*. On January 5,' Ebbe Strange (Socialist People's Party) noted that immigrants had always been well taken care of in Denmark in the past, and this should be the case now respecting the Iranians. Criticism was again directed toward Ninn-Hansen:

The right-wing politicians, led by the Minister of Justice, constantly repeat that there are so many asylum-seekers because of the new law on aliens. Fortunately, the Social Democrats have stated clearly that they are not prepared to countenance a change in the law, so the Minister might as well give up.

Several news reports accused the authorities of dragging their feet in asylum cases and of using incompetent interpreters. Around January 20 1985 there were items concerning the allegedly threatening behaviour of a policeman during hearings for the Iranians, and *Politiken* announced that the Social Democrat MP Erik B. Smith would request that the Minister of Justice would make himself available for consultation in the Justice Committee. Towards the end of the month there were protests that the police took into custody asylum-seekers threatened with expulsion, to prevent them going underground.

On January 20 the paper published an article on the debate in the Liberal party that went on during a meeting of local party chairmen, mayors and MPs held at Christiansborg, the Parliamentary building. The Foreign Minister, Uffe Ellemann-Jensen (V), was quoted as saying:

It is clear that there are different views within the Liberal party on the problem, but I'm glad that the majority agree with me that it is important that we are prepared to accept genuine refugees.

He added, 'Discussion of the issue of so-called economic migrants must not be allowed to overshadow the problem of genuine refugees'.

The paper[25] described the parliamentary negotiations of March 22 under

25. It should be noted that *Politiken* was affected by a major strike for much of March 1985.

the headline 'Asylum seekers gain a respite'. Weight was placed in this report on the fact that the opposition parties, including the Social Liberals, had proposed that the Minister of Justice should have the power to grant temporary residence permits on humanitarian grounds. The possibility of a quick settlement of manifestly unfounded appeal cases was described as an efficiency measure. The paper emphasized that the Social Democrats and the other opposition parties insisted that the civil rights of refugees should be guaranteed.

In July 1985, *Politiken* strongly condemned the violence in Kalundborg. A leader on July 30 claimed without reservation: 'It cannot be denied that this was the product of racism. The actions are the result of a number of sad truths about the attitudes of some parts of the population.'

In December, the tightening of the law on aliens was presented under the headline 'Criticism of new asylum legislation'. The paper quoted the opponents of the change as saying that it would result in a weakening of civil rights and would also damage Denmark's international image. 'It is tragic that the Government has chosen the UN's Human Rights Day to introduce a curtailment of asylum-seekers' civil rights' pronounced Bernard Baunsgaard, whilst the most left-wing opposition parties demanded a usable definition of 'manifestly unfounded'.

6.2.5 *Information*

As with *Politiken*, opinion expressed in *Information* was overwhelmingly in favour of retaining the 1983 legislation. For example, on January 2 1985 the newspaper reported the outcome of a parliamentary question from the Left-wing Socialist Party to the Minister of Justice in the words 'Ninn-Hansen does not know how many economic migrants there are among the refugees,' and on January 13, *Information* reported from Geneva that the possible expulsion of the Iranians had awoken international attention and concern. Sources in the UN High Commission for Refugees stated that no country had as yet sent Iranians back to their homeland. Other articles backed the Iranians' case in Denmark.[26]

On January 15, a leader headed 'The price of openness' was published. The leader expressed the view that the decision to deport the two Iranians had further intensified the already bitter argument over the new refugee policy. According to the paper, it was clear that the two asylum-seekers were not political refugees in the normal sense. 'Their real challenge to the Ayatollah's regime in Tehran lies in the fact that *after* leaving Iran, they came to Denmark and asked for asylum'. In other words, the Directorate for Aliens was faced with the problem that some asylum-seekers only became refugees at the mo-

---

26. 'Iranians fear execution' (January 15) and 'The Socialist People's Party says: Let the Iranians stay in Denmark' (January 28 1985).

ment when they requested asylum. However, this was not a new situation, said the article. The same thing happened in the case of Polish refugees in the 1960s. At that time, politicians had never hesitated to grant asylum; the request for asylum was in fact 'in itself a political act which had to be taken into account in considering the case'. The only valid criterion after that, said the paper, was the degree of political oppression in the asylum-seekers' homeland, and since Iran and Iraq both had repressive regimes, it would only be in very rare cases that it would be possible to refuse asylum under the new refugee law. The paper also claimed that this was a common European problem, since 'the situation regarding refugees in Europe is approaching total anarchy' (January 24 1985).

In an interview published the same day, Poul Hartling stated that Denmark had not accepted as many refugees as Sweden, or indeed as some of the poorer countries. It was, however, a problem that because of the pressure, Denmark was taking so long to evaluate individual cases that 'it becomes harder to send them back'. A few days later there was an interview with Candida Toscani, the head of the European section of the UN High Commission for Refugees. She reported that there were Iranians everywhere.

On June 26, *Information* put out a whole supplement filled with articles taking an opposing stance to hatred of foreigners in Denmark and in other countries. Headlines included 'The racism in our hearts' and 'Turks are Germany's new Jews'. On December 11 1985, *Information* announced, 'Aliens law tightened up', and the criticisms of opponents were given full coverage in an otherwise neutral article.

6.2.6 *Ekstra Bladet*

There was full editorial support in *Ekstra Bladet* for the sentiments which the Queen expressed in her speech, and during January a number of items were published warning strongly against racism in Denmark. In several articles, criticism of racism was used as a springboard for attacks on the right wing in general and the Progress Party in particular.[27]

The Queen's New Year message was published on the front page on January 2 1985 under the headline 'Victims of racial hatred say "Thanks, Margrethe"'. Next day the paper interpreted the speech as showing that she was the Queen of the weak and oppressed, putting herself 'at a yet clearer distance from the political right'. *Ekstra Bladet* also referred to the New Year's speech at the beginning of 1981, in which, according to the paper, she 'lashed out at the Progress Party and their views on the question of immigrant

---

27. In addition to those articles named in the text, see the following: 'Glistrup starts new witch-hunt against refugees' (January 14), and 'Racist whining from Progress Party dogs: "Don't preach at us, Margrethe"' (January 25 1985).

workers'. The party was not actually named, but there could be no mistaking the intended target. On that occasion, the Queen's speech came in the wake of the poisonous remarks concerning rats and immigrant workers made by a member of the Progress Party. Queen Margrethe appealed instead for people to show solidarity and to get to know the foreign workers and help them to adapt.

In its news coverage of the refugee issue, *Ekstra Bladet* was notable for its sympathetic coverage concerning the fate of the Iranians,[28] and the paper was active in reporting on and publishing critical items on the alleged racism displayed by the police during case hearings. Corresponding sympathy and solidarity were noticeable in a number of leaders, such as that of January 15 headed 'The refugee test', which again included a strong attack on the Progress Party. On January 19, the paper published a leader entitled 'Hatred of foreigners' in which the sympathy was expressed as follows: 'It may well be that there really are many Danes who believe that book-keeping, finance and cold calculation of figures should guide our fortunate little country in every detail. But we must have freedom! If we are not allowed to share our good fortune with those who are in need, then perhaps we should be thinking of leaving Denmark.' The author Sven Holm wrote in a feature article, 'We are on our way to becoming a remarkably self-righteous people. And in our peevish priggishness we take a watchdog's satisfaction in denying entry to people who have fled from inhuman regimes to stand at our gates.' (January 12 1985).

On March 3, the front page of *Ekstra Bladet* returned to the Queen's New Year message: 'Margrethe despises Glistrup. The Queen's New Year message was a warning to the Progress Party's guru against making political capital out of xenophobia.' The paper also declared that 'appealing to the bastard in Danes has produced political advantage time and again'. On June 1, the paper reported that 'Those condemned to death are allowed to stay in Denmark. The politicians have saved the Iranians — even though they cannot be given refugee status.' In a leader published the same day, the paper welcomed 'in the name of humanity' the fact that the minister, Erik Ninn-Hansen 'will in future be obliged to issue a temporary residence permit for all the politically persecuted Iranians who end up in Denmark in their flight from the lunatic Khomeini'. That day's *Ekstra Bladet* also published a report from a village in southern Jutland called Øster Højst, where a group of residents had threatened to block the roads into the village when a group of refugees were

---

28. Examples include 'Refugees shiver' (January 8), 'Condemned to death by Denmark (January 12), 'Awaiting judgement' (January 16), 'They are depending on us' (January 19), 'Our flight from death to life' (January 19) and 'Don't throw us out: The gallows are waiting' (January 29 1985).

to be housed in the disused inn. Now the Iranians had arrived. 'First Khomeini. Now Øster Højst. Village klansmen drive Iranians away.' The article spoke of 'the burning racial hatred' that had burst out in the little town. It was reported that a group of Iranians had left the village again, driven into flight by 'this town that describes them as knife-wielders and fears for the safety of their children and the aged'.

In December 1985 *Ekstra Bladet* did not write specifically about Parliament's tightening of the Aliens Act, but the editorial sympathy of the paper was evident in articles such as 'They are to be sent home to Khomeini. Justice Ministry official suddenly gets cold feet in incomprehensible deportation case' (December 12 1985).

6.2.7 *Aktuelt*

If we turn now to consider *Aktuelt*, we find that the paper also supported the sentiments expressed in the Queen's speech, with front-page stories such as 'Enthusiasm over New Year's message' and 'Margrethe receives lots of praise'. On January 2, interviews with some immigrants were published, in which they expressed their great delight about the initiative. The paper had also interviewed Vibeke Storm Rasmussen, the chairwoman of the Social Democrats' immigrant committee and a local politician, whose support was perhaps a little more restrained:

I agree with the Queen in her rejection of Danish 'humour' which is directed against people who are different in some way... . But I think there is high degree of solidarity among those who, for example, stand in the unemployment queues together with the immigrants. We have not paid sufficient attention to the fact that we have created large concentrations of both immigrants and refugees in the municipalities around Copenhagen, as a result of which the problem is somewhat different there to that in the rest of the country.

A leader on January 3 gave this political signal: 'The Queen's warning is timely. Just when the political right are trying with all their might to change Danish refugee policy, because it is beginning to cost money.' In an article the same day the argument was put forward that Denmark had accepted fewer refugees than other western European countries. This report was based on the reply to a Parliamentary question from Torben Lund (Social Democrat) to Ninn-Hansen, which had confirmed that this was the case. Torben Lund concluded: 'That's why we should uphold the Aliens Act, which the Minister of Justice voted for himself, as it stands.'

Many other items published in *Aktuelt* during the course of January showed continued support of the 1983 legislation, and a number of articles defended the Iranians threatened with expulsion. One particularly passionate article described in detail how an Iranian man had been subjected to severe torture,[29] and other journalists and writers attacked what was now being interpreted as manifest Danish racism. For example, Jacques Blum wrote an article published on January 28 on 'Racist snakes in the Danish paradise'. However, many of the letters to the editor published in the paper were strongly opposed to the policy on refugees, and one could well have formed the impression that the opinions of the editors were not fully in tune with those of their readers.

When the negotiations on the tightening of the Aliens Act were in progress at the end of May 1985, the paper described these negotiations under the headline 'Parliament rages against refugee witch-hunt'.[30] It was stated that 'all the Parliamentary parties, with the exception of the Progress Party, condemn the witch-hunt which is being directed from a number of factions against the refugees who have been given permission to stay here in Denmark'. The attack by Torben Lund (Social Democrat) on the Progress Party received especially detailed attention in the report,[31] and it was also reported that developments in Øster Højst had caused alarm among MPs.

In December 1985, with the year's significant tightening of the legislation on aliens, *Aktuelt* described the changes very briefly. The idea was that the new law would mean quicker processing of cases. The opposition parties' criticisms were given in summary form.

6.3 1986: Another round in the battle over legislation on aliens

The year 1986 had hardly begun when the debate started up again, generally focusing to a lesser or greater extent on either attacking or defending the current legislation on aliens. On January 1 *Ekstra Bladet* published an article entitled 'Block to refugees a tragedy'. The article in particular reported on a new agreement with the DDR whereby asylum-seekers' access to Denmark via that country would be barred. 'The consequence will be hundreds of human tragedies.' The article also announced that a group of Danes wanted to start an association, to be called 'The Friends of Refugees'. *Berlingske Tidende* published an article about the new organization on the same day, and quoted Bernhard Baunsgaard as saying:

I can well understand people wanting to help refugees when the Danish authorities have declined to do so. There have been times before in history when it has been necessary to break the law to help people in need.

Several of Denmark's bishops criticized the tightening of the law in *Politiken*

29. 'He survived unbelievable torture', *Aktuelt*, January 13 1985.
30. *Aktuelt*, June 1 1985.
31. Earlier in the year, a letter to the editor published in *Aktuelt* had claimed: 'Glistrup's programme has been stolen from Hitler' (March 20 1985).

on January 2 1986. 'We must be open and tolerant. There is no cause for us to moan. We are a rich society, and if we don't think we have the means to take care of refugees, then we can always pay a little more in tax,' said Bishop Henrik Christiansen. Bishop Thorkild Græsholt added: 'It's something of a compliment to us that refugees want to come here.'

It was in the context of such a turbulent debate that *Vestkysten* published on January 2 a commentary by Laurits Tørnæs, the Liberals' political spokesman, concerning the new agreement with the DDR: 'We shouldn't be scared over the agreement with the DDR.' Tørnæs rejected criticism from the Refugee Council, and went on:

The central rule should now be that a plan to take a certain number of refugees is included in the budget. These refugees must be approved by the UN High Commission and should come from the UN's refugee camps.

The debate rumbled on through 1986. A fairly widespread conception among those in the political centre that there was a continued pressure on the Danish borders led to yet another amendment to the law in October 1986 (see below). Another factor contributing to the law being changed was that both the Government and the Social Democrats pointed out that stricter rules in Sweden and West Germany necessitated a tightening of the Danish regulations (Pedersen, 1991 p. 194).

On October 11, *Aktuelt* published an article on the new parliamentary negotiations entitled 'Asylum rules to be tightened up: Tough debate on refugees'. The report said that 'the much-discussed refugee debate has ended up in the way that all politicians were equally anxious to avoid — as a party political slanging match on refugee policy'. According to the article, Ole Espersen had given the impression that the Social Democrats would be willing to enter into a compromise with the Government if 'certain amendments' were made to the Government proposal. The amendment to the law was among other things to lay down that asylum-seekers who came from transit countries where they were in fact perfectly safe should in future be turned away at the border, and also that valid passports and visas would be required for entry to the country. The *Aktuelt* article also stated that the spokesmen for the older parties had made yet another attack on the Progress Party. Pia Kjærsgaard herself had spoken of 'people who are deathly tired of the whole refugee circus, which has brought violence and terror to Denmark on a scale never known before'. Ninn-Hansen had then 'clearly distanced himself from the Progress Party'.

An article in *Berlingske Tidende* published the same day painted a similar picture, but laid stress on the Conservative Minister of Justice's exact words: 'At one point, so many asylum-seekers were strolling across the border into Denmark that it took on the character of a migration.' But the paper also published the critical response of Helveg Petersen (Social-Liberal): 'That sort of talk creates a bad climate around the subject.' *Berlingske* also explained what divided the Government and Social Democrat positions. The Government wished that the *de facto* refugees — refugees who were not covered by any re-fugee convention, but who nevertheless were in danger — should no longer have a legal right to a residence permit. Ole Espersen expressed the Social De-mocrats' opposition to this:

We agree with the Government that a revision of the law is required. Our precondition is that we do not want thereby to send any asylum-seekers home to a perilous existence; but this is not what the Government wants either (*Berlingske Tidende*, October 11 1986).

Hagen Hagensen was quoted as saying: 'We recognize our obligations to-wards genuine refugees — but we also have obligations to the Danish people.'

In *Information's* coverage of the negotiations, Ole Espersen was quoted as saying that it was only with regret that the Social Democrats had agreed to changes in the rules:

We agree with the Government that the situation has changed to an extent where we cannot simply remain passive. But we are very sorry that it will be necessary to revise the current legislation, which is and which should be a model for other countries to follow.

The Socialist People's party and the Left-wing Socialists were reported to have flatly rejected the proposal, which they saw as returning to the legal situation that pertained before the 1983 legislation. Ole Espersen's regrets were also quoted by *Jyllands-Posten* on October 11 1986:

We agree with the Government that there should be a reduction in the number of asylum-seekers. The situation has changed to an extent where we cannot simply remain passive. We risk arriving at a situation where we have to take panic measures to put a total stop to refugee entry.

In its editorial coverage, *Jyllands-Posten* wrote: 'The background to the Govern-ment proposal is the rapidly increasing number of asylum-seekers at the Da-nish borders.'

Politiken discussed the negotiations under the heading 'Opposition to the asylum law' (October 11 1986), stressing that the Government could not get its proposal passed without amendments, but that compromise would be difficult, as Ninn-Hansen insisted that the proposal had to be accepted as a whole. *Politiken* also emphasized that the Social-Liberals were not willing to support the proposal in its current form, and

neither are the Social Democrats, according to the former Minister of Justice Ole Espersen. The Socialist People's party and the Left-wing Socialists will certainly not put their
names to limiting the number of asylum-seekers.

Like *Politiken*, *Vestkysten* quoted Ninn-Hansen as saying that the proposal had
to be taken as a whole: 'If we start to mess about with it, it will end up
having next to no effect, and we'll be back where we started' (October11
1986). The misgivings of the Social democrats and Social-Liberals were mentioned, and Pia Kjærsgaard was quoted as saying 'the refugee legislation has
become a taboo, and asylum-seekers are economic migrants and deserters.
They should be kicked out of the country.' In reports from the paper's own
area, *Vestkysten* continued to describe the situation of the refugees in Ribe
county, often with a sympathetic angle, as in the article 'Fear of beatings
isolates refugees'. The paper also reported on episodes where refugees had
been threatened or suffered harassment in some way or other.

On October 13 1986, *Berlingske Tidende* announced agreement between the
Government and the Social Democrats on a stricter asylum law, since the Government had given in to the Social Democrats' demands over *de facto* refugees. It was stated that there was opposition to the new tightening of the
1983 legislation in some sections of the Social Democratic group. Similarly,
Jyllands-Posten's coverage on October 13 reported that a compromise was in
sight, as the Government had given in to the demand to change the legal status of *de facto* refugees,[32] and *Aktuelt* echoed, 'Broad compromise on refugees
now in sight'. The article mentioned that during the negotiations in the
parliamentary committee, Ninn-Hansen had forcefully rejected a request from
the Refugee Council that they should assist the police in the cases that would
arise when refugees arrived at the border:

The Danish Refugee Council is a private organization, and this is a question of border
control. It must be absolutely clear as a general principle that private organizations will
not be allowed to assist the state in this control.

Politiken described the negotiations from the angle 'Tougher for refugees'
(*Politiken*, October 13 1986). The most significant change was again seen to be
the fact that refugees could now be turned away at the border if they came
from a country where they had actually been living in safety.

The amendments to the legislation were passed by a majority comprising
the Government parties, the Progress Party and the Social Democrats, while
the Social-Liberals, The Socialist People's party and the Left-wing Socialists

---

32. The press discussion that day also made it clear that under the new law, the Government would be able to fine airlines and shipping companies who transported
foreigners to Denmark without passports or visas.

voted against. During the final debate in Parliament, the Social Democrats in particular were criticized by the three parties who voted against for abandoning the line on which the four parties had been united before the passage of the 1983 legislation (Pedersen 1991:194). An article in *Jyllands-Posten* the same day could be read as suggesting that a certain tightening of the law was justified, since the current system was probably reaching the limits of what it could handle. In the course of the coming month, said the article, 2,000 people granted asylum would be handed on to the Refugee Council, 'or five times as many as has been the case in recent months'. The newspaper suggested that that would create almost insurmountable problems in housing the refugees and in putting them through the normal 18-month integration programme.

As early as October 20, *Politiken* published an article describing how refugees were being stopped at Kastrup (Copenhagen) Airport. The Airport Police Chief described the effect of the change in the law:

Last Sunday we received 40 asylum-seekers. Of the nine who arrived yesterday, five had landed in transit at a West European airport, and these were sent back there. The other four Iranians had come directly from Turkey, and they were sent to the refugee camp at Sandholm.

The Chairman of the Refugee Council, Thor A. Bak, showed no surprise at these developments: 'Rumours spread quickly, and that's why so many refugees came here to try to get accepted. The refugees hurried to get here before the law was passed.' On the same day, *Jyllands-Posten* carried a similar report from Kastrup Airport. There would very probably be a need to increase the size of the administrative apparatus, but the tightening of the law had worked as intended. *Vestkysten* reported on October 22 that the police believed that the stream of refugees was in part organized by immigrant-smugglers. The police said that the situation was unclear at that time, but that was no reason to reduce the level of preparedness.[33]

The Government and the Social Democrats recognized the need to spread information about the new rules. This recognition was reflected in a feature by Ninn-Hansen in *Berlingske Tidende* and a piece by Ole Espersen in *Aktuelt*, both published on October 20.

Ninn-Hansen stressed that the 1983 legislation had provided extensive civil rights to the refugees, and Denmark had committed herself to a greater extent than any other country to giving residence permits to refugees. The original law was passed, according to the Minister, on the assumption that other countries would also accept similar obligations, but that had not happened. As the problems had grown to massive proportions, so the need for a revision

33. The previous day, *Jyllands-Posten* had described how the countries of the EC had decided at a meeting of ministers of justice and internal affairs to tighten border controls and develop a common policy over the misuse of the asylum system.

had become acute. The Minister pointed out that the figures for arrivals for September 1986 had been so high that they were equivalent to an annual influx of thirty to thirty-five thousand asylum-seekers. The Government's solution was an ongoing adjustment of the legislation by means of a new paragraph in the law which said that asylum-seekers could be turned back at the border if they came from certain safe countries. Ninn-Hansen argued that this rule was in accordance with the 1951 Convention, and the basis on which an asylum-seeker could be recognized as a refugee had not altered. In the future, the Minister stated, the complex problem of refugees would need an international solution. The article concluded with a reference to the sovereignty of the nation state:

We now have a law which once more makes it possible for us in Denmark to decide which foreigners we want to accept into our country. I think that's splendid. But there should be no doubt that in the future we want to help those people that are in need around the world ... We shall continue to accept refugees here, both those who arrive on their own and those accepted under UN quotas. Our goal must be to ensure good conditions for the refugees that we will still be accepting in numbers that just a few years ago would have seemed enormous.

Ole Espersen's article in *Aktuelt* was entitled 'Modest reform of the law on foreigners'. He stated that the Social Democrats regarded the changes as fully defensible, 'though naturally we would have preferred not to have found the changes necessary. We must however never forget that our obligation is first and foremost to find room for those in genuine need.'

On October 20 *Jyllands-Posten* published a major contribution to the debate by Søren Krarup. On that day he focused especially on the treatment of non-Danish-speaking children in the compulsory school system:

Of course, Denmark should continue to be a Danish state, where the Danish language and history and culture will be the indisputable basis of school teaching and where knowledge of these things will be a necessary precondition for obtaining Danish nationality!

The pastor also used as a springboard for his argument conditions in England and Germany, where as a result of these countries' past history they had accepted 'floods' of foreigners:

And that would be catastrophic for us. What sort of Europe would we have if England and Germany were to disintegrate? How can the western world survive as a democratic society, built upon Christian respect for the individual's freedom and responsibility, if the leading countries go under in chaos and internal anarchy?

On October 25, a leader in *Jyllands-Posten* rejected a suggestion by Social Democrat MP Jytte Hilden for the establishment of a Ministry of Immigrants.

Jytte Hilden's comments in the debate, in which according to the leader she had declared that Denmark did not understand how to integrate these new citizens into society, were described as being both incorrect and confused. The leader pointed out that 'many refugees are here temporarily and have no wish to integrate into Danish society. Consequently, they have to accept things as they are.' Integration was an issue solely for the foreigners who stayed permanently in the country, and the leader accepted that:

The integration experiment might fail, but this is not necessarily the fault of the host country. There are examples of foreigners who have lived in Denmark for decades and who have never learned to speak comprehensible Danish, and of course it's not very easy for them to fit into society.

6.4 In appropriate numbers? Debate and party political differences concerning the revised Aliens Act

The entire process concerning the three revisions of the 1983 Act indicated that the debate was unlikely to reach a conclusion in autumn 1986 with the implementation of the third and most stringent set of restrictions. The parties of the left wing had expressed dissatisfaction, as had the Social-Liberals. Furthermore, the Progress Party had also — although for completely different motives — been vociferous in its criticism of the refugee policy, even though the party had voted in favour of the October 1986 revision. However, there was also a degree of internal disagreement within the government and the Social Democratic Party.

On 14 August 1987, *Information* published the existence of such a split within the ranks of the right-wing government. Party Chairman Flemming Kofoed-Svendsen, the Christian People's Party, confirmed to *Information* that Denmark should accept around five thousand refugees per year, but Erik Ninn-Hansen, the Conservative Minister of Justice, only wished to guarantee to the United Nations that Denmark would accept two hundred and fifty quota refugees per year[34]. Moreover, discontent was brewing among the ranks of the Social Democrats. On September 5, immediately before the general election in September 1987, and the day before the party's annual congress, *Det fri Aktuelt* put the cat among the pigeons with a front page splash under the heading: 'Social Democrats bury critical report'. The newspaper article commented on the way in which the executive committee of the party had delayed the central committee's reading of a report from the party's committee on refugees and immigration.

A report from within the Social Democratic Party strongly attacking refugee organizations in Denmark has been shelved by the party's executive committee until after

34. This figure did not include spontaneous asylum-seekers.

the general election ... The report accuses the Danish Red Cross and the Refugee Council of making the handling of refugees into a commercial enterprise. At the expense of the state and without public knowledge or control.

The committee was chaired by Vibeke Storm Rasmussen, a county and municipal politician, who 'had been working with problems concerning refugees and immigrants for ten years via her seat on Albertslund Municipal Council and Copenhagen County Council'. From the report, the article quotes a demand that immigrants should be required to adapt to the conditions of Danish society to a far greater extent, as well as for much tighter rules concerning when refugees and immigrants should be permitted to marry citizens from their country of origin. The report also proposed setting a maximum limit for the number of foreign citizens entering from countries outside the EC. It also mentioned 'attitudes, actions and conditions among immigrants and refugees that are unacceptable to Social Democrats'. All in all, the committee was pressing for a political standpoint concerning the groups of aliens that Denmark should accommodate.

On September 6 1987, *Jyllands-Posten* stated: 'Social Democrats pave the way for a tightening of policy on refugees.' The article described a number of the new restrictions that the committee advocated and, at the same time, quoted the party chairman Anker Jørgensen as saying: 'Denmark is a small country, so we must avoid being overrun by foreigners. Accepting too many refugees will damage Denmark both economically and culturally.' The chairman would also prefer to see Denmark accommodating more UN refugees and fewer spontaneous asylum-seekers.

On October 13 1987, *Information* published an interview with Vibeke Storm Rasmussen. The interview again made it clear that, in fact, the report contained proposals for tightening a number of existing regulations, and included the proposal that young immigrants should not immediately be allowed to marry 'a cousin from their country of origin or bring their spouse to Denmark unless both husband and wife can prove that they have learned the Danish language'. In addition, the report suggested a ceiling of 5,000 immigrants per annum, and that this total should include both refugees themselves and other family members who might seek reunification with their relatives in Denmark. The report also included a draft proposal for the possibility of offering immigrants and refugees a sum of money if they wished to return to their homeland. To a question from the *Information* journalist as to whether marriage control in fact constituted 'negative special treatment of immigrants', Vibeke Storm Rasmussen answered:

Yes, it does involve treating people differently on the basis of whether or not they are Danish citizens. However, it is an attempt to find a solution to the current situation. There are many problems involved, but it is difficult to find other solutions that provide fair protection for young people, and that is why we have made this suggestion.

On October 18 1987, *Politiken* wrote: 'Social Democrats in turmoil about refugees'. The article mentioned that the party's confidential report contained points of view that many people 'lumped together with Pastor Søren Krarup's view on the matter. But now it is time to clear the air.' According to *Politiken*, Svend Auken, the new party chairman, had thus made ready to dismiss Vibeke Storm Rasmussen. A new and politically 'weightier' committee was to formulate a cohesive policy on immigration and refugees for the Social Democrats. Auken also expressed his opinion that it was time for an 'anti-racism campaign' aimed at changing attitudes, a campaign which has the support of the entire union movement. He said that it was also necessary to 'build models to ensure a more even distribution of the expenses linked to accepting and accommodating aliens'. The party chairman argued that:

Unemployment is increasing rapidly, and that is why I want to solve this problem now. We must avoid the risk of a 'scapegoat mentality', i.e. blaming immigrants and refugees for our own problems, and using the integration problems they face as an excuse for conditions that exist in our own society.

On October 18 1987, *Jyllands-Posten* published the fact that, under any circumstances, there were administrative difficulties linked to the large number of asylum-seekers. A survey carried out by the newspaper of the Danish Red Cross showed that, even a year after the Aliens Act had been tightened, there was still a considerable backlog of cases dating back to the 'refugee flood' of 1986. One applicant had waited no less than three years for a decision. However, the article also made it clear that the modifications to the act had slowed the stream of refugees 'far more effectively than the politicians had originally imagined'. The following day, *Jyllands-Posten* revealed the fact that airlines in the United Arab Emirates — probably for a sufficient bribe — allowed stateless Palestinians to board flights bound for Copenhagen. In this way, the article served as an attempt to document the fact that the business of organized illegal immigration still flourished, and a warning to the authorities to be vigilant. At the same time, the article argued that requiring immigrants to present a valid passport and visa when entering Denmark was a particularly well-considered decision — otherwise the country would have to deal with a massive influx of refugees and immigrants; stateless Palestinians, for example.

On October 19, *Information* broke the news: 'Social Democrats to introduce anti-racist information campaign' and published an interview with Ole Espersen, who stated that one of the aims of the campaign was to eradicate the 'quasi-racist' political parties in Denmark. Asked whether the party's participation in the 1986 Act had not, in effect, been a concession to this self-same racism, Espersen answered:

Either you say that everyone has the right to seek asylum and has the right to live here while their applications are processed, or you have to say that we will grant entry to everyone who does not have a safe place to live elsewhere. That is what we have chosen to do now.

On February 18 1988, *Berlingske Tidende* announced that 'a new commission on aliens' had in fact been set up by the Social Democrats with the aim of drawing up concrete proposals for a conciliatory agreement with the government parties, as the 1986 revision contained provisions stating that the act was to be revised after two years. However, Elsebeth Kock-Petersen, the spokeswoman on the immigration question for the Liberal Party, believed that the leaders of the Social Democrats would have to implement a radical change in policy if they wanted such an agreement. The following day, the newspaper actually ran the headline: 'Threat from the Conservatives: general election'. The Conservative Members of Parliament had agreed at a meeting to work to press for a referendum on immigration policy — a proposal that had been aired by the Progress Party — if a majority of politicians outside the government parties wished to ease the restrictions that had been introduced in October 1986.[35] The newspaper referred to the fact that Ole Espersen had spoken in favour of an administrative relaxation on a number of occasions. In addition, *Berlingske Tidende* commented that tightening the provisions of the Act had led to a considerable fall in the number of asylum-seekers:

The government believes that the arrangement is working according to plan while organizations including the Refugee Council criticize the Act for sending refugees back to the countries where they are persecuted. Both the Socialist People's Party and the Social Liberal Party are appealing to the Social Democrats to alter the law to avoid erroneous expulsions (*Berlingske Tidende*, February 19 1988).

On the same day, the journalists Anna Winding and Jan Jørgensen also revealed that:

The truth behind the myth of the hordes of refugees that have flooded in over the

---

35. The public had been giving consideration to this thought ever since autumn 1986. For example, on October 18 1986, a reader wrote to *Jyllands-Posten*, making the following demand: 'Let us vote on the immigration question'. 'This is much more important than the matter of whether or not to join the EC. It seems that we are well on the way to destroying Denmark from the inside, and this is worse than being at war'. On October 18 1987, another reader asked in the same newspaper: 'Since when has it been so bad to listen to the people?'

borders is that only 21,500 of them entered the country in the 1980s. In fact, they would not fill one end of the national football stadium (*Berlingske Tidende*, February 19 1988).

Søren Jessen-Petersen, the leader of the UN Refugee Commission for Scandinavia stated that 'we can see that our refugees are in a tough situation'. However, Jessen-Petersen conceded that the 2–3,000 refugees to whom the country granted entry over a period of just a few months in 1985 and 1986 were clearly more than the Danish society could accept. 'But as the situation is now, there is a glaring contrast between the humanitarian values that Denmark wishes to stand for, and the policies it enforces with regard to refugees.' The UN official also pointed out that work should be done to find international solutions and that in this case Denmark could reasonably be expected to accommodate 3–5,000 refugees per year. The article revealed that it had been stated during the current debate about the revision of the Act that 'both the parties in government and the Social Democrats had mentioned the figure of 3–5,000 as an "appropriate" number'.

On February 19 1988, *Vestkysten* wrote about the existing disagreement within the government concerning the possibility of a referendum,

while the Liberals and the Conservatives are not really afraid of a referendum, the two minor parties in the government — the Centre Democrats and the Christian People's Party — are a little more cautious .... The Centre Democrats have no intention of moving in that direction. 'It doesn't really suit us to hang on to the shirt tails of the Progress Party in this matter'

said Arne Melchior, the Centre Democrats' party chairman, to *Vestkysten*.

Elsebeth Kock-Petersen was quoted as saying that she 'can well understand the idea' behind the proposal for a referendum.

On February 20 1988, *Berlingske Tidende* published a verbatim account of the immigration debate in the Danish Parliament the previous day. During the debate, the Social Democrat Torben Lund made it clear that his party did not, in fact, wish to relax the restrictions of the Aliens Act, whereupon Grethe Fenger Møller of the Conservatives conceded that her party was therefore willing to drop its backing of the move towards a referendum. During the debate, most parties again attacked the Progress Party. Mogens Glistrup of the Progress Party had thus been met with 'overwhelming contempt from all sides' when he compared the influence of Muslim refugees on Denmark with the effects of arsenic in a glass of water. The summary of the debate published in *Vestkysten* on the same day revealed that the left-wing 'Common Way' (Fælles Kurs) coalition was the only group not to have rejected the Progress Party's proposals out of hand.

On February 28 1988, the editorial in *Berlingske Tidende* laid out the paper's official evaluation. Firstly, the paper firmly reiterated that Denmark had accepted refugees for centuries, and that these refugees had introduced valuable qualities to Danish society. Recently however, the Danish policy on aliens had 'unfortunately given rise to a debate that has occasionally been tarnished with a hint of racism and which has often demonstrated what could easily be termed malice'. According to the paper, the Danish Parliament was particularly responsible for this. In fact, the 1983 Act had exacerbated an already bad situation:

It gave everyone waiting at the borders the right to demand entry to the country and to stay here while their applications were processed. The flood of refugees became so big that it overwhelmed any possibility that might have existed for dealing with the purely practical problems. The Act was more far-reaching than any of Denmark's international obligations.

As a result of the flood of refugees, the Danish Parliament was obliged to introduce restrictions to the Act, and the number of refugees seeking residence has since decreased. Finally, the editorial criticized the Progress Party for profiting from an unfortunate wave of public opinion. The Social-Liberals, and especially Bernhard Baunsgaard, were also criticized. The extreme points of view could, in fact, undermine the possibility of generating public understanding of the refugee policy.

Somewhat late in the day, with regard to events in Parliament, Pastor Søren Krarup wrote in an article in *Ekstra Bladet* on February 22 under the heading 'Yes to a referendum' that it was clear that 'more and more we have to face the fact that the parties and the politicians that belong to them can act as a kind of occupying army oppressing the people'. According to the pastor, the politicians' ability to represent the people left something to be desired in the matter of immigrants. 'Because Denmark is not a country of immigrants. It is the Danes' fatherland'. However, the article should not be considered an expression of the paper's opinion, as at this time, a number of articles spoke in favour of the immigrants' and refugees' case. For example, an article published on February 25 criticized the internment of refugees in Danish detention centres.

In January 1991, *Politiken* warned of the threat of new problems arising in connection with the imminent influx of people from the former communist countries, as these people had a clear picture of the possibilities offered by the rich West. Actually, the background to the article entitled 'Rich Europe raises the drawbridge'[36] was a conference held by the European Commission with the aim of establishing a common European policy on immigration. According

36. *Politiken*, October 17 1984.

to *Politiken*, this conference resulted in a number of proposals for common and more restrictive rules for immigration. However, these had already been implemented by the individual countries in a large number of cases. Furthermore, the article mentioned that possibly the most important reason behind the restrictions was a growing feeling of resentment towards these aliens in Western Europe, but it was also the case that this immigration actually influenced the social order in the west, because immigrants worked illicitly and were used by employers to push wages down. At the same time, the journalist could see a link between the influx of tens of thousands of young men with no ties to society and a rise in criminality. Even though the article contained a certain amount of criticism of the double standards displayed by many countries in this regard, it could be regarded as a contribution to the domestic debate, with *Politiken* sending out partially new signals.

At the same time, there was talk of the possibility of a stream of genuine refugees arriving in the country resulting from the unrest in the Baltic States caused by these countries' attempts to achieve national independence.

On January 27 1991, *Politiken* published a Vilstrup survey that showed that there was a high level of public support for Denmark granting asylum to refugees from Estonia, Latvia and Lithuania. The right-wing government had already announced that Denmark was prepared to grant entry to refugees from the Baltic, who would be welcome in Denmark. However, when these refugees first began to arrive in Denmark via Sweden, the Aliens Act actually proved to be an obstacle to granting them entry, as Sweden simply had to be considered a first safe country of refuge. On January 27, Foreign Minister Uffe Ellemann-Jensen (V) stated to *Politiken*: 'The law is too inflexible. We have no opportunity to decide whom to accept.' Thus the right-wing parties that helped to form the government had also — somewhat unexpectedly — voiced their opinion that the law was in need of revision.

6.5 The municipal dimension

Finding room for the numerous refugees in municipalities throughout the country revealed major differences from region to region, with some local authorities accommodating large numbers of refugees, while others were un-willing to accept more than a few. As the distribution of guest workers also revealed major variations, with a relatively high concentration in a limited number of municipalities controlled by the Social Democrats — in the County of Copenhagen, and in the municipalities of Aarhus and Odense — a heated debate was almost guaranteed as the number of refugees increased. Or, perhaps more precisely: To the re-emergence of a debate that had roots stretching back to 1980, when Erik Mørk, the then town clerk of the municipality of Ishøj, had stated: 'Other municipalities export immigrants and social problems to us.'[37]

On January 8 1985, on the basis of a report from Ritzau's news agency, *Vestkysten* published an article dealing with the way in which some municipalities had used a number of excuses to support their refusal to house refugees, and as mentioned above in section 6.2.2, *Jyllands-Posten* took a closer look at the problems in Vejle and Kolding. It was clear from the reports in both papers that the National Association of Local Authorities in Denmark was pushing for the state to provide the local authorities with financial compensation. In autumn 1986, the municipalities of Kalundborg and Holbæk refused to accommodate more refugees on the Swedish hotel ship which the leader of the centre in the County of West Zealand planned to moor at one of the county's harbours.[38]

In August 1987, Per Madsen, the Social Democrat Mayor of Ishøj, put himself in the spotlight by voicing strong criticism of what he interpreted as the Muslim immigrants' unwillingness to adapt to Danish society, using the slogan 'when in Rome, do as the Romans do.' The mayor received backing from *Ekstra Bladet* on August 11 1987 in a lead story about 'Little Turkey' and in an article entitled 'Ishøj split: Mohammed or Madsen'[39]. The lead story picked up the pieces from the 1970s and made it clear that Denmark had never managed to draw up a policy on immigration. This meant that such immigration as had taken place had developed according to 'the principle of self-service'. The Danes should accept

a fair number of refugees who are threatened with torture or execution, but we cannot take the pressure off the Turkish unemployment queues without this having far-reaching political, economic and cultural effects.

In other words, the nation should not turn a blind eye to 'the exploitation of our social system, for which some Turks have acquired a taste'. In the article, Per Madsen was quoted as having made statements about Turkish immigrants grossly abusing the social services. According to the mayor, the worst problem was that the Turkish children in Ishøj were being married off to Turks in Turkey, and so all of a sudden, their in-laws were living in the municipality, too. 'In 1978 there were 644 Turks living here — today, there are 1,440.'

The situation in Ishøj was the subject of a report in *Vestkysten* on August 11 1987. The report carried a detailed summary of Per Madsen's arguments as well as an interview with Knud Enggaard, the Liberal Minister of the In-

37. Quoted here from *Politiken*, December 14 1994 which published an article that day charting the 'Outbreak of the 18-year-old ghetto debate'.
38. See for example, *Jyllands-Posten* October 19 1986.
39. Quoted from Gaasholt and Togeby 1996, p. 29.

terior, who stated that, in fact, the municipality of Ishøj received huge financial compensation for the extra costs it incurred due to the large numbers of
aliens it housed. Erik B. Smith, the Social Democrat's spokesman on social security, was also quoted as saying: 'what Per Madsen is saying here can in no
way be taken as an expression of the Social Democrats' policy'. The editorial
in *Vestkysten* on the same day examined the question and expressed sympathy
for the initiative taken by Per Madsen. When Pia Kjærsgaard appeared on the
scene with 'her irresistible urge to pander to cheap, uncommitted points of
view', *Vestkysten* had to distance itself from this, but it was necessary to

discuss seriously the problem that the Mayor of Ishøj aired on the radio news yesterday. It is obvious that if around 14% of the population of a municipality are immigrants
from other countries, primarily countries that have a different cultural background,
then this will inevitably create problems. Especially when the immigrants are unwilling
to accept the initiatives to facilitate integration that the host country is striving to
establish.

The editorial ended by claiming that immigrants would do better to stay at
home if 'they feel themselves tainted by any and every contact with Danish
culture, Danish norms and Danish tradition ... And they should be made
aware of this. Even hospitality has its limits.'

On August 17 1987, *Information* reported on an internal conference for the
Social Democrats which was attended by the party's Members of Parliament,
the executive committee and a number of leading municipal politicians. The
conference was held as a part of the Social Democrats' preparations for the
approaching election, and a central theme of the meeting was the party's
stance on the question of immigrants and refugees. Ole Espersen gave
Information the following summary of the discussions: 'Everyone agrees that
we should grant entry to refugees. However, the problem is the extremely
concentrated placement of refugees and immigrants in some municipalities.'
Per Madsen had been granted a conditional support at the meeting as his
fellow mayors had backed his assertion that there were problems in Ishøj and
other municipalities. However, the party refuted the mayor's statements about
a 'Khomenification'. In practice, the Social Democrats wished to work for a
proposal for county-by-county distribution of refugees in accordance with a
quota system. Thorkild Simonsen (S), at that time chairman of the National
Association of Local Authorities in Denmark, pointed out to *Information* that
there was a proposal from his organization concerning municipal rights of re-
quisition — including the right to allocate privately-owned leased properties.
This could help to even out the spread of refugees throughout the country.
However, an article in *Information* on the same day reported that the right-
wing government rejected this approach. Thor Pedersen, Minster of Housing,
said: 'That would completely ruin any refugee's possibilities of achieving

reasonable living conditions. Situations can quickly arise in which the police may have to protect immigrants from protesting owners and tenants.'

On October 27 1987, Per Madsen repeated to *Politiken* his criticism of the unwillingness of immigrants to integrate in connection with a report that the municipality had just published: 'It is a problem that we cannot live with in the long run. Not only does the municipality contain a large population of immigrants, but they make no effort to integrate with the Danish population'. The report had traced the histories of 23 immigrants — chosen at random — who had lived in the municipality since their arrival in 1970. The survey showed that in 1987, the group of 23 had increased in size to 371. The following day, the mayor was rebuked in the same paper by a representative of the Ishøj Committee against Xenophobia. The spokesman criticized the report and claimed that the municipality had deliberately chosen to highlight extreme cases. In addition, the immigrants had extensive social needs that 'could best be fulfilled by starting a family. Who, apart from Per Madsen, could wonder that they choose to marry people from their home countries?'

In February 1988, the debate arose again when the Mayor of Ishøj requested a statement from the municipal council concerning the question of the extent to which the municipality should work to allow more aliens to move to Ishøj. On February 29 1988, Per Madsen said to *Berlingske Tidende*: 'Experience from other countries shows that a municipal population of 10% immigrants should be considered the permissible maximum if problems are to be avoided.' At that time, 12.5% of the municipal population was of non-Danish origin.

On the same day, Per Madsen again received support from *Ekstra Bladet*, which published a leading article interpreting his outspoken contribution as a 'stand against racism':

He could just as well have asked: 'Should we fight tooth and nail against having more aliens moving to Ishøj?' Because that is what he believes is required now — regardless of the fact that in reality municipal powers for such a housing prohibition are restricted.

Ekstra Bladet thus clearly stated that it believed that the municipality had already done its utmost to accommodate its share of aliens. Per Madsen's initiative was therefore seen as a rebellion against conditions that would really nurture racism. On the other hand it was possible 'easily to demonstrate that racism is alive and well — albeit discreetly — in other municipalities', such as those in the region to the north of Copenhagen. The article ended by urging the government and the National Association of Local Authorities in Denmark to find a solution to the municipal distribution of immigrants as quickly as possible.

Vestkysten covered the story on the basis of a report from the Ritzau agency under the heading: 'Balancing immigrant distribution clearly illegal' (February 29 1988). Thor Pedersen, the Liberal Minister of the Interior, implied that Per Madsen's initiative was illegal:

Municipalities must not discriminate against people who are legal residents in this country. Municipalities are not empowered to decide which categories of people they wish to have living within their boundaries.[40]

In summer 1993, it was Britta Christensen, the Lady Mayor of Hvidovre who made the headlines by announcing that the municipality would not accept any more refugees. *Politiken* reported the events in Hvidovre on July 22 1993 under the headline: 'She is being provocative. Hvidovre Mayor says no to more refugees.' The paper added an editorial comment to a subsequent interview with the mayor : 'The way in which the Municipality of Hvidovre deals with the refugees who have moved there — or, rather, the refugees seeking residence there — gives a hollow ring to the Social Democrats' fine words.' The mayor stated that the municipality naturally did not wish to break the law, but referred to the fact that over the years, and without any noticeable effects, the Municipalities of Hvidovre, Ishøj, Høje-Taastrup and Albertslund had delivered around 70 reports to the government detailing the special problems relating to refugees and immigrants. The desired system for a fairer distribution of refugees had therefore yet to be established. The interview concluded with the following statement:

To live in peace is all about respecting each others' differences, but if these differences begin to dominate, then it is bound to go badly wrong. And in Hvidovre, we have reached the limit of what we can deal with.

Jyllands-Posten reported on the Hvidovre matter on July 24,1993 as, following a decision by the Supervising Authority in Copenhagen, the Social Democrat municipal politicians had been threatened with fines if the town council upheld its decision to refuse to house more refugees. It appeared that the municipality had 'tried in vain to set up an agreement with the Danish Refugee Council for a maximum limit of 90 new refugees per year'. Several Social Democrats on the town council stated that the high concentration of refugees in the municipality threatened to undermine its economy, and that essential municipal tasks such as child-minding arrangements and municipal services for the elderly risked deterioration.

    The discussion about municipal distribution continued throughout the summer and into early autumn 1993 with talk of the emergence of ghettos in

40. As early as 1976, the Municipality of Ishøj had already decided to try to disperse immigrants by introducing quotas for the housing associations. At that time, Ombudsman Lars Nordskov Nielsen had chosen not to become involved.

council housing gradually becoming a well-known refrain. Gaasholt and Togeby mention that:

The Social Democrats were again put under pressure by a number of mayors hostile
to immigrants, and Prime Minister Poul Nyrup Rasmussen blamed the party's poor
Gallup figures on the immigrant problem (Gaasholt and Togeby, 1996:30)[41].

At the turn of 1994/95, the problem re-emerged, this time greatly exacerbated
by the likelihood that the status of 18,000 refugees from former Yugoslavia
would change from temporary residence to asylum.

6.6 The debate about refugees from former Yugoslavia

Søren Pedersen's chapter explained that the rules for family reunification were
tightened in 1992. This, added to the restrictions to the 1983 Act introduced
in 1985 and 1986 could possibly otherwise have led to a deceleration of the
rise in the number of citizens of other countries living in Denmark in the following years. This, in turn, could have dampened the debate.

However, in summer 1993, the newspapers continued to report:[42] 'The
number of immigrants is rising' and 'Denmark still attracts foreigners'. In fact,
1992 saw the second-highest annual intake on record of foreigners into
Denmark — exceeded only by that of 1986. One of the conclusions reached by
Jyllands-Posten was that 'on the whole, tightening the rules for family reunification has not had a noticeable effect'. This conclusion applied in particular to the group of genuine refugees. *Politiken* reported on the group of
around 9,000 refugees from former Yugoslavia who had arrived in Denmark
in 1992.[43]

As regards the press coverage of the Yugoslav refugees, in summer 1992
it was possible to recognize a similar pattern to that applying to the entry of
the Iranian refugees in summer 1984. There was thus a 'very positive attitude
among the Danish population towards the necessity of helping the civilian
victims of the civil war that was raging in Yugoslavia' — before the refugees
began to make their way towards Denmark in large numbers, that is. During
autumn 1992, a 'degree of discord' gradually began to appear, and a number
of articles expressed the fear of more widespread racism and of the development of 'German conditions' with the newspapers citing the arson

---

41. Poul Nyrup Rasmussen led the administration from January 1993
42. *Jyllands-Posten*, July 22 and *Politiken*, July 22 1993.
43. John Aggergaard Larsen (1998) has analysed the way in which the media defined
    this new group of refugees, and this source is used as reference in the following
    sections.

murders in Solingen, Lübeck and Rostock.[44] In Denmark, too, there were incidents involving attacks on refugee centres, and these were covered in depth
by the media. In addition to this, the media gave extensive coverage to a number of incidents in which refugees had been caught stealing, and these articles
initiated a war of words in readers' letters columns. Many articles in the
media hinted at the fact that the Danish population did not consider Yugoslavs to be 'real' refugees:

The negative statements from Danes are based on the lack of concordance between the
mental image that Danes had of refugees and the real refugees they met. The Danes'
expectations were based on images related to the Second World War, when starving
people fled in bare feet with their possessions in bags on their shoulders.[45]

It could perhaps be added that the 1980s debate about 'genuine refugees' and
'luxury refugees' could quickly rise again.

However, according to John Aggergaard Larsen, the comprehensive media
coverage of the war in Bosnia in late autumn 1992 led to a dramatic change
in public opinion. It was then that it became clear to most people that the Yugoslav refugees really *were* refugees from war. In fact, the expression — *the
Bosnian war refugees* — was introduced in summer 1993. This expression
further underlined that these refugees had a legitimate claim to seek protection in Denmark.

At the same time, several newspapers reported that large groups of
Yugoslav refugees were, in fact, already living in Denmark on temporary
residence permits.[46] On July 25 1993, *Jyllands-Posten* reported that around
10,000 Bosnian refugees had received residence permits of this kind, and that
from:

August onwards, around 1,000 more are expected to arrive in Denmark every month.
Many are Muslims who have been driven from areas controlled by the Serbian or
Croatian forces. However, no-one knows exactly how many there are, says Søren
Axelsen, Vice-Chairman of the Danish Immigration Service.

The article also made it clear that Denmark could only refuse to grant asylum
to these ethnic refugees if the persecution of Muslims in Bosnia were to
cease.Two days previously, *Jyllands-Posten* had printed an empathetic descrip-

44. *Ibid*, p. 14.
45. *Ibid*, p. 16.
46. In 1992, the Danish Parliament had passed a law concerning temporary residence
    permits for certain people from former Yugoslavia. This meant that the authorities
    could postpone the processing of asylum applications from these people for up to
    two years. During this time, the people in question could live in Denmark on their
    temporary residence permits.

tion of life in one of the tent villages that the Danish authorities had been obliged, for practical reasons, to set up in summer 1993 to house the large numbers of refugees: 'Refugee life under canvas'. The article stated that the recent tightening of the visa regulations meant that the Bosnian women feared that their husbands would be unable to join them in Denmark. The article described the conditions under which the refugees lived in the camps as extremely spartan, but also made it clear that the Bosnian women were doing what they could to make light of their hardships. In addition, the article emphasized that many of the Bosnians had previously lived comfortable lives, owning houses and cars, and that the men had had good jobs before the war broke out. Here, Aggergaard Larsen is pointing out the fact that in general, this was a part of the picture the media drew of the Bosnian refugees. In fact, it was a question of 'the refugees of today' from a society that was not so far removed in either time or space from Denmark, and the media placed special emphasis on the fact that anyone in Denmark could just as well have been subjected to the same fate. This further promoted acceptance, and a positive attitude towards this new group of refugees subsequently grew.[47]

This positive view held for a while, but when, in December 1994, it seemed likely that around 18,000 refugees from former Yugoslavia were on the point of having their status changed from temporary residence to full asylum, the debate erupted again.

In reality, the debate about the likelihood of large new groups of refugees being granted permanent asylum coincided with a new chapter of the debate that the mayors of municipalities with large immigrant populations had kept running for almost ten years. On November 27 1994, the front page of *Jyllands-Posten* carried the following story:

Kjeld Rasmussen, the Social Democrat Mayor of Brøndby, who is also chairman of the Association of Local Authorities in the County of Copenhagen believes that immigrant families with several children receive positive special treatment in relation to Danish families.

According to the mayor, only immigrants with large numbers of children — due to child benefit allowances and rent subsidies — could afford to live in large flats in social housing projects. On December 1 1994, the newspaper followed up the story with an article under the headline, 'Social Democrat Mayor: alien policy flawed': '"Danes are not ready to accept so many foreigners. That is why the policy on refugees and immigrants has missed its mark," says Thorkild Simonsen, Social Democrat Mayor of Aarhus.'

On December 4 1994, *Jyllands-Posten* published an article headed, 'Mayors demand debate about foreigners': 'Politicians in Parliament have helped to

---

47. John Aggergaard Larsen, (1998) p. 17.

foster xenophobia in Denmark because they have suppressed the debate about foreigners, ghetto problems and conflicts of culture.' Anders Bak, Social Democrat Mayor of the Municipality of Høje-Taastrup said:

Those politicians who are not prepared to do anything about the problems are helping to promote racism. Parliament should have dealt with this matter years ago. Instead, politicians have simply mouthed empty promises and handed the problems over to us in the local authorities.

Thorkild Simonsen was quoted as more-or-less agreeing with the criticism: 'The politicians have not been honest. Now people are just beginning to be aware of the problems that exist with refugees and immigrants, and we are facing very strong reactions from citizens from all social groups.' Vibeke Storm Rasmussen, who had since become Mayor of the County of Copenhagen, also returned to the aliens debate:

Many politicians from my own party did not want to hear such things. They did not want to hear anything about problems with immigrants; but the problems do exist and they have become more serious because we did not deal with them early enough.

In the same article, the chairman of INDSAM (The Association of Ethnic Minorities) stated that Denmark was becoming a multi-ethnic society, but the politicians had not dared to initiate a debate about the composition of this society as they were afraid of losing votes: 'Now the Danes are unprepared, and that means that immigrants and refugees are meeting with prejudice and xenophobic attitudes.'

This particular point of view, that the debate about the multi-ethnic society had been suppressed, was the theme of a leading article published in *Jyllands-Posten* that same day: 'Promote the aliens debate'. The article put forward the point of view that the centre parties had neglected to initiate a debate about

the problems linked to the increasing numbers of refugees and immigrants in Denmark. Insofar as any debate has been held about the far-reaching consequences of this, it has more-or-less been left to the extreme parties.

It was therefore no longer sufficient like the Social Democrat spokesman Dorthe Bennedsen, 'to think that it is so nice to buy your groceries from a Turkish shopkeeper'. The article called on the centre parties — the Social Democrats in particular — to state whether they wanted a multiethnic society[48]. And if so: how this society should develop.

48. In another article published on December 4 1994, *Jyllands-Posten* defined the concept: 'The 'multi-ethnic' concept covers a country in which the different ethnic groups — Turks, Pakistanis, Palestinians and Somalians — live side by side. And in which no single group is dominant. It is a society in which the foreigners maintain their own culture, religion and characteristics'.

On December 5 1994, *Jyllands-Posten* stated: 'Bosnians have nowhere to live'. A number of mayors of small towns and village communities in Jutland did not think that there were vacant houses in their municipalities for the Bosnian refugees, even though 'Birte Weiss, Social Democrat Minister of the Interior, expects most of the 18,000 Bosnian refugees in Denmark to settle in Jutland'. 'The politicians in Parliament haven't got a clue what they're talking about. In fact, there are no empty residences. The only solution is for the state to build houses for the Bosnian refugees', said Erik Tychsen, Liberal Mayor of Billund.

On December 7 1994, Ralf Pittelkow[49] analyzed the situation after Parliament had discussed the situation of the 18,000 Bosnians on the previous day. According to Pittelkow, the Liberals and the Conservatives wanted simply to extend the temporary residence status and did not want to give the refugees the chance to integrate. In other words, they still wanted the Bosnians to return home as soon as conditions allowed. In contrast to this, the Social Democrat government wanted to initiate normal asylum procedures. Pittelkow's principal point of view was that the Bosnians should be allowed to stay with temporary residence permits, but should also be given the chance to have their own homes and to seek employment and education.

On December 11 1994, *Jyllands-Posten* carried the following news on its front page:

'Mayor Thorkild Simonsen on foreigners: Glistrup is being proved right': Thorkild Simonsen, Social Democrat Mayor of Aarhus, believes that the predictions about the development of the numbers of immigrants and refugees in Denmark made by Mogens Glistrup, the former leader of the Progress Party, are coming true. Thorkild Simonsen criticizes Parliament for not taking appeals from mayors of municipalities with developing ghettos and large populations of refugees and immigrants seriously.

Thorkild Simonsen was also quoted as saying that the fact that Glistrup 'said it so incisively and so vehemently at the start of the 1970s' forced the population to distance itself from the issue, and people were subsequently unwilling to join the debate. 'That was unfortunate', says Thorkild Simonsen, who took his share of the blame for rejecting Glistrup's claims:

I was one of those people who did not believe that so many foreigners would come to the country, and that the number of immigrants would become so large that it would cause problems.

An article inside the paper stated: 'The ghettos are booming'. 13.8% of the

---

49. For years, Ralf Pittelkow had been the Social Democrats' international secretary. He then became personal adviser to Poul Nyrup Rasmussen. In December 1994 he was involved with *Jyllands-Posten* as a regular freelance writer.

population of the Municipality of Ishøj now consisted of refugees or immigrants. The corresponding figures for the Municipalities of Albertslund and Brøndby were 9.2 and 8.7%, respectively. The figure for the Municipality of Aarhus was 4.4%.

Berlingske Tidende started its coverage of 'the mayoral rebellion' on November 29 1994 with several mayors — from in and around the capital in particular — stating that they could not deal with any more aliens in their municipalities. The mayors also feared that the Bosnians would become a burden on the municipalities as soon as they had completed the state-financed integration programme, as they would be unable to find work. On December 1 1994, *Berlingske Tidende* rejoined the debate with a leading article entitled, 'The right to be Danish'. The premise for this article was the fact that the Liberals and the Conservatives had demanded the right to refuse to grant Danish citizenship to foreigners who had previously been found guilty of homicide or other violent crimes. The article gave full backing to this demand — 'in fact, it is surely most natural to ask why in the world they are allowed to stay in the country after serving a sentence for homicide, rape, serious violence or drug-related crimes' — and then turned its attention to the current debate about the Bosnian refugees. Here, the paper claimed that it was problematic to give the '19,000 guests from former Yugoslavia' the opportunity to seek asylum:

It was a clear precondition for the two-year-old emergency act that it was a matter of temporarily playing host to people in dire need. The idea was that they should stay here as guests but should not learn Danish nor be integrated ... . If temporary residence permits are converted to permanent residence permits and normal asylum proceedings, then it is pointless to maintain the special legislation. This is a shame, because in itself, the guarantee of temporary residence opens the door to more flexible help than that which can be provided in accordance with normal asylum procedures.

In a news analysis on December 13 1994, *Berlingske Tidende* established that, following Thorkild Simonsen's statements, the Social Democrat leaders found themselves in a dilemma equivalent to the party's chances of taking action on the EU question: The party leaders wanted one thing, while in reality, the core voters — who supported Simonsen — wanted something completely different. According to the analysis, Poul Nyrup Ramussen would have been in a stronger position

if only it had been Ishøj's Per Madsen, Brøndby's Kjeld Rasmussen or Hvidovre's Britta Christensen who had made the controversial statements. Such statements from these people have become par for the course in the debate about Danish society and no longer have the power to embarrass anyone.

In a new leading article on December 13 1994, the paper had calculated that the cost of the Danish efforts to help refugees was on a steeply rising curve that had 'long since' passed the DKK 7 billion (Euro 0.94 billion) per annum mark. And even though Danes were fundamentally considered to be a helpful people, the article did not believe that the population wanted 'to open themselves to ridicule':

Criminal elements and parasites feeding off asylum legislation should therefore be encouraged to leave the country as quickly as possible so that they do not poison the climate for those who really need help and behave in the way that is expected of guests. And who are prepared to adapt to the rules of Danish society with all its benefits and disadvantages if they should be granted permanent residence.

The article also welcomed Thorkild Simonsen's contribution to the debate. The mayor had 'a God-given ability to rock the boat and force people who would rather ignore reality to open their eyes and look around them' even though his input met with massive resistance from Social Democrat leaders, with Social Democrat ministers attempting to 'gag' him. On December 14 1994, the paper announced 'Social Democrat leaders disagree on aliens policy' According to *Berlingske Tidende*, the Prime Minister wished to play down the internal split over refugees, while 'the Social Democrat minister Mogens Lykketoft expressed understanding for the criticisms that a number of Social Democrat mayors had levelled at the party leadership'. In an interview with the paper he said that it was 'completely grotesque' that in the western region of Copenhagen unemployment among Turks was running at 56%:

Many of them will find themselves outside the union unemployment system in the coming years. This means that the municipalities will be burdened with the social expenses. I can well understand that this is a major problem.

On December 16 1994, *Berlingske Tidende* reported on 'The day of hate in Parliament'. The debate about the Bosnian refugees had resulted in a clear right/left-wing split in Parliament with regard to the question of immigrants, and, according to the summary published in the media, the debate had been unusually heated. The paper concluded:

The Socialist People's Party and the Unity List (Enhedslisten, a very left-wing party) had good reason to be satisfied yesterday. Deep trenches were dug between the government and the right-wing opposition parties.

According to the summary, Pia Kjærsgaard was apparently also satisfied with the result: 'For the first time in many years, the Progress Party is not alone. But I am still not tempted to say: "I told you so".'

In its report *Vestkysten* described how the 'mayoral rebellion' was spreading and, on December 12 1994, the paper quoted the *Jyllands-Posten* interview with Thorkild Simonsen: 'Aarhus Mayor ready to concede that Glistrup was right'. This summary concluded:

Parliament must give careful consideration to the question of whether we can accept any more guests from foreign countries. However, this is one of the worst possible things that can be said to Parliament, as the members' humanitarian attitude dictates that new groups of refugees should be granted entry to Denmark. Nevertheless, I think that in five years they will admit that I was right' says the Mayor of Aarhus.

Concurrently with reporting the mayor's criticism, the newspaper published details of the development of the work towards the 'Bosnians Act', with summaries of the political parties' attitudes — without, however, clearly stating the opinion of the newspaper itself. However, this situation changed on December 15 1994, when the paper published a leading article in which it maintained that 'in the clear light of hindsight' the government should thank the right-wing opposition as

passing the Bosnians Act it seems very hurried, unfinished and, not least, out of step with public opinion... . Danes understand and empathize with the Bosnian refugees. Nonetheless, we should not turn a blind eye to the fact that Danish hospitality is closely linked to the fact that the Bosnians have only been granted a breathing space here — and not permanent residence. The three largest right-wing parties understand this point. The government has not understood it, and this means that it is good that the government has time to reflect on the situation until the start of the new year before reaching a final decision on the Bosnians Act.

In its editorial coverage of 'the aliens' during December, *Ekstra Bladet* attempted to draw a distinction between the Bosnian war refugees and immigrants in general. As regards refugees, the picture was clear in that the paper took a standpoint equivalent to the one it took in connection with the debate about Iranian refugees in 1985 and 1986. This meant that the paper criticized the right-wing parties for reneging on previous agreements concerning the Bosnians, and claimed that the Bosnians, who had already been subjected to a brutal war, had now become the innocent victims of machinations in the area of domestic policy. For example, on December 9, 1994, the newspaper published an article written by Birte Weiss, the Social Democrat Minister of the Interior, who explained the background for the 'Act concerning the residence status of certain people from former Yugoslavia, etc.' of 1992 and made it clear that, in any case, it was the Conservative Minister of Justice, Hans Engell, who was responsible for the law and that the law had not given the Bosnians any special privileges but had in fact

taken away their constitutional right to have their asylum applications processed in Denmark. Not for ever, but for exactly two years. After that time, the authorities were obliged to start an evaluation of each individual case in order to establish whether ethnic cleansing was sufficient grounds for asylum.

If Danes were in doubt as to whether the Bosnians were genuine refugees, Weiss encouraged them to:

Follow the daily reports of the Yugoslavian nightmare on television and then judge for yourselves. Or visit an asylum centre and meet a complete family — five, six or seven people living together in one room. And then judge for yourselves.

The paper's opinions was published on December 14 in an editorial headlined 'Hostages in Denmark'.

It is with disgust that we have observed the Liberals, the Conservatives and the Progress Party gathering signatures in Parliament with the intention of postponing a decision about the permanent residence of the Bosnian refugees until after Christmas.[50]

The article claimed that this postponement was nothing but political tactics:

The Liberals, the Conservatives and the Progress Party are counting on the famous Social Democratic trait of disagreement concerning refugees and immigrants continuing through the traditionally uneventful Christmas holidays and growing to create an unbreachable divide, which, finally, can split the party that is holding up the government, thus creating a split in the government itself.

The editorial also referred to 'the right-wing hostage-taking' and asked:

What have the right-wing parties considered doing about the Bosnians who are already in Denmark? Are they to live like battery hens in refugee camps until peace is restored to Yugoslavia in five, ten or fifteen years? Or are they to be sent back to the slaughterhouse that Bosnia will surely become when the UN finally admits defeat and withdraws its troops?

In the same article, the newspaper further claimed that the postponement would have a 'shocking effect on the most vulnerable nerves in Denmark — those of the Bosnian war refugees'.

However, the readers' letters column of the paper bore witness to the clarity of the general discontent that existed towards the country's policy on refugees. Letters with headers such as 'Red card for Weiss', 'Don't forget the Danes' and 'listen to Thorkild Simonsen' — with one reader even going as far

50. The initiative was carried out on the basis of §41, item 3 of the Danish Constitution which states that two-fifths of the Members of Parliament may, in writing, request the postponement of the final approval of an act until 12 working days after its second reading. In all, the three parties had 80 seats in the Danish Parliament.

as to suggest: 'Let us elect Thorkild Simonsen Prime Minister as soon as possible' — were common. In addition, the paper's coverage of material concerning the immigration question was far from the unambiguity of the editorial attitudes that applied to the Bosnian refugees. The paper highlighted a number of incidents of racism and discrimination against immigrants but, at the same time, also published a number of fairly aggressive articles targeted at Islamic fundamentalism in Denmark and the abuse of the public social security systems. An example of the former was the article entitled 'Birte Weiss — you are naïve', which was published on December 19 1994. In this article, a former school teacher and a teacher from a

'Koranic School' on the outskirts of Gellerup Park in Aarhus explain how the school's Arabic board — the members of which, by the way, did not send their children to the school — 'squeeze as much as possible out of the Danish system, but this is just a cover-up of the other issue… We noted many unpleasant factors. Everyday, the members of the Arabic school board sat at the school smoking fat cigars. As if they were in a recreational room. They controlled everything and made all the decisions. They cut Danish books up into thousands of tiny pieces because there were pictures of pigs in them. As well as the books that contained pictures of angels… It was almost impossible to believe.

In general, according to the former employees, the school was distinguished by extreme regimentation, which, instead of integration, resulted in 'disintegration'. 'They were so extreme that they have withdrawn from Danish society — and this is what they teach the pupils.' When the teachers were asked whether they believed that there was a fundamentalist group in Gellerup Park, one replied: 'Yes there is, and I would also like to state its name: Hamas.'[51]

In an interview entitled 'We should not be so naive' with a card-carrying Social Democrat and former resident of the big Aarhus housing complex, the

51. On October 21 1994, *Jyllands-Posten* carried the front page headline: 'Hamas terrorists have a base in Denmark'. On the basis of information from the Danish Police Intelligence Agency, the paper reported that 'the feared Hamas movement, which is responsible for the bloody terrorist acts in Israel, has established groups in Denmark, which supply the militant activists with money and forged documents'. It was also stated that in at least one situation, the police had investigated the 'militant training of young people in Gellerup Park in Aarhus, a training programme that was supposedly organized by Hamas'. The paper also mentioned that the Hamas Groups have prepared passports to enable terrorists who fear exposure in Israel to slip away. When they apply for asylum, their papers have 'officially' disappeared. They can be re-used. The front page article concluded: 'In the first nine months of the year, no fewer than 468 Palestinians applied for asylum in Denmark'. Inside, the paper wrote that 'respect and fear of the Hamas terrorist organization hangs like a heavy cloud above the Palestinians in Denmark'. *Jydske Vestkysten* likewise reported on possible Hamas activities in Denmark on October 22 1994.

interviewee highlighted a number of positive behavioural characteristics in the immigrants.[52] But there were manifest problems, too:

I am opposed to all these arranged marriages — and particularly to the *pro forma* ceremonies we know so well. Those spouses that just come up here for the money should be sent back home. However, the door should always be open to those in genuine need. The others? The economic migrants? Send them back home straight away.

In an article printed next to the interview entitled 'Voices from the Ghetto', what could be termed 'the voice of the people' could be heard. 'How can it be that my neighbour's mother — an old Palestinian woman — can have her Danish pension sent to her in Lebanon? While she lived here, she never spoke a word of Danish' and 'How can foreigners, year in and year out, get help from public funds when they don't speak a word of Danish?'

In *Det fri Aktuelt*, the 'mayoral rebellion' was, not surprisingly, the month's hottest topic for debate and reflected a far-reaching and clearly stated difference of opinion between the top executives of the Social Democratic Party and many of its voters, who supported the criticisms levelled by the mayors.

On December 5 1994, the paper carried the following story on its front page: 'Bosnians to live outside the bigger cities', which can be interpreted as a concession to the party's rebel mayors. Inside the paper, it was mentioned that the towns or parts of towns that housed large numbers of ethnic minorities would not be expected to accommodate any of the 18,000 Bosnians. This applied, for example, to the western region of Copenhagen and to Aarhus. However, in the same article, Birte Weiss categorically refuted what she termed the right-wing parties' attempt to manipulate the mayors' contributions to the debate: 'There is a wide difference between the wonderful support that we receive from the decentralized and humanist Denmark, and the attempt at political posturing we see from the right-wing parties.' In a summary of an 'end of the day meeting' at *Det fri Aktuelt* on December 5 1994, Weiss made the following statement: 'The mayors' talk about fear of contact is completely unfounded. It is rather an expression of the fact that they disagree with the policy followed by the government.'[53]

However, by necessity, the municipal political opposition had to be expressed in full in the columns of *Det fri Aktuelt* — for example on December 5, when a municipal politician from Brøndby asked in a political commentary:

Is there no-one in Parliament who knows what is going on outside in society? Here in Brøndby, throughout the Greater Copenhagen area, in fact, we have major ethnic and financial problems. And where is the help from our party colleagues in Christiansborg?

52. *Ekstra Bladet*, December 18 1994.
53. *Det fri Aktuelt*, December 6 1994.

On December 13 1994, it became known that Hilmar Sølund, the Social Democrat Mayor of Herning, supported Thorkild Simonsen, and other articles published later that month in the same newspaper stated that support was being
strengthened by the Mayors of Køge and Svendborg. In fact, Hilmar Sølund
actually regretted that Denmark was obliged to live up to international conventions.

Two features which the editors highlighted as being written by two of the
party's 'foot-soldiers' also addressed the issue of the Danish policy on immigrants and refugees and the Social Democrats' share in the responsibility
for this. The age-old fear within the Labour movement that the immigrant
workforce would push wages down, reared its head once again:[54]

For the majority of the population, reticence about aliens was quickly replaced by a certain degree of ill-will, and the expression 'foreign worker' took on unfortunate con-
notations. The lobby for the immigration of a cheap workforce rapidly adopted the
term 'guest worker'. When it became abundantly clear that the Danish worker was to
be undercut by very permanent 'guests', the term 'guest worker' had outlived its purpose. The focus of the debate was now turned towards refugees. Decency dictated that
we had to accept these immigrants, and the resistance to foreign or guest workers was
drowned in a flood of humanitarianism.

The writer also saw a link to the EU, as immigration and emigration should
'ease the introduction of a common labour market with the same goals'. The
writer thus feared that waves of foreign workers could be expected from the
former colonies of the British and French empires 'not to mention the immigration from the countries of Eastern Europe, just as soon as they become
members of the EU'. The feature articles also reflected an attitude whereby the
top executives of the Social Democrats found themselves on a highfaluting
theoretical level as 'the leading voice in favour of continued immigration to
this country'. However, the writer claimed, the party executives lived in a
world far removed from the man on the street, and the attitude of the party
leadership scared the 'ordinary' Social Democrats from taking part in the
debate. As dissatisfaction could not be expressed within the party, the party
naturally lost ground in the polls.

On December 14 1994, the newspaper reported: 'Social Democrat group
divided on refugees'. It was stated that Poul Nyrup Rasmussen had 'launched
an attack on the Social Democrat mayors who have criticized the party's
policy on refugees'. The mayors should 'give it a rest' and instead take part
in the committee work, which, according to the paper, should solve the problems. However, the paper also stated that by no means all the parliamentary
group agreed with the head of the government. In fact, the Social Democrat

---

54. 'A taboo subject must be discussed' (December 14 1994) and 'A scaffolder's view of
    refugees and immigrants' (December 15 1994).

Per Kaalund directly advocated immigrant quotas: 'If we want integration, certain municipalities must have the right to say no to more immigrants.'

Thorkild Simonsen was interviewed on the same day. To start with, he distanced himself to a degree from the interview in *Jyllands-Posten*:

I would never have talked about Glistrup if the journalist had not brought him into the discussion. My honesty prohibited me from saying that everything that Glistrup has said has been utter rubbish. Some of what he said has turned out to be true.

According to the interview, the mayor's main concern was that the gulf between the parliamentary politicians and the people would grow so wide that it would allow racism to flourish. And the mayor sensed the beginnings of xenophobia. When asked about the current situation with the Bosnian refugees, he said:

I think that it was right to accept the Bosnian refugees. I experienced a strong feeling of solidarity from most people in this regard. However, people still maintained that they should only be allowed to stay in Denmark for two years. I remember a meeting at a school at which Ritt Bjerregaard said that it would never work. Birte Weiss gave her a verbal dressing down. However, Ritt Bjerregaard was proved right, and people remember that today. What was promised on the basis of the very best intentions has never become reality.

Thorkild Simonsen also made it clear that he would rather have seen broad agreement and compromise on the subject of the Bosnian refugees with the participation of the Liberals and the Conservatives 'that would have strengthened the population's respect for the decision to a fantastic extent'.

However, the greatest number of column inches throughout the month were devoted to the party's official policy on refugees, as displayed in the Danish Parliament's negotiations about the Bosnians' future in Denmark. On December 6 1994, a comment from Søren Søndergård of the Unity List made it clear that the law would build a 'ceiling over uncertainty about the future'. The right-wing parties' attempt to extend the temporary residence period to up to seven years[55] was considered to be completely indecent and inhuman.

On December 12 1994, the newspaper wrote that 'Glistrup and the Progress Party thank Thorkild'. Birte Weiss was quoted as having said that Thorkild Simonsen must have misunderstood the new asylum law, adding 'you can't expect the Mayor of Aarhus to keep up with everything'. Thorkild Simonsen's relationship to Glistrup was also the theme of a leading article on the same day. In this article, the paper claimed that:

55. After which they could apply for citizenship according to the usual conditions.

The question of immigration did not play a central role in the latest general election campaigns as most of the population do not consider it to be important. There are hundreds of associations and thousands of people throughout the country who are participating in a beneficial working relationship and reaping the benefits of the fact that Denmark is also a multi-ethnic society.

On the subject of Thorkild Simonsen, it was mentioned that his criticism 'purely on the basis of respect for his integrity and good political judgement' would be considered important and

the members of the Progress Party will know how to abuse it. An experienced debater such as Simonsen should know that. One area in which he is right is that the Danish debate about refugees and immigrants is far too polarized, as every form of critical debate is immediately shouted down as an expression of racism.

On December 13 1994, the paper concluded: 'Social Democrat grass roots reject Thorkild Simonsen'. The paper stated that Poul Nyrup Rasmussen had refused

to comment on immigration policy at all. He refers to Birte Weiss, the Social Democrat Minister of the Interior, who has little time for the Mayor of Aarhus' points of view. In Birte Weiss' opinion, the immigration debate is conducted excellently within the ranks of the Social Democrats and she thinks that the much vaunted problems are highly exaggerated.

Poul Øland, Chairman of the Copenhagen Social Democrats, expressed his disappointment over Thorkild Simonsen having hinted that Glistrup's predictions were about to come true — 'that's way off the mark'. Several members of the party executive were quoted as saying that Denmark could not stop the flow of refugees without breaking international conventions. Another article stated that: 'HK [The Union of Commercial and Clerical Employees in Denmark] will fight prejudice.'

The refugee theme appeared in yet another leading article on December 14 1994, which stated that the Prime Minister was attempting to take the mayoral rebellion into consideration by encouraging mayors throughout the country to come up with concrete proposals for solutions to the problems surrounding refugees and immigrants. The Prime Minister was quoted as warning against hysteria and, according to the article, made the point that 'the flow of refugees to Denmark has more-or-less dried up'. The article claimed that these were all wise words, but chose also to draw attention to the fact that the question was so explosive in 'his own party that he should unconditionally use the chairman's powers necessary to deal properly with the debate'.

However, this partial concession to opposition within the party was not completely consistent. In fact, during the paper's coverage of the negotiations in Parliament, emphasis was placed on the fact that the three right-wing parties were consciously speculating in the 'imminent refugee rebellion among the Social Democrat mayors'. On December 15 1994, the summaries also highlighted the fact that 'Weiss stands firm on Bosnians Act: The Bosnians Act will be passed without amendment on January 12 1995 when the three right-wing parties' postponement of the third reading expires'. Birte Weiss again took advantage of the opportunity to criticize the mayors:

There are great differences between the cards that the municipalities hold when attempting to integrate immigrants. And I hope that the municipalities will carefully consider and improve their efforts in the area of immigrant integration now this debate is over.

Torben Lund, the party's political parliamentary spokesman added: 'Thorkild Simonsen has a credibility problem in this case and I am surprised by the way in which certain Social Democrat mayors have chosen to discuss the matter.' On December 16 1994, *Det fri Aktuelt* reported that the USA was prepared to accommodate 200 of the Bosnian families that had arrived in Denmark. In the USA, the refugees would be assured a home, education and a job, while the Danish Parliament only discussed their subsequent fate. It was therefore possible to interpret the development of the debate as indicating that the Social Democrats wished to end the month by putting the lid on the issue of discontent within the party.[56]

In the special Friday Column in *Politiken* on December 2 1994, Torben Krogh managed to squeeze in the re-opened debate under the header: 'When racism turns really nasty'. Torben Krogh found that 'the statement quoted from the Mayor of Brøndby was a clear-cut example of a manipulative appeal to racial prejudice'. In a commentary published on December 4 1994, Ole Olsen, member of the Social-Liberals' Executive Committee said, 'they've done it again'. 'The two Social Democrat Mayors in the western region of Copenhagen, Kjeld Rasmussen and Per Madsen, have done it again. They have launched an attack on aliens without any kind of documentation.' The trend continued in the days leading up to Christmas, on December 10, for example, with a contribution to the debate under the heading, 'Give refugees something to do. Years of passivity wear people down' and on December 13, 'Illegal imprisonment of asylum-seekers'.

However, on December 14 1994, *Politiken* stated that the likely arrival of

---

56. Among the refugee and immigrant-friendly articles published in *Det fri Aktuelt* in December 1994, we refer to: 'The new citizens' (December 15), 'American conditions that mean business' (chronicle on December 16), 'Pathetic to hear mayors whining' (December 16), 'Social Democratic pettiness' (December 17) and 'Refugees and moral leadership' (December 17 1994).

'18,000 new citizens adds fuel to the debate — several mayors are demanding an end to the flow of refugees, claiming that they cannot cope with any more'. At this point, the Municipality of Odense announced that the strain was too great. According to the article, a large number of immigrants via family re-unifications would have to be added to the original figure of 18,000 over the coming years. Likewise, the protest from Aarhus was followed up:

Social Democrat Thorkild Simonsen has now also criticized the government for al-lowing the Bosnians to enter Danish Society. And in a previously unheard of sharp tone. Thorkild Simonsen reacts to the imbalanced *distribution* of refugees in Denmark. It is true that Birte Weiss, the Social Democrat Minister of the Interior, has promised that the Bosnians will be placed outside large towns, and that the local authorities involved will receive financial compensation — but, as Thorkild Simonsen points out, many of the Bosnians will subsequently move into the large towns. And no-one can stop them.

It was also stated that the Chairman of the National Association of Local Authorities in Denmark, Liberal Mayor Evan Jensen was advocating stopping the flow of refugees into Denmark, as, in his opinion, the local authorities could not manage to integrate the 18,000 Bosnians and the other refugees who would be coming to the country in the following years. However, in a com-mentary in *Politiken* on the same day, Journalist Søren Nielsen rejected the mayors' considerations. 'Town kings' diagnosis pure routine'.

Another article in *Politiken* on December 14 reported that Thorkild Simon-sen himself did not find the problems with foreigners to be 'as big as the debate makes them appear'. But the population was uneasy, and this was the reason why the mayor demanded action from the government and parliament. It was precisely popular disquiet that had, over the years, had the following result:

I have learnt a great deal over the years. Ghettos become assembly points for the weakest immigrants, while those who are better off move away. We do not want to create a social ghetto. The second point is that the schools are reporting a rise in the number of children who cannot speak Danish. The third point is that a number of school boards in town are now warning that the proportion of non-Danish speakers at several schools is rising. This does not bother me — but it does bother me if the citizens of Aarhus say that it is unacceptable.

In a leading article published the following day, the paper admitted

that it has taken a few days for us at *Politiken* to inform our readers thoroughly about the political upheaval that a number of mayors have caused in the aliens debate. This is not because we, here at the paper, suppress dissenting opinions or do not want to have the widest possible debate on the subject of refugees, immigrants and victims of the war in Bosnia ... Our hesitation is due to the fact that there is no sense in the statements made by Kjeld Rasmussen in Brøndby, Per Madsen in Ishøj and, of late, Thorkild Simonsen in Aarhus.

The article noted that it was true that there were socially disadvantaged housing complexes in both Copenhagen and Aarhus, but also asked a question as to whether this had anything to do with the fact that there were 18,000 Bosnians in the country living in centres 'where they have less available space than in our prisons'. The article then noted that in any case, the local authorities had been provided for financially and that it was therefore nothing less than 'unadulterated whining' when the mayors complained, and as the municipal elections were not within sight, the initiative could only be interpreted as 'a tasteless attempt to dip their snouts even further into the state coffers'. There was thus no real reason for

the storm that the mayors have whipped up and which the three right-wing parties have seized upon as a reason for delaying a piece of legislation that Parliament has long since discussed in detail from start to finish.

The article ended by putting forward the point of view that Danes owed it to the war refugees to set aside 'that little part of our shared resources that is necessary and offer them a humane future'.

In another article that same day, it was also stated that 'Denmark has a duty to help refugees'. In fact — due to its commitments to international conventions — Denmark was not free to choose how to act in the area of refugees and immigrants. A number of politicians from the Liberal Party would therefore not be successful in their attempts to prove that Denmark was free to choose its own policy in this area — even though, according to *Politiken*, they had tried. It was also stated that the government felt that it had been 'grossly let down' by the Social Democrat mayors who 'demand a political showdown with refugee ghettos. The same mayors have repeatedly asked Parliament not to get involved in matters relating to exactly this area.' Torben Lund, the Social Democrats' political spokesman, noted that the mayors could rest assured that the government was ready to implement a centrally controlled solution to the problems and made it clear that 'only respect for the autonomy of the local authorities and their stated will to solve the problems themselves had delayed central involvement'. Peter Brixtofte, the Liberal Mayor of Farum, was quoted as saying that he knew very well where he would place the Bosnians — in camps — and that

he would definitely prefer it if these camps were located in former Yugoslavia rather than in Denmark. That is why he whole-heartedly supported his party's attempt to prevent 18,000 Bosnians from being granted asylum in Denmark.

The mayor hinted that if the Municipality of Farum was forced to accept more refugees, it would have an adverse effect on the social welfare services supplied to the municipality's own citizens.

During the rest of the month, the 'distancing' articles continued in *Politiken*, opposed to stopping the flow of refugees and also refuting the mayors' criticism.[57] On December 18 1994, a guest worker's family and a family of refugees from former Yugoslavia were interviewed. Both families explained how the intense debate was ruining their everyday lives, but the interviews also demonstrated a pronounced ability to adapt and a strong will for self sufficiency.

During the first days of 1995, *Politiken* rounded off the debate. For example, on January 1 1995, the paper announced that the Prime Minister, Poul Nyrup Rasmussen, would give the Danish people a 'good New Year's telling-off . Poul Nyrup attacks hostility to foreigners in New Year speech.'[58] On the same day, the paper published a lengthy contribution to the debate by Knud Vilby, Chairman of the Danish Association for International Co-operation: 'Now is the time for composure'. Here, the politicians were encouraged to avoid letting themselves be carried away by what Vilby termed incomplete and manipulative information:

Ever since the Liberal Party Chairman said that integration of the Bosnians risked undermining the popular will to operate a humane refugee policy, it has become clear that the greatest threat to popular will is incorrect and panic-inducing information from responsible politicians — locally in the municipalities and nationally in parliament — and, unfortunately, the passivity of a large group of local politicians.

57. See, for example, 'Brutalization in Danish politics' (December 16 1994), 'Vengeful debate on right to asylum' (December 16 1994) and 'Embarrassing and hysterical' (December 16 1994). The following can, for example, be quoted from the last contribution to the debate by Elisabeth Arnold, the Radical Liberal Member of Parliament: 'That is why the Liberals' action is the war cry of the male baboon: distinguished by its great symbolic value but with little effect — the greatest effect being the pain it inflicts on the Bosnian refugees (...) The opposition role has changed some of the right-wing politicians into genuinely demagogic propaganda machines. They forget their previous opinions — and they follow whatever they believe to be popular opinion. Totally without principles'.
58. On January 2 1995, *Politiken* published the speech itself: 'There are only five million people in Denmark. I can well understand that many people are concerned and worried about the future of Denmark in a world dominated by immigration flows. After all, we have so much to lose. But we have both the assets and the strength to tackle this challenge. And think how it would be if the roles were reversed. We need to do our share. It is our duty as people living in a humanitarian society to provide all the support we can. If we do not, then this is a victory for cynicism. The discussion must not flounder on the question of whether there is room in Denmark to accommodate needy refugee families'.

Information published an indirect contribution to the ongoing debate on December 6 1994 in the form of an article entitled 'Set up a refugee republic' by the artist Ingo Gunther. The artist pointed out that nations such as the USA, Canada and Australia had formerly competed earnestly to attract refugees. Now almost all countries — on the basis of short-sighted interests — considered refugees to be a burden. The following day, the paper reported on how 'the government receives help from the right-wing parties for the restrictive aspect, and from the Socialist People's Party and the Unity List for the humanitarian aspect' of the work of making ongoing legislative modifications to the refugee policy. From the previous day's parliamentary debate on the first reading of a bill proposing allowing the Bosnians to change their status from living in Denmark on temporary residence permits to seeking asylum, the paper quoted Birthe Rønn Hornbech, the Liberal Party spokeswoman, as having criticized the government for 'instantly turning refugees into immigrants', and she predicted that processing asylum applications from 18,000 Bosnians would cause major problems. Elisabeth Arnold of the Social Liberals had commented on the Liberal Party's position on the matter in the following manner: 'there must be members of the Liberal Party who are not pleased with the direction the party's refugee policy has taken'.

On December 14 1994, *Information* commented on the top level political conflicts regarding the refugee question. The standpoint adopted by the Liberal Party was characterized as: 'Birthe Rønn Hornbech's usual prudishness and Ellemann-Jensen's insupportable mock concern'. The article continued:

As the former foreign minister says, we must not risk 'undermining the popular will for operating a humanitarian refugee policy'. No indeed. Much better to turn people away at the border, which you can also attempt to do by demanding a postponement of the legislation regarding the Bosnians' long-term asylum.

Furthermore, the article spoke of 'the Social Democrats' own populist regional bigwigs, certain mayors apparently being willing to score cheap points off concern about the refugee question'. On the other hand, Poul Nyrup Rasmussen was praised for being prepared to battle against this tendency in the party.

In an interview on the same day, the paper gave Thorkild Simonsen the opportunity to elaborate on his points of view, including the opinion that the mayor

has nothing against citizens with unpronounceable foreign names and foreign passports in their pockets ... But he understands that the Danish population are not keen on seeing an increase in the proportion of their fellow citizens who come from foreign countries. Xenophobia is on the rise.

In particular, the mayor objected to the fact that

when moving (to Aarhus), 77% of the foreigners arriving from outside the cultural circle of Western Europe chose to set up home in just four council housing complexes. Fifty-nine % of these foreigners live in just two of the 28 local communities in Aarhus.

According to the mayor, this created a ghetto consisting of the least integrated foreigners and the least advantaged Danes.[59] During the interview, Thorkild Simonsen also expressed his opinion that discrimination and common malice towards foreigners among Danes could result in these foreigners being forced to live — as the interviewing journalist put it — 'on the outskirts of society'. The mayor himself wanted the Prime Minister to enter the debate by addressing the attitude of the Danish people. The Prime Minister should thus explain to the people exactly what the government had actually done to promote integration. The interview also made it clear that the mayor

regretted a couple of the statements he had made during the past few days. One of these was the remark that the statements that Glistrup made in the 1970s had been right. During an interview with *Jyllands-Posten*, the journalist introduced Glistrup into the conversation and Simonsen let himself be carried away and answered yes to the question of whether Glistrup was right.

On December 15 1994, *Information* reported: 'Mayors have good experience with Bosnians'. 'Mayors of municipalities that include asylum centres report friendly relations between Danes and Bosnians — but it will be hard to find sufficient housing.' On the same day, the paper also reported on a split between the Liberals and the Conservatives, as the Liberals were contemplating pressing for a referendum if the government changed the status of the Bosnians from temporary residence to permanent asylum:

At Conservative Headquarters, Helge Adam Møller, the party's political administration spokesman is shaking his head. The Conservatives are not working with the idea of a referendum.

Finally, in a leading article published on December 16 1994, the paper distanced itself in particular from *Jyllands-Posten's* contribution to the debate and from the debate that had been initiated by the mayors and the National Association of Local Authorities in Denmark.

---

59. This information came from a memo that the mayor's office had sent to Prime Minister Poul Nyrup Rasmussen.

6.7 Summary

In collectively evaluating the voluminous newspaper material about refugees in the period from 1983 until the first half of the 1990s — the selection of which is based on criteria including the dates of important legislative amendments — it is clear that the editorial attitudes are somewhat less unambiguous than they were found to be with regard to the debate on immigrants. However, a pattern appears, according to which, newspapers such as *Politiken* more-or-less consistently defended the rights of the foreigners in relation to the Danish State throughout the period. This was expressed as early as the time of the first attempts to revise the 1983 Act in autumn 1984, and the editorial line held firm during the following two years for the legislative modifications that were actually introduced in 1985 and 1986. In the same way, throughout the remainder of the period in question, the paper published several articles with a recurring theme, namely that of defending liberal legislation and stressing the humanitarian obligations that Denmark should meet. For example, the arguments chosen included highlighting the fact that the numbers of aliens in Denmark were still only small, stressing that by following the refugee policy it had adopted, Denmark was doing no more than living up to clearly defined international obligations and that failing to meet these obligations would damage Denmark's reputation abroad, and making the point that, from an historical point of view, Danish society was the result of a series of previous migrations.

A similar pattern applies to *Information*, which, throughout the period, published a string of articles defending the legitimacy of lenient legislation. *Det fri Aktuelt* also sought to maintain the 1983 Act and to insist on the civil rights of the foreigners. However, the paper also occasionally carried critical articles from the grass roots of the Social Democratic Party, expressed, for example, by its commentary on the critical report from the party's Immigration Committee in 1987, which it printed on the front page. At the end of the period in question, the paper covered in detail the split that had developed within the Social Democrats as a result of the immigrant question.

As regards the three right-wing papers — *Berlingske Tidende, Jyllands-Posten* and *Vestkysten* — the picture is less clear-cut. In a paper such as *Berlingske Tidende*, it is possibly par for the course to expect that the right-wing government's desire for a revision — i.e. a tightening — of the 1983 Act should be expressed more-or-less directly via an interview with the then Minister of Justice, Erik Ninn-Hansen, who time and again expressed concern about the new Aliens Act, and who also insisted that a distinction be made between genuine refugees and economic migrants. Various politicians and civil servants also spoke — via the paper — in favour of stricter legislation that could differentiate between these two groups of refugees. However, at the same time, the paper also published — perhaps most obviously after the Queen's

New Year's speech at the turn of 1984 — a long series of articles pleading the case for Denmark maintaining the 1983 Act in its original form and expressing sympathy for the Iranians' situation, for example. This paper, too, carried a recurring argument, namely that there were not particularly many refugees in Denmark and that Denmark should accept its obvious humanitarian and international obligations.

Vestkysten does not deviate appreciably from the picture presented here of *Berlingske Tidende*, and throughout the period, *Jyllands-Posten* — which is, in fact, the paper that consistently carried the most high-profile articles against an open policy on refugees — published articles, including leading articles, which insisted that the rights of the refugees should be upheld. A consistent feature of the right-wing papers' presentation of their opinions was, however, a demand for amendment of the Act itself and the current administration so as to differentiate between economic migrants and genuine refugees. Furthermore, the paper also stated on numerous occasions that many of the refugees were not really refugees at all. Another oft-repeated demand was that criminal aliens who had been convicted of crimes of violence or offences related to drugs should be expelled from the country.

During the period under review, the editorial position of *Ekstra Bladet* moved from staunch defence of all refugees and immigrants to an acceptance of the Social Democrat mayors' critical attitude to the immigrant question. The paper even went as far as to claim that certain groups of immigrants deliberately exploited the Danish welfare state. At the end of the period, the editorial team had returned to their previously well-established position of defending the Bosnian refugees while maintaining a generally critical approach to the immigrant question.

6.8 Overall conclusions

A comprehensive overview of 30 years' debate on aliens in this analysis of major Danish newspapers makes it clear that there were a number of right-wing papers and the social-liberal paper *Politiken*, which, at the start of the 1960s argued in favour of the use of a foreign workforce.

It appears that the background for this attitude was the prosperity of the 1960s and an occasionally pronounced shortage of unskilled workers in particular. *Aktuelt* argued continuously against importing workers in this way, as the union movement was both afraid that the condition of full employment would not last, and was also uneasy about the likelihood that the use of cheap foreign workers would postpone necessary investments in Danish business. In addition, the unions were naturally also concerned that the presence of large numbers of unskilled foreign workers might push wage levels down.

As the guest workers arrived in the country, *Aktuelt* began to change its position slightly, in that the paper increasingly began to focus on the difficult social situation of the foreigners — many of whom joined unskilled workers' unions. In the same way, *Information, Ekstra Bladet* and, to a certain extent, *Politiken* followed suit, publishing articles that revealed unfair treatment of guest workers in both the work and housing markets.

Around 1980, when the period of prosperity was long since over, an increasing number of articles in the right-wing press began to hint that the foreigners should conform to certain demands from society, and that it would be wise to take steps to ensure that the foreign workers could not abuse certain aspects of the Danish system of taxation. In addition, the papers generally agreed that Danish society should live up to a number of obligations to an underprivileged group of the population.

In analyzing the debate about asylum-seekers from 1983 to 1995, it is clear that, to start with, the majority of the papers were positively disposed towards the new liberal Aliens Act adopted in 1983 with the Conservative Minister of Justice as the only high-level opponent in the contributions to the debate examined here.

Subsequently, however, as pressure at the Danish borders increased, more and more critical articles were published in *Jyllands-Posten, Berlingske Tidende* and *Vestkysten* — calling in particular for a tightening of the Act so as to make it easier to distinguish between what several articles termed 'economic migrants' and 'genuine refugees'. As this was indeed a debate, the picture was not completely clear. Thus a number of articles defended the rights of the refugees in relation to the Danish State.

However, faced with the right-wing papers' insistent pressure in favour of slowing immigration down, papers such as *Politiken* and *Information* argued against tightening up the relevant legislation, while *Aktuelt* stated that the Social Democrats only agreed to the ongoing amendments to the Act under extreme pressure, even though a section of the Social Democrat grass roots membership was clearly opposed to the line followed by the party in Parliament. An editorial shift in approach could be observed at *Ekstra Bladet*, in that the paper moved away from strongly emotional articles supporting refugees and immigrants, and began publishing much more critical contributions towards the end of the 1980s.

In general, the development of affairs surrounding the Iranian refugees in 1984 and 1985 clearly showed that the debate became more intense and its character changed as the number of Iranians applying for asylum increased. This was repeated in the period 1992–95 with regard to the arrival of the refugees from the war in former Yugoslavia. First, general goodwill, subsequently replaced by an increasing number of more critical articles.

This study also seems to suggest that, both in the debate and in the public domain, it is easiest to accept a liberal policy on refugees as long as there is not excessive pressure at the Danish borders.

References

Andersen, Jørgen Goul, Hans Jørgen Nielsen, Niels Thomsen and Jörgen Westerståhl, with contributions from Henrik Christoffersen, Jan Beyer Schmidt-Sørensen and Jette D. Søllinge (1992). *Vi og vore politikere. En kortlægning af forholdet mellem befolkningen og politikerne i dagens Danmark.* Copenhagen: Spektrum.

Andersen, Karen (1979). *Gæstearbejder, udlænding, indvandrer, dansker! Migration til Danmark 1968-78.* Copenhagen: Gyldendal.

Arbejdsministeriet (1971). *Betænkning om udenlandske arbejderes forhold i Danmark*, Betænkning no. 589. Copenhagen: Statens Trykningskontor.

Blüdnikow, Bent (ed.), (1987). *Fremmede i Danmark. 400 års fremmedpolitik.* Odense: Odense University Press.

Christensen, Lone B., Niels Henrik Christensen, Gunnar Homann, Lene Johannessen, Ellen Brinch Jørgensen, Kim U. Kjær, Morten Kjærum, Nina Lassen and Jens Vedsted-Hansen (1995). *Udlændingeret.* Copenhagen: Jurist- og Økonomforbundets Forlag.

Coleman, David and Eskil Wadensjö, contributions from Bent Jensen and Søren Pedersen (1999). *Indvandringen til Danmark. Internationale og nationale perspektiver.* Copenhagen: Spektrum.

Danmarks Statistik (1995). *50-års oversigten.* Copenhagen.

Gaasholt, Øystein and Lise Togeby. (1996). *I syv sind. Danskernes holdninger til flygtninge og indvandrere.* Århus: Politica.

Hammer, Ole (1976). *De nye danskere. Om udenlandske arbejdere i Danmark.* Copenhagen: Mellemfolkeligt Samvirke.

Hammer, Ole (1984). Ryd forsiden, indvandrerne er her... også! En undersøgelse af indvandrerstoffet i dagspressen. *Dokumentation om indvandrere*, 1984, vol. 3. Copenhagen: Mellemfolkeligt Samvirke.

Hansen, Svend Aage and Ingrid Henriksen (1980). Velfærdsstaten 1940-78. In *Dansk socialhistorie*, vol. 7. Copenhagen: Gyldendal.

Henriksen, Ingrid (1985). *Indvandrernes levevilkår i Danmark.* Copenhagen: Socialforskningsinstituttet.

Højsteen, Signe (1992). Dansk udlændingelovgivning med særligt henblik på perioden 1968-1986. Unpublished dissertation, Department of History, University of Copenhagen.

Larsen, John Aggergaard (1998). Holdninger til de fremmede — forestillingen om bosniske krigsflygtninge i den danske offentlighed. *Dansk Sociologi*, 1998, vol. 1.

Martinsen, Harald R. and Chr. Estrup (1973). *Fremmedarbejdere som faktor i dansk økonomi: En cost-benefit analyse.* Copenhagen: Tidsskriftet Management.

Matthiessen, Poul Chr. (1998). *Befolkning og samfund.* Copenhagen: Handelshøjskolens Forlag.

Nellemann, George (1981). *Polske landarbejdere i Danmark og deres efterkommere. Et studie af landarbejder-indvandringen 1893-1929 og indvandrernes integration i det danske samfund i to generationer.* Copenhagen: Nationalmuseet.

Nissen, Henrik S. (1991). Landet blev by. 1950-1970, vol 14 of Olaf Olsen (ed.), *Gyldendal og Politikens Danmarkshistorie.* Copenhagen: Gyldendal.

Pedersen, Ole Karup (1991). Danmark og verden. 1970-1990, vol. 15 of Olaf Olsen (ed.), *Gyldendal og Politikens Danmarkshistorie.* Copenhagen: Gyldendal.

Pedersen, Søren (1999). Udviklingen i vandringen til og fra Danmark i perioden 1960-1997. In David Coleman *et al.*, 1999.

Søllinge, Jette D. (1995). Pressede blade i en skov af antenner. Den trykte presse i et vekslende mediebillede gennem et lige så vekslende århundrede — en kortfattet introduktion til nyere dansk pressehistorie. *Information*, anniversary issue, May 4-5 1995, pp. 14-15.

Søllinge, Jette D. (1994). Træk af udviklingen i dansk politisk journalistik 1900-1991. *Rotunden* 1994, vol. 3. Copenhagen: Statsbiblioteket.

Søllinge, Jette D. and Niels Thomsen (1991). De danske aviser 1634-1989/91. Vol. 3: 1918-1991. Odense: Odense University Press.

Sørensen, Jørgen Würtz (1988a). *'Der kom fremmede'. Migration, Højkonjunktur, Kultursammenstød. Fremmedarbejderne i Danmark frem til 1970.* Århus: Center for Kulturforskning ved Aarhus Universitet.

Sørensen, Jørgen Würtz (1988b). *Hvor dansk? Så dansk! Den politiske debat om indvandrerintegration i 70-erne og 80-erne.* Århus: Center for Kulturforskning ved Aarhus Universitet.

Tonsgaard, O. (1989). Flygtninge og indvandrere — et politisk spørgsmål? In J. Elklit and O. Tonsgaard (eds), *To Folketingsvalg. Vælgerholdninger og vælgeradfærd i 1987 og 1988.* Århus: Politica.

Togeby, Lise (1997): *Fremmedhed og fremmedhad i Danmark. Teorier til forklaring af etnocentrisme.* Columbus.

Togeby, Lise (1998). Prejudice and tolerance in a period of increasing ethnic diversity and growing unemployment: Denmark since 1970, *Ethnic and Racial Studies* 21/6, November 1998.

Tygesen, Peter (1985). Ytringsfrihed og hjælpsomhed, Supplement to *Information*, June 26 1985.

Willerslev, Richard (1983). *Den glemte indvandring. Den svenske indvandring til Danmark 1850-1914.* Copenhagen: Gyldendal.

CHAPTER 7

Economic Effects of Immigration[*]

Eskil Wadensjö

7.1 Introduction

International migration can result from economic, but also from other, circumstances. Refugees account for a large amount of the international migration seen in recent decades. Also in Denmark refugees have come to form a large group. Family members joining relatives who have already migrated comprise an even larger group of immigrants in Denmark.[1] Whatever the cause of migration, the phenomenon produces economic effects in the host country and elsewhere. Immigration can influence the economy of the host country in several different ways, both directly and indirectly. Directly, immigration can influence wages and prices. Among the indirect effects of immigration are those which influence the public sector and economic policy. These indirect effects can be divided into two groups. The first group results from the fact that the public sector redistributes resources among individuals and groups of individuals, on the basis of factors such as family status, age and labour market circumstances. The immigration of a group involves a transfer from and to the group, via taxes, transfers and public consumption. This can result in net transfers to and from the rest of the population. The second group of factors which affect public policy results from the fact that immigration can influence a country's economy and, thereby, also indirectly influence the circumstances on which economic policy is based, as well as that policy itself. Finally, there are other kinds of indirect effects which are not related to the public sector and policy.

In this chapter, the effects of immigration will be divided into four categories: 1) effects on wages and prices, 2) effects on public sector redistribution, 3) macro-effects (effects on unemployment and inflation and thus also on the basis upon which economic policy is formed), and 4) various kinds of indirect

---

[*]. I will use the term 'immigrants' consistently to refer to all people who move to a country. Refugees thus comprise one sub-category of immigrants, migrant workers a second sub-category, and immigrants joining family members a third.

1. Chapter 4, by Søren Pedersen, contains a review of immigration to Denmark in recent decades, in which immigrants are divided into categories such as migrant workers, refugees, family members, etc.

effects. This chapter reviews international studies on the various areas and attempts to relate this scholarship to immigration in Denmark, but also provides an in-depth analysis of the effects of immigration on the public sector redistribution of resources in Denmark.

Immigration not only influences the economy of the host country, but also the economic situation of individual immigrants and the economies of the countries of origin. An immigrant's own situation can be transformed as a result of migrating to a new country. The typical immigration of foreigners in search of work is precisely this kind of migration from unemployment or risk of unemployment and low wages to employment and higher wages. This does not mean that all who immigrate in order to secure a better job actually end up earning higher wages — merely that an expectation of higher earnings is a motivating factor in the migration. In the case of refugees, considerations other than economic factors lie behind the decision to migrate. Even in such cases, however, a higher economic standard can result from the migration, and the economic situation in potential host countries can be a factor in the choice of the country to which the refugee will migrate. Countries from which immigrants migrate can, in the same way as the new country, be influenced economically via direct and indirect effects. Wages and prices can be influenced, and emigration can have fiscal effects and economic effects that influence public economic policy. Economic effects on immigrants themselves and on the countries from which immigrants migrate will not be treated in this chapter, although a more thorough evaluation of the economic effects of international migration would have to take these factors into account.

7.2 Effects on Wages and Prices

Let us begin by discussing the effects of immigration on wages and prices, with the help of a traditional economic model, while temporarily ignoring the existence of a public sector that is involved in various resource-redistribution schemes. A country's output depends on the level of factors of production (labour and capital), on the relationship between the factors of production and production itself (which, in turn, is dependent upon the country's level of technological and organisational advancement), and on the degree to which the productive factors are utilised (unemployment and unutilised production capacity are signs that the productive factors are not being fully utilised). Immigration increases the size of the labour force in the host country. The balance between the productive factors is altered if immigration is not accompanied by an equivalent influx of capital. The number of workers per unit of capital increases. This, in turn, has consequences for wages, returns on capital, and also for the cost of goods and services. Equally important are potential changes in the structure of the labour force. Labour is not a uniform production factor, but can be divided according to occupations and regions.

7.2.1 Labour and capital

Immigration, then, means that the size of the labour force in the host country increases. This, in turn, leads to a fall in wages and a rise in returns on capital. Wage levels will fall provided that three basic conditions are met: 1) that the immigration is not accompanied by a parallel influx of capital to ensure that the capital intensity of the country is maintained, 2) that wages equal the value of the marginal product of labour, and 3) the absence of economies of scale in the economy.

Let us briefly examine these three conditions.

The first condition is that immigration is not accompanied by an influx of capital that is large enough to allow the capital intensity to be maintained. It is not self-evident that this condition is always met. Historically, for example, emigration to North America was accompanied by a parallel injection of capital into North America, even if the capital did not always originate in the same country as the immigrants.[2] Today's international migration provides also examples of a close relationship between the mobility of the labour force and that of capital. This is especially true of the 'new Asian emigration' from countries such as Hong Kong, Taiwan, Singapore and South Korea. This particular migratory trend is partly based on the fact that some countries grant immigration visas to immigrants who also invest in the economy of the host country.[3] Even setting aside this type of very close connection between the movement of labour and capital, the argument can be made that capital today is so mobile that movements of labour, and the accompanying altered wage relations, lead to movements of capital in the same direction. However, no empirical research into the existence or extent of this relationship between the movement of labour and capital in the 1990s has yet been conducted.

That wages match the value of the marginal contribution of labour is a standard assumption in economics that is also open to question. The Scandinavian economies display a considerable rigidity in wage formation, so that an increase in the number of workers does not lead directly to lower wages. Powerful trade unions and implicit or explicit wage contracts generally prevent, in any case, nominal wages from falling when the number of workers rises.[4] Still, the effect can be that wages rise less quickly than they would have

---

2. Brinley Thomas has examined this particular issue most thoroughly. See, for example, Thomas (1972).
3. See Teng (1997) for a review of the problem and an investigation of this type of migration from Taiwan.
4. It might even be the case that trade unions, in order to prevent the immigration of foreign workers at an enlargement of the common labour market, and aware of the fact that it is the number of available jobs more than wage levels that influence immigration, are inclined to keep wages high, so as to reduce the incentive for people from other countries to move to the country. See Lundborg (1997).

had the size of the labour force not increased due to immigration, and thus that wages do adjust, but over a longer period of time. One might also argue that wages paid to immigrants are lower than the market rate (i.e. their wages are lower than the value of their contribution) because, for example, of discrimination. In this case, the economic gain reaped by the country's native population is larger.[5]

As regards the third condition, that there are no economies of scale in the country's production, it is hardly probable that any clear economies of scale will be available in countries that form a customs union. A company's 'domestic' market in such cases will include not only the market in the home country but that in all the countries in the union. On the other hand, economies of scale can be seen in certain types of public consumption. We will return to this matter later.

Immigration means that economic production capacity rises. Since remuneration falls when the size of the labour force grows, the wages earned by immigrants do not entirely match the increase in production that immigration creates, given that wages are equal to the value of the marginal contribution.[6] This means that the existing population in the host country will reap a fiscal gain from immigration. While it is true that the native labour force will see a decrease in wages, this decrease will be more than compensated by an increase in returns on capital. The way in which this affects individual members of the society depends on how capital is distributed. If one imagines that capital is distributed equally among the entire native labour force, then the result would be that everyone wins. A more realistic picture is that capital is distributed in such a way that some segments of the labour force win, while others lose.

To what extent does immigration affect wages? This depends on how wage-sensitive the demand for labour is. Wage-sensitivity can be measured by the degree of elasticity in the demand for labour. The results of estimates of the demand elasticity for labour vary widely, but a fairly reasonable estimation is that it is about 0.3.[7] This means that an immigration equal to 10 percent of the labour force would cause a decrease in wages of about 3 percent. The number of immigrants and second generation immigrants taken together constituted 6.6 percent of the population in Denmark in 1998 and those who arrived in Denmark during the past decade (1988-97) and who still live there constitute approximately 2 percent of the population.[8] The effect of

---

5. See Dex (1992) for a review of research on discrimination against immigrants.
6. This is the standard result. See, however, Lundborg & Segerstrom (1998) for an analysis of a model (with endogenous economic growth) where the result is a fall in the return on capital.
7. See Hamermesh (1993) for a general survey of research on labour demand.
8. See Ejby Poulsen & Lange (1998) and Emerek, Jacobsen & Dahl (1998).

this immigration on wages should thus be c. 0.6 percent, i.e. the effect is quite small in the light of wage increases as a whole during this period. The effect is even smaller if immigrant participation in the labour force is low.

7.2.2 Different groups of workers

Probably more important than the fact that immigration influences the capital intensity is the fact that it also influences the composition of the labour force. This influence is important, as research on the demand for labour shows that a simplified analysis using only a single type of labour fails to reveal important relations. One result is that different types of labour are not, in many cases, substitutes, but in fact complements in the production process. If a certain part of the labour force grows due to immigration, and wages then fall for this group, it may also imply an increase in demand and higher wages for other groups that complement the first group in the production process.

We have long been aware that the way in which immigrants divide into various trades and professions has an impact on wages, and this knowledge has influenced immigration policy in various countries. Ashley Timmer and Jeffrey Williamson (1998) have produced an interesting historical study of immigration policy in Argentina, Australia, Brazil, Canada and the United States during the period 1860-30. Their hypothesis — which they also manage to support — is that immigration policy during this period was formed so as to preserve the relative wage differentials between the skilled and unskilled workers. We can also study the debate about immigration that took place in the 1960s in countries such as Denmark and Sweden. Resistance to immigration in both countries was strongest among groups whose wages were most likely to be influenced by job-related immigration, i.e. primarily among unskilled workers.[9]

One way in which we might analyse a case of two different groups on the labour market might be to work with a model with two production factors, namely two different types of workers: skilled workers and unskilled workers. Immigrants are presumed to belong to the second group (or presumed not to be able to use their education in Denmark for various reasons). We can then produce an analysis which is consistent with that in the previous section, where the production factors were labour and capital. The result is that skilled workers see an increase in wages, while unskilled see lower wages because of immigration.

One problem with this analysis is that it does not allow for the possibility that these groups can be complements, as well as substitutes. It thus makes

---

9. See Bent Jensen's chapter in the present volume (Chapter 5) on the debate in Denmark during the period 1963-80, and Wadensjö (1973) for the debate in Sweden during the 1960s.

more sense to employ a model with (at least) three production factors: capital, skilled workers, and unskilled workers. Estimates indicate that the two categories of workers complement each other in production (while capital and unskilled workers are substitutes).

An examination of the way in which immigrants can be divided into various trades and professions in different countries suggests that immigrants are over-represented in certain jobs that only require a brief period of training, but also in certain professions that require a lengthy education (under-re-presentation is especially pronounced in jobs that fall between these categories). Immigrants are under-represented above all in jobs that require highly advanced skills in the language, culture or formal and informal rules of the host country. This is the case, for example, with many white-collar occupations. In Denmark, as in other Nordic countries, immigrants from countries with more highly developed economies are over-represented among the highest-paid workers, while immigrants from countries with less developed economies are over-represented among the lowest-paid workers.[10]

Immigrants are, in general, also highly over-represented in certain regions. In most countries, immigrants are primarily over-represented in large cities. In Denmark, an average of 6.6 percent of the population consists of immigrants and their children.[11] In the Danish capital, Copenhagen, and surrounding areas, this percentage is significantly higher (10.5) and in some municipalities within this area — for instance in the Municipality of Copenhagen (15.8), and suburbs such as Ishøj (22.1), Brøndby (19.7) and Albertslund (18.2) — it is even higher. Outside the Copenhagen region, the percentage is especially high in larger cities such as Århus and Odense, and in some of the municipalities along the border with Germany. These figures do not reveal the fact that percentages can be much higher in particular areas of these municipalities.[12]

The effects on wages can be greater for some occupations, educational groups and regions than for the labour force as a whole, due to the selectivity of immigration. The wage effect depends, among other things, on the degree of geographic and job-related mobility among the native labour force. Increased movement away from regional labour markets with a high density of immigrants and decreased settlement in such markets can thus reduce the effect on wages. The mobility among the immigrants and the selectivity as regards region, occupation and education can, among those of the immigrants leaving Denmark, also influence the effects on wages.

There are two basic types of studies of the effects of immigration on

10. See Ejby Poulsen & Lange (1998) and Emerek, Jacobsen & Dahl (1998).
11. Figures taken from Ejby Poulsen & Lange (1998).
12. See Hummelgaard *et al.* (1995) for a discussion of the concentration of immigrants within certain residential areas.

wages.[13] The first type is based on differences between the percentage of immigrants living in various regions or in different occupations. This type of study generally shows only a minimal effect on wages.[14] One explanation of why the expected effects do not appear might be that a movement of immigrants to an area is entirely or partly countered by changes to the settlement patterns of the native population, and by a movement of capital to the area to which the immigrants have moved. The other type of study is based on a view of the country as a single economic entity. The study of this entity is then based on the fact that variations in the composition of production factors can be traced over time. In this type of study, immigration appears to have a considerably greater effect on wages.

An interesting question is that of whether immigrants comprise a non-competitive group, by occupying a segment of the labour market and holding jobs that the native population does not want and, thereby, widening the range of goods and services on the market. Daniel Hamermesh's (1997) study of the American labour market fails to find any evidence to support this hypothesis. The group that, to a certain extent, holds these kinds of jobs consists of non-immigrants, namely African-Americans. It should, however, be noted that Hamermesh's analysis does not take into account illegal immigrants, who are perhaps more likely to hold such jobs (but for whom statistics are lacking), nor does it include the self-employed. We will return to self-employed immigrants later.

It could be interesting to study in more detail the effects of immigration on wages, also with respect to the Danish labour market. Since the Danish labour market is relatively small geographically speaking, the second method — the production factor composition approach — should be the most suitable.

7.2.3 Immigrants, the wage structure and income distribution

For several decades following the end of World War II, wages and incomes underwent a process of levelling out in industrialised countries. During the past two decades, however, this trend has been reversed, and differences have been increasing. In analyses of this development, attention has been drawn mainly to the question of labour demand, but also to some extent to that of labour supply.

As to the question of labour demand, three explanatory factors have figured prominently in the debate: An increasing internationalisation of

---

13. See Borjas, Freeman & Katz (1996) for a discussion of both types of studies.

14. A recently published study of the United States, Enchautegui (1997), indicates, however, that immigration accounts for only a small part of the decrease in wages for high school dropouts nationally, but that it has a larger effect on areas where large numbers of immigrants live.

economies (globalization),[15] technological advances and changes in the structure of labour.

The deregulation of international trade (lower tariffs, fewer and less restrictive non-tariff barriers) and lower transport costs have led to greater international competition and thus increased specialisation. Industrial countries with more highly developed economies ('the North') have come to specialise in making products that require a relatively large highly educated labour force (which is relatively plentiful in these countries), while countries with less developed economies ('the South') have specialised in making products that require a relatively large labour force without such education (who are plentiful in these countries). This has resulted, relatively speaking, in an increased demand for more highly educated workers in more highly developed countries such as Denmark.

Technological development does not take any particular direction through physical necessity. It can tend towards the use of relatively larger numbers of workers with less formal education or towards the use of larger numbers of highly educated workers. In recent decades, the trend in technological development seems to be to make do with fewer workers with less education, and the demand for this type of worker has thus been falling, while employers are seeking more workers who are more highly educated. This development influences demand in both more and less developed countries.

The third factor influencing changes in labour demand is related to the way in which labour is organised at the workplace. The development has gone from a more hierarchical form of labour organisation with clearly defined tasks for different jobs to a less hierarchical form of organisation where employees carry out more loosely defined tasks and are assumed to change tasks more frequently, and which demands greater social and communicative skills from employees. Also this type of change leads to an increased demand for a more highly educated labour force. Such changes in the way in which labour is organised can also lead to a decrease in the demand for immigrant workers due to the increased requirements in skills in the host country's language.[16]

The development of demand has been moving in the direction of an increase in demand for more highly educated workers. In isolation, that could be expected to lead to greater wage differentials between more highly educated workers and those with less education. That is counteracted by that,

15. Globalization is not a new phenomenon. On the contrary, increasing globalization is a distinguishing feature of the 19th and early 20th centuries, until the outbreak of World War I. Global migration played a considerably greater role in this period of globalisation than in the present period. Following an initial period marked by increasing differences in wages between countries, most of the period before World War I saw decreasing differences in wages. See Williamson (1998).

16. See Broomé, Bäcklund, Lundh & Ohlsson (1996).

due to an increase in the education of young people, the labour supply has come, to a greater extent, to consist of more highly educated people. In many countries, however, this expansion in education appears not to have been comprehensive enough or to have taken place quickly enough to be able to neutralise the change in labour demand. This change in the composition of the labour force towards a greater portion of the workers being more highly educated can also, in some countries, have been countered by the fact that many immigrants are less highly educated than the host country's population (or have an education that cannot be used on the labour market in the host country).

It has been suggested that the development in the United States has led primarily to an increase in wage differences, while the development in Europe has led mainly to an increase in unemployment differences. The causes of the difference between these two parts of the world might be that wages are more flexible in the United States than in Europe, due to weaker trade unions in the United States. In both cases, however, the result is an increase in income differences. Immigration can, by putting a check on labour supply adjustments, contribute to an increase in wage differences, and by leading to an increase in returns on capital, lead to further differences in income. Especially in the United States, the role that immigrants may play as a factor in growing wage differences has been the subject of lively debate.

If returns on education rise, then differences between the average wage earned by the native population and that earned by immigrants will also increase, given the difference in educational level between the two groups. In the case of the United States, increased returns on education have been very important in explaining growing differences between the average wage earned by the native population and that earned by immigrants.[17]

The development of the immigrants' labour market in Denmark is described in more detail in Søren Pedersen's chapter (Chapter 4) in the present volume. The labour force participation of all of active age has largely remained stable during the past two decades in Denmark, although there has been a slight decline in the last few years. The decline in labour force participation has been dramatic, however, for groups of immigrants who mainly consist of migrant workers and who have been in the country for a long period of time, such as immigrants from Turkey and Pakistan. The 1990s have seen an even more dramatic development for immigrants from the former Yugoslavia. The cause of this development, however, lies primarily in the very low labour force participation by immigrants from Bosnia who arrived in the 1990s.

17. See Butcher & DiNardo (1998) for an empirical investigation of the development in the USA.

While it is true that unemployment among the different groups of immigrants rises and falls with unemployment for the population at large, the unemployment rate is much higher among immigrants from countries with less developed economies than the average unemployment rate for the country as a whole, and there is a trend towards greater unemployment among these immigrants.

Statistics on the position of immigrants on the labour market in Denmark cover only the 1980s and 1990s. It is probable, however, that their position on the labour market during the 1960s resembles that of immigrants in Sweden during the same period: A high labour force participation and relatively low unemployment.

An increase in the relative demand for more highly educated workers — and in places where a change in demand is not countered by an equivalent change in the labour supply — leads to an increase in wage differences or an increase in unemployment differences. Greater differences in wages and employment status can, but do not necessarily, lead to greater inequalities as regards disposable income. The majority of countries have also witnessed such an increase in the inequality of disposable incomes. Denmark, however, is one of a few countries that have seen development in the opposite direction, and where the inequality of disposable incomes has rather grown smaller during the period 1983-95.[18] Differences in private income have increased during this period, and differences in gross income have remained almost unchanged, but differences in disposable income have decreased. The explanation of this development lies in the system of taxation and transfers and changes to that system.[19]

7.2.4 Immigration and prices

Immigration can, via effects on the wage structure, influence prices, for example by increasing the supply of labour in certain sectors producing for the domestic market and thereby putting pressure on prices of those goods and services which they produce. If the immigrants' structure of demand differs from that of the non-immigrant population this can influence the relative prices. Immigration can also lead to the establishment of markets for goods or services that were not previously available. In many countries, immigrants will typically establish themselves as entrepreneurs in certain sectors of the economy. One reason for this can be that they find it difficult to enter the normal labour market. They are not able to secure employment by offering to work for low wages — minimum wages, trade union agree-

18. See Økonomiministeriet (1997), Finansministeriet (1997) and Danmarks Statistik (1998).
19. See Finansministeriet (1997).

ments or social conventions about what constitutes reasonable remuneration for work prevent their doing so. An alternative for them is then to start their own businesses. Restrictions on what constitutes a minimum hourly wage do not apply to people who are self-employed. Many small business owners work a great many hours for a very low hourly wage. In many cases, other family members also work in businesses owned by immigrants. Another reason why many immigrants start their own businesses is that some groups of immigrants uphold traditions and have knowledge from their home country about how businesses should be run, and perhaps also that starting a business can make them more independent.

Businesses run by immigrants are often concentrated in particular sectors, such as restaurants, retail shops and household services. A common feature of all of these businesses is that not much start-up capital is required in order to establish one. In Denmark, a significantly higher proportion of immigrants from less highly developed countries of those employed run their own businesses than other groups among all employed.[20] The figures are 16 percent for immigrants from less highly developed countries, 10 percent for immigrants from more highly developed countries and 8 percent for Danes.[21] The pattern for the sectors in which the self-employed work varies greatly from group to group, especially between immigrants from countries with less developed economies and Danes. Among immigrants from these countries, the majority — 71 percent — are in retail trade or the hotel or restaurant business, while self-employed Danes are distributed more evenly across the sectors, with the largest number (28 percent) in farming.

The establishment of businesses run by immigrants can also give rise to effects on income distribution. The appearance of these effects depends in part on who the customers of such businesses are, in part on the kinds of businesses with which immigrant-run businesses compete.

Which groups buy most goods and services from businesses run by immigrants? Some immigrant businesses are set up to serve the needs of the immigrants themselves. In many countries, there is a tendency for immigrant enclaves to develop, where many of the businesses are run by the immigrants themselves. Yet businesses run by immigrants do not cater to other immigrants alone. In many cases, the immigrant business will serve as a low-cost alternative, selling goods and certain types of services, and will perhaps therefore cater primarily to low-income groups such as students.

20. If we examine the entire population within the respective groups, the proportion of self-employed is approximately the same, 4 percent. The discrepancy between this figure and those in the text is due to the fact that a much lower percentage of immigrants from countries with less highly developed economies are employed, and so the self-employed constitute a larger portion of the total number of employed of the group.

21. See Ejby Poulsen & Lange (1998).

The establishment of businesses that pay low hourly wages to the owner and family members can threaten the existence of other businesses whose owners view the issue of remuneration for labour differently.[22] Yet in many cases, immigrant businesses establish themselves in areas where there is no competition and where they almost seem to be competing with and replacing work normally carried out in the household, for example, eating out rather than at home or sending out sewing to a tailor.

7.3 Redistribution via the Public Sector: Principles[23]

In the preceding section, the effects of immigration, aside from the existence of the public sector, were discussed. In this section, we will instead focus on the process of redistribution that is carried out via the public sector. The underlying question is: What effects does an influx of immigrants have on the population already residing in the country in terms of the income and expenditure of the public sector? The basic idea is that if income rises more than expenditure, then resources will be redistributed in favour of the existing population, while the opposite will result if expenditure rises more than income.

This section will deal with more basic issues and previous research in this area, in order to provide the background for an examination in the following section of the results of the study of this problem in Denmark. These more basic issues will be covered in a few simple steps. We begin by discussing the structure of the entire system of redistribution, and then examine the various types of public sector activities. We will examine the different costs related to public consumption and public transfers, as well as income (i.e. tax revenues). We will then proceed to examine the demarcation of the population in order to discuss some alternative analytical principles. Finally, at the end of this section, we will present the results of some previous studies of this area conducted in different countries.

7.3.1 The structure of the entire system of redistribution

Individuals are consumers throughout their entire lives, but are only active in production for part of this time. Children are not allowed to take employment, and the age at which individuals enter the labour force has gradually been rising. After a period of employment, individuals typically enjoy a number of

22. A study by Farlie & Meyer (1997) deals with the question of whether immigrant businesses (especially those owned by Asian immigrants) threaten the existence of businesses owned by African Americans. They do not find any evidence to support this hypothesis.
23. For a good theoretical and empirical discussion of the basis for this type of study, see MaCurdy, Nechyba & Bhattacharya (1998).

years as pensioners. What they produce during their 'active' lives must not only meet the needs of their own consumption, but also cover consumption expenses for people of a 'passive' age, i.e. children and the elderly. This is made possible by means of a process of redistribution between the generations. This process takes place in three fundamentally different ways: Via the family (for example, parents who provide for their children), via the market (for example, working individuals who invest in a pension insurance) or via the public sector (two examples would be publicly financed schools and a pension system funded by tax revenues). Redistribution via the public sector has come to be of ever greater importance in the Scandinavian societies.

In societies such as Denmark, the redistribution of resources is carried out not only between generations, but also between individuals of an active age. An important form of this type of redistribution is that which takes place between those who are employed and those who are not employed or who hold a job but cannot work, for example, due to illness. Resources are also redistributed from people earning high wages or having a high income to those earning low wages and with low incomes, in part via a tax system in which the amount of tax paid increases along with an increase in income (even more so if the tax system is progressive), while certain types of individual-oriented public consumption are not dependent upon the individual's income, in part via the transfer system.

Immigration can influence the different forms of redistribution in various ways. In most societies, immigrants are generally over-represented among those of an active age. This should imply that resources are transferred from them to the rest of society, provided that all factors other than age are equal for both groups. On the other hand, employment levels are lower among immigrants, and their average wage level is lower, all of which would suggest a transfer to the immigrants. The matter of the direction in which resources are actually transferred is an empirical question, the answer to which varies from country to country and within a given country over a period of time.

7.3.2 Public consumption

Public sector consumption can be divided into several different parts: 1) a part which is independent of the size of the population, 2) a part where the extent of public sector activity depends upon the size and composition of the population, but where it is not possible to tie a particular unit to a particular person and 3) a part which can be viewed as publicly financed private goods. It is also possible to distinguish a fourth group as public sector activities directly connected to immigrants.

When the cost of public sector goods is independent of the size of the population, and when their value for each resident of the country does not depend on the total number of people residing in the country (no crowding effects), these goods are generally referred to as 'public goods'. Common examples of this are expenses related to maintaining the royal family, diplomatic representation, defence and border control. However, it is not self-evident that these costs do not vary in accordance with the size of the population. Defence is a good example. Denmark is a member of NATO and contributes with its own forces to NATO's common defence force. The contribution expected from a given country probably depends upon the size of the country's population. If the population of Denmark were twice its present size, NATO would expect a greater defence contribution, and defence expenses would probably be higher. A certain degree of inertia is, nevertheless, associated with this area. The same is also true of investments in infrastructure such as highways and bridges.

Another type of public sector activity is dependent in a more obvious way upon the size of the population. This is the case, for example, with expenses related to maintaining road networks. If the size of the population grows, more residential areas are built, and more infrastructure for residential areas (for example, local road networks) is needed.

A third category of public consumption can be tied to individuals. This is the case for, for example, education and health care. If there is an increase in the number of schoolchildren, costs will also rise, and it is easy to see the direct financial effect of the increase.

A fourth kind of public consumption is that which is provided specifically for immigrants, and whose costs can be directly related to the immigrants. In certain cases, these costs can be attributed to particular individuals, and sometimes they can be tied to the immigrants as a group. An example of an activity whose costs can be related to particular individuals would be the instruction of immigrants in the Danish language. Another example would be initiatives specifically directed at pre-school and school-aged children of immigrants.[24] Public support of immigrant associations is an example of a cost which is difficult to relate to specific individuals, but which can be related to immigrants as a group. Measures such as these can be referred to as *immigrant* policy, as opposed to *immigration* policy, which is something altogether different. Immigration policy consists of measures aimed at regulating the number of immigrants who arrive and are permitted to remain in the country.

It is very important to distinguish between immigrant policy — which is related to the fact that immigrants are living in a country and which is generally aimed at assisting immigrants in various ways — and immigration policy, which regulates the influx of immigrants to the country. The expenses related to dealing with people seeking asylum and to returning refugees who are not granted asylum in Denmark to their countries of origin are covered

---

24. For an example, see Mehlbye (1994).

under border control activities, and form a part of immigration policy, but not of immigrant policy.

7.3.3 Transfers

Transfers intended for specific individuals are easy to distribute. They are simply traced to the individual in question. It is more difficult, however, to find an appropriate principle for the granting of subsidies to businesses (in many cases it might not be appropriate to distribute them on individuals). Each of these transfers must be examined separately to see what the relevant principle of distribution is.

It is possible to find a simplified method for the analysis of the social insurance systems. This is primarily the case for systems in which compensation is actuarially correct, i.e. where the insurance is run according to the same principles as a private insurance. This can be the case for certain pension systems. If so, both disbursements and receipts can be eliminated from the calculations. There are also other cases in which the element of redistribution within national insurance can be distinguished from the element that is calculated in an actuarially correct manner, and where only the subsidy element (with a negative or positive sum for a given individual) can be included in the calculations. One step in this direction is to carry out a thorough analysis of various national insurance systems in order to see which elements relate to insurance and which elements constitute redistribution in the system.[25]

7.3.4 Interest on the national debt[26]

In some countries, the costs associated with a national debt are considerable. The question is to whom these costs should be attributed — should they be counted as part of expenses related to immigrants as well as for the native population, or should they be distributed in another manner? The answer depends in part upon the dates involved. Assume that a country has a considerable national debt at the beginning of a given year, and that immigrants arrive in the country at the beginning of the same year. Their arrival does not influence the existing national debt, and the costs associated with the debt neither rise nor fall. On the other hand, an increase in debt-related expenditure should be counted if this is due to any increase in the national debt that occurs while immigrants are living in the country, and which is due to a situation where the amount of taxes paid by immigrants fails to cover the

25. See Gustman & Steinmeier (1998) for an analysis of redistribution between immigrants and people born in the United States within the American social security system. Hammarstedt (1998) analyses immigrants in the Swedish national insurance system.

26. See MaCurdy, Nechyba & Bhattacharya (1998) for an analysis.

costs of transfers to those same immigrants and other expenditure on public sector activities related to their presence in the country.

A problem with cross sectional studies can arise in this connection, as it is difficult to ensure accurate dating in the calculations.

7.3.5 Taxes

Immigrants contribute to public sector finances by paying taxes and various special fees, such as those paid for unemployment insurance and pensions. One problem in relating taxes to various individuals and groups is that the issue of who actually pays the taxes is not always clear. This is easy to determine with some taxes. Income tax, for example, can be attributed to the person who pays the tax. A fairly easy solution can also be found in the case of certain other taxes. Value-added tax and selective purchase tax can be allocated in proportion to the consumption level of different individuals and households, and general payroll taxes can be distributed in proportion to wages. The most difficult taxes to distribute are business taxes (taxes on profits, environment taxes, etc.). The degree of uncertainty surrounding this point, as well as many others, means that the type of calculations in which we are engaged should be interpreted cautiously.

7.3.6 The distribution of expenditures and income per individual

As regards the discussion of the various expenditure items within the public sector, it is clear that the most important principle is that expenditure should be tied as closely as possible to specific individuals. This is easy in the case of certain items — for instance, when information is available about who attends a particular school, who has been admitted to a hospital, and so on. It is even easier in the case of transfers, as a direct connection can most often be made. Sometimes this information is lacking, even in cases where individual-oriented public consumption is involved, and it then becomes necessary to work with general patterns, for example, in order to distribute expenditure evenly for all individuals in a particular age group. Certain kinds of expenditure cannot, as previously mentioned, even theoretically be related to specific individuals, even if the expenditure varies in accordance with the number of individuals in the economy. In such cases, general patterns and averages are the only way forward.

The fact that not all expenditure can be tied to specific individuals can give rise to particular problems, and has in fact done so in Swedish studies of immigration. One problem arises because of the fact that people do not always notify the authorities when they leave a country, and thus appear in records to be residing in the country even after they have moved. In the case of Sweden, it is important to take this problem into account, because of a significant under-reporting of emigration from the country among immigrants from countries other than the Nordic countries.[27] If all taxes, transfers and public sector expenditure can be directly tied to payments or the use of services, then this lag in the reporting of emigration would not constitute a problem. Now, however, a greater or smaller portion of expenditure must be distributed on the basis of general patterns, while taxes can, in essence, be tied directly to individuals. The result of the calculations can be that, in the case of individuals who move out of the country, public sector income (i.e. tax revenues) will fall, while public sector expenditure remains the same, and that this will, in terms of the analysis as a whole, mean that estimates of net transfers to these immigrants and to immigrants as a group are too high. Even without this lag, incorrect estimates can be produced for individuals who emigrate during the year for which the estimate is calculated. The problem with such lags and with emigration during the year under study increases the higher the rate of emigration, and the greater the lag in reporting emigration and the proportion of expenditure that is distributed based on general patterns.[28]

7.3.7 Basic points of departure for the analysis

The way in which an analysis is carried out should depend upon the questions to be answered. The basic question in much of the discussion is: What effect does a marginal increase (or a non-marginal increase) in the number of immigrants moving to Denmark have on public sector finances? An alternative question is the following: What does the redistribution pattern between Danes and immigrants look like in a given year?

If one wishes to attempt to answer the first question, one solution might be to follow a particular cohort, such as all people who immigrated to Denmark in 1960, and then to examine the redistribution pattern between this particular group and the rest of the population for each year, and attempt to make a projection of what will happen in years to come. One could then repeat the analysis cohort by cohort. It is important not to limit the period of study for the respective cohorts in such a way as to distort the analysis. Children of immigrants must be included (second and third generation immigrants) in any case for a period of time that is long enough for any differences between the immigrant cohort and the native population to have dis-

27. See Greijer (1995), (1996), (1997a) and (1997b) and Nilsson (1995). According to these reports, cases of failure to report emigration constitute between 3 and 10 percent of the population of immigrants from non-Nordic countries.
28. According to a conversation with Anita Lange, Statistics Denmark, follow-up routines with respect to an individual's residence status are better in Denmark than in Sweden, and thus the problem is less serious. However, I have not had access to any report on the size of the overestimation of the immigrant population in Denmark.

appeared (i.e. for the cohort to have become assimilated). Children born out of marriages between immigrants and Danes must also be counted, even if this group should be distributed equally between the immigrant and native populations.

The type of study described above where cohorts are followed and projections made requires a great deal of data, and useful information is generally only available for recent years. This means that, in practise, cohorts can be followed only for a few years. On the other hand, it is possible to construct artificial cohorts and to attempt to make assumptions that are as realistic as possible based on the study of cross sectional information.[29] We will not, however, be concerned with this option in the present chapter.

A typical feature of studies of cohorts (both real and artificial) is that the result is highly dependent on the age composition of the immigrants under study. In general, a large proportion of people who immigrate are of younger active age or the children of these immigrants. By contrast, relatively few are older (older but still active or over pension age). If one examines only those who have themselves immigrated (excluding children born after their parents have already immigrated), then one examines a group of people who gradually grow older. If children (and future generations) are included, the age composition of the group gradually comes more and more to resemble that of the native population. Provided that the immigrants find employment, we also see a net transfer from the immigrants for a number of years subsequent to their immigration, and that these transfers then gradually cease. What is emphasised in this type of model is that immigrants who are of younger active age when they arrive have already had their childhood and youth expenses paid in their country of origin, and that they arrive as members of an age group from which transfers generally occur to those who are below (children and youth) or above (the elderly) an active age. An even clearer illustration of this type of redistribution is found in countries that have adopted a 'guest worker' system, and where immigrants only reside in the country for a year or a few years while they are of active age.

With respect to the problem of data, cross sectional investigation is the method most frequently employed in studies of the effects of immigration on public sector redistribution. Such studies examine the occurrence of redistribution over the course of a year (or more) between the immigrants and the native population. Here it is important to include the children of immigrants. If they are not included, only a portion of the effects of the increase in population enter into the calculations. Data problems associated with this can arise in connection with the descendants of earlier groups of immigrants. A possible solution is to limit the investigation to a group of immigrants who

---

29. See, for example, Storesletten (1998) and Gustafsson & Larsson (1998, section 6) for two cohort-based analyses.

arrived in the country after a particular year (after 1970, for example). The problem then is that one can generally see whatever redistribution occurs during the first decades after the immigration, but not after that (for example studying redistribution when people are 20-50 years old but not when they are older).

7.3.8 The public sector on different levels

When we refer to transfers carried out via the public sector, we generally ignore the fact that the public sector is divided into different, often highly independent, levels. In Scandinavian countries, we can generally distinguish between three or four levels — first the state level, then the regional level (county level), and finally the municipal level. A fourth level or form of organisation often having a separate economy is the social insurance sector. Immigration influences the different levels in different ways, depending upon the tax system and various fees, etc.

It may seem only to be a minor problem to add up the different levels of the public sector, and if a study of the totality of effects is all that is required, then proceeding in such a manner might be reasonable. Yet arguments can be made in favour of dividing the various entities that make up the public sector.

The first of these arguments is that results for the respective levels can influence behaviour. Let us imagine two different cases and assume that the total effect is the same in both cases: 1) in the first case, the state wins, while the municipality loses; 2) in the second case, the municipality wins, while the state loses. We cannot dismiss the possibility that the two types of results will influence the actions of the municipality with respect to measures that influence the number of immigrants who settle in the municipality. If, to take an extreme example, the municipalities must bear the expenses and the state reaps the benefits, the municipalities could feasibly attempt to direct immigrants towards other municipalities.[30]

A second argument is that the system ought to take a neutral position to redistribution with respect to effects on people who live in different parts of the country. The overall level of immigration is determined by the state. In a country such as Denmark, a large portion of newly arrived immigrants are refugees, and the rules governing who will be accepted as refugees are established centrally (i.e. on the state level). Those who are granted permission to enter the country are thus accepted and must settle somewhere in the country. Finding acceptance in a given municipality can be more difficult if the distribution of expenses between the municipality and the state results in a si-

---

30. There are numerous examples in nineteenth century Sweden of municipalities attempting by means of relocation assistance to move costly families into other municipalities.

tuation where the municipality is responsible for a large portion of the expenses, while income (tax revenue) is received at the state level.

Both of these arguments indicate the fact that it is important to acquire knowledge about the actual distribution as well as to have a way of compensating municipalities that accept refugees to provide them with reasonable incentives to do so.

The fact that the fiscal effects can actually vary from level to level has been demonstrated in investigations of immigrants in two states in the USA, California and New Jersey. These studies indicate a small net income for the Federal level but a net expenditure on the state and local levels.[31]

One Danish study sheds at least some light on the question.[32] The study deals with the Danish municipalities' net expenditure for 1995 and is based on information from 23 municipalities. This net expenditure is primarily influenced by the fact that immigrants show a different demographic composition, but also by special provisions for immigrants as a group. The net expenditure amounts to DKK 7300 per immigrant (DKK 6800 per refugee and DKK 7700 per immigrant defined as a non-refugee immigrant). No consideration has been made for taxes paid by immigrants (compared to those paid by the native population) nor to the fact that this expenditure influences tax rate equalisation measures and also various contributions from the state to the municipality. It is thus not possible to form a complete picture of how the municipalities are influenced based on this particular study.

A report produced by the Danish Ministry of the Interior's Finance Committee deals with the present system of redistribution between different municipalities and counties, and attempts to calculate the effects of the presence of foreign citizens in a municipality on the municipality's expenditure.[33] In the present system of redistribution between municipalities, the number of foreigners from third-world countries — who, for the purposes of this system, include the citizens of all countries other than the Nordic countries, members of the European Union and North America[34]: 1 — are included as one of the factors that determine socially conditioned redistribution. This can be viewed as an indicator of which factors influence socially conditioned expenditure needs in the municipalities. In this particular redistribution system, the number of foreign citizens equals a factor which represents 10 percent of all redistribution. Since socially conditioned redistribution constitutes 20 percent of the redistribution basis (most of it is dependent on age composition), this means that the foreign citizen factor is attributed a weighting of 2 percent in

---

31. See Clune (1998), Garvey & Espenshade (1998) and Smith & Edmonston (1997).
32. See Christoffersen & Mørch Andersen (1997).
33. See Indenrigsministeriet (1998).
34. Citizens of countries such as Switzerland, Australia, New Zealand and Japan are counted as immigrants from third-world countries.

the redistribution system as a whole. There is, in addition, a form of redistribution which is tied directly to the fact that foreign citizens of this group of countries reside in the municipality and which provides a subsidy of a particular amount per person. This amount varies according to age and the length of the period of residence in the country in the case of refugees (the longer this period, the lower the subsidy), and a certain low amount is also paid per asylum seeker. This type of subsidy amounts to a total of DKK 4 billion.

The report also contains a regression analysis in which the actual expenditure in a municipality per resident or per resident belonging to a particular (age)-group that is relevant to the type of expenditure in question is explained by making use of certain variables, where the percentage of foreign residents from third-world countries is one of the factors. It appears that the effect of the number of foreign citizens on the level of expenditure is statistically significant in three areas: Library and leisure-time expenditure, state school expenditure for students aged 7-16, and housing subsidy expenditure for people between 20-59. In all of these cases, expenditure is higher if the percentage of foreign residents is higher, which indicates that the redistribution that has taken place is supported by actual differences in expenditure (although it cannot be determined on the basis of this study whether the redistribution corresponds to the actual differences in costs).

The result of this investigation indicates the importance of carrying out further research in this area, in order to form a better basis for decision-making regarding the design of the redistribution system.

7.3.9 Experience in Denmark and other countries

A number of studies of the fiscal effects of immigration based on cross sectional analyses have been carried out in different countries. We will discuss studies carried out in the United States, Sweden, Norway and Denmark.

A review of previous American studies shows that the fiscal effects of immigration in all cases are negative. However, all of these studies lack important details of the precise accounting for expenditure and income. This makes them difficult to interpret. Studies carried out within the framework of the National Research Council's recent comprehensive report on the effects of immigration, and which are considerably more thorough as regards the system of accounting for expenditure and income, still produce similar results.[35] The net fiscal effect is negative, even when — as was previously mentioned — the net effect is positive on the Federal level.

The experience in Sweden is that results have changed over time, as immigration itself has changed from being an immigration of workers to primarily refugee immigration, and as the Swedish economy has also undergone

---

35. See Clune (1998), Garvey & Espenshade (1998) and Smith & Edmonston (1997).

considerable transformation. A study of labour immigration during the 1960s, and where the fiscal calculations relate to the year 1969, indicates a considerable net transfer from the immigrants to the rest of the population.[36] Of decisive importance for the results of this study was the fact that the immigrants who were studied had a very high level of labour force participation. A study of immigrants in the 1970s suggests that there was at that time still a net transfer from the immigrants, but that it was considerably smaller. Later studies show a fairly considerable net transfer to the immigrants.[37, 38] According to a recent study by Jan Ekberg (1999) the net transfer amounts to between 1 and 2 per cent of GDP per year. There are large differences between different groups of immigrants.

Knut Arild Larsen and Erik Bruce (1998) have carried out a study of redistribution via the public sector in Norway. Their results indicate a significant redistribution to refugee immigrants, while there is a smaller transfer from other immigrants.[39] The factor that, to a great extent, determines these results is the poor labour market situation for especially refugee immigrants. If immigrants were employed at the same levels as the rest of the population in the same age group, the net transfer to refugees would fall significantly, and the net fiscal transfer from other immigrants would rise sharply.

A new Danish study of fiscal effects of immigrants in 1995, produced by the Ministry of Economic Affairs, attempts to a very great extent to allocate both tax revenues and expenditure directly to individuals.[40] This should make the study more reliable than many others conducted in other countries, and also less sensitive to the issue of people leaving the country without being registered as having done so.

The total fiscal effects amount to DKK 1 billion *from* group 1 immigrants (immigrants from EU countries, Norway, Iceland, Switzerland, North America, Australia and New Zealand), DKK 11.3 billion *to* immigrants from group 2 countries (all other countries) and DKK 58.9 billion *from* the rest of the population. The figures per person over 18 are DKK +10,600, DKK -82,000 and DKK +15,000. A distinction is also made between those who are employed full time and those employed part time or not employed at all. The result shows that the fiscal transfers to group 2 immigrants go to individuals who are not employed full time, and that the total effect is governed to a great extent by the fact that the level of employment in this group is low.

36. See Wadensjö (1973).
37. See Ekberg (1998) for a review of different studies.
38. According to a study by Gustafsson & Larsson (1998), this reversal occurred in the early 1990s, at the same time that unemployment rose quickly in Sweden.
39. The groups included in the study are primarily first and second generation immigrants in Norway.
40. See Økonomiministeriet (1997) and Christensen (1998).

We are now in a position to describe in greater detail redistribution via the public sector in Denmark. This question will be dealt with in section 7.4.

7.4 Redistribution via the Public Sector in Denmark: Empirical Data

Let us now look more closely at patterns of redistribution of resources between immigrants and the native population in Denmark. We can do this for three different years, 1991, 1995 and 1996, using data from the Danish Ministry of Economic Affairs' Law model.[41] This will extend the study carried out by the Ministry of Economic Affairs, which only covered 1995. There are a number of reasons why it is important to look at several different years. One reason is that the results of a single year can be influenced to a far extent by random effects. One such element of chance is the fact that the results are based on a sample of immigrants, and when the data is divided into subgroups, the results are based on relatively few observations. Another is that the variations in the labour market situation between years can be of great significance. By examining three different years, at least some variation in the labour market will be included, and this can also provide clues about the importance of the labour market to the final result. The fact that we use data from different years also enables us, to a certain extent, to follow cohorts. Those who had been in Denmark from 0 to 5 years in 1991 had in 1996 been in the country from 6 to 10 years, assuming, of course, that they remained in Denmark at all.

One problem with the database is that most descendants of immigrants who were born before 1960 are not included, but fall into the same category as the rest (Danish part) of the population. The same is true for immigrants and descendants of immigrants who became Danish citizens prior to 1978. This means that more than a few of those immigrants who are most successfully integrated into the Danish labour market will not be categorised as immigrants.

The results for the different population groups appear in table 7.1. In contrast to the Ministry of Economic Affairs' report, expenditure related to the period before asylum is granted is not included among the expenditures, as this expenditure should be considered a part of border control policy rather than a transfer of resources to immigrants.

Table 7.1 indicates a net transfer (in part to cover expenditures related to collective public goods such as defence) from the Danish population, but also from immigrants from group 1 countries (EU countries, Norway, Switzerland, Iceland, North America, Australia and New Zealand). This is the case for all

---

41. I am grateful for all the assistance with data that the Danish Ministry of Economic Affairs has provided.

Table 7.1 Net transfers per person for different groups (amounts given in Danish *kroner*) **for the years 1991, 1995 and 1996.**

Group	1991	1995	1996
Danish population (excluding those with one immigrant parent)	13,600	15,800	18,600
Danish population (including those with one immigrant parent)	13,600	15,900	18,700
Second generation — one Danish parent and one immigrant parent from group 1 country	17,700	25,700	29,600
Second generation — one Danish parent and one immigrant parent from group 2 country	4,900	14,500	12,400
Immigrants from group 1 country	14,900	10,700	12,300
Immigrants from group 2 country	−48,000	−62,600	−63,700
Second generation — parents from group 1 country	19,600	18,900	27,500
Second generation — parents from group 2 country	700	−29,300	−10,700
Total	12,000	12,600	15,000

Note: Group 1 countries are EU countries, Norway, Switzerland, Iceland, North America, Australia and New Zealand; Group 2 countries are all other countries.

Table 7.2 Rate of employment (full-time and full-year employment = 1.0) for the years 1991, 1995 and 1996.

Group	1991	1995	1996
Danish population (excluding those with one immigrant parent)	0.48	0.53	0.54
Danish population (including those with one immigrant parent)	0.48	0.53	0.54
Second generation — one Danish parent and one immigrant parent from group 1 country	0.56	0.59	0.60
Second generation — one Danish parent and one immigrant parent from group 2 country	0.48	0.52	0.49
Immigrants from group 1 country	0.39	0.41	0.44
Immigrants from group 2 country	0.25	0.25	0.26
Second generation — parents from group 1 country	0.45	0.51	0.52
Second generation — parents from group 2 country	0.42	0.32	0.44
Total	0.47	0.52	0.53

Note: Group 1 countries are EU countries, Norway, Switzerland, Iceland, North America, Australia and New Zealand; Group 2 countries are all other countries.

Table 7.3 Age distribution in the different groups in 1996 (percentage distribution).

Group	-24	25-29	30-39	40-49	50-59	60-66	67-
Danish population (excluding those with one immigrant parent)	11.6	8.7	18.5	18.3	16.7	8.4	17.7
Danish population (including those with one immigrant parent)	12.0	8.9	18.7	18.2	16.5	8.3	17.6
Second generation — one Danish parent and one immigrant parent from group 1 country	34.1	23.5	35.1	7.3	0.1	-	-
Second generation — one Danish parent and one immigrant parent from group 2 country	50.0	23.8	19.5	6.7	-	-	-
Immigrants from group 1 country	8.3	9.3	20.1	19.8	19.5	7.5	15.2
Immigrants from group 2 country	17.2	16.5	30.3	17.8	9.3	4.0	4.7
Second generation — parents from group 1 country	19.4	8.1	29.0	21.0	6.8	4.8	10.8
Second generation — parents from group 2 country	78.7	8.3	11.1	1.4	-	-	0.4
Total	12.1	9.2	19.1	18.2	16.3	8.1	16.9

Note: Group 1 countries are EU countries, Norway, Switzerland, Iceland, North America, Australia and New Zealand; Group 2 countries are all other countries.

three years included in the study. By contrast, the table shows a significant transfer to immigrants from group 2 countries (all other countries). The transfer per person is greater in 1995 and 1996 than in 1991, even if changes in the price level are taken into account. It is of particular interest to note that a clearly positive net transfer can be seen in the case of children born from marriages between a Dane and an immigrant (considerably greater than for children of two immigrants). This would indicate that such ties can be important for assimilation into Danish society.

Several explanations can be offered for the pattern shown in table 7.1. The most important factor, however, is that the rate of employment varies greatly from group to group.[42] Table 7.2 shows that the rate of employment for group 2 immigrants is far lower (by approximately half) than that for the Danish population, and also much lower than for group 1 immigrants.

The lower rate of employment here cannot be explained by differences in

42. See Søren Pedersen's chapter and the next section of the present chapter for information and an analysis of the development of the labour market situation for immigrants in Denmark.

Table 7.4 Net transfers per person from group 2 countries according to length of stay in Denmark (amounts in Danish *kroner*) for the years 1991, 1995 and 1996.

Length of stay*	1991	1995	1996
Less than one year	−45,200	−82,000	−55,800
1–3 years	−63,200	−56,600	−89,900
3–5 years	−65,400	−76,300	−79,300
5–7 years	−70,300	−79,300	−83,600
7–10 years	−40,400	−76,600	−82,100
10 years or more	−34,100	−49,000	−46,700
Second generation	700	−29,300	−10,700
Total	−48,000	−62,600	−63,700

* The division according to length of stay is based on exact age, so that the 'less than one year' in the column for the year 1996 includes those who immigrated on 1 January 1996 or later, '1–3 years' includes those who immigrated between 1 January 1994 and 31 December 1995, etc.

age composition. On the contrary, a considerably larger proportion of the adult immigrants from group 2 countries are of an active age than is the case for the Danish population and for immigrants in group 1. The age composition for the various groups for one year, 1996, is shown in table 7.3.

The second generation immigrants included in the study are, as table 7.3 shows, relatively young, and many of them are still of an age where many — Danes as well as immigrants — have not yet firmly established themselves on the labour market. It is important to bear in mind that a large number of older children of immigrants do not appear in the group due to gaps in the statistical basis.

The results shown in tables 7.1 and 7.2 indicate the importance of investigating in particular the conditions for immigrants from group 2 countries, i.e. from countries with less developed economies. Table 7.4 presents information about net transfers for this group of immigrants, divided up according to the length of their stay in Denmark. It is striking that all of the values are negative. Research in other countries has shown considerable differences between categories based on the length of stay in the host country. Here there are differences, but the values are consistently negative, and the differences are not very great. Even in the case of children of immigrants, two of the years show negative values. This can be compared with the values for those who have one immigrant and one Danish parent.

The main determining factor in these results can be seen in table 7.5. The rate of employment is low, not only for the first year — which is reasonable considering that many only stayed in Denmark for part of a year — but also

Table 7.5 Rate of employment per person from group 2 countries according to length of stay in Denmark (full-time and full-year employment = 1.0) for the years 1991, 1995 and 1996.

Length of stay	1991	1995	1996
Less than one year	0.03	0.02	0.05
1-3 years	0.13	0.17	0.11
3-5 years	0.20	0.17	0.17
5-7 years	0.23	0.22	0.20
7-10 years	0.24	0.27	0.25
10 years or more	0.33	0.35	0.36
Second generation	0.42	0.32	0.44
Total	0.25	0.25	0.26

These results indicate that the integration of immigrants into the labour market is the central issue, and that analyses of why the position of immigrants on the labour market is so weak, as well as studies of measures that can influence their rate of employment, are urgently needed. For this reason, we will deal in the following section with the immigrants' situation with respect to the labour market.

---

for those who have stayed in Denmark over a longer period of time. If we examine those who, in 1991, had been in Denmark for 0-5 years, and compare them with the group who, in 1996, had been in Denmark for 5-10 years, we find that the rate of employment has increased, but is still very low. The rate of employment of all immigrants from group 2 countries is in all three years close to 0.25.

Compared to the study carried out by the Ministry of Economic Affairs, the transfer to immigrants from group 2 countries is smaller, due to the elimination of costs related to the pre-asylum period. By studying transfers over the course of three years, and with a gap of a few years, we can see that transfers to immigrants from countries with less developed economies have not decreased during the 1990s. We can also see that transfers do not decrease rapidly with an increase in length of stay in Denmark.

7.5 Employment, Unemployment and Inflation

We have already seen the significance of the immigrants' employment situation, as well as the discouraging figures for Denmark. In this section, we will first attempt to place the Danish situation within the context of the EU as a whole, in order to then examine some explanations for the worsening situation and, finally, to determine how the low levels of employment should be interpreted from a macro-economic perspective.

Table 7.6 Labour force participation of 25-49-year-olds in 1997 according to nationality.

	Men			Women		
	Citizens of the country (%)	*Citizens of another EU country (%)*	*Citizens of a non-EU country (%)*	*Citizens of the country (%)*	*Citizens of another EU country (%)*	*Citizens of a non-EU country (%)*
Austria	94.3	92.2	94.6	77.3	69.8	71.4
Belgium	94.5	91.5	76.2	76.1	62.7	30.9
Denmark	94.1	78.2	72.3	84.8	88.6	51.1
France	95.9	95.6	90.7	80.4	73.7	47.1
Germany	94.2	95.4	87.0	77.8	71.0	47.7
The Netherlands	95.5	91.4	65.8	73.7	74.4	36.7
Sweden	91.4	90.8	70.9	87.2	86.3	58.6
United Kingdom	92.9	87.5	84.2	76.4	73.2	54.1
EUR 15	93.7	93.1	86.5	72.7	71.1	50.2

Note: EUR 15 gives the percentage for all EU countries considered as a whole.
Source: Eurostat (1998).

As table 7.6 shows, a similar pattern to that in Denmark can also be detected in other EU countries. The table provides statistics for men and women aged 25-49, an age group with a generally high level of participation in the labour force. Labour force participation is, with a few exceptions, highest among people who are citizens of the country in which they live, somewhat lower for citizens of another EU country and lowest for people from countries outside the EU. Denmark is, along with the Netherlands and Sweden, one of those countries which show the greatest differences in labour force participation among men who are citizens of different countries. It is important to note that the table categorises people according to citizenship, and not according to country of birth, since the ease with which immigrants can acquire citizenship in the host country varies considerably from country to country. Being granted citizenship is a relatively simple matter in countries such as Denmark and Sweden, but extremely difficult in a country like Germany.[43] This means that of the citizens of foreign countries living in Denmark and Sweden, most have arrived during the past decade, while a large portion of foreign citizens in Germany have lived there for a very long

43. See Chapter 4 by Søren Pedersen for information regarding the rules by which Danish citizenship is granted and regarding the extent of the number of those who apply for, and are granted, citizenship in Denmark.

time. The most important conclusion, however, is that the great differences in levels of employment between the native population and immigrants, and also between different groups of immigrants, that are found in Denmark can also be found in other countries.

If we examine a cross section of immigrants in Denmark, the employment situation is more favourable for those who arrived in the country earlier. This might be interpreted to mean that, after a period of time in the country, immigrants gradually begin to see an improvement in their employment situation. The debate in the United States suggests, however, that this interpretation is incorrect. It may be instructive to review this particular debate briefly.

The employment situation for a cross section of immigrants to the United States appeared, in studies based on the 1970 census, to be better for immigrants who had been living in the country for a longer period of time than for those who had been there for a shorter period. When Barry Chiswick first presented these results, he interpreted them to suggest precisely this kind of adjustment over time on the part of immigrants who had arrived in the country.[44] This interpretation was later subjected to a critique most notably by George Borjas, who proposed the alternative explanation that different cohorts of immigrants had different educational backgrounds, and that those who arrived most recently were less educated.[45] Other hypotheses and explanations regarding the differences that can be seen in cross sections include the notion of self-selective re-emigration (those who succeed stay, those who fail move home) and the idea that the labour market has gradually become more difficult to enter for immigrants, due to higher educational requirements.

This debate has led to a considerable amount of research in the United States on the differences between different cohorts upon their arrival in the country, as well as on how the various cohorts fare there. Current research suggests that successive waves of immigrants are more educated, but that the educational level of the native population is rising more rapidly.[46] The immigrants' educational level has thus deteriorated in relative terms, although a rising relative level of education among immigrants can be seen beginning in the mid-1980s.[47] This later turnabout could possibly be the result of changes in immigration policy that, relatively speaking, promote the immigration of more highly educated individuals.

The employment situation for immigrants in Denmark is not good. Labour force participation is low, and unemployment is high among those in the

44. The first study in this tradition is Chiswick (1978).
45. One of the most recent of Borjas' many studies of this problem is Borjas (1998). A useful review of the argument can be found in Borjas (1990).
46. See Betts & Lofstrom (1998).
47. See Jasso, Rosenzweig & Smith (1998).

labour force. This is the case primarily for immigrants from countries with less developed economies.

A study by Hans Hummelgaard *et al.* (1995) of immigrants and refugees from countries with less developed economies indicates that the average rate of unemployment among refugees rose dramatically in the beginning of the 1990s in Denmark. Unemployment was also high before then, but at that time the difference between immigrant unemployment levels and those of the rest of the population began to increase. The high rate of unemployment among immigrants and refugees from these countries can be explained to a considerable extent by the fact that they run a generally higher risk of becoming unemployed. This risk is greater for those who have been in the country for only a short period of time than for those who have stayed longer. The difference in the rate of unemployment between the group of immigrants who were studied and the population as a whole is also dependent upon the fact that immigrants tend to remain unemployed for longer periods of time. Differences in the length of the period of unemployment between immigrants and the population as a whole decrease noticeably, however, when the education level is taken into account, and they disappear altogether for those who are highly educated. Another interesting point made in this study is that a larger percentage of immigrants will end periods of unemployment by exiting the labour force, while the rest of the population will more often leave unemployment in order to take a job.

We should look for explanations that are not specific to Denmark, as the state and development of the immigrants' labour market situation is similar in Norway and Sweden.[48] What is the explanation for the higher level of unemployment among immigrants? There are two types of explanations. The first of these is based on the unique characteristics of immigration, its composition, the way in which the economy adjusts to immigration, and the notion that all of this adds up to generally higher levels of unemployment in the economy as a whole and a higher rate of unemployment among immigrants. In the case of Denmark, a large portion of immigration during the last decades has consisted of refugee immigration and the immigration of relatives joining family members already in the country.[49] This type of immigration has not — unlike job-related immigration — been governed by the availability of jobs for new immigrants. The second explanation is based on the fact that unemployment is determined by macro-economic factors, and that immigrants are generally not as successful as the native population in competing for jobs when there is a certain amount of unemployment.

---

48. For Norway, see, for example, Blom & Ritland (1997), and for Sweden see, for example, Lundh & Ohlsson (1994).
49. Søren Pedersen's Chapter 4 contains a review of the development of the composition of immigration in Denmark.

Immigration can influence unemployment. The exact nature of this influence, however, is not clear. It depends upon the way in which the structure of labour demand and labour supply are influenced by the immigration. One case that has been dealt with in various studies is the way in which immigration influences the state of the economy, or more generally whether immigration helps to exaggerate swings in the economy, or contributes to promoting stability. How do investments (private, public), consumption (private, public) and production look in the period immediately following a wave of immigration? Immigration can, for example, lead to investment in industry (companies see a chance to expand), residential property and infrastructure, so that the total level of demand rises.

Do a larger wave of immigration and an increase in the immigrant population lead to greater unemployment? A superficial investigation does not support this hypothesis. It seems as if unemployment levels are determined by other factors, for example by a political desire to keep inflation at bay. Lower unemployment levels lead to higher inflation. In a way, one could say that the contribution that unemployment makes to the economy is to fight inflation, and that the unemployed are, in part, compensated for their efforts and, in part, contribute to it themselves by having a lower standard of living. The question is whether an unemployed immigrant contributes as much to holding inflation down as an unemployed Dane. (Actually, this is a matter that it should be possible to research, by including unemployment among Danes and that among immigrants separately in the wage equations). If the immigrant does contribute as much, one could say that the Danish population has managed to attain a certain given (low) inflation level along with lower unemployment for themselves by allowing the immigrants to 'take over' a part of the unemployment that is needed to fight inflation.

It might also be the case that immigration leads to an increase in structural unemployment. Immigration leads to an increase in the labour supply in certain occupations and not so much in other occupations. This can, at least in the short term, lead to imbalances in the labour market if no adjustment of relative wages occurs via changes of relative wages, or via mobility between different occupations. Without an adjustment, the total level of unemployment may increase at any given level of inflation.

7.6 Other Indirect Effects

Thus far, we have dealt with the direct effects of immigration on wages and prices, and with its indirect effects via the public sector and influence on economic policy. There are also other types of indirect effects which ought to be discussed.

Immigration is not simply a migration of labour, but also a migration of people with skills that are not always present in the host country. There are examples in the history of many countries of governments actively working to entice particular groups of people with certain kinds of desired skills to immigrate, to make it possible for new industries to be established in the host country. We can, in such cases, not only observe the direct productive activity of these immigrants, but also a rise in the productivity of other people, due to skills imported into the country by the immigrants. The fact that many countries have, at various points in their history, given immigration priority to people with certain kinds of special training or working in particular trades and professions in order to assist in the establishment of new industries can also be interpreted in this manner.

Even if we ignore these kinds of conscious attempts to grant priority to people with particular skills, there are numerous examples of cases where labour migration or refugee migration has meant a transfer of new skills and contributed to the establishment of new kinds of businesses.

In the debate in recent years, the value of ethnic diversity — and the fact that such diversity can lead to the renewal and further development of commercial activities — has also been emphasised.

In most countries, immigrants settle in large cities. Many of them arrive directly in large cities, and others, who had previously arrived or been placed in other parts of a country, eventually make their way to the large cities. In Denmark, there is a considerable amount of refugee relocation to the Copenhagen area or to Århus from other parts of the country.[50]

The phenomenon of the concentration of immigrants in particular cities and certain areas within these cities has been the subject of debate during recent years within several international organisations, often under the general headings of 'social exclusion' and 'marginalisation'. It is not a clear-cut matter that the concentration of immigrants in large cities is a negative development.[51] On the contrary, urban immigration has contributed to the revitalisation of large cities in various countries. Examples of cities that have been mentioned in this regard are New York, London and Vancouver. Immigrant communities can also provide a way by which immigrants can begin their lives in a new society by living close to fellow countrymen, perhaps then moving on to other areas at a later stage. In certain cases, however, immigrants do not end up moving away from the immigrant community, which can result in the formation of ethnic ghettos. This can lead to the creation of social boundaries between immigrants and the native population, and to antagonism between immigrants and the native population and between different ethnic groups — antagonism which sometimes finds expression in

50. See Hummelgaard *et al.* (1995), chapter 6. For Sweden see Storrie & Nättorp (1997).
51. See OECD (1998) for a number of articles that deal with the question of the concentration of immigrants in large cities. Denmark is not among the countries under study in this collection of essays.

violence. Differences between different neighbourhoods in a large city can be extreme. An obvious example is the city of Los Angeles, which includes both a very advanced 'high-tech' district and areas inhabited mainly by immigrants from the third world.[52]

Another issue to which a great deal of attention has been paid is the relatively high amount of crime among immigrants compared to that among the native population. Part of the cost of crime is included in the calculations of transfers via the public sector. Other effects of crime — for example, the costs of the consequences of crime that are borne by individual households, and the preventative measures taken by households — are not included in the calculations. It is important, in this connection, to draw attention to a number of difficulties associated with making comparisons of the levels of criminality for different groups. In the first place, it is important to ensure that the appropriate population group is identified — immigrants settled in the host country. A portion of crime committed by foreigners is committed by individuals who are visiting the country temporarily (formally as tourists). These crimes and the costs associated with them should not be attributed to the immigrant population. In the second place, it is important to note that crimes are committed, above all, by particular demographic groups (primarily younger men) in which immigrants are generally over-represented. In carrying out a comparative study, it is important to account for age and gender, as well, perhaps, as for other variables such as social class. In the third place, it is important to bear in mind that the risk of being caught varies from crime to crime, and that immigrants and the native population do not generally show the same distribution of crimes committed, and that the risk of being caught for committing a given crime can vary between the immigrant and native populations (the rate of detection can vary).

Most studies indicate a higher rate of criminality among immigrants than among the native population, even when differences in age composition, etc. are taken into account. This fact is perhaps related to the migration process itself, and to the difficulties it causes those involved, particularly the second-generation immigrants who grow up in the country. Yet not all studies produce this kind of result.

A review of American research indicates great differences between different groups of immigrants, but, above all, that the differences are relatively minor between immigrants on average and the native population.[53] The authors of this study stress the degree of uncertainty involved in their results, partly due to incomplete data on origins and an unknown and probably variable rate of detection. A more recent American study shows that the portion of men aged 20-44 who are placed in institutions (prisons, in the

---

52. See Sabagh (1993) for an interesting description.
53. See Hagan & Palloni (1998).

majority of cases) is considerably higher among the native population than among immigrants as a group.[54] The rate is especially low among newly arrived immigrants. These results differ from those of earlier studies. They emphasise the importance of continually conducting these kinds of studies.

In one study of criminality in Federal States over a number of years in Germany, the percentage of foreign citizens is included as an explanatory variable. The results indicate that the number of thefts increases along with a higher percentage of foreign citizens, but that the number of other crimes does not increase.[55]

In the case of Sweden, previous studies have been conducted on criminality among foreign citizens,[56] who, however, only constitute a portion of all immigrants. This fact means that the results of such studies can be misleading if they are generalised to apply to the entire immigrant population. Jan Ahlberg (1996) conducted a study of criminality among both immigrants and the children of immigrants during a five-year period from 1985 to 1989. The study suggests that, even when age, gender and place of residence are taken into account, criminality is considerably higher among immigrants and the children of immigrants than among Swedes. Criminality is significantly higher among immigrants than among children of immigrants, a result that is different from that in many other countries. Children with one immigrant and one Swedish parent show a significantly lower rate of criminality than do children whose parents are both immigrants. This may be an indication of the difficulties that immigrants and their children face in establishing themselves in Swedish society. There are considerable differences in the rate of criminality among immigrants from different countries. The lowest levels of criminality are seen among immigrants from East and Southeast Asia, the United States, and some countries of Western Europe such as Great Britain. The levels are high for immigrants from, among other places, countries in Eastern Europe, South America and the Middle East and North Africa. Criminality is not higher in Denmark than in Sweden, but Danish immigrants in Sweden show a level of criminality that is nearly twice that of Swedes, even when age, gender and place of residence are taken into account. Possible explanations for this include selectivity in immigration and the difficulties associated with immigration itself, even between neighbouring countries.

Danish experience indicates a relatively higher level of criminality among immigrants than among the native population, even when factors such as age and gender, etc. are taken into account.[57] Criminality among the descendants

---

54. See Butcher & Piehl (1997).
55. The authors, Entorf & Spengler (1998), themselves admit that it would be better to have data on individuals. However, such data is not available.
56. See, for example, Eriksson & Tham (1983).
57. See Ejby Poulsen & Lange (1998) for a review of the differences.

of immigrants appears to be especially high. The statistics show that the distribution into different categories of crime is markedly different for immigrants than for the population as a whole. Immigrants and their descendants are especially over-represented in crimes involving property, but under-represented in traffic crimes.

The effects of immigration that have been dealt with in this section cannot in any simple manner be added to, for example, the redistribution of resources that takes place via the public sector. Such effects can be important nevertheless, and an especially great amount of interest in them has been shown in the general debate, which indicates how important it is to survey them properly and perhaps thus also to reduce the emotive content of such issues.

7.7 Conclusions

Immigration to a country entails economic effects, regardless of whether the reasons for the migration are economic, political or related to other factors. An understanding of these economic effects is important, since it can form the basis of more effective policies both for immigrants and the native population.

Immigration can affect the economy by influencing relative wages and prices. Through the influence of immigration on wages and prices, incomes rise for the existing population. A decisive factor in these results is that the amount of capital per worker falls, and that the composition of the labour market with respect to different occupations and age groups, etc. changes due to immigration. If the capital intensity does not fall due to a parallel influx of capital, and if the composition of the labour force does not change through immigration, then neither will the income level of the native population increase as a result of immigration's effects on wages and prices.

Of equal interest are the fiscal effects of immigration. Studies conducted in different countries in recent years indicate that a redistribution of resources to immigrants occurs via the public sector, especially to immigrants from countries that differ most in terms of economy from the host country. The studies also indicate that these results are highly dependent on the fact that these particular groups of immigrants have a very low rate of employment.

A study on the fiscal effects in Denmark produces similar results. The transfers to immigrants from group 2 countries, i.e. immigrants from countries other than those with the most highly developed economies, are considerable. On the other hand, there is a net transfer from immigrants from group 1 countries, i.e. those who come from countries with more highly developed economies. This pattern appears to have been stable during the 1990s. However, net transfers to immigrants from countries with less developed economies increased during the period 1991-95/96, when immigrants who had been in Denmark for an equal length of time are compared.

The study also indicates the great importance of the poor employment situation for the relatively large fiscal transfers to immigrants from countries with less developed economies. An important factor underlying these results may be that many of these immigrants have come to Denmark as refugees or to join family members, rather than as job-related immigrants.

The results of the fiscal study indicate the central role that the labour market plays in determining the effects that immigration has on redistribution via the public sector, and also for the position of the immigrants themselves in Danish society.

Labour force participation is very low among immigrants from less developed countries. Different studies suggest that the situation has gradually deteriorated. The percentage of immigrants from these countries who are unemployed, among those in the labour force, is higher than that among the population as a whole. The unemployment rate among this group of immigrants varies in accordance with the general state of the economy, just as it does for the population as a whole, but there is a trend towards rising unemployment among immigrants.

The higher level of unemployment can be due in part to the fact that immigrants take a large part of the amount of unemployment needed to keep inflation low, but it can also be due to the fact that immigrants contribute to an increase in structural unemployment, which in turn can be explained by various forms of inertia in the labour market. It is important to ensure that the position of immigrants on the labour market and the reasons behind that position are given proper attention in research.

This chapter has also dealt with other aspects of immigration that have been the centre of attention in the general debate in many countries in Europe. This is the case for the transfer of new ideas via immigration, the value of ethnic diversity, ethnic conflicts and differences in the levels of criminality between immigrants and the native population. It is important that research addresses these questions as well.

References

Ahlberg, Jan (1996). *Invandrares och invandrares barns brottslighet*. Brårapport 1996:2. Stockholm: Fritzes.

Bager, Torben & Shahamak Rezaei (eds.) (1998). *Invandringens økonomiske konsekvenser i Skandinavien*. Esbjerg: Sydjysk Universitetsforlag.

Betts, Julian R. & Magnus Lofstrom (1998). The Educational Attainment of Immigrants: Trends and Implications. NBER Working Papers 6757, October.

Blom, Svein & Agnes Aall Ritland (1997). Levekår blant ikke-vestlige innvandrere: Trang økonomi, men færre enn antatt opplever diskriminering. *Samfunnsspeilet*, Vol. 11, no. 1, pp. 2-16.

Borjas, George J. (1990). *Friends or Strangers. The Impact of Immigrants on the U.S. Economy*. New York: Basic Books.

Borjas, George J. (1994). The Economics of Immigration. *The Journal of Economic Literature*, Vol. 32, pp. 1667-1717.

Borjas, George J. (1998). The Economic Progress of Immigrants. NBER Working Papers 6506, April.

Borjas, George J., Richard B. Freeman & Lawrence Katz (1996). Searching for the Effect of Immigration on the Labor Market. *American Economic Review*, Papers and Proceedings, May, pp. 246-51.

Broomé, Per, Ann-Kathrin Bäcklund, Christer Lundh & Rolf Ohlsson (1996). *Varför sitter 'brassen' på bänken? Eller Varför har invandrarna så svårt att få jobb?* Stockholm: SNS Förlag.

Butcher, Kristin F. & John Dinardo (1998). The Immigrant and Native-Born Wage Distribution: Evidence from United States Censuses. NBER Working Papers 6630, July.

Butcher, Kristin F. & Anne Morrison Piehl (1997). Recent Immigrants: Unexpected Implications or Crime and Incarceration. NBER Working Papers 6067, June.

Card, David, John DiNardo & Eugena Estes (1998). The More Things Change: Immigrants and the Children of Immigrants in the 1940s, the 1970s, and the 1990s. NBER Working Papers 6519, April.

Chiswick, Barry R. (1978). The Effects of Americanization on the Earnings of Foreign-Born Men. *Journal of Political Economy*, Vol. 86, October, pp. 897-921.

Christensen, Lars (1998). Immigration, arbejdsmarkedet og de offentlige finanser i Danmark. In Torben Bager & Shahamak Rezaei (eds.) (1998).

Christoffersen, Henrik & Laura Mørch Andersen (1997). *Kommunaløkonomi, flygtninge og indvandrere.* AKF rapport, København: AKF Forlaget.

Clune, Michael P. (1998). The Fiscal Impacts of Immigrants: A California Case Study. In James P. Smith & Barry Edmonston (eds.) (1998).

Danmarks Statistik (1998). *Statistisk tiårsoversigt*, København: Danmarks Statistik.

Det økonomiske Råd (1996). *Dansk økonomi. Efterår 1996.* København: Det økonomiske Råd.

Dex, Shirley (1992). The costs of discriminating against migrant workers: An international review. World Employment Programme Research. Geneva: ILO.

Ekberg, Jan (1998). Hur påverkar invandring inkomster för infödda? In Torben Bager & Shahamak Rezaei (eds.) (1998).

Ekberg, Jan (1999). Immigration and the public sector: Income effects for the native population in Sweden. *Journal of Population Economics*, Vol. 12, pp. 278-97.

Ejby Poulsen, Marius & Anita Lange (1998). *Indvandrere i Danmark.* København: Danmarks statistik.

Emerek, Ruth, Vibeke Jacobsen & Jeanette E. Dahl (1998). Indvandrare og det danske arbejdsmarked. In Torben Bager & Shahamak Rezaei (eds.) (1998).

Enchautegui, Maria E. (1997). Immigration and wage changes of high school dropouts. *Monthly Labor Review*, Vol. 120, no. 10, pp. 3-9.

Entorf, Horst & Hannes Spengler (1998). Socio-economic and demographic factors of crime in Germany: Evidence from panel data of the German states. ZEW Discussion Paper, No. 98-16.

Eriksson, Ulla-Britt & Henrik Tham (eds.), (1983). *Utlänningarna och brottsligheten*, Brårapport 1983:4. Stockholm: BRÅ.

Eurostat (1998). *Labour Force Survey. Results from 1997.* Luxembourg: Office for publications of the European Communities.

Farlie, Robert W. & Bruce D. Meyer (1997). Does Immigration Hurt African-American Self-Employment? NBER Working Papers 6265, November.

Finansministeriet (1997). *Finansredegørelse 97.* København: Finansministeriet.

Garvey, Deborah L. & Thomas J. Espenshade (1998). Fiscal Impacts of Immigrant and Native Households: A New Jersey Case Study. In James P. Smith & Barry Edmonston (eds.) (1998).

Greijer, Åsa (1995). Uppskattningen av övertäckningen i RTB avseende utlandsfödda med hjälp av AKU. Metodrapport från BoR-avdelningen 1995:3. Örebro: SCB.

Greijer, Åsa (1996). Övertäckningen i Registret över totalbefolkningen — en studie av postreturer. Metodrapport från BoR-avdelningen 1996:7. Örebro: SCB.

Greijer, Åsa (1997a). Skattning av övertäckningen i folkbokföringen med hjälp av SCB:s inkomstregister. Metodrapport från BoR-avdelningen 1997:11, Örebro: SCB.

Greijer, Åsa (1997b). Uppskattningen av övertäckningen i RTB avseende utlandsfödda med hjälp av AKU, 1997. Metodrapport från BoR-avdelningen 1997:12. Örebro: SCB.

Gustafsson, Björn & Torun Larsson (1998). Ritva, Mohamad och det offentligas kassa. In Torben Bager & Shahamak Rezaei (eds.) (1998).

Gustman, Alan L. & Thomas L. Steinmeier (1998). Social Security Benefits of Immigrants and U.S. Born. NBER Working Papers 6478, March.

Hagan, John & Alberto Palloni (1998). Immigration and Crime in the United States. In James P. Smith & Barry Edmonston (eds.) (1998).

Hamermesh, Daniel S. (1993). *Labor Demand.* Princeton NJ: Princeton University Press.

Hamermesh, Daniel S. (1997). Immigration and the Quality of Jobs. NBER Working Papers 6195, September.

Hammarstedt, Mats (1998). Studier kring invandrares arbetsinkomster och inkomsttrygghet. Licentiatavhandling. Rapporter från Högskolan i Växjö, nr 12.

Hummelgaard, Hans *et al.* (1995). *Etniske minoriteter, integration og mobilitet.* København: AKF Forlaget.

Indenrigsministeriet (1998). *Betænkning om kommunernes udgiftsbehov.* Redegørelse fra arbejdsgruppe under Indenrigsministeriets Finansieringsudvalg, Betænkning nr. 1361. København: Indenrigsministeriet.

Jasso, Guillermina, Mark R. Rosenzweig & James P. Smith (1998). The Changing Skills of New Immigrants to the United States: Recent Trends and their Determinants. NBER Working Papers 6764, October.

Larsen, Knut Arild & Erik Bruce (1998). Virkninger av innvandring på de offentlige finanser i Norge. In Torben Bager & Shahamak Rezaei (eds.) (1998).

Lundborg, Per (1997). Fri arbetskraftsrörlighet mellan Sverige och nya EU-länder. Bilaga till SOU 1997:153, *Arbetskraftens fria rörlighet — trygghet och jämställdhet,* Betänkande av kommittén om EU:s utvidgning: konsekvenser av personers fria rörlighet m.m.

Lundborg, Per & Paul P. Segerstrom (1998). The Growth and Welfare Effects of International Mass Migration. FIEF, Working Paper No. 146. Stockholm.

Lundh, Christer & Rolf Ohlsson (1994). *Från arbetskraftsimport till flyktinginvandring.* Stockholm: SNS Förlag.

MaCurdy, Thomas, Thomas Nechyba & Jay Bhattacharya (1998). An Economic Framework for Assessing the Fiscal Impacts of Immigration. In James P. Smith & Barry Edmonston (eds.) (1998).

Mehlbye, Jill (1994). *Tosprogede børn og unge i Albertslund*. AKF rapport. København: AKF Forlag.

Nilsson, Åke (1995). Brister i folkbokföringen — övertäckningen bland utomnordiska medborgare. Metodrapport från BoR-avdelningen 1995:2. Örebro: SCB.

OECD (1998). *Immigrants, Integration and Cities. Exploring the Links*. Paris: OECD.

Sabagh, Georges (1993). Los Angeles, a World of New Immigrants. In Giacomo Luciani (ed.), *Migration Polices in Europe and the United States*. Dordrecht: Kluwer Academic Publishers.

Smith, James P. & Barry Edmonston (eds.) (1997). *The New Americans. Economic, Demographic, and Fiscal Effects of Immigration*. Washington, D.C.: National Academy Press.

Smith, James P. & Barry Edmonston (eds.) (1998). *The Immigration Debate. Studies on the Economic, Demographic, and Fiscal Effects of Immigration*. Washington, D.C.: National Academy Press.

Storesletten, Kjetil (1998). Nettoeffekten av invandringen på offentliga finanser — en nuvärdesberäkning för Sverige. In Torben Bager & Shahamak Rezaei (eds.) (1998).

Storrie, Donald & Bengt Nättorp (1997). *Starthjälp. Geografisk rörlighet 1978-1995 och en utvärdering av starthjälpen*, Rapporter från EFA nr 49. Stockholm: Arbetsmarknadsdepartementet.

Thomas, Brinley (1972). *Migration and Urban Development*. London: Methuen & Co.

Timmer, Ashley P. & Jeffrey G. Williamson (1996). Racism, Xenophobia or Markets? The Political Economy of Immigration Policy Prior to the Thirties. NBER Working Papers 5867, December.

Tseng, Yen-Fen (1997). Immigration Industry: Immigration Consulting Firms in the Process of Taiwanese Business Immigration. *Asian and Pacific Migration Journal*, Vol. 6, pp. 275-94.

Wadensjö, Eskil (1973). *Immigration och samhällsekonomi*. Lund: Studentlitteratur.

Williamson, Jeffrey G. (1998). Globalization, Labor Markets and Policy Backlash in the Past. *The Journal of Economic Perspectives*, Vol. 12, no. 4.

Økonomiministeriet (1997). *Økonomisk oversigt. December 1997*. København: Økonomiministeriet.

Appendices

Appendix Table 1.1. Population Characteristics of Europe's Neighbours, around 1995.

Country	Population size (1000s)	Births 1000s	Deaths 1000s	Population growth per 1000	Crude birth rate per 1000	Crude death rate per 1000	Rate of natural increase per 1000	Net migration per 1000	Total fertility rate	$e_0 m$	$e_0 f$	Population projections 2025 (millions)	Population projections 2050 (millions)
Algeria	28,109	816	172	24.00	29.03	6.12	22.91	1.09	4.30	66.0	68.3	47	59
Libya	5,407	208	40	34.70	38.47	7.40	31.07	3.63	6.39	61.6	65.0	13	19
Mauritania	2,274	85	31	25.40	37.38	13.63	23.75	1.65	5.40	49.9	53.1	4	6
Morocco	26,524	729	193	19.60	27.48	7.28	20.21	-0.61	3.75	62.8	66.2	40	47
Tunisia	8,987	220	55	19.30	24.48	6.12	18.36	0.94	3.25	66.9	68.7	14	16
Maghreb	*71,301*	*2,058*	*491*	*22.63*	*28.86*	*6.89*	*21.98*	*0.65*	*4.16*	*64.08*	*66.83*	*118*	*147*
Egypt	62,096	1,696	479	19.60	27.31	7.71	19.60	0.00	3.80	62.4	64.8	96	115
Sudan	26,707	881	351	20.90	32.99	13.14	19.84	1.06	5.00	49.6	52.4	47	60
Nile Valley	*88,803*	*2,577*	*830*	*19.99*	*29.02*	*9.35*	*19.67*	*0.32*	*4.16*	*58.55*	*61.07*	*143*	*175*
Gaza	0,792	38	5	46.60	47.98	6.31	41.67	4.93	8.80	64.2	67.8	2	4
Iraq	20,095	732	199	21.10	36.43	9.90	26.52	-5.42	5.70	57.6	60.0	42	56
Israel	5,525	109	33	20.41	19.73	5.97	13.76	6.65	2.90	75.3	78.7	8	9
Jordan	5,373	187	26	46.50	34.80	4.84	29.96	16.54	5.57	66.2	69.8	12	17
Lebanon	3,009	75	20	32.70	24.93	6.65	18.28	14.42	3.09	66.6	70.5	4	5
Syria	14,203	441	74	27.40	31.05	5.21	25.84	1.56	4.70	65.2	69.2	26	34
North Middle East	*48,997*	*1,582*	*357*	*26.76*	*32.29*	*7.29*	*25.00*	*1.76*	*4.97*	*63.40*	*66.62*	*95*	*126*
Bahrein	0,557	13	2	25.60	23.34	3.59	19.75	5.85	3.40	69.8	74.1	1	1
Kuwait	1,691	46	4	-47.40	27.20	2.37	24.84	-72.24	3.10	73.3	77.2	3	3
Qatar	0,548	10	2	24.30	18.25	3.65	14.60	9.70	4.10	68.8	74.2	1	1
Oman	2,207	87	9	42.50	39.42	4.08	35.34	7.16	7.20	67.7	71.8	7	11
Saudi Arabia	18,255	601	80	25.80	32.92	4.38	28.54	-2.74	6.37	68.4	71.4	42	60
UAR	2,210	43	5	28.10	19.46	2.26	17.19	10.91	3.80	72.9	75.3	3	4
Yemen	15,027	647	160	51.60	43.06	10.65	32.41	19.19	7.60	54.9	55.9	40	61
Arabian Peninsula	*40,495*	*1,447*	*262*	*26.86*	*35.73*	*6.47*	*29.26*	*-2.40*	*6.48*	*63.83*	*66.20*	*96*	*141*

continued on facing page

continued from preceding page

										e_0m	e_0f		
Iran	68,365	2,411	432	28.70	35.27	6.32	28.95	-0.25	5.30	67.0	68.0	128	170
Turkey	62,171	1,379	408	17.36	22.18	6.56	15.62	1.74	2.55	69.9	74.7	86	98
Asia Minor	*130,536*	*3,790*	*840*	*23.30*	*29.03*	*6.44*	*22.60*	*0.70*	*3.99*	*68.38*	*71.19*	*214*	*268*
Armenia	3,760	49	25	3.39	13.02	6.65	6.37	-2.98	1.60	69.3	76.2	4	4
Azerbaijan	7,208	143	53	-0.03	19.88	7.33	12.56	-12.58	2.30	66.3	74.5	10	11
Georgia	5,418	56	38	-3.65	10.40	6.99	3.41	-7.06	1.81	68.7	76.1	6	6
Transcaucasia	*16,386*	*249*	*116*	*-0.46*	*15.17*	*7.08*	*8.01*	*-8.55*	*1.97*	*67.78*	*75.42*	*20*	*21*
Kazakhstan	16,540	277	163	-11.90	16.75	9.87	6.88	-18.78	1.90	62.8	72.5	20	22
Kyrgyzstan	4,514	117	37	9.23	25.99	8.18	17.82	-8.58	2.80	63.4	71.9	6	7
Tajikistan	5,745	162	40	18.98	28.23	6.95	21.27	-2.29	2.90	64.2	70.2	10	12
Turkmenistan	4,075	124	30	20.41	30.43	7.36	23.07	-2.66	2.90	61.2	68.0	6	8
Uzbekistan	21,948	657	145	22.97	29.94	6.62	23.32	-0.35	3.20	64.3	70.7	37	45
Central Asia	*52,821*	*1,338*	*415*	*10.01*	*25.32*	*7.86*	*17.46*	*-7.45*	*2.70*	*63.50*	*71.10*	*79*	*95*
All	*449,339*	*13,040*	*3,312*		*29.02*	*7.37*	*21.65*					*764*	*974*

Sources: Mostly Council of Europe, Eurostat, national statistical yearbooks except for Central Asia (UN ECE, for 1995) and Israel and Turkey (UN, for 1995).

Note: 'Net migration' is simply natural increase subtracted from population growth. The figures are highly approximate and substantially affected, in the Middle East, by the effects of the Gulf War.

UN World Population Prospects 1996 revision.

Definitions: population given is usually mid-year total. Latest data for Central Europe usually 1994 or 1995.

Abbreviations in headings: e_0m, e_0f: Expectation of life at birth (males, females).

Appendix Table 1.2. Basic population data for European countries and selected others, around 1996.

Country	Population size (1000s)	Births 1000s	Deaths 1000s	Population growth per 1000	Crude birth rate per 1000	Crude death rate per 1000	Rate of natural increase per 1000	Net migration per 1000	Total fertility rate	Life expectancy e_om	e_of	Population projections 2025 (millions)	2050
Blr	10,280	101	134	-2.75	9.84	12.90	-3.06	0.31	1.39	62.9	74.3	10	9
Bul	8,363	72	117	-5.14	8.63	14.00	-5.37	0.23	1.24	67.2	74.4	7	7
Czr	10,315	90	113	-1.17	8.76	10.93	-2.17	1.00	1.18	70.5	77.5	10	9
Hun	10,193	105	143	-3.48	10.33	14.04	-3.71	0.23	1.46	66.1	74.7	9	8
Mol	4,327	52	50	-2.67	11.99	11.50	0.49	-3.16	1.76	62.9	70.4	5	5
Pol	38,624	428	385	0.76	11.09	9.98	1.11	-0.35	1.60	68.5	77.0	40	40
Rom	22,619	231	286	-2.88	10.23	12.65	-2.42	-0.46	1.30	65.3	73.1	21	19
Rus	147,774	1,364	2,204	-1.31	9.23	14.90	-5.67	4.36	1.34	61.0	73.1	131	114
Slk	5,373	60	51	2.12	11.19	9.54	1.65	0.47	1.47	68.8	76.7	5	5
Ukr	51,558	493	432	-2.10	9.56	15.40	-5.84	3.74	1.40	62.8	73.2	46	41
Eastern Europe	309,427	2,997	3,915	-1.48	9.69	12.65	-2.97	1.49	1.39	63.4	73.9	284	256
Esp	39,270	352	337	1.55	8.97	8.59	0.38	1.17	1.15	74.4	81.5	38	32
Gre	10,475	102	101	2.02	9.69	9.59	0.10	1.92	1.31	75.1	80.3	10	9
Ita	57,397	521	547	1.68	9.10	9.50	-0.40	2.08	1.22	74.1	80.5	52	42
Por	9,927	110	107	1.11	11.11	10.77	0.34	0.77	1.44	71.3	78.9	9	9
Alb	3,168	71	18	-3.55	23.23	5.25	17.98	-21.53	2.77	69.6	75.5	4	5
Bos	4,554	63	30	7.85	13.80	6.55	7.25	0.60	1.70	69.7	75.2	4	4
Cro	4,786	54	51	1.91	10.49	10.56	-0.07	1.98	1.58	68.6	75.9	4	4
FYRMac	2,075	31	16	4.36	16.14	7.60	8.54	-4.18	1.93	70.1	74.0	3	3
Slo	1,989	19	19	-0.62	9.44	9.36	0.08	-0.70	1.28	71.0	78.6	2	1
Yug	10,552	137	111	3.10	13.31	10.19	3.12	-0.02	1.88	68.9	74.7	11	11
Southern Europe	144,193	1,461	1,336	1.82	10.13	9.27	0.86	0.96	1.34	73.2	79.7	137	119

continued on next page

continued from preceding page

Aut	8,061	89	81	1.74	11.01	10.02	0.99	0.75	1.42	74.3	80.6	8	7
Bel	10,157	116	105	1.96	11.44	10.37	1.07	0.89	1.55	74.0	80.8	10	10
Fra	58,380	734	536	4.01	12.57	9.18	3.39	0.62	1.72	73.6	81.7	60	58
Ger	81,678	796	883	2.94	9.37	10.70	-1.33	4.27	1.29	73.0	79.5	81	70
Lux	0,416	6	4	14.28	13.69	9.37	4.32	9.96	1.76	73.5	79.6	0	0
Nl	15,531	190	138	4.63	12.21	8.86	3.35	1.28	1.53	74.7	80.4	16	15
Swi	7,073	83	63	4.67	11.74	8.86	2.88	1.79	1.50	76.1	82.2	8	7
Western Europe	181,294	2,013	1,809	3.42	11.10	9.98	1.13	2.29	1.48	73.6	80.1	184	167
Den	5,263	68	61	5.68	12.86	11.61	1.25	4.43	1.81	72.9	78.0	5	5
Est	1,469	13	19	-9.92	9.05	12.95	-3.90	-6.02	1.30	64.7	76.0	1	1
Fin	5,125	61	49	3.29	11.85	9.59	2.26	1.03	1.76	73.4	80.5	5	5
Ice	0,269	4	2	5.41	16.10	6.99	9.11	-3.70	2.12	76.4	81.3	0	0
Ire	3,626	50	32	5.80	13.90	8.69	5.21	0.59	1.91	72.3	77.9	4	4
Lat	2,491	20	34	-9.86	7.94	13.78	-5.84	-4.02	1.16	64.2	75.9	2	2
Lit	3,710	39	43	-1.42	10.56	11.56	-1.00	-0.42	1.43	65.9	76.8	4	3
Nor	4,381	61	44	5.08	13.91	10.01	3.90	1.18	1.89	75.5	81.0	5	5
Swe	8,841	95	94	1.59	10.78	10.65	0.13	1.46	1.61	76.5	81.5	10	10
UK	58,778	733	639	3.08	12.48	10.87	1.61	1.47	1.71	74.3	79.5	60	59
Northern Europe	93,952	1,145	1,017	2.57	12.19	10.82	1.36	1.21	1.69	73.6	79.4	95	94
Can	29,606	383	213	12.13	12.94	7.19	5.75	6.38	1.81	74.5	80.5	36	36
USA	264,965	3,900	2,312	8.41	14.84	8.80	6.04	2.37	2.03	72.5	78.9	332	348
North America	294,571	4,283	2,525	8.78	14.54	8.57	5.97	2.82	2.01	72.7	79.1	369	384

continued on next page

continued from preceding page

Armenia	3,760	49	25	3.49	13.02	6.56	6.47	-2.98	1.80	69.3	76.2	4	4
Azerbaijan	7,208	143	53	-0.03	19.88	7.33	12.56	-12.58	2.30	66.3	74.5	10	11
Georgia	5,418	56	38	-3.65	10.40	6.99	3.41	-7.06	1.80	68.7	76.1	6	6
Israel	5,525	109	33	20.41	19.73	5.97	13.76	6.65	2.90	75.3	78.7	8	9
Turkey	62,171	1379	408	17.36	22.18	6.56	15.62	1.74	2.55	69.9	74.7	86	98
West Asia	*84,082*	*1,737*	*556*	*14.04*	*20.65*	*6.62*	*14.04*	*0.01*	*2.45*	*69.8*	*75.1*	*113*	*128*
Kazakhstan	16,540	277	163	-11.90	16.75	9.87	6.88	-18.78	1.90	62.8	72.5	20	22
Kyrgyzstan	4,514	117	37	9.23	25.99	8.18	17.82	-8.58	2.80	63.4	71.9	6	7
Tajikistan	5,745	162	40	18.98	28.23	6.95	21.27	-2.29	2.90	64.2	70.2	10	12
Turkmenistan	4,075	124	30	20.41	30.43	7.36	23.07	-2.66	2.90	61.2	68.0	6	8
Uzbekistan	21,948	657	145	22.97	29.94	6.62	23.32	-0.35	3.20	64.3	70.7	37	45
Central Asia	*52,821*	*1,338*	*415*	*10.01*	*25.32*	*7.86*	*17.46*	*-7.45*	*2.70*	*63.5*	*71.1*	*79*	*95*
Aus	18,049	256	125	11.81	14.19	6.93	7.26	4.55	1.82	74.7	80.6	24	25
NZl	3,618	57	28	14.34	15.78	7.80	7.98	6.36	2.12	73.6	79.5	5	5
Australia and N. Zealand	*21,667*	*313*	*153*	*13.44*	*14.46*	*7.08*	*7.38*	*6.06*	*1.87*	*74.5*	*80.4*	*29*	*31*
Jap	125,864	1,187	876	6.64	9.43	6.96	2.90	3.74	1.45	77.0	83.6	121	110
Kor	45,248	710	240	8.85	15.69	5.29	10.85	-2.00	1.71	67.3	74.8	53	52
Tai	21,525	326	122	7.87	15.12	5.69	9.47	-1.60	1.76	71.9	77.8		
HK	6,156	69	32	20.00	11.15	5.12	6.15	13.85	1.15	75.6	81.3	7	6
Sin	2,987	49	16	19.21	16.28	5.21	11.06	8.15	1.71	74.2	78.7	4	4
East and South East Asia	*201,780*	*2,340*	*1,285*	*7.85*	*11.60*	*6.37*	*5.23*	*2.62*	*1.53*	*74.2*	*80.9*	*185*	*172*
Dev. World total	*1,246,884*	*11,478*	*12,041*	*4.10*	*9.21*	*9.66*	*-0.45*	*4.55*	*1.63*	*70.8*	*78.4*	*1282*	*1222*

Sources: Mostly Council of Europe, Eurostat, national statistical yearbooks except for Central Asia (UN ECE, for 1995) and Israel and Turkey (UN, for 1995).

WHO (1997). The world health report; UN World Population Prospects 1996 revision.

Definitions: population given is usually mid-year total. Latest data for Central Europe usually 1994 or 1995. Further definitions as in Appendix Table 1.1.

Appendix Table 2.1 Gross inflows of foreign population into Western Countries 1980-96 (selected countries only). Thousands. Asylum-seekers not included, except where indicated.

Country	1980	1981	1982	1983	1984	1985	1986	1987	1988
Austria	...	...	...	...	...	...	...	...	...
Belgium	46.8	41.3	36.2	34.3	37.2	37.5	39.3	40.1	38.2
Denmark[1]	...	...	13.0	11.6	17.9	15.6	17.6	15.2	13.8
Finland[2]									
France[3]	59.4	75.0	144.4	64.2	51.4	43.4	38.3	39.0	44.0
Germany[5]	523.6	451.7	275.5	273.2	331.1	398.2	478.3	473.3	648.6
Greece	...	...	...	...	...	...	...	...	...
Hungary	...	...	...	...	...	...	...	...	...
Ireland[4]	...	...	...	...	...	...	...	17.2	19.2
Italy	...	...	...	...	...	...	...	...	...
Luxemburg	7.4	6.9	6.4	6.2	6.0	6.6	7.4	7.2	8.2
Netherlands[6]	78.5	49.6	39.7	36.4	37.3	46.2	52.8	60.9	58.3
Norway[7]	11.8	13.1	14.0	13.1	12.8	15.0	16.8	23.8	23.2
Spain	...	...	...	...	...	6.2	4.3	5.3	9.7
Sweden[8]	...	...	...	22.3	26.1	27.9	34.0	37.1	44.5
Switzerland[9]	70.5	80.3	74.7	58.3	58.6	59.4	66.8	71.5	76.1
UK[10]	69.8	59.1	53.9	53.5	51.0	55.4	47.8	46.0	49.3
UK[11]	173.7	153.3	201.7	201.9	201.1	232.2	250.3	212.2	216.0
Canada	143.1	128.6	121.1	89.2	88.2	83.3	99.2	152.1	161.9
USA	530.6	596.6	594.1	559.8	543.9	570.0	601.7	601.5	643.0
Total for European countries above excl. Austria, Denmark, Finland, Greece, Hungary, Ireland, Italy and Spain									
Total (see above	867.8	777.0	644.8	539.2	585.4	661.7	747.5	761.8	945.9
Germany %	60.3	58.1	42.7	50.7	56.6	60.2	64.0	62.1	68.6
Total for N. America	673.8	725.2	715.3	648.9	632.1	653.3	700.9	753.6	804.9

continued on next page

Appendix Table 2.1 continued ...

Country	1989	1990	1991	1992	1993	1994	1995	1996	Total
Austria	...	...	...	...	280.5	276.9	308.6	224.2	1090.2
Belgium	43.5	50.5	54.1	55.1	53.0	56.0	53.1	51.9	768.1
Denmark[1]	15.1	15.1	17.5	16.9	15.4	15.6	33.0		233.3
Finland[2]	4.2	6.5	12.4	10.4	10.9	7.6	7.3	7.3	66.6
France[3]	53.2	102.4	109.9	116.6	99.2	91.5	77.0	74.0	1282.9
Germany[5]	770.8	842.0	920.5	1207.6	986.9	774.0	788.3	708.3	10851.8
Greece	...	25.0	13.4	...	...	...	...	...	38.4
Hungary	33.7	37.2	23.0	15.1	16.4	12.8	13.2	9.4	184.3
Ireland[4]	26.7	33.3	33.3	40.9	35.0				205.6
Italy	81.2	96.7	...	...	...	...	...	...	177.9
Luxemburg	8.4	9.3	10.0	9.8	10.1	9.2	9.6	...	128.7
Netherlands[6]	65.4	81.3	84.3	83.0	87.6	68.4	67.0	77.2	1073.9
Norway[7]	18.5	15.7	16.1	17.2	22.3	17.9	16.5	17.2	285.0
Spain	14.4	13.7	...	...	...	...	...	...	53.6
Sweden[8]	58.9	53.2	43.9	39.5	54.8	74.7	36.1	29.3	582.3
Switzerland[9]	80.4	101.4	109.8	112.1	104.0	91.7	87.9	74.3	1377.8
UK[10]	49.7	52.4	53.9	52.6	55.5	55.1	55.5	61.7	921.9
UK[11]	249.8	266.8	266.5	215.9	190.3	193.6	206.3	216.4	3648.0
Canada	192.0	214.2	230.8	252.8	255.8	223.9	212.2	226.1	2874.6
USA	1090.9	1536.5	1827.2	974.2	904.3	804.4	720.5	915.9	14015.1
Total for European countries above excl. Austria, Denmark, Finland, Greece, Hungary, Ireland, Italy and Spain									
Total for Europe	1089.8	1255.0	1358.6	1654.0	1418.6	1163.8	1154.9	1064.6	16690.1
Germany %	70.7	67.1	67.8	73.0	69.6	66.5	68.3	66.5	65.0
Total for N. America	1282.9	1750.7	2058.0	1227.0	1160.1	1028.3	932.7	1142.0	16889.7

Notes, see next page

Notes to Appendix Table 2.1

Notes: Data generally from population registers except for Austria, France, UK, Canada, USA. Data from annual SOPEMI reports can differ substantially from data given in earlier reports (e.g. Norway, Sweden).

1. Entries of foreigners staying in Denmark for more than one year. Asylum seekers and refugees with provisional permit not included.

2. Persons intending to stay in Finland for over one year.

3. Up to 1989, includes entries of new foreign workers with permanent and provisional work permits, and family reunification. After 1990, provisional work permits not included, but spouses of French nationals, parents of French children, refugees and those eligible for a residence permit are included.

4. Mostly returning Irish citizens. Net migration negative in all years but 1992. Source: Sexton 1994 Table 5.

5. Data includes reunited Germany after 1990.

6. Register data include asylum-seekers with provisional stay permits, recognized refugees, those admitted on humanitarian grounds. Asylum seekers in reception centres excluded.

7. Foreigners intending to spend more than 6 months in Norway.

8. Residence notification entries for less than one year are not included (mostly citizens of other Nordic countries).

9. Foreigners with annual residence permits and permanent permits returning to Switzerland after a temporary stay abroad. Includes (up to 31 Dec 1992) holders of permits of less than 12 months duration. Seasonal and frontier workers excluded.

10. Data from Home Office Control of Immigration Statistics; 'Accepted for Settlement' only. Most persons 'accepted' will have actually entered the UK in previous years.

11. Data from the International Passenger Survey. Sample of persons (all nationalities) intending to (re)enter the UK for at least 12 months. OPCS Series MN table 2.

£. Asylum-seekers not included except for the small number recognized and accepted for settlement.

No overall gross inflow data available for Austria for (only net, and labour).

£. New entries excluding temporary visitors, which include registered immigrants who declare the intention to stay for more than 90 days (sic)

Other sources: Greece, Italy, Spain: Salt 1994, Table 7.5. Otherwise OECD 1998 and earlier SOPEMI. Statistics Canada Report on the Demographic Situation in Canada, 1994, Table A 8.

Appendix Table 2.2. Fertility of foreign populations.

Year	All	Swedes	Foreign	Sweden (by nationality) Finns	Turks	Yugoslavs	Greeks
1970	1.92	1.90	2.44	2.40	..	2.71	3.30
1971	1.97	1.94	2.44	2.35	..	2.69	3.56
1972	1.91	1.90	2.32	2.22	..	2.49	3.20
1973	1.87	1.86	2.21	2.03	..	2.50	3.16
1974	1.89	1.86	2.25	2.08	4.68	2.27	3.08
1975	1.78	1.75	2.23	1.98	4.61	2.33	2.69
1976	1.69	1.65	2.24	1.93	6.23	2.26	3.08
1977	1.65	1.61	2.14	1.84	5.93	2.01	2.53
1978	1.60	1.56	2.12	1.79	5.23	2.10	2.71
1979	1.66	1.62	2.16	1.80	5.32	2.12	2.29
1980	1.68	1.64	2.19	1.86	5.02	2.00	2.62
1981	1.63	1.60	2.09	1.77	4.87	1.80	2.04
1982	1.62	1.59	2.06	1.73	4.03	1.75	2.18
1983	1.61	1.59	1.96	1.66	3.88	1.50	1.82
1984	1.65	1.62	2.08	1.73	3.84	1.71	1.90
1985	1.73	1.70	2.17	1.80	3.91	1.78	1.81
1986	1.79	1.76	2.24	1.83	3.67	1.84	1.79
1987	1.84	1.81	2.34	1.75	3.71	2.01	1.84
1988	1.96	1.93	2.49	1.92	3.74	2.08	1.74
1989	2.02	1.98	2.49	1.94	3.41	2.12	1.57
1990	2.14	2.10	2.68	2.19	3.34	2.46	1.66
1991	2.12	2.07	2.70	2.01	3.33	2.05	1.79
1992	2.09	2.02	2.46	2.03	2.96	2.08	1.28
1993	2.00	1.91	2.49	2.08	2.83	1.94	1.44
1994	1.88	1.81	2.79	1.94	2.82	2.02	1.40

continued on next page

Appendix table 2.2 continued ...

Switzerland (by nationality)

Year	All resident	Swiss	All foreigners	Germans	French	Italians	Spaniards	Turks
1971	2.02	1.82	2.90	...	...	...	...	...
1972	1.90	1.68	2.83	...	...	...	...	...
1973	1.80	1.58	2.73	...	...	...	...	...
1974	1.72	1.50	2.66	...	...	...	...	...
1975	1.60	1.42	2.46	...	...	...	...	...
1976	1.54	1.39	2.32	...	...	...	...	...
1977	1.52	1.38	2.32	...	...	...	...	...
1978	1.50	1.45	1.85	...	...	...	...	...
1979	1.52	1.50	1.68	...	...	...	...	...
1980	1.55	1.53	1.69	...	...	...	...	...
1981	1.54	1.52	1.69	0.78	0.80	1.88	1.83	3.36
1982	1.55	1.53	1.70	0.71	0.83	1.80	1.88	3.44
1983	1.51	1.51	1.58	0.71	0.84	1.66	1.65	3.04
1984	1.52	1.52	1.58	0.74	0.86	1.64	1.58	2.9
1985	1.51	1.51	1.54	0.71	0.93	1.55	1.53	2.86
1986	1.53	1.52	1.58	0.80	1.01	1.53	1.48	2.79
1987	1.51	1.51	1.54	0.74	0.97	1.42	1.43	2.96
1988	1.57	1.56	1.61	0.85	1.09	1.39	1.52	3.18
1989	1.57	1.55	1.65	0.86	1.10	1.35	1.44	3.34
1990	1.59	1.55	1.67	0.87	1.19	1.37	1.26	2.76
1991	1.58	1.50	1.77	0.95	1.13	1.32	1.36	2.83
1992	1.58	1.48	1.85	0.99	1.27	1.36	1.39	2.67
1993	1.51	1.40	1.74	1.06	1.22	1.28	1.24	2.33
1994	1.49	1.37	1.71	1.22	1.34	1.27	1.26	2.19

continued on next page

Appendix table 2.2 continued ...

Netherlands (by nationality or birthplace)

Year	All	Dutch	All non-Dutch	Turks	Moroccans	Born Surinamese	Born Antillean	Yugoslavs	Spaniards	Italians
1976	1.64	1.60	2.97	4.55	7.95	...	...	2.30	2.82	5.87
1977	1.59	1.54	3.36	5.03	7.98	1.65	...	2.19	2.91	5.37
1978	1.59	1.54	3.38	4.95	7.34	1.68	...	2.64	2.69	4.25
1979	1.57	1.51	3.39	4.80	7.23	1.70	...	2.43	2.42	4.30
1980	1.60	1.54	3.47	4.76	6.97	1.89	...	2.51	2.58	4.65
1981	1.56	1.49	3.46	4.59	6.66	1.80	...	2.42	2.32	4.65
1982	1.50	1.43	3.13	3.73	6.28	1.79		2.00	1.93	3.31
1983	1.47	1.41	3.08	3.53	5.95	1.80	1.31	1.92	1.83	3.51
1984	1.49	1.44	2.97	3.30	5.85	1.90	1.30	1.80	1.65	3.12
1985	1.51	1.48	2.43	3.04	5.48	1.99	1.43	1.59	1.07	1.05
1986	1.55	1.53	2.27	2.92	5.21	1.95	...	1.50	0.76	0.81
1987	1.56	1.53	2.28	3.09	5.27	1.85	...	...	...	...
1988	1.55	1.52	2.25	3.23	5.13	1.91	1.50	...	...	...
1989	1.55	1.53	2.22	3.18	4.98	1.81	...	...	...	...
1990	1.62	1.59	2.17	3.09	4.71	1.86	...	...	...	...
1991	1.61	1.60	2.01	2.93	4.18	1.79	...	...	...	...
1992	1.59	1.58	1.92	2.73	4.14	1.66	...	...	...	...
1993	1.57	1.57	1.73	2.52	3.53	1.59	...	...	...	...

continued on next page

Appendix Table 2.2. continued

England and Wales (birthplace of mother)

Year	All birth-places	UK	New Commonwealth	West Indies	India	Pakistan & Bangladesh	Bangladesh	Pakistan	Other Asian	Africa	Mediterranian
1971	2.37	2.3	3.9	3.4	4.3	9.3			2.7	4.2	2.9
1980	1.84	...	3.5	2.5	3.9	7.1					
1981	1.80	1.7	2.9	2.0	3.1	6.5	8.0	6.1	2.1	3.4	2.1
1982	1.76	1.7	2.9	2.0	3.0	6.3	8.0	5.9	2.1	3.2	2.2
1983	1.76	1.7	2.9	1.9	2.9	6.1	8.3	5.7	2.0	2.9	2.3
1984	1.75	1.7	2.9	1.9	2.9	5.9	7.7	5.5	2.1	2.7	2.6
1985	1.78	1.7	3.0	1.9	3.1	5.6	7.2	5.5	2.1	2.7	2.7
1986	1.77	1.7	3.0	2.0	3.1	5.6	7.3	5.4	2.1	2.5	2.7
1987	1.81	1.8	3.0	2.2	3.1	5.2	6.8	5.1	2.1	2.7	2.7
1988	1.82	1.8	3.1	2.3	3.2	4.9	6.2	5.0	2.1	2.8	3.0
1989	1.80	1.8	3.0	2.1	2.8	4.7	5.9	4.8	2.0	3.2	3.0
1990	1.86	1.8	2.9	2.0	2.6	4.7	6.0	4.7	2.0	3.1	2.8
1991	1.82	1.8	2.8	1.9	2.5	5.0	5.3	4.8	1.9	3.1	2.0
1992	1.80	1.8	2.9	2.0	2.4	4.8	4.8	4.8	1.9	3.3	2.1
1993	1.76	1.7	2.9	2.0	2.4		4.7	4.9	1.8	3.2	2.0
1994	1.75	1.7	3.0	2.2	2.2		4.6	4.9	1.9	3.4	1.9
1995	1.72	1.6	3.0	2.3	2.2		4.7	4.8	1.8	3.6	1.9

Sources: National statistical yearbooks and national SOPEMI reports.

Appendix Table 3.1 Summary of means of regulating immigration.

Labour migration (work permit)	Conditions for permits to be given to employers made more stringent in some countries by administrative means (e.g. UK). Little legislation in Europe. Expanded (at the expense of family migration) in US by 1990 IA.
Guest workers and temporary workers	Guest worker schemes generally ended in Europe around 1973. Continued in Austria, Switzerland, especially for temporary/seasonal workers. Renewed in Germany from 1992 through special bilateral agreements with Poland and other Central/East European countries. Border workers also encouraged by Germany and generally between 'Schengen' countries.
Family reconstitution	Subject to increasingly strict conditions on availability of suitable (sometimes private) accommodation, no dependence on state welfare (e.g. Italy, Germany, Netherlands).
Family formation	Subject to increasingly strict conditions on marriage being 'genuine' and partners living together after marriage (Netherlands, UK) and availability of suitable accommodation.
Ethnic return	Continues as before except that quotas imposed by Germany along with subsidies to persuade intending Aussiedler emigrants to remain. Bilateral agreements between Russia and 'near abroad' to minimize forced migration.
Other (non-nuclear relatives)	Only applies to US and Canada except in exceptional cases. In 1990 US has increased labour stream at the expense of family stream, but latter remains predominant.
Repatriation	Germany, France, Netherlands, Belgium, UK (tiny and obscure scheme) have had schemes on and off for years. Emphasis now is on removal of illegal entrants and rejected asylum-claimants (Germany, France), often following bilateral agreements.
Quotas	Part of US and Canadian legislation (but not for 'restrictionist' purposes). Residence and labour permits in Austria and Switzerland, overall annual quotas in Estonia, Italy, Austria.
Foreign investment to encourage local employment of potential migrants	Widely supported, most active countries are Germany (in Eastern Europe) and the United States (in Mexico, through *maquiladoras* and North American Free Trade Area (NAFTA)).

Appendix Table 3.2 Summary of means of reducing illegal immigration.

Visas	Visa requirement very generally applied by most European UN ECE countries to large numbers of potential claimant-sending countries. Some relaxation by Germany in respect of Poland and other Central European countries.
Restriction on places where claims of asylum may be made	Some countries now normally restrict claims to overseas consulates or embassies. Others require that claims may only be made on arrival, not after residence in the country (Italy, Belgium). Others, however still permit claims to be made after arrival and by post (UK).
Restriction on characteristics of claimant	Claims may not be considered by some countries in respect of persons with criminal records or who have used criminal means to further political causes or who have entered the country illegally.
Restriction on breadth of grounds	Most countries now only accept refugees under Convention criteria (although some courts are widening their interpretation of those criteria to include, for example, sexual orientation). However, permission to remain on humanitarian grounds, without formal refugee status, remains common.
Restriction in respect of documents	Some countries now refuse consideration to persons known to have destroyed their documents.
Safe third countries	Increasing numbers of countries will not consider claims when the claimant has arrived from another 'safe' country in which he or she could have claimed asylum (because that country has acceded to the Geneva Convention). Arrangements for return have been developed through international agreements (e.g. Dublin Convention).
Safe countries	Increasing numbers of countries will automatically reject claims made from specified countries deemed not to generate genuine asylum problems by virtue of their democratic and judicial systems. Only Germany has a formal 'white' list; others have less formal a priori arrangements (such as those proposed in the UK Asylum and Immigration Bill 1996).
Accelerated screening procedures for manifestly unfounded claims	Most countries attempt to screen out the great majority of claims not considered worthy of the expensive and time-consuming process of full investigation. That includes the application of safe third country and safe country principles, and the application of fingerprint checks to eliminate duplicate claims in other countries.
Detention and confinement	An increasing number of countries require claimants to reside in given places for their claims to be considered (Germany). Others confine some claimants thought to be at risk of absconding (UK), or confine all of them (Belgium), or are working towards that end, either when claims are considered or for rejected claimants to prevent their absconding.

Appendix Table 3.2 continued ...

Appeal procedures	While most countries have an appeal system, their widespread use by claimants can greatly increase the cost and duration of the processing of claims. Some steps are being made to simplify and shorten any appeals process, or to require that appeals be conducted from outside the country.
Repatriation arrangements	Numerous bilateral arrangements have been negotiated for the return of rejected claimants, their provision with documents and acceptance as citizens of the sending countries, sometimes associated with aid packages to help re-settlement. A number of countries pay expenses or premiums to asylum-seekers to return (Belgium; over 1000 in 1993, Germany).
Entitlements of claimants	Many countries have removed the right of claimants to seek work entirely (France) or for a specified time (Germany), or are considering doing so. Welfare and cheap housing entitlements have been restricted, for example to persons who claimed on arrival (UK), or replaced in part or entirely by free accommodation from which mobility is restricted.
Collaborative measures	A number of agreements between groups of countries operate to minimize asylum-claiming. The EU Dublin convention made general the safe third country principle. Visa lists and regulations are being harmonized. The Schengen countries agreed on a common asylum decision; a person rejected by one could not apply to the others.

Appendix 5.1 A description of the newspapers used in the analysis, based on the work of press historian Jette D. Søllinge

Berlingske Tidende began publication in 1749. The paper was consistently conservative in outlook until 1949, even though the political affiliation never showed strongly. In 1949 the paper declared itself to be independently conservative, with the aim of being the paper of the business community and the bourgeoisie. Today, the paper regularly sells 90% of its print run in the eastern part of Denmark, and largely within urban areas. Readers are mainly independent business people, senior management and echelon civil servants.

Politiken started publication in 1884 and was at first linked to radical circles in the Danish Liberal Party (the so-called "European" Liberals). In 1905 it formally espoused the cause of the Social-Liberal Party, and in 1970 the paper declared itself to be "independently radical social-liberal". The newspaper aims at being culturally-oriented, and cultivates an image as the paper for intellectuals. Half the provincial sales are made on Zealand and Lolland-Falster. The readership represents a wide range in socio-demographic terms, but is primarily urban. The paper is increasingly read by white-collar workers.

Aktuelt was called *Socialisten* ("The Socialist") when it was first published in 1872, and from 1874 was known as *Social-Demokraten* ("The Social Democrat"). It took the name *Aktuelt* from 1959, though from 1987-1997 it was called *Det fri Aktuelt* ("The Independent Aktuelt"). It has from the outset been the paper of the Social Democratic Party. It has always carried a significantly greater proportion of political material than the most of the Danish press, and it also tends to draw a less distinct line between news and comment. The paper has had difficulty in maintaining its circulation, particularly since the Second World War, because it never followed the other papers in becoming less party-political in outlook. The pattern of circulation has varied considerably over time, depending particularly on the number of different provincial editions published. The readership is concentrated in the lower income groups (skilled and unskilled workers), and from 1950 onwards the paper has also increasingly been read by pensioners and white-collar workers.

Information started publication in 1945 as a continuation of the activities of a news service of the same name which had operated underground during the German occupation. From the outset it was completely independent of party politics, and it has never attempted to align the views of its leader writers. In the early days the newspaper supported Denmark's membership of NATO and had views close to the neo-liberal stance of Thorkil Kristensen; later, during the 1960s, its standpoint was close to that of the "New Left". Until 1969 it was published as an evening paper; as such, and particularly during its first 5-10 years of its existence, it emphasized comment and debate. Later, it increasingly focused on publishing analysis of and background to the news. In the past 2-3 years the emphasis has switched back again to opinion. The content focuses on politics, in particular on foreign politics, and on culture. Readers are mainly highly educated.

Ekstra Bladet first appeared in 1904 during the Russo-Japanese war under the name *Ekstrablad til Politiken* ("Supplement to *Politiken*"), but it achieved independent status and its new name in 1905. It belongs to the category of tabloid popular press. It was originally aligned politically with the Danish Liberal party, and then with the Social

Liberals from 1905 to 1954/63. From then on it became politically independent, though with a continued radical orientation; from 1963/70 it was independently social-liberal, though without any specific party loyalty. Since its re-launch in 1963 in particular the paper has been notable for its lack of respect for both authority of any kind and for what it regards as old-fashioned morality and taboos. The content and journalistic style are marked by sensationalism, with a heavy emphasis on violent death and crime, and also on scandal of all kinds – though the paper has a particular appetite for political or sexual scandal. Circulation was originally concentrated to the Copenhagen area, spreading later to the other large towns, and from the 1970s out to the provinces as well. At first the readership was mainly the Copenhagen middle classes; later the readership became much broader, but with a high proportion of workers and low-level white-collar staff.

Jyllands-Posten was first published in Aarhus in 1871 as a newspaper for the whole of Jutland. A supporter of the Conservative Party from 1877-1938, the paper then switched to being independently bourgeois. It has consistently held to a bourgeois/Danish Liberal line and has been critical of centralized government, powerful organizations, and social welfare authorities. In 1969 the paper changed its name to *Morgenavisen Jyllands-Posten* and made a push for sales in eastern Denmark, thus becoming a truly national paper.

Vestkysten (Esbjerg) was founded in 1918 through the merger of two small local papers. Its circulation increased rapidly. The paper was a notable mouthpiece for the Danish Liberal Party, and after 1950 it was the party's most important press supporter. In January of 1991 the paper amalgamated with the conservative *Jydske Tidende* to form *Jydske Vestkysten*, an independent bourgeois paper and the only daily covering the whole of southern Jutland (the area south of Varde/Kolding).

Appendix Table 5.1 (below) gives the circulation figures for these papers.

Appendix Table 5.1. Daily circulation figures for the national newspapers used in the analysis. Thousands.

	Berlingske T.	Politiken	Aktuelt	Inform.	EB	Jyll.P.	Vestkysten
1963	*171.0	137.0	41.0	21.5	79.2	61.9	44.1
1973	146.0	121.0	53.0	22.7	245.0	79.2	54.0
1983	118.0	149.8	54.6	32.9	247.7	102.2	55.8
1993	134.4	152.0	41.3	24.4	182.4	145.6	**96.2

Source: Søllinge and Thomsen, 1991. The figures for 1993 have been calculated by Jette D. Søllinge from *Dansk Oplagsstatistik.*
Notes:
*   Morning edition.
** *Jydske Vestkysten.*

Publications from the Rockwool Foundation Research Unit

Time and Consumption
Edited by Gunnar Viby Mogensen. With contributions by Søren Brodersen,
Thomas Gelting, Niels Buus Kristensen, Eszter Körmendi, Lisbeth Pedersen,
Benedicte Madsen, Niels Ploug, Erik Ib Schmidt, Rewal Schmidt Sørensen
and Gunnar Viby Mogensen (Statistics Denmark, Copenhagen).

Welfare and Work Incentives. A North European Perspective
Edited by A.B. Atkinson and Gunnar Viby Mogensen. With contributions
from A.B. Atkinson, Richard Blundell, Björn Gustafsson, Anders
Klevmarken, Peder J. Pedersen and Klaus Zimmermann (Oxford University
Press).

Solidarity or Egoism?
By Douglas A. Hibbs (Aarhus University Press).

Danes and Their Politicians
By Gunnar Viby Mogensen (Aarhus University Press).

Unemployment and Flexibility on the Danish Labour Market
By Gunnar Viby Mogensen (Statistics Denmark, Copenhagen).

The Shadow Economy in Denmark 1994. Measurement and Results
By Gunnar Viby Mogensen, Hans Kurt Kvist, Eszter Körmendi and Søren
Pedersen (Statistics Denmark, Copenhagen).

On the Measurement of a Welfare Indicator for Denmark 1970-1990
By Peter Rørmose Jensen and Elisabeth Møllgaard (Statistics Denmark,
Copenhagen).

Work Incentives in the Danish Welfare State. New Empirical Evidence
Edited by Gunnar Viby Mogensen. With contributions by Søren Brodersen,
Lisbeth Pedersen, Peder J. Pedersen, Søren Pedersen and Nina Smith
(Aarhus University Press).

Actual and Potential Recipients of Welfare Benefits, with a Focus on Housing Benefits
By Hans Hansen and Marie Louise Hultin (Statistics Denmark, Copenhagen).

The Shadow Economy in Western Europe. Measurement and Results for Selected Countries
By Søren Pedersen, with contributions by Esben Dalgaard and Gunnar Viby Mogensen (Statistics Denmark, Copenhagen).

Immigration to Denmark. International and national Perspectives
By David Coleman and Eskil Wadensjö, with contributions by Bent Jensen and Søren Pedersen (Aarhus University Press).